PRENTICE HALL

WORLD HISTORY

THE MODERN ERA

Reading and Note Taking Study Guide

Boston, Massachusetts
Upper Saddle River, New Jersey

Boston, Massachusetts
Upper Saddle River, New Jersey

ISBN 0-13-133346-1
2 3 4 5 6 7 8 9 10 09 08 07 06

Contents

How to Use This Book

The **Reading and Note Taking Study Guide** will help you better understand the content of *Prentice Hall World History.* This book will also develop your reading, vocabulary, and note taking skills.

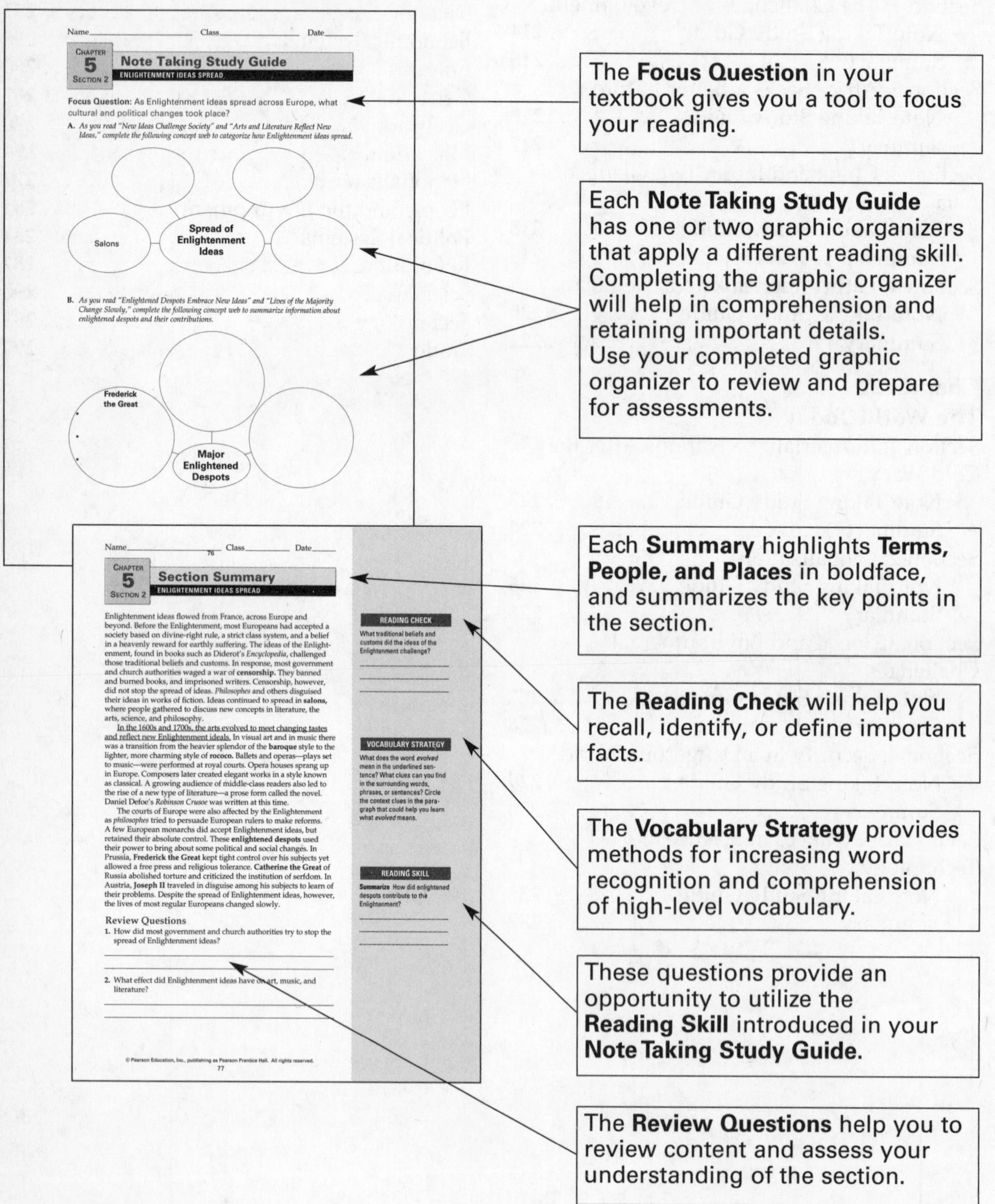
Name______ Class______ Date______

CHAPTER 5 SECTION 2

Note Taking Study Guide

ENLIGHTENMENT IDEAS SPREAD

Focus Question: As Enlightenment ideas spread across Europe, what cultural and political changes took place?

A. *As you read "New Ideas Challenge Society" and "Arts and Literature Reflect New Ideas," complete the following concept web to categorize how Enlightenment ideas spread.*

Spread of Enlightenment Ideas

Salons

B. *As you read "Enlightened Despots Embrace New Ideas" and "Lives of the Majority Change Slowly," complete the following concept web to summarize information about enlightened despots and their contributions.*

Major Enlightened Despots

Frederick the Great

76

Name______ Class______ Date______

CHAPTER 5 SECTION 2

Section Summary

ENLIGHTENMENT IDEAS SPREAD

Enlightenment ideas flowed from France, across Europe and beyond. Before the Enlightenment, most Europeans had accepted a society based on divine-right rule, a strict class system, and a belief in a heavenly reward for earthly suffering. The ideas of the Enlightenment, found in books such as Diderot's *Encyclopedia*, challenged those traditional beliefs and customs. In response, most government and church authorities waged a war of **censorship.** They banned and burned books, and imprisoned writers. Censorship, however, did not stop the spread of ideas. *Philosophes* and others disguised their ideas in works of fiction. Ideas continued to spread in **salons,** where people gathered to discuss new concepts in literature, the arts, science, and philosophy.

In the 1600s and 1700s, the arts evolved to meet changing tastes and reflect new Enlightenment ideals. In visual art and in music there was a transition from the heavier splendor of the **baroque** style to the lighter, more charming style of **rococo.** Ballets and operas—plays set to music—were performed at royal courts. Opera houses sprang up in Europe. Composers later created elegant works in a style known as classical. A growing audience of middle-class readers also led to the rise of a new type of literature—a prose form called the novel. Daniel Defoe's *Robinson Crusoe* was written at this time.

The courts of Europe were also affected by the Enlightenment as *philosophes* tried to persuade European rulers to make reforms. A few European monarchs did accept Enlightenment ideas, but retained their absolute control. These **enlightened despots** used their power to bring about some political and social changes. In Prussia, **Frederick the Great** kept tight control over his subjects yet allowed a free press and religious tolerance. **Catherine the Great** of Russia abolished torture and criticized the institution of serfdom. In Austria, **Joseph II** traveled in disguise among his subjects to learn of their problems. Despite the spread of Enlightenment ideas, however, the lives of most regular Europeans changed slowly.

Review Questions

1. How did most government and church authorities try to stop the spread of Enlightenment ideas?

2. What effect did Enlightenment ideas have on art, music, and literature?

READING CHECK

What traditional beliefs and customs did the ideas of the Enlightenment challenge?

VOCABULARY STRATEGY

What does the word *evolved* mean in the underlined sentence? What clues can you find in the surrounding words, phrases, or sentences? Circle the context clues in the paragraph that could help you learn what *evolved* means.

READING SKILL

Summarize How did enlightened despots contribute to the Enlightenment?

© Pearson Education, Inc., publishing as Pearson Prentice Hall. All rights reserved.

77

Concept Connector Worksheets support the **Concept Connector** features and the **Concept Connector Cumulative Review** found in each chapter of your text, as well as the **Concept Connector Handbook** found at the end of your textbook. These worksheets will help you to compare key concepts and events and to see patterns and make connections across time. The thematic essay portion of each worksheet will prepare you for social studies exams and assessments.

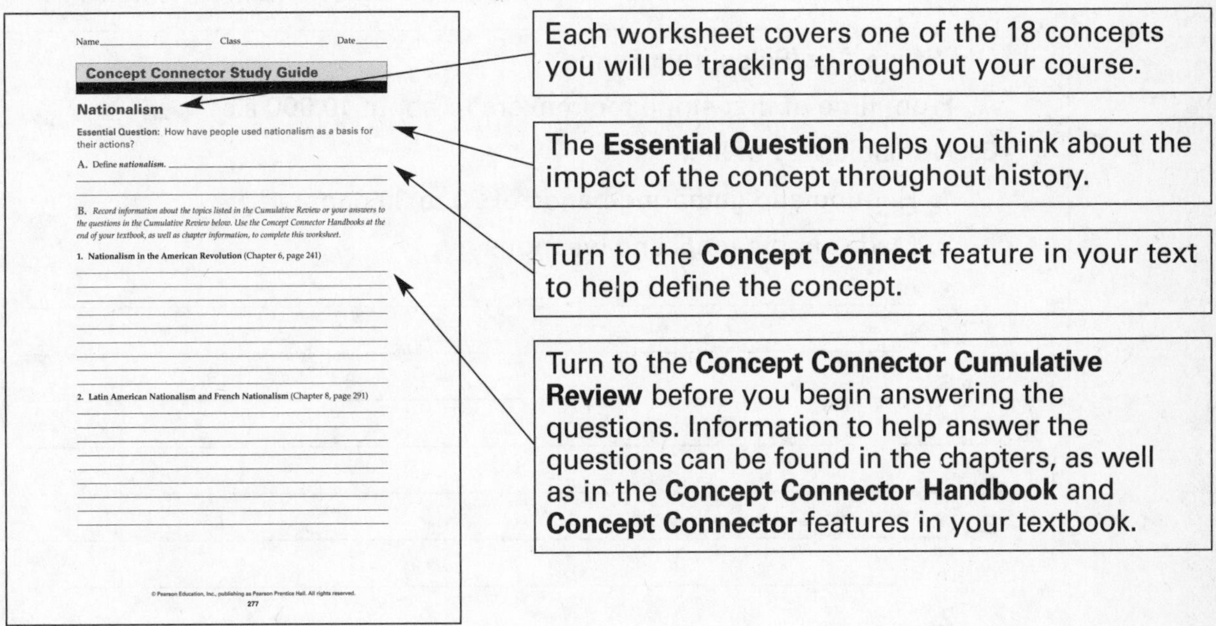
Name________ Class________ Date________

Concept Connector Study Guide

Nationalism

Essential Question: How have people used nationalism as a basis for their actions?

A. Define *nationalism*.

B. *Record information about the topics listed in the Cumulative Review or your answers to the questions in the Cumulative Review below. Use the Concept Connector Handbooks at the end of your textbook, as well as chapter information, to complete this worksheet.*

1. **Nationalism in the American Revolution** (Chapter 6, page 241)

2. **Latin American Nationalism and French Nationalism** (Chapter 8, page 291)

© Pearson Education, Inc., publishing as Pearson Prentice Hall. All rights reserved.

277

Thematic essays are an important part of social studies exams and assessment tests. This portion of the Concept Connector Worksheet provides sample topics for thematic essays.

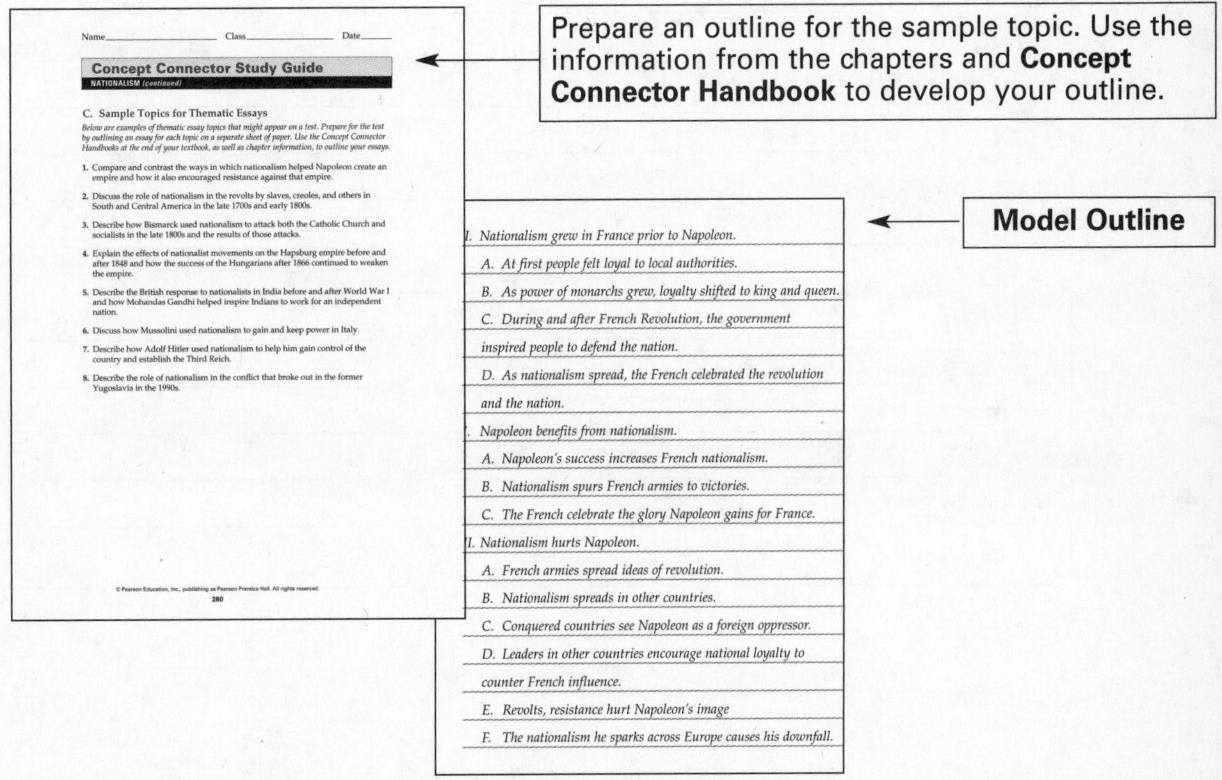
Name________ Class________ Date________

Concept Connector Study Guide

NATIONALISM *(continued)*

C. Sample Topics for Thematic Essays

Below are examples of thematic essay topics that might appear on a test. Prepare for the test by outlining an essay for each topic on a separate sheet of paper. Use the Concept Connector Handbooks at the end of your textbook, as well as chapter information, to outline your essays.

1. Compare and contrast the ways in which nationalism helped Napoleon create an empire and how it also encouraged resistance against that empire.
2. Discuss the role of nationalism in the revolts by slaves, creoles, and others in South and Central America in the late 1700s and early 1800s.
3. Describe how Bismarck used nationalism to attack both the Catholic Church and socialists in the late 1800s and the results of those attacks.
4. Explain the effects of nationalist movements on the Hapsburg empire before and after 1848 and how the success of the Hungarians after 1866 continued to weaken the empire.
5. Describe the British response to nationalists in India before and after World War I and how Mohandas Gandhi helped inspire Indians to work for an independent nation.
6. Discuss how Mussolini used nationalism to gain and keep power in Italy.
7. Describe how Adolf Hitler used nationalism to help him gain control of the country and establish the Third Reich.
8. Describe the role of nationalism in the conflict that broke out in the former Yugoslavia in the 1990s.

© Pearson Education, Inc., publishing as Pearson Prentice Hall. All rights reserved.

280

I. Nationalism grew in France prior to Napoleon.
A. At first people felt loyal to local authorities.
B. As power of monarchs grew, loyalty shifted to king and queen.
C. During and after French Revolution, the government inspired people to defend the nation.
D. As nationalism spread, the French celebrated the revolution and the nation.
. Napoleon benefits from nationalism.
A. Napoleon's success increases French nationalism.
B. Nationalism spurs French armies to victories.
C. The French celebrate the glory Napoleon gains for France.
I. Nationalism hurts Napoleon.
A. French armies spread ideas of revolution.
B. Nationalism spreads in other countries.
C. Conquered countries see Napoleon as a foreign oppressor.
D. Leaders in other countries encourage national loyalty to counter French influence.
E. Revolts, resistance hurt Napoleon's image
F. The nationalism he sparks across Europe causes his downfall.

Name____________________ Class____________________ Date__________

PART 1.1

Note Taking Study Guide

TOWARD CIVILIZATION

As you read this section in your textbook, complete the outline below to summarize information about the periods of early human history and the development of civilizations.

I. Old Stone Age/Paleolithic Period

- **A.** From time of first stone toolmakers to about 10,000 B.C.
- **B.** Nomadic way of life
    - **1.** Hunting and gathering bands of 20 to 30 people
    - **2.** Made simple tools and weapons
    - **3.** ____________________
    - **4.** ____________________
    - **5.** ____________________

II. ____________________

- **A.** ____________________
- **B.** ____________________
    - **1.** ____________________
    - **2.** ____________________
    - **3.** ____________________
    - **4.** ____________________

III. ____________________

- **A.** ____________________
- **B.** ____________________
- **C.** ____________________
    - **1.** ____________________
    - **2.** ____________________
- **D.** ____________________
    - **1.** ____________________
    - **2.** ____________________
- **E.** ____________________
    - **1.** ____________________
    - **2.** ____________________

Name________________________ Class__________ Date______

PART 1.1

Section Summary

TOWARD CIVILIZATION

The period from the time of the first stone toolmakers to about 10,000 B.C. is known as the **Old Stone Age,** or the Paleolithic Period. Paleolithic people were **nomads,** or people who move from place to place to hunt for animals and edible plants. They lived in bands of 20 to 30 people and made simple tools and weapons. They developed spoken language, invented clothing made from animal skins, and learned to build fires.

About 10,000 years ago, nomadic bands learned to farm. This allowed them to remain in one place, which ushered in the **New Stone Age,** or Neolithic Age. Neolithic people established permanent villages and learned to tame animals. Village life reshaped the roles of men and women. During times of want, warfare increased. Success in battle enabled some men to gain status as warriors, which gave them power over both women and other men. The status of women declined.

About 5,000 years ago, the advances made by early farming communities led to the rise of civilizations. Historians have identified seven basic features common to most early civilizations: well-organized central governments, complex religions, job specialization, social classes, arts and architecture, public works, and writing.

Food surpluses in the river valleys of Africa and Asia helped populations to expand. As populations increased, some villages grew into cities. The challenge of farming in a river valley contributed to the development of city governments. Projects to control flooding and channel waters to fields required organization. Over time, city governments became more complex, and government **bureaucracies** grew.

Social organization also became more complex. People were ranked according to their jobs. Priests and nobles were usually at the top, followed by merchants and **artisans,** or skilled craftworkers. Below them were the peasant farmers and slaves at the very bottom. Priests developed writing to record information. Early writing was made up of **pictographs,** or simple drawings that represented ideas.

As ancient rulers gained more and more power, they conquered territories beyond their cities. Some conquered many cities and villages, creating **empires,** or groups of states, territories, and peoples ruled by one person.

Review Questions

1. Why did city governments develop in river valleys?

____

____

2. How were people ranked socially in early civilizations?

____

____

READING CHECK

Who are nomads?

____

____

____

VOCABULARY STRATEGY

What does the word *status* mean in the underlined sentence? Note that the word *status* is repeated in the next sentence. As men gained *status* as warriors, the *status* of women declined. How does this help you understand the meaning of the word *status*?

READING SKILL

Identify Causes and Effects Create a 4-step flowchart to show how the development of farming led to the growth of cities in river valleys. Begin your flowchart with "Nomadic bands learned to farm."

Name______________________ Class__________________ Date________

PART
1.2
Note Taking Study Guide
FIRST CIVILIZATIONS: AFRICA AND ASIA

As you read this section in your textbook, complete the outline below to summarize information about the first civilizations in North Africa and the Middle East.

I. Ancient Kingdoms of the Nile
  A. Villages in Nile River valley joined into two kingdoms.
  B. ______________________________
  C. Old Kingdom (about 2575–2130 B.C.)
  D. ______________________________
  E. ______________________________
II. ______________________________
  A. ______________________________
  B. ______________________________
III. ______________________________
  A. ______________________________
  B. ______________________________
    1. ______________________________
    2. ______________________________
    3. ______________________________
  C. ______________________________
    1. ______________________________
    2. ______________________________
IV. ______________________________
  A. ______________________________
  B. ______________________________
  C. ______________________________
  D. ______________________________
V. ______________________________
  A. ______________________________
  B. ______________________________
  C. ______________________________
  D. ______________________________
  E. ______________________________

Name____________________ Class__________ Date_____

PART **1.2**

Section Summary

FIRST CIVILIZATIONS: AFRICA AND ASIA

The first civilizations emerged in river valleys and developed complex ways of life. In the **Nile River** valley in Egypt, villages joined together into two kingdoms. These kingdoms were later united under King Menes.

The history of ancient Egypt after King Menes is divided into three periods, the Old, Middle, and New Kingdoms. During the Old Kingdom, the Egyptian rulers, or **pharaohs,** organized a strong central government and built pyramids as tombs. During the Middle and New Kingdoms, trade and warfare brought Egypt into contact with other civilizations, which led to **cultural diffusion.**

Egyptians worshiped many gods and goddesses and built tombs to preserve their bodies for the afterlife. Egyptian society was organized into classes. At the top was the pharaoh, who was considered both a king and a god.

Another civilization, the **city-states** of Sumer, developed along the Tigris and Euphrates rivers. This area was called **Mesopotamia,** and was located in the **Fertile Crescent.** The city-states often fought for control of land and water. War leaders eventually became rulers, and a social **hierarchy** emerged. The Sumerians built dikes, irrigation ditches, and **ziggurats,** or pyramid-temples. They also invented the earliest form of writing, called **cuneiform,** which **scribes** learned how to read and write.

About 2300 B.C., Sargon, the ruler of Akkad, conquered the city-states of Sumer. He built the world's first empire. About 1790 B.C., Hammurabi, king of Babylon, conquered much of Mesopotamia. His law code was the first major collection of laws in history.

About 2000 B.C., the **Hebrews** migrated from Mesopotamia to Canaan. They developed Judaism, a **monotheistic** religion based on the belief in one God. They recorded events and laws in the Torah, their most sacred text. **Prophets** preached a strong code of **ethics** and urged the Hebrews to obey God's law. The Hebrews established the kingdom of Israel, which eventually split into two parts. Invading armies captured the Hebrews, who later became known as Jews. About 2,000 years ago, many Jews were forced to leave their homeland. This scattering of the Jewish people is known as the **diaspora.**

Review Questions

1. Why did Egyptian rulers build pyramids?

____

____

2. Who invented the earliest form of writing, and what was it called?

____

____

READING CHECK

What was the diaspora?

____

____

____

VOCABULARY STRATEGY

Find the word *complex* in the underlined sentence. What do you think it means? The word *simple* is an antonym of the word *complex.* Use this clue to help you figure out the meaning of *complex.*

READING SKILL

Compare and Contrast Compare and contrast the geography of civilizations in Egypt and in Sumer.

____

____

____

Name________________ Class________________ Date________

PART **1.3**

Note Taking Study Guide

EARLY CIVILIZATIONS IN INDIA AND CHINA

As you read this section in your textbook, complete the outline below to summarize information about early civilizations in India and China.

I. Cities of the Indus Valley

A. India's first civilization arose in Indus River valley about 2600 B.C.

B. Two main cities were Mohenjo-Daro and Harappa.

C. ________________

II. ________________

A. ________________

1. ________________

2. ________________

B. ________________

1. ________________

2. ________________

C. ________________

1. ________________

2. ________________

3. ________________

III. ________________

A. ________________

1. ________________

2. ________________

B. ________________

1. ________________

2. ________________

C. ________________

1. ________________

2. ________________

3. ________________

D. ________________

1. ________________

2. ________________

3. ________________

Name________________________ Class____________ Date______

PART 1.3

Section Summary

EARLY CIVILIZATIONS IN INDIA AND CHINA

India's first civilization emerged in the Indus River valley about 2500 B.C. This civilization flourished for 1,000 years and covered the largest area of any in ancient times. Its two main cities, **Mohenjo-Daro** and Harappa, were carefully planned, with plumbing systems and underground sewers.

About 1500 B.C., nomadic people from the north, called **Aryans,** overran the cities of the Indus region. They spread eastward to the Ganges River basin. By 500 B.C., a new Indian civilization, with many rival kingdoms, had emerged.

Most of what we know about the Aryans comes from the **Vedas,** a collection of prayers, hymns, and religious teachings. The Aryans divided themselves into social classes by occupation. Over time, these divisions grew into a system of **castes.** These are social groups into which people are born and cannot leave. We also know that the Aryans were **polytheistic,** or believed in many gods. They eventually came to believe in a single spiritual power, called **brahman,** which lived in all things. Some Aryans became **mystics,** who devoted their lives to seeking spiritual truth.

The ancient Chinese believed that China was at the center of Earth and the sole source of civilization. Physical barriers, including mountains and deserts, separated China from the rest of the world and contributed to this belief.

Chinese civilization began in the Huang He valley. About 1650 B.C., a Chinese people called the Shang came to power in northern China. In 1027 B.C., the **Zhou** people overthrew the Shang. The Zhou **dynasty,** or ruling family, lasted until 256 B.C. They promoted the idea of the Mandate of Heaven, or the divine right to rule. This idea was later used to explain the **dynastic cycle,** or the rise and fall of dynasties.

The Chinese prayed to many gods and nature spirits. Over time, these religious practices came to center on respect for ancestors. The Chinese also believed that the universe reflected a balance between two forces, yin and yang. They studied the planets and eclipses and created an accurate calendar. They also developed bronzemaking and silkmaking and made the first books.

Review Questions

1. When and where did India's first civilization emerge?

____

____

2. Name three achievements of the ancient Chinese.

____

READING CHECK

What are castes?

____

____

____

VOCABULARY STRATEGY

What does the word *barriers* mean in the underlined sentence? Two examples of physical *barriers* are given in the sentence. How do these examples help you understand the meaning of *barriers*?

READING SKILL

Identify Main Ideas List four main ideas about the Aryans from the second paragraph of the Summary.

____

____

____

____

Name____________________ Class____________________ Date__________

PART 2.1

Note Taking Study Guide

EMPIRES OF INDIA AND CHINA

As you read this section in your textbook, complete the outline below to summarize information about the religions and empires of India and China.

I. Hinduism and Buddhism

- **A.** Both developed in ancient India.
- **B.** Hinduism
  - **1.** ____________________
  - **2.** ____________________
- **C.** ____________________
  - **1.** ____________________
  - **2.** ____________________

II. ____________________

- **A.** ____________________
  - **1.** ____________________
  - **2.** ____________________
- **B.** ____________________
- **C.** ____________________
  - **1.** ____________________
  - **2.** ____________________

III. ____________________

- **A.** ____________________
  - **1.** ____________________
  - **2.** ____________________
- **B.** ____________________
  - **1.** ____________________
  - **2.** ____________________
- **C.** ____________________
  - **1.** ____________________
  - **2.** ____________________

IV. ____________________

- **A.** ____________________
- **B.** ____________________
  - **1.** ____________________
  - **2.** ____________________

Name__________________________ Class____________ Date______

PART **2.1**

Section Summary

EMPIRES OF INDIA AND CHINA

Hinduism and Buddhism both developed in ancient India. Hinduism has no single founder and no single sacred text. Hindus believe that everything is part of the spiritual force called brahman. The rebirth of the soul in another body, or **reincarnation,** allows people to work toward the goal of union with brahman.

Unlike Hinduism, Buddhism had a single founder, **Siddhartha Gautama,** known as the Buddha. Buddhism urges people to seek enlightenment through meditation, rather than through the priests, rituals, and many gods of Hinduism. The goal of Buddhism is **nirvana,** or union with the universe and release from the cycle of reincarnation.

In 321 B.C., Chandragupta Maurya forged the first great Indian empire. The Maurya dynasty eventually conquered much of India. The greatest Maurya emperor was Asoka, Chandragupta's grandson. He converted to Buddhism, and his policies brought peace and wealth. After his death, rivals battled for power.

About 500 years after the Mauryas, the Gupta dynasty reunited much of India. Under the Guptas, India enjoyed a golden age of peace and achievement. Most Indians of that period were village peasants. The village and the family maintained order, and caste rules governed every part of life.

Important philosophies and religions in ancient China also developed. China's most influential philosopher, **Confucius,** was born in 551 B.C. He was concerned with social order and good government. He put **filial piety,** or respect for parents, above all other duties. His ideas came to influence every area of Chinese life. Another Chinese philosopher, Hanfeizi, insisted that strict laws and harsh punishments were needed to maintain order. Hanfeizi's teachings came to be known as Legalism. A third philosophy, Daoism, arose around the same time. Daoists sought to live in harmony with nature and viewed government as unnatural.

When the Zhou dynasty weakened, a new ruler, **Shi Huangdi,** rose to unify all of China. He built a strong government, as well as the Great Wall. After his death, a new dynasty, the **Han,** was founded. Under the Han, the Chinese made huge advances in trade, government, technology, and the arts. Under the Han, the Silk Road linked China to the Fertile Crescent.

Review Questions

1. According to Hindus, what is the purpose of reincarnation?

____

____

2. Name three philosophies that developed in ancient China.

____

____

READING CHECK

What major building project took place under Shi Huangdi?

____

____

____

VOCABULARY STRATEGY

What does the word *converted* mean in the underlined sentence? The verb *convert* comes from the Latin word *vertere,* which means "to turn." The verb *convert* is often used to describe a religious experience. Use these clues to help you understand the meaning of *converted.*

READING SKILL

Contrast List some main differences between Hinduism and Buddhism.

____

____

____

Name______________________ Class________________ Date__________

PART **2.2**

Note Taking Study Guide

ANCIENT GREECE

As you read this section in your textbook, complete the outline below to summarize the information about ancient Greece.

I. Early People of the Aegean

A. Minoans

1. Traders on the island of Crete
2. ______________________________

B. ______________________________

1. ______________________________
2. ______________________________

II. ______________________________

A. ______________________________

B. ______________________________

1. ______________________________
2. ______________________________

C. ______________________________

1. ______________________________
2. ______________________________
3. ______________________________

D. ______________________________

1. ______________________________
2. ______________________________

E. ______________________________

1. ______________________________
2. ______________________________

III. ______________________________

A. ______________________________

B. ______________________________

C. ______________________________

IV. ______________________________

A. ______________________________

B. ______________________________

Name________________________ Class____________ Date______

PART **2.2**

Section Summary

ANCIENT GREECE

The Minoans created the earliest civilization in the Aegean region. They were traders from the island of Crete who adapted Egyptian and Mesopotamian ideas to their own culture. Minoan civilization reached its height between about 1600 and 1500 B.C., but had vanished by 1400 B.C. The Mycenaeans, another civilization of sea traders, soon dominated Crete and the Greek mainland. They are best remembered for their part in the Trojan War, which was described by **Homer** in the *Iliad* and the *Odyssey*.

After Mycenaean civilization declined, the Greeks lived in small, isolated farming villages. Eventually, they began to build many small city-states. They often warred among themselves, but they shared a common culture, including their language, religion, and festivals. The Greeks evolved a unique version of the city-state, called the **polis.** Their cities often had two levels. They built temples on the **acropolis,** or high city, above the main city. At first, the ruler of the polis was a king. This type of government is called a **monarchy.** Power slowly shifted to a landholding elite, or **aristocracy.** Wealthy merchants, farmers, and artisans came to rule some city-states. The result was a form of government called an **oligarchy,** or rule by a small, powerful elite.

Two of the most important Greek city-states were Sparta and Athens. Sparta was a warrior society. Athens was a **democracy,** or government by the people. When the Persians threatened the Greeks, the city-states joined together to defend themselves. After the Persian Wars, Athens thrived. Under the leadership of **Pericles,** Athenian culture flourished. Athens also developed a **direct democracy,** in which a large number of citizens took part in day-to-day government.

Philosophers like Socrates, Plato, and Aristotle developed new ideas about truth, reason, and government. They used observation and reason to find causes for events. Greeks also developed new styles of art, architecture, poetry, and drama.

Greece was eventually controlled by King Philip of Macedonia. After his death, his son **Alexander** the Great conquered a vast area and spread Greek civilization. Greek culture blended with Persian, Egyptian, and Indian cultures to create the Hellenistic civilization.

Review Questions

1. For what event are the Mycenaeans best remembered?

____

____

2. How did Greek philosophers find causes for events?

____

____

READING CHECK

What civilization resulted from the blending of Greek, Persian, Egyptian, and Indian cultures under Alexander the Great?

____

____

____

VOCABULARY STRATEGY

Find the word *thrived* in the underlined sentence. What does it mean? The sentence that follows the underlined sentence contains a synonym for the word *thrived.* What is that synonym?

READING SKILL

Categorize In which of the following categories does Athenian government under Pericles belong? Circle all that are correct.

city-state

warrior society

monarchy

aristocracy

oligarchy

democracy

Name______________________ Class________________ Date________

PART **2.3**

Note Taking Study Guide

ANCIENT ROME AND THE RISE OF CHRISTIANITY

As you read this section in the textbook, complete the outline below to summarize information about ancient Rome and the rise of Christianity.

I. The Roman World Takes Shape

A. Rome began as a small city-state in Italy.

B. Romans overthrew Etruscan king and set up a republic.

1. At first, patricians controlled the government.

2. ______________________

C. ______________________

II. ______________________

A. ______________________

B. ______________________

1. ______________________

2. ______________________

3. ______________________

III. ______________________

A. ______________________

B. ______________________

C. ______________________

IV. ______________________

A. ______________________

1. ______________________

2. ______________________

3. ______________________

B. ______________________

1. ______________________

2. ______________________

3. ______________________

V. ______________________

A. ______________________

B. ______________________

1. ______________________

2. ______________________

3. ______________________

Name________________________ Class___________ Date______

PART 2.3

Section Summary

ANCIENT ROME AND THE RISE OF CHRISTIANITY

Rome began as a small city-state in Italy. In 509 B.C., the Romans overthrew the Etruscan king who ruled their area. They set up a **republic,** a government in which the people choose the officials. At first, **patricians,** or members of the upper class, controlled the government. Eventually, commoners, or **plebeians,** were elected to the Roman senate. Meanwhile, Rome's armies expanded Roman control until it reached from Spain to Egypt.

Rome's conquests made it very wealthy, but this wealth led to corruption. Rome faced many civil wars. Eventually, a Roman general named Octavian restored order and took the name **Augustus.** He exercised absolute power, and his rule changed Rome from a republic to an empire. Roman emperors brought peace and order to the lands they controlled. As a result, the 200 years from Augustus to Marcus Aurelius are known as the ***Pax Romana,*** or "Roman Peace."

The Romans admired Greek culture and borrowed Greek ideas. Rome spread this blend of cultures, known as Greco-Roman civilization, to distant lands. Romans also excelled as engineers, building roads, bridges, and aqueducts. Probably the greatest legacy of Rome was its commitment to law and justice.

Early in the *Pax Romana,* Christianity began in the Middle East. A Jew named **Jesus** was born about 4 B.C. in Bethlehem. He called himself the Son of God and taught that his mission was to bring salvation and eternal life. Some people saw Jesus as a troublemaker. He was executed, but his disciples believed he had risen from the dead. Jews who believed that Jesus was the **messiah,** or savior sent by God, became the first Christians. For a while, Christianity remained a **sect** within Judaism. Then Paul spread Christianity to non-Jews. At first, Rome persecuted Christians, but later accepted Christian beliefs.

The Roman empire eventually split into two parts, east and west. In the west, corruption, poverty, and declining moral values contributed to the empire's decline. Germanic invaders finally conquered Rome in 476. However, the eastern Roman empire prospered and became known as the Byzantine empire.

Review Questions

1. In the Roman republic, what group originally controlled the government?

____

____

2. After Jesus was executed, what did his disciples believe happened?

____

____

READING CHECK

What was the *Pax Romana*?

____

____

____

VOCABULARY STRATEGY

Find the word *exercised* in the underlined sentence. The word *exercise* often refers to physical activity or training, but it has a different meaning here. To help you understand the meaning of the word *exercised,* complete the sentence below, using a word other than *exercised.*

Augustus did not just have absolute power, he also ______________ it.

READING SKILL

Recognize Multiple Causes Name three causes that led to the decline of the western Roman empire.

____

____

____

Name______________________ Class__________________ Date______

PART
2.4

Note Taking Study Guide

CIVILIZATIONS OF THE AMERICAS

As you read this section in the textbook, complete the outline below to summarize the information about the early civilizations in the Americas.

I. Olmecs, the First American Civilization

A. ______________________________

B. ______________________________

II. Civilizations of Middle America

A. First settlers were nomadic hunters.

1. ______________________________

2. ______________________________

B. ______________________________

1. ______________________________

2. ______________________________

C. ______________________________

1. ______________________________

2. ______________________________

III. ______________________________

A. ______________________________

B. ______________________________

C. ______________________________

1. ______________________________

2. ______________________________

D. ______________________________

1. ______________________________

2. ______________________________

IV. ______________________________

A. ______________________________

1. ______________________________

2. ______________________________

B. ______________________________

1. ______________________________

2. ______________________________

C. ______________________________

D. ______________________________

Name________________________ Class__________ Date______

PART 2.4

Section Summary

CIVILIZATIONS OF THE AMERICAS

The first settlers in the Americas were nomads who probably migrated across a land bridge between Siberia and Alaska. They gradually spread throughout the Americas. The first American civilization, the **Olmec,** began along the Mexican Gulf Coast. It lasted from about 1500 to 500 B.C.

Later, other civilizations developed in Central and South America. The **Maya,** for example, built city-states in Mesoamerica. They created pyramid temples, a writing system, and an accurate calendar. Each city-state had its own ruling chief. Several hundred years after the Maya declined, the **Aztecs** conquered most of Mexico. The Aztec empire grew wealthy from **tribute,** or payment from conquered people. Conquered people were also the source of human sacrifices for Aztec religious rituals. The Aztecs developed a complex social structure with a single ruler, the emperor, at the top.

In the 1400s, the **Inca** came down from the Andes mountains of Peru. Led by Pachacuti, they conquered an empire 2,500 miles wide. The Inca emperor claimed to be divine and had absolute power. His officials kept records on quipus, or collections of knotted colored strings. The Inca united their empire by imposing their language and religion on the people they conquered. They also created one of the greatest road systems in history.

Before 1500, many different culture groups lived in North America. In the desert southwest, the **Anasazi** built large villages, or pueblos, of stone and adobe brick. At the center of their village life was the **kiva,** a large underground chamber used for religious rituals. In the Mississippi and Ohio river valleys, farming cultures emerged as early as 1000 B.C. The Hopewell people left behind giant earthen mounds. <u>Objects found in the mounds suggest that trade networks stretched from the Gulf of Mexico to the Great Lakes.</u> Hopewell culture was replaced by the **Mississippians,** who built large towns and ceremonial centers.

Variations in climate and resources encouraged the development of different cultures in other parts of North America. In the far north, for example, the Inuits adapted to frozen terrain. In the Northeast, warring tribes eventually settled their differences and formed the Iroquois League.

Review Questions

1. How did the first settlers probably get to the Americas?

____

____

2. Why were there so many different culture groups in North America?

____

____

READING CHECK

What is tribute?

____

____

____

VOCABULARY STRATEGY

What does the word *networks* mean in the underlined sentence? With what other *networks* are you familiar? What do *networks* have in common? This sentence refers to "trade" *networks.* Use your prior knowledge of other *networks* to help you understand what a trade *network* would be like.

READING SKILL

Compare and Contrast Compare and contrast the governments of the Maya, Aztecs, and Inca.

____

____

____

____

____

____

Name________________________ Class__________________ Date________

PART **3.1**

Note Taking Study Guide

THE RISE OF EUROPE

As you read this section in the textbook, complete the outline below to summarize the information about Europe during the Middle Ages.

I. Germanic Civilization

A. ____________________

B. ____________________

II. The Early Middle Ages

A. Charlemagne reunited much of Western Europe.

1. ____________________

2. ____________________

B. ____________________

C. ____________________

D. ____________________

III. ____________________

A. ____________________

1. ____________________

2. ____________________

3. ____________________

B. ____________________

1. ____________________

2. ____________________

a. ____________________

b. ____________________

IV. ____________________

A. ____________________

B. ____________________

1. ____________________

2. ____________________

V. ____________________

A. ____________________

B. ____________________

1. ____________________

2. ____________________

Name______________________ Class__________ Date______

PART 3.1

Section Summary

THE RISE OF EUROPE

When **Germanic peoples** ended Roman rule in the West, they began to create a new civilization. They had no cities and no written laws. Instead, they lived in small communities ruled by elected kings. Europe became a fragmented region.

Around 800, **Charlemagne** reunited much of Europe. He revived learning and extended Christian civilization into northern Europe. <u>He also set up a strong, efficient government.</u> After Charlemagne's death, his grandsons divided his empire into three regions. Muslims, Magyars, and Vikings all attacked these regions. A new system, called **feudalism,** evolved in response to the need for protection from the invaders.

Under feudalism, powerful lords gave land to lesser lords, or **vassals.** A lord granted his vassal a **fief,** or estate, which included the peasants who worked the land. In exchange for land and protection, vassals pledged service and loyalty to the greater lord. Because feudal lords battled constantly, many nobles trained as **knights,** or mounted warriors. They adopted a code of conduct called **chivalry,** which required them to be brave, loyal, and true to their word.

The **manor,** or lord's estate, was the heart of the medieval economy. Most manors included one or more villages and surrounding lands. Most of the peasants on a manor were **serfs.** They could not be sold like enslaved people, but they spent their lives working for the lord of the manor. In return, the lord gave them protection and the right to farm some land for themselves.

After the fall of Rome, the Christian Church split into an eastern and a western church. The western church, headed by the pope, became known as the **Roman Catholic Church.** As the Church grew stronger and wealthier, it became the most powerful **secular,** or worldly, force in medieval Europe. Because the Church administered the sacraments, it also had absolute power in religious matters.

By the 1000s, advances in agriculture and commerce spurred economic revival in Europe. Farming was improved by new iron plows and the three-field system. New trade routes and goods also increased wealth. Merchant **guilds,** or associations, came to dominate life in medieval towns.

Review Questions

1. Why did feudalism evolve?

____

____

2. Why did the Roman Catholic Church have absolute power in religious matters?

____

____

READING CHECK

What is chivalry?

____

____

____

VOCABULARY STRATEGY

What does the word *efficient* mean in the underlined sentence? *Efficient* comes from the Latin word *efficere,* which means "to bring to pass" or "accomplish." If a government is *efficient,* what would you expect it to be able to do? Use these clues to understand the meaning of *efficient* in this sentence.

READING SKILL

Identify Supporting Details Identify the details in the Summary that support the following idea: By the 1000s, advances in agriculture and commerce spurred economic revival in Europe.

____

____

____

Name________________________ Class____________________ Date________

PART **3.2**

Note Taking Study Guide

THE HIGH AND LATE MIDDLE AGES

As you read this section in the textbook, complete the outline below to summarize the information about the High and Late Middle Ages.

I. Growth of Royal Power in England

A. ______________________________

B. ______________________________

C. Evolving traditions

1. Kings had conflicts with nobles and the Church.

2. ______________________________

D. ______________________________

1. ______________________________

2. ______________________________

II. ______________________________

A. ______________________________

B. ______________________________

C. ______________________________

1. ______________________________

2. ______________________________

III. ______________________________

A. ______________________________

1. ______________________________

2. ______________________________

3. ______________________________

B. ______________________________

1. ______________________________

2. ______________________________

IV. ______________________________

A. ______________________________

B. ______________________________

C. ______________________________

V. ______________________________

A. ______________________________

B. ______________________________

Name________________________ Class___________ Date______

PART 3.2

Section Summary

THE HIGH AND LATE MIDDLE AGES

When William the Conqueror took the throne of England in 1066, he helped unify England and strengthen the monarchy. Other kings developed the basis for English **common law,** or law that is the same for all people. A jury system also developed. A **jury,** or group of men sworn to speak the truth, determined which cases should be brought to trial. In the early 1200s, a group of nobles forced England's King John to sign the **Magna Carta,** or Great Charter. The Magna Carta contained two basic ideas. First, it said that nobles had certain rights. Second, it made clear that the monarch must also obey the law.

The **Holy Roman Empire** arose from the many Germanic kingdoms that formed after the death of Charlemagne. When a single ruler united these kingdoms, the pope crowned him "emperor." His successors took the title "Holy Roman Emperor." Popes soon clashed with the Holy Roman emperors. Refusal to obey the Church could result in **excommunication.** This meant that someone could not receive the **sacraments,** or sacred rituals of the Church.

In the 1050s, Muslim Turks invaded the Byzantine empire. The Byzantine emperor asked the pope in Rome for help. Soon, thousands of Christian knights left for the Holy Land to fight **crusades,** or holy wars. The Crusades failed in their chief goal—the conquest of the Holy Land. Instead, they left behind a legacy of religious hatred. However, the Crusades increased European trade, papal power, and the power of monarchs. Contacts with the Muslim world also introduced Christians to regions they had not known existed.

A revival of learning took place in the High Middle Ages. Schools sprang up around cathedrals, eventually becoming the first universities. Ideas and texts from ancient Greece reached the universities through the works of Muslim scholars. New writings began to be produced in the **vernacular,** or everyday language of ordinary people.

In the late Middle Ages, bubonic plague, also called the **Black Death,** spread through Europe. One in three people died, and the plague brought social and economic upheaval. Famine and war added to the turmoil of the period.

Review Questions

1. How did nobles in the early 1200s limit the power of the English king?

____

____

2. What made excommunication such a serious punishment?

____

____

READING CHECK

What is the vernacular?

____

____

____

VOCABULARY STRATEGY

What does the word *unify* mean in the underlined sentence? *Uni-* is a root word meaning "one" and *-fy* is a suffix meaning "make" or "cause to become." Use these word-part clues to figure out the meaning of *unify.*

READING SKILL

Understand Effects Name five effects of the Crusades.

____

____

____

____

____

Name______________________ Class__________________ Date________

PART 3.3

Note Taking Study Guide

THE BYZANTINE EMPIRE AND RUSSIA

As you read this section in the textbook, complete the outline below to summarize the information about the Byzantine empire, Russia, and Eastern Europe.

I. The Byzantine Empire

A. Roman emperor Constantine rebuilt Byzantium and renamed it Constantinople.

1. Eastern Roman empire became known as Byzantine empire.

2. ______________________

B. ______________________

1. ______________________

2. ______________________

C. ______________________

1. ______________________

2. ______________________

D. ______________________

1. ______________________

2. ______________________

II. ______________________

A. ______________________

B. ______________________

C. ______________________

D. ______________________

E. ______________________

F. ______________________

1. ______________________

2. ______________________

3. ______________________

III. ______________________

A. ______________________

B. ______________________

Name________________________ Class____________ Date______

PART 3.3

Section Summary

THE BYZANTINE EMPIRE AND RUSSIA

By 330 A.D. the Roman emperor Constantine had rebuilt the city of Byzantium as his capital and renamed it **Constantinople**. The city thrived because of trade. The eastern Roman empire eventually became known as the Byzantine empire. The Byzantine emperor **Justinian** had the laws of ancient Rome organized into a collection, known as Justinian's Code. <u>This code preserved and spread the heritage of Roman law.</u>

In the Byzantine empire, the emperor controlled Church affairs, rejecting the pope's claim to authority over all Christians. By 1054, controversies caused a **schism,** or permanent split, between the Eastern (Greek) Orthodox and Roman Catholic churches.

Byzantine civilization blended Christian beliefs with Greek science, philosophy, and the arts. When the empire fell in the 1400s, Greek scholars took Greek manuscripts and their knowledge of Greek and Byzantine culture to the West.

During Roman times, a people called the Slavs moved into southern Russia. In the 700s and 800s, the Vikings began to trade with the Slavs. The city of **Kiev** became a trade center and the center of the first Russian state. Missionaries from Constantinople brought Christianity to Russia and developed an alphabet for the Slavic languages. In the early 1200s, the Mongols overran Russia. The absolute power of the Mongols served as a model for later Russian rulers. Eventually, the princes of Moscow gained power and defeated the Mongols. Between 1462 and 1505, **Ivan III,** or Ivan the Great, brought much of northern Russia under his control. He took the title **tsar,** the Russian word for *Caesar*. His grandson, known as Ivan the Terrible, introduced Russia to a tradition of extreme absolute power.

Many ethnic groups, including Slavs, Asians, and Germanic peoples, settled in Eastern Europe. An **ethnic group** is a large group of people who share the same language and cultural heritage. Byzantine missionaries brought Eastern Orthodox Christianity and Byzantine culture to the Balkans. German knights and missionaries spread Roman Catholic Christianity to the area. In the late Middle Ages, many Jewish settlers came to Eastern Europe to escape persecution. Many kingdoms and small states arose in Eastern Europe, including Poland, Hungary, and Serbia.

Review Questions

1. Who controlled Church affairs in the Byzantine empire?

____

____

2. What two peoples came together to form the first Russian state?

____

____

READING CHECK

What is an ethnic group?

____

____

____

VOCABULARY STRATEGY

What does the word *preserved* mean in the underlined sentence? An antonym of *preserved* is *destroyed.* Use this clue to help you understand the meaning of *preserved.*

READING SKILL

Recognize Sequence Number the following events from Russian history to show the correct sequence:

____ Kiev becomes the center of the first Russian state.

____ Mongols overrun Russia.

____ Slavs move into southern Russia.

____ Ivan the Great takes the title of tsar.

____ Princes of Moscow defeat the Mongols.

____ Ivan the Terrible reigns.

____ Vikings begin to trade with Slavs.

Name______________________ Class__________________ Date________

PART **3.4**

Note Taking Study Guide

MUSLIM CIVILIZATIONS

As you read this section in the textbook, complete the outline below to summarize the information about the rise of Islam and Muslim civilizations.

I. Rise of Islam
- A. Muhammad
  1. Born in Mecca in western Arabia about 570
  2. ______________________
  3. ______________________
- B. ______________________
  1. ______________________
  2. ______________________
  3. ______________________

II. ______________________
- A. ______________________
- B. ______________________
- C. ______________________

III. ______________________
- A. ______________________
- B. ______________________
- C. ______________________
- D. ______________________

IV. ______________________
- A. ______________________
- B. ______________________
- C. ______________________
  1. ______________________
  2. ______________________
- D. ______________________
  1. ______________________
  2. ______________________

V. ______________________
- A. ______________________
  1. ______________________
  2. ______________________
- B. ______________________
  1. ______________________
  2. ______________________

Name________________________ Class___________ Date______

PART
3.4 Section Summary
MUSLIM CIVILIZATIONS

Muhammad was born in Arabia about 570. According to Muslim belief, he was called in a vision to become God's messenger. He spent the rest of his life spreading Islam. Like Judaism and Christianity, Islam is a monotheistic religion. All Muslims accept five duties, known as the Five Pillars of Islam. These include belief in one God, daily prayer, charity to the poor, fasting, and the **hajj,** or pilgrimage to Mecca. Muslims believe that the Quran contains the word of God and is the final authority on all matters.

When Muhammad died, Abu Bakr was elected to be the first **caliph,** or successor to Muhammad. He was the first in a series of rulers who led military conquests that expanded Islam to the Atlantic and to the Indus Valley. Muslim merchants established a vast trading network that also spread Islamic ideas. Eventually, the Abbasid dynasty made **Baghdad** the capital of Islam, which became a great center of learning. Muslims pioneered the study of algebra and made advances in medicine and other fields. Islamic artists and architects created elaborate mosaics and beautiful **mosques,** or houses of worship.

In the late 1100s, a **sultan,** or Muslim ruler, defeated Hindu armies in India. His successors founded the Delhi sultanate. Muslim rule brought changes to India. Destruction of Buddhist monasteries led to the decline of Buddhism as a major religion in India. Many Hindus were killed. In 1526, Turkish and Mongol invaders, led by Babur, poured into India. They ended the Delhi sultanate and set up the **Mughal dynasty,** which ruled from 1526 to 1857.

In 1453, the Ottomans captured Constantinople and renamed it Istanbul. The **Ottoman empire** was a powerful force for 500 years. At its height, it stretched from Hungary to Arabia and across North Africa. Under Suleiman, who ruled from 1520 to 1566, the Ottoman empire enjoyed its golden age. <u>Ottoman poets adapted Persian and Arab models to produce works in the Turkish language.</u>

Another Muslim dynasty, the Safavid, united a strong empire in present-day Iran. Shah Abbas the Great ruled from 1588 to 1629 and revived the glory of ancient Persia.

Review Questions

1. What do Judaism, Christianity, and Islam have in common?

____

____

2. Name two ways in which Islam and Islamic ideas were spread.

____

____

READING CHECK

What is a sultan?

____

____

____

VOCABULARY STRATEGY

What does the word *adapted* mean in the underlined sentence? *Adapt* comes from the Latin word *adaptare*, which means "to fit to." Use this word-origins clue to help you understand the meaning of *adapted* in this sentence.

READING SKILL

Identify Supporting Details List two sentences from the Summary that support the following idea: Muslim rule brought changes to India.

____

____

____

Name________________________ Class____________________ Date_______

PART **3.5**

Note Taking Study Guide

KINGDOMS AND TRADING STATES OF AFRICA

As you read this section in the textbook, complete the outline below to summarize the information about the kingdoms and trading states of Africa.

I. Bantu Migrations

II. Early Civilizations of Africa

- **A.** The Kingdom of Nubia
  - **1.** ____________________
  - **2.** ____________________
  - **3.** ____________________
- **B.** ____________________
  - **1.** ____________________
  - **2.** ____________________
  - **3.** ____________________

III. ____________________

- **A.** ____________________
- **B.** ____________________
- **C.** ____________________
  - **1.** ____________________
  - **2.** ____________________
  - **3.** ____________________
- **D.** ____________________
  - **1.** ____________________
  - **2.** ____________________
- **E.** ____________________
  - **1.** ____________________
  - **2.** ____________________

IV. ____________________

- **A.** ____________________
- **B.** ____________________

V. ____________________

- **A.** ____________________
- **B.** ____________________
- **C.** ____________________
- **D.** ____________________

Name____________________ Class__________ Date______

PART
3.5 Section Summary
KINGDOMS AND TRADING STATES OF AFRICA

Two important civilizations developed along the Nile River in Africa. One was Egypt. The other was **Nubia,** or Kush. Powerful kings ruled Nubia for thousands of years. The Egyptians sometimes conquered Nubia, and Nubians adopted many Egyptian traditions. About A.D. 350, armies from the kingdom of Axum overran Nubia.

Egypt and North Africa were ruled, for a time, by the Greeks and then the Romans. Linked to a global trade network, North African ports prospered. Camels that had been brought to North Africa from Asia revolutionized trade across the Sahara. Gold and salt were the main trade items. North Africans wanted gold to buy European goods. West Africans traded gold to North Africans in exchange for salt, which they needed to stay healthy.

By A.D. 800, the kingdom of **Ghana** had been formed in West Africa. The king controlled the gold-salt trade routes. Muslim merchants brought Islam to Ghana. Ghana declined in the late 1100s and was overtaken by the kingdom of Mali. Mali controlled both the gold-mining regions and the salt supplies of the Sahara. The greatest emperor of Mali was **Mansa Musa.** As Mali weakened in the 1400s, a new West African kingdom, Songhai, arose. Songhai was the largest state that had ever existed in West Africa. The kingdom controlled trade routes and wealthy cities like Timbuktu.

By the time **Axum** conquered Nubia, Axum had long been an important trading center. It linked trade routes from Africa, India, and the Mediterranean world. As Axum declined, other trading centers rose along the East African coast. By 1000, East African port cities were thriving from trade across the Indian Ocean.

Early African societies varied depending on geography, climate, and other factors. In some societies, the **nuclear family** was typical, while in other communities, the family included several generations. Religious beliefs were also varied. Some Africans followed traditional beliefs and were polytheistic. Others followed Christianity or Islam. **Griots,** or professional storytellers, preserved African values and history by reciting ancient stories. Migrations contributed to the diversity of cultures. The **Bantu migrations,** for example, spread Bantu languages throughout much of southern Africa.

Review Questions

1. Why did West Africans trade gold in exchange for salt?

____

____

2. What role did griots play in African society?

____

____

READING CHECK

What effect did camels have on trade in Africa?

____

____

____

VOCABULARY STRATEGY

What does the word *global* mean in the underlined sentence? *Global* comes from the word *globe.* Use this word-family clue to help you understand the meaning of the word *global.*

READING SKILL

Identify Causes Why did cities along the East African coast thrive?

____

____

____

Name____________________ Class________________ Date________

PART **3.6**

Note Taking Study Guide

SPREAD OF CIVILIZATIONS IN EAST ASIA

As you read this section in the textbook, complete the outline below to summarize the information about the civilizations in East Asia.

I. Sui Dynasty

- **A.** ____________________
- **B.** ____________________

II. Two Golden Ages of China

- **A.** Tang dynasty (618–907)
  - **1.** ____________________
  - **2.** ____________________
- **B.** ____________________
  - **1.** ____________________
  - **2.** ____________________
- **C.** ____________________
  - **1.** ____________________
  - **2.** ____________________
- **D.** ____________________
  - **1.** ____________________
  - **2.** ____________________

III. ____________________

- **A.** ____________________
- **B.** ____________________
- **C.** ____________________
  - **1.** ____________________
  - **2.** ____________________

IV. ____________________

- **A.** ____________________
- **B.** ____________________

V. ____________________

- **A.** ____________________
- **B.** ____________________

VI. ____________________

- **A.** ____________________
- **B.** ____________________
- **C.** ____________________

Name______________________ Class__________ Date______

PART 3.6

Section Summary

SPREAD OF CIVILIZATIONS IN EAST ASIA

In the 500s, the Sui dynasty reunited China. Then a Sui general and his son, Tang Taizong, established their own dynasty, the **Tang.** Tang armies forced neighboring lands to become **tributary states.** These states remained independent, but had to send tribute to the Tang emperor. Tang emperors restored the bureaucracy and redistributed land to the peasants.

The Tang dynasty collapsed in 907, and the **Song** dynasty soon rose to take its place. The Song period was a golden age of wealth and culture. Under both the Tang and Song, China was a well-ordered society. The two main classes were the gentry and the peasantry. The gentry were wealthy landowners. Most scholar-officials came from this class. Painting and calligraphy became essential skills for the gentry.

In the 1200s, the **Mongols** invaded China and toppled the weakened Song dynasty. They established peace and order, and trade flourished along the Silk Road. In 1368, a rebel army drove the Mongols out of China. A new dynasty, the **Ming,** sought to reassert Chinese greatness. Under the Ming, Zheng He led a series of sea voyages into distant waters.

China influenced other peoples. Korea, for example, absorbed many Chinese traditions. Yet it maintained its own identity and even improved on a number of Chinese inventions, such as book printing and an alphabet. Japan also felt the influence of Chinese civilization. However, the surrounding seas protected and isolated Japan and allowed it to maintain its own distinct culture. However, in the early 600s, rulers of the Yamato dynasty sent young nobles to study in China. For a time, the Japanese modeled much of their society on Chinese ideas.

Japan eventually evolved into a feudal society. In theory, the emperor was at the top. <u>In fact, he was a powerless, though revered, figurehead.</u> The **shogun**, or supreme military commander, had the real power. He gave land to warrior lords who agreed to support him with their armies. These lords were called **daimyo.** They, in turn, gave land to lesser warriors called **samurai.** In 1603, Tokugawa Ieyasu founded the **Tokugawa** shogunate, which brought peace and stability to Japan.

Review Questions

1. How did Mongol rule affect trade?

____

____

2. What role did land play in the relationships between the shogun, daimyo, and samurai?

____

____

READING CHECK

What were tributary states?

____

____

____

VOCABULARY STRATEGY

What does the word *revered* mean in the underlined sentence? *Revere* comes from the Latin word *revereri*, which means "to feel awe." Use this word-origins clue to help you understand the meaning of *revered.*

READING SKILL

Recognize Sequence Number the dynasties listed below to show the correct sequence.

___ Ming

___ Song

___ Sui

___ Mongol

___ Tang

Name______________________ Class__________________ Date________

CHAPTER 1
SECTION 1

Note Taking Study Guide

THE RENAISSANCE IN ITALY

Focus Question: What were the ideals of the Renaissance, and how did Italian artists and writers reflect these ideals?

As you read this section in your textbook, complete the following outline to identify main ideas and supporting details about the Italian Renaissance.

I. What was the Renaissance?

- **A.** A changing worldview
  - **1.** ______________________
  - **2.** ______________________
- **B.** A spirit of adventure
  - **1.** ______________________
  - **2.** ______________________
- **C.** ______________________
  - **1.** ______________________
  - **2.** ______________________

II. ______________________

- **A.** ______________________
  - **1.** ______________________
  - **2.** ______________________
  - **3.** ______________________
- **B.** ______________________
  - **1.** ______________________
  - **2.** ______________________

III. ______________________

- **A.** ______________________
  - **1.** ______________________
  - **2.** ______________________
- **B.** ______________________
  - **1.** ______________________
  - **2.** ______________________

(Outline continues on the next page.)

Name______________________ Class__________________ Date________

CHAPTER 1 SECTION 1

Note Taking Study Guide

THE RENAISSANCE IN ITALY

(Continued from page 34)

C. ______________________________
  1. ______________________________
  2. ______________________________

D. ______________________________
  1. ______________________________
  2. ______________________________

E. ______________________________
  1. ______________________________
  2. ______________________________

F. ______________________________
  1. ______________________________
  2. ______________________________

IV. ______________________________

A. ______________________________
  1. ______________________________
  2. ______________________________

B. ______________________________
  1. ______________________________
  2. ______________________________

Name__________ Class________ Date______

CHAPTER 1 SECTION 1

Section Summary

THE RENAISSANCE IN ITALY

READING CHECK

What was significant about the discovery of perspective?

____

____

____

VOCABULARY STRATEGY

What does *comprehend* mean in the underlined sentence? What clues can you find in the surrounding text? Circle the words in the paragraph that could help you learn what *comprehend* means.

READING SKILL

Identify Main Ideas Identify three of the main characteristics of the Renaissance.

____

____

____

A new age called the Renaissance, meaning "rebirth," marked a great change in culture, politics, society, and economics. In Italy, it began in the 1300s and reached its peak around 1500. Instead of focusing on religion, as in the Middle Ages, the Renaissance explored the human experience. At the same time, there was a new emphasis on individual achievement. At the heart of the Renaissance was an intellectual movement called **humanism.** <u>Renaissance humanists studied the classical culture of Greece and Rome to try to comprehend their own times.</u> They wanted to broaden their understanding. They emphasized the **humanities**—subjects such as rhetoric, poetry, and history. Poet Francesco **Petrarch** was an early Renaissance humanist. He gathered a library of Greek and Roman manuscripts. This opened the works of Cicero, Homer, and Virgil to Western Europeans.

Italy was the birthplace of the Renaissance for many reasons. It had been the center of the Roman empire; remains of that ancient culture were all around. Rome was also the seat of the Roman Catholic Church, an important **patron** of the arts. Furthermore, Italy's location encouraged trade with markets on the Mediterranean, in Africa, and in Europe. Trade provided the wealth that fueled the Renaissance. In Italy's city-states, powerful merchant families, such as the Medici family of **Florence,** lent political and economic leadership and supported the arts.

Renaissance art reflected humanism. Renaissance painters returned to the realism of classical times by developing improved ways to represent humans and landscapes. For example, the discovery of **perspective** allowed artists to create realistic art and to paint scenes that appeared three-dimensional. The greatest of the Renaissance artists were **Leonardo** da Vinci, **Michelangelo,** and **Raphael.**

Some Italian writers wrote guidebooks to help ambitious people who wanted to rise in the Renaissance world. The most widely read of these was *The Book of the Courtier*, by **Baldassare Castiglione.** His ideal courtier was a well-educated, well-mannered aristocrat who mastered many fields. **Niccolò Machiavelli** wrote a guide for rulers, titled *The Prince*, on how to gain and maintain power.

Review Questions

1. How did the focus of study change between the Middle Ages and the Renaissance?

____

____

2. Identify two reasons why the Renaissance began in Italy.

____

____

Name________________________ Class____________________ Date________

CHAPTER 1
SECTION 2

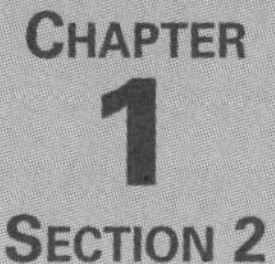

Note Taking Study Guide

THE RENAISSANCE IN THE NORTH

Focus Question: How did the Renaissance develop in northern Europe?

As you read this section in your textbook, complete the following chart to record the main ideas about the Renaissance in the North.

Renaissance in the North		
	Humanists	• • • •
	Artists and Writers	• • • •
	Printing Revolution	• • • •

Name________________________ Class____________ Date______

CHAPTER 1 SECTION 2

Section Summary

THE RENAISSANCE IN THE NORTH

READING CHECK

Where did the northern Renaissance begin?

____

____

____

By the 1400s, northern Europe began to enjoy the economic growth needed to develop its own Renaissance. An astounding invention—the printing press—helped to spread Renaissance ideas. In about 1455, **Johann Gutenberg** printed the first complete edition of the Bible using the new printing press. The printing press caused a printing revolution. Before, books were made by hand. They were rare and expensive. Printed books were cheaper and easier to produce. Now more books were available, so more people learned to read. Printed books exposed Europeans to new ideas and new places.

The northern Renaissance began in the prosperous cities of **Flanders,** a thriving center of trade. Flemish painters pursued realism in their art. One of the most important Flemish painters was Jan van Eyck. He portrayed townspeople and religious scenes in rich detail. Pieter Bruegel used vibrant color to portray lively scenes of peasant life. Peter Paul Rubens blended the tradition of Flemish realism with themes from mythology, the Bible, and history. German painter **Albrecht Dürer** traveled to Italy to study the techniques of the Italian masters. He soon became a pioneer in spreading Renaissance ideas to northern Europe. Dürer applied the painting techniques he learned in Italy to **engraving.** Many of his engravings and paintings portray the theme of religious upheaval.

VOCABULARY STRATEGY

What does the word *prosperous* mean in the underlined sentence? Ask yourself what is meant by a "thriving center of trade." Use that information to help you figure out what *prosperous* means.

Northern European humanists and writers also helped spread Renaissance ideas. The Dutch priest and humanist Desiderius **Erasmus** called for a translation of the Bible into the **vernacular** so that it could be read by a wider audience. The English humanist **Sir Thomas More** called for social reform in the form of a **utopian,** or ideal, society in which people live together in peace and harmony.

The towering figure of Renaissance literature, however, was the English poet and playwright William **Shakespeare.** His 37 plays are still performed around the world. Shakespeare's genius was in expressing universal themes, such as the complexity of the individual, in everyday, realistic settings. He used language that people understand and enjoy. Shakespeare's love of words also enriched the English language with 1,700 new words.

READING SKILL

Identify Main Ideas Write the sentence from the second paragraph of the Summary that states the main idea of that paragraph.

____

____

____

Review Questions

1. What changes did the invention of the printing press bring about?

____

____

2. What theme did Dürer explore in many of his paintings and engravings?

____

____

Name________________________ Class____________________ Date________

Note Taking Study Guide

THE PROTESTANT REFORMATION

Focus Question: How did revolts against the Roman Catholic Church affect northern European society?

As you read this section in your textbook, complete the following concept web to identify main ideas about the Protestant Reformation.

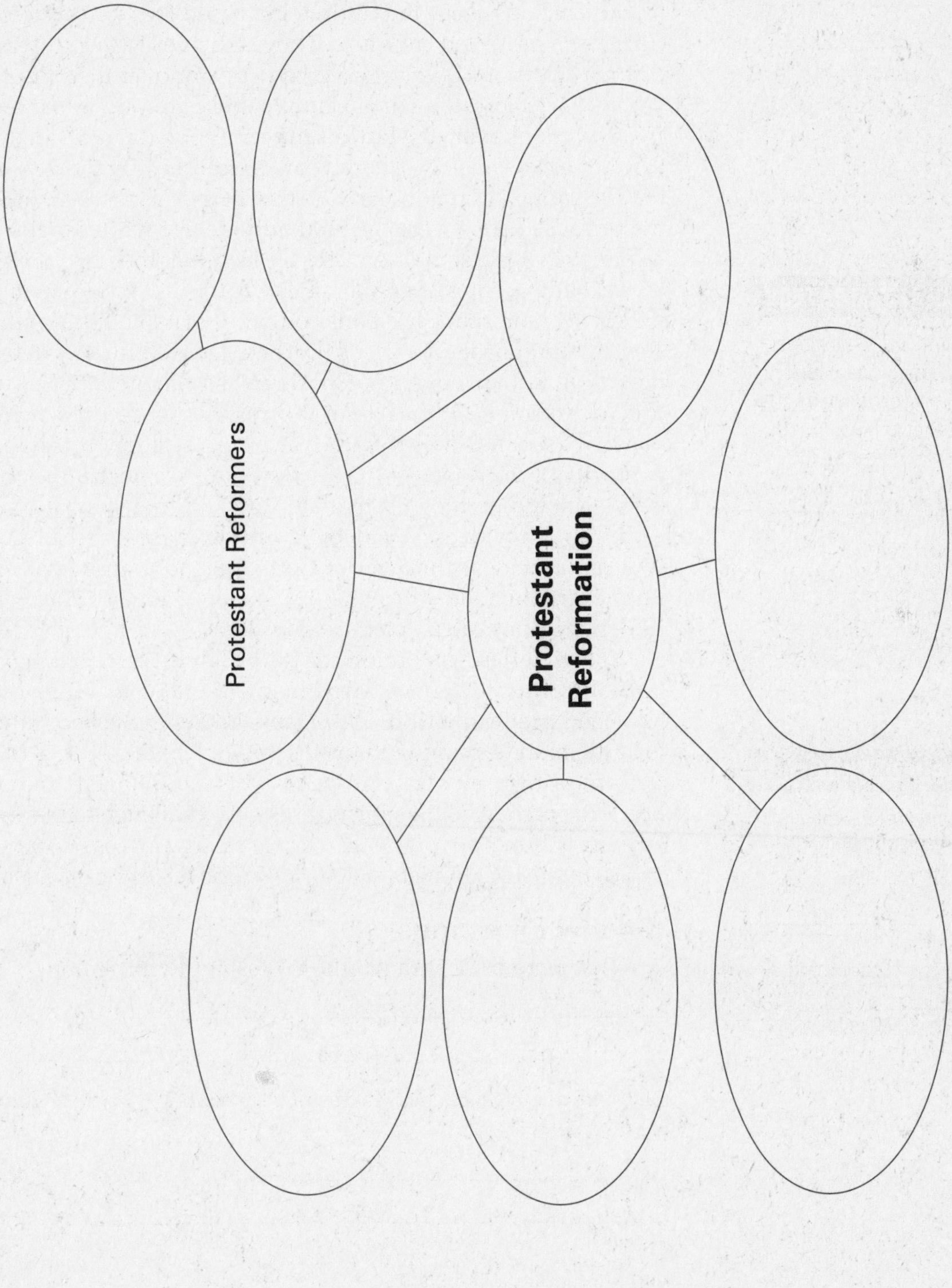

Protestant Reformers

Protestant Reformation

Name______________________ Class__________ Date______

CHAPTER 1 SECTION 3

Section Summary

THE PROTESTANT REFORMATION

In the 1500s, the Renaissance in northern Europe sparked a religious upheaval that affected Christians at all levels of society. This movement is known as the Protestant Reformation. In the late Middle Ages, the Catholic Church had become caught up in worldly affairs. Popes led lavish lives and hired artists to enhance churches. To finance such projects, the Church increased fees for services. Many Christians protested such acts. They also questioned why the Church in distant Rome should have power over their lives.

In 1517, protests against Church abuses turned into a revolt. A German monk named **Martin Luther** triggered it over an event in **Wittenberg,** Germany. There, a priest sold **indulgences** to Christians to raise money to rebuild St. Peter's Cathedral in Rome. To Luther, the priest's actions were the final outrage. He wrote 95 Theses, or arguments, against indulgences. He said that they had no biblical basis, that the pope did not have the authority to release souls from purgatory, and that Christians could be saved only through faith. Throughout Europe, Luther's 95 Theses stirred furious debate. The new Holy Roman emperor, **Charles V,** summoned Luther to the **diet,** or assembly, at the city of Worms. Luther refused to change his views. Thousands hailed Luther as a hero and renounced the authority of the pope. <u>At the heart of Luther's doctrines were several beliefs, including the idea that all Christians have equal access to God through faith and the Bible.</u> Printing presses spread Luther's writings and ideas throughout Germany and Scandinavia. By 1530, Luther's many followers were using a new name, "Protestants," for those who "protested" papal authority.

In Switzerland, the reformer **John Calvin** also challenged the Catholic Church. Calvin shared many of Luther's beliefs, but also preached **predestination.** Protestants in **Geneva** asked Calvin to lead them. In keeping with his teachings, Calvin set up a **theocracy.** Reformers from all over Europe visited Geneva and then returned home to spread Calvin's ideas. This new challenge to the Roman Catholic Church set off fierce wars of religion across Europe. In the 1600s, English Calvinists sailed to America to escape persecution.

READING CHECK

Who was John Calvin?

____

____

____

VOCABULARY STRATEGY

What does the word *doctrine* mean in the underlined sentence? The word comes from a Latin word that means "teaching" or "instruction." Use the word's origin to help you figure out what *doctrine* means.

READING SKILL

Identify Main Ideas What was one of the main beliefs at the heart of Luther's doctrines?

____

____

____

Review Questions

1. What factors encouraged the Protestant Reformation?

____

____

2. What arguments did Martin Luther make against indulgences in the 95 Theses?

____

____

Name______________________ Class__________________ Date________

CHAPTER 1 SECTION 4

Note Taking Study Guide

REFORMATION IDEAS SPREAD

Focus Question: How did the Reformation bring about two different religious paths in Europe?

As you read this section in your textbook, complete the following flowchart to identify main ideas about the spread of the Protestant Reformation in Europe.

Name________________________ Class____________ Date______

CHAPTER 1 SECTION 4

Section Summary

REFORMATION IDEAS SPREAD

READING CHECK

What happened at the Council of Trent?

____

____

____

VOCABULARY STRATEGY

What does the word *rigorous* mean in the underlined sentence? What clues can you find in nearby words? Circle the words in the sentence that could help you figure out what *rigorous* means.

READING SKILL

Identify Main Ideas How did Elizabeth restore unity to England?

____

____

____

As the Reformation continued, hundreds of new Protestant **sects** arose, influencing Protestant thinking in many countries. In England, the break with the Catholic Church came from **Henry VIII.** He and his wife, Catherine of Aragon, had one child, **Mary Tudor.** Henry wanted to divorce Catherine and marry another woman whom he hoped would bear him a male heir. However, the pope refused to annul Henry's marriage. Furious, Henry had Parliament pass laws to take the English church from the pope's control. Henry appointed **Thomas Cranmer** archbishop of the new English church. Cranmer annulled the king's marriage. In 1534, Parliament passed the Act of Supremacy, making Henry the head of the Church of England.

Many Catholics, including Sir Thomas More, refused to accept the Act of Supremacy and were executed. The Catholic Church later **canonized** More for his stand against Henry. When Henry died in 1547, his son Edward VI inherited the throne. Under Edward, Parliament passed laws bringing more Protestant reforms to England. When Edward died, his half-sister Mary Tudor, a Catholic, became queen. She wanted to return England to the Catholic faith. Hundreds of English Protestants were burned at the stake.

On Mary's death in 1558, the throne passed to her half-sister, **Elizabeth.** She made reforms that became known as the Elizabethan settlement—a **compromise** between Protestant and Catholic practices. Elizabeth restored unity to England; she kept many Catholic traditions, but made England a Protestant nation.

As the Protestant Reformation swept northern Europe, the Catholic Church began a Counter Reformation. The pope's **Council of Trent** reaffirmed Catholic beliefs that Protestants had challenged. **Ignatius of Loyola** founded a new religious order, the Jesuits. <u>They followed a rigorous program of strict discipline, thorough religious training, and absolute obedience to the Church.</u> **Teresa of Avila** established her own order of nuns dedicated to prayer and meditation. Both Catholics and Protestants fostered intolerance, and persecuted radical sects. Innocent people were executed for witchcraft. In Venice, Jews were pressured to convert and forced to live in a separate part of the city called the **ghetto.**

Review Questions

1. What caused Henry VIII to break with the Catholic Church and establish the Church of England?

____

____

2. How did many Catholics in England respond to the Act of Supremacy?

____

____

Name________________________ Class____________________ Date________

Note Taking Study Guide

THE SCIENTIFIC REVOLUTION

Focus Question: How did discoveries in science lead to a new way of thinking for Europeans?

As you read this section in your textbook, complete the following to identify main ideas about the Scientific Revolution in Europe.

Thinkers of the Scientific Revolution	
Nicolaus Copernicus	Developed sun-centered universe theory

Name______________________ Class__________ Date______

CHAPTER 1 SECTION 5

Section Summary

THE SCIENTIFIC REVOLUTION

READING CHECK

What did Isaac Newton call the force that keeps planets in their orbits around the sun?

____

____

____

VOCABULARY STRATEGY

What does the word *contradicted* mean in the underlined sentence? The prefix *contra-* means "against." Use the meaning of the word's prefix to help you figure out what *contradict* means.

READING SKILL

Identify Main Ideas How did Copernicus's proposed model of the solar system differ from earlier beliefs?

____

____

____

In the mid-1500s, a big shift in scientific thinking caused the Scientific Revolution. At the heart of this movement was the idea that mathematical laws governed nature and the universe. Before the Renaissance, Europeans thought that Earth was the center of everything in the heavens. In 1543, Polish scholar **Nicolaus Copernicus** proposed a **heliocentric,** or sun-centered, model of the solar system. In the late 1500s, the Danish astronomer **Tycho Brahe** provided evidence that supported Copernicus's theory. The German astronomer and mathematician **Johannes Kepler** used Brahe's data to calculate the orbits of the planets revolving around the sun. His calculations also supported Copernicus's heliocentric view.

Scientists from different lands built on the foundations laid by Copernicus and Kepler. In Italy, **Galileo** assembled a telescope and observed that the four moons of Jupiter move slowly around that planet. He realized that these moons moved the same way that Copernicus had said that Earth moves around the sun. Galileo's findings caused an uproar. Other scholars attacked him because his observations contradicted ancient views about the world. The Church condemned him because his ideas challenged the Christian teaching that the heavenly bodies were fixed in relation to Earth, and perfect.

Despite the opposition of the Church, a new approach to science had emerged, based upon observation and experimentation. To explain their data, scientists used reasoning to propose a logical **hypothesis,** or possible explanation. This process became known as the **scientific method.** The new scientific method was a revolution in thought. Two giants of this revolution were the Englishman **Francis Bacon** and the Frenchman **René Descartes.** Both were devoted to understanding how truth is determined, but they differed in their approaches. Bacon stressed experimentation and observation. Descartes focused on reasoning.

The 1500s and 1600s saw dramatic changes in many branches of science. English chemist **Robert Boyle** explained that matter is composed of particles that behave in knowable ways. **Isaac Newton** used mathematics to show that a single force keeps the planets in their orbits around the sun. He called this force **gravity.** To help explain his laws, Newton developed a branch of mathematics called **calculus.**

Review Questions

1. What assumption was at the heart of the Scientific Revolution?

____

____

2. Why did the Church condemn Galileo?

____

____

Name________________ Class________________ Date________

CHAPTER 2 SECTION 1

Note Taking Study Guide

THE SEARCH FOR SPICES

Focus Question: How did the search for spices lead to global exploration?

As you read this section in your textbook, complete the following flowchart to identify causes and effects of European exploration.

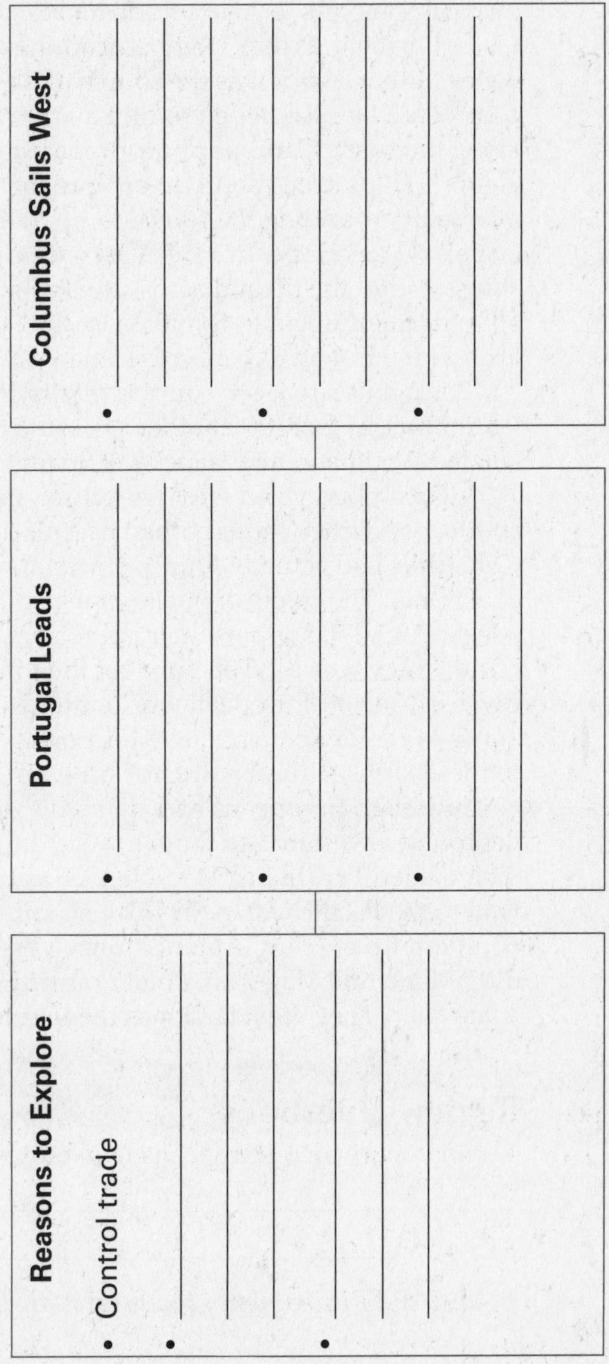

Name________________________ Class____________ Date______

CHAPTER 2 SECTION 1

Section Summary

THE SEARCH FOR SPICES

By the 1400s, Europe's population and its demand for trade goods from Asia were growing. Especially desirable were spices. The chief source of spices was the **Moluccas,** an island chain in present-day Indonesia. Arab and Italian merchants controlled most trade between Asia and Europe. Europeans outside Italy wanted their own direct access to Asia's trade goods.

In Portugal, **Prince Henry** encouraged sea exploration. He believed that Africa was the source of the riches the Muslim traders controlled. He also hoped to find a way to reach Asia by sailing along the coast. **Cartographers** prepared maps for the voyages. Henry's ships sailed south to explore the western coast of Africa, eventually rounding the southern tip, which became known as the Cape of Good Hope. In 1497, **Vasco da Gama** led four Portuguese ships around the tip and across the Indian Ocean to reach the great spice port of Calicut in India. Soon, the Portuguese seized ports around the Indian Ocean, creating a vast trading empire.

Portugal's successes spurred others, including **Christopher Columbus,** to look for another sea route to Asia. Columbus persuaded Ferdinand and Isabella of Spain to finance his voyage. In 1492, Columbus sailed west with three small ships. When the crew spotted land, they thought they had reached the Indies. What Columbus had actually found, however, were previously unknown continents. <u>The rulers of Spain appealed to the Spanish-born Pope Alexander VI to support their authority, or power, to claim the lands of this "new world."</u> The pope set the **Line of Demarcation,** which divided the non-European world into two trading and exploration zones—one for Spain and one for Portugal. The two nations agreed to these terms in the **Treaty of Tordesillas.**

Although Europeans had claimed vast territories, they had not yet found a western sea route to Asia. In 1519, a Portuguese nobleman named **Ferdinand Magellan** set out west from Spain to find a way to the Pacific Ocean. In 1520, he found a passageway at the Southern tip of South America. Survivors of the long voyage, who did not include Magellan, finally returned to Spain nearly three years later. They were hailed as the first to **circumnavigate** the world.

Review Questions

1. What motivated Europeans to explore the seas?

____

____

2. Why did Prince Henry focus on Africa for his explorers' voyages?

____

____

READING CHECK

What was the Line of Demarcation?

____

____

____

VOCABULARY STRATEGY

What does the word *authority* mean in the underlined sentence? What context clues can you find in the surrounding words? Circle the words in the same sentence that could help you learn what *authority* means.

READING SKILL

Identify Causes and Effects

Identify one cause of European exploration.

____

____

Identify two effects of Prince Henry's encouragement of sea exploration.

____

____

____

____

Name________________________ Class________________ Date________

CHAPTER 2 SECTION 2

Note Taking Study Guide

TURBULENT CENTURIES IN AFRICA

Focus Question: What effects did European exploration have on the people of Africa?

As you read this section in your textbook, complete the following chart to identify the effects of European exploration on Africa.

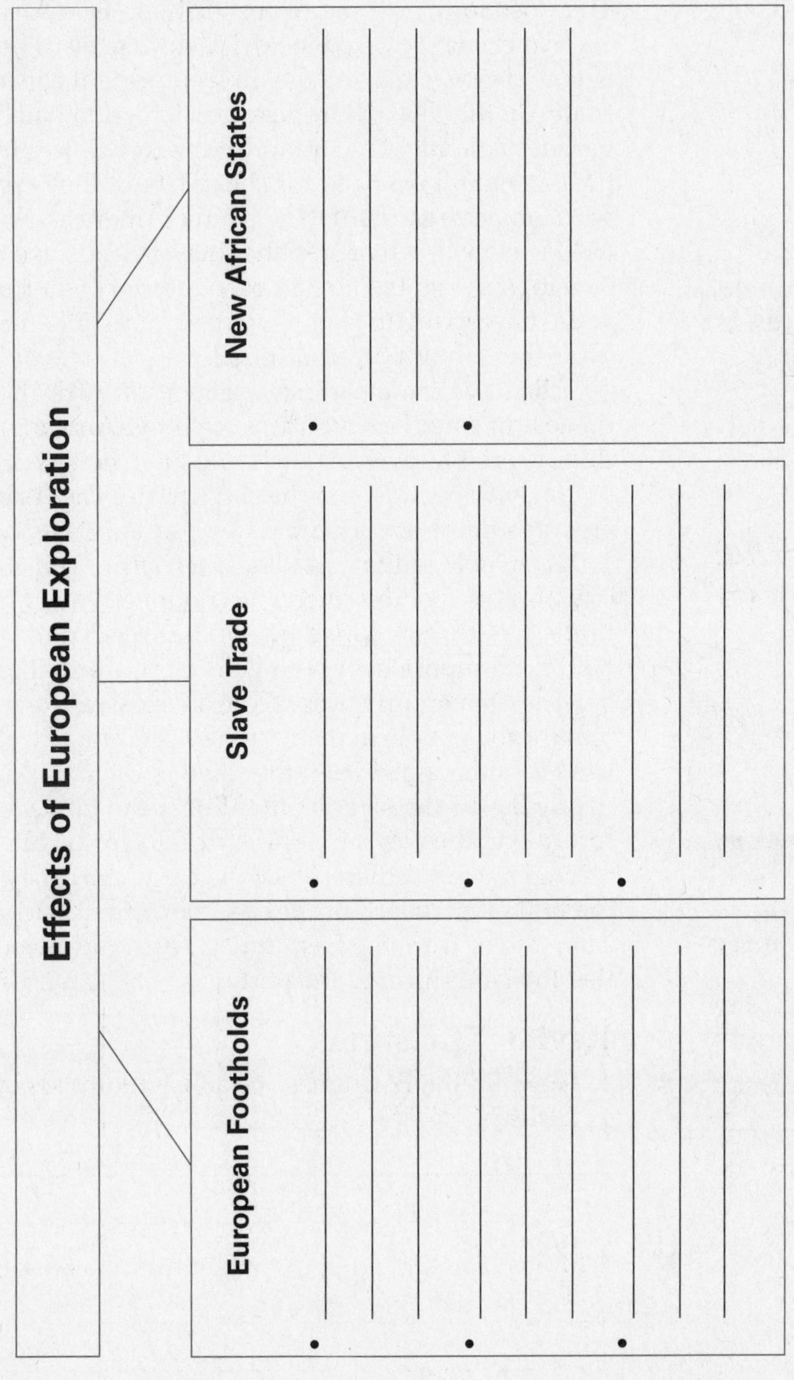

Name________________________ Class____________ Date______

CHAPTER 2 SECTION 2

Section Summary

TURBULENT CENTURIES IN AFRICA

READING CHECK

Why did the Portuguese and other Europeans want slaves?

____

____

____

VOCABULARY STRATEGY

What does the word *unified* mean in the underlined sentence? What clue can you find in the word's prefix, *uni-?* Think of other words you may know that start with *uni-*. Use what you may know about related words to help you figure out what *unified* means.

READING SKILL

Identify Effects Identify two effects the slave trade had on African states.

____

____

____

The Portuguese established footholds on the coast of West Africa, building small forts and trading posts. From West Africa, they sailed around the continent. They continued to establish forts and trading posts, but they also attacked coastal cities of East Africa, such as **Mombasa** and **Malindi,** which were hubs of international trade. They also took over the Arabs' thriving East African trade network.

Slavery had existed in Africa since ancient times. Europeans began to view slaves as the most important aspect of the African trade. By the 1500s, European participation had encouraged a much broader Atlantic slave trade, and it grew into a huge and profitable business to fill the need for cheap labor. They especially needed workers on their **plantations** in the Americas. Some African leaders tried to slow down or stop the transatlantic slave trade. The ruler of Kongo, **Affonso I,** who had been tutored by Portuguese **missionaries,** wanted to maintain contact with Europe but end the slave trade. The slave trade, however, continued.

The slave trade had major effects on African states. Because of the loss of countless numbers of young Africans, some small states disappeared forever. At the same time, new states arose, with ways of life that depended on the slave trade. The **Asante kingdom** emerged in the area occupied by present-day Ghana. In the late 1600s, an able military leader, **Osei Tutu,** won control of the trading city of Kumasi. From there, he conquered neighboring peoples and unified the Asante kingdom. Under Osei Tutu, the Asante kingdom held a **monopoly** over both gold mining and the slave trade.

The **Oyo empire** arose from successive waves of settlement by the Yoruba people in the region of present-day Nigeria. Its leaders used wealth gained from the slave trade to build a strong army.

By the 1600s, several other European powers had established forts along the west coast of Africa. In 1652, Dutch immigrants arrived at the southern tip of the continent. They built **Cape Town,** the first permanent European settlement in Africa, to supply ships sailing to or from the East Indies. Dutch farmers, called **Boers,** settled the lands around the port.

Review Questions

1. How did the Portuguese establish footholds on the coasts of Africa?

____

____

2. Who created the first permanent European settlement in Africa?

____

____

Name____________________ Class________________ Date________

CHAPTER 2 SECTION 3

Note Taking Study Guide

EUROPEAN FOOTHOLDS IN SOUTH AND SOUTHEAST ASIA

Focus Question: How did European nations build empires in South and Southeast Asia?

As you read this section in your textbook, complete the flowchart below to identify causes and effects of European exploration in South and Southeast Asia.

Portugal	• •
Netherlands	• •
Spain	• •
Britain	• •

Name________________________ Class____________ Date______

CHAPTER 2 SECTION 3

Section Summary

EUROPEAN FOOTHOLDS IN SOUTH AND SOUTHEAST ASIA

READING CHECK

What was the Dutch East India Company?

____

____

____

VOCABULARY STRATEGY

What does the word *strategic* mean in the underlined sentence? Note that *strategic* is an adjective describing the settlement of Cape Town. The sentence following the underlined sentence gives you more information about Cape Town. Based on these context clues, what do you think *strategic* means?

READING SKILL

Identify Causes and Effects Identify one cause and one effect of the Mughal emperors' decision to grant trading rights to Europeans.

____

____

____

After Vasco da Gama's voyage to India, the Portuguese, under the command of **Afonso de Albuquerque,** burst into the Indian Ocean. By then, Muslim rulers had established the **Mughal empire** throughout much of India. The Portuguese gained footholds in southern India, however, by promising local princes aid against other European rulers. In 1510, the Portuguese seized the island of **Goa** off the coast of India. Then, they took **Malacca.** In less than 50 years, the Portuguese built a trading empire with military and merchant **outposts.** For most of the 1500s, they controlled the spice trade between Europe and Asia.

The Dutch challenged Portuguese domination of Asian trade. In 1599, a Dutch fleet from Asia returned with a cargo of spices. Soon after, Dutch warships and trading vessels made the Netherlands a leader in European commerce. <u>The Dutch set up colonies and trading posts around the world, including their strategic settlement at Cape Town.</u> Cape Town's location gave the Dutch a secure presence in the region. In 1602, a group of wealthy Dutch merchants formed the **Dutch East India Company,** which had full **sovereign** powers. With its power to build armies, wage war, negotiate peace treaties, and govern overseas territory, the Dutch East India Company dominated Southeast Asia. Meanwhile, Spain took over the **Philippines,** which became a key link in Spain's colonial empire.

India was the center of the valuable spice trade. The Mughal empire was larger, richer, and more powerful than any kingdom in Europe. When Europeans sought trading rights, Mughal emperors saw no threat in granting them. The Portuguese—and later the Dutch, British, and French—were permitted to build forts and warehouses in coastal towns. Over time, the Mughal empire weakened, and French and British traders fought for power. Like the Dutch, both the British and the French had established East India companies. Each nation's trading company organized its own army of **sepoys,** or Indian troops. By the late 1700s, however, the British East India Company controlled most of India.

Review Questions

1. How did Portugal build a trading empire in South and Southeast Asia?

____

____

2. How did the Dutch come to dominate trade in Southeast Asia?

____

____

Name________________________ Class__________________ Date________

CHAPTER 2
SECTION 4

Note Taking Study Guide

ENCOUNTERS IN EAST ASIA

Focus Question: How were European encounters in East Asia shaped by the worldviews of both Europeans and Asians?

As you read this section in your textbook, complete the following chart to understand the effects of European contacts in East Asia.

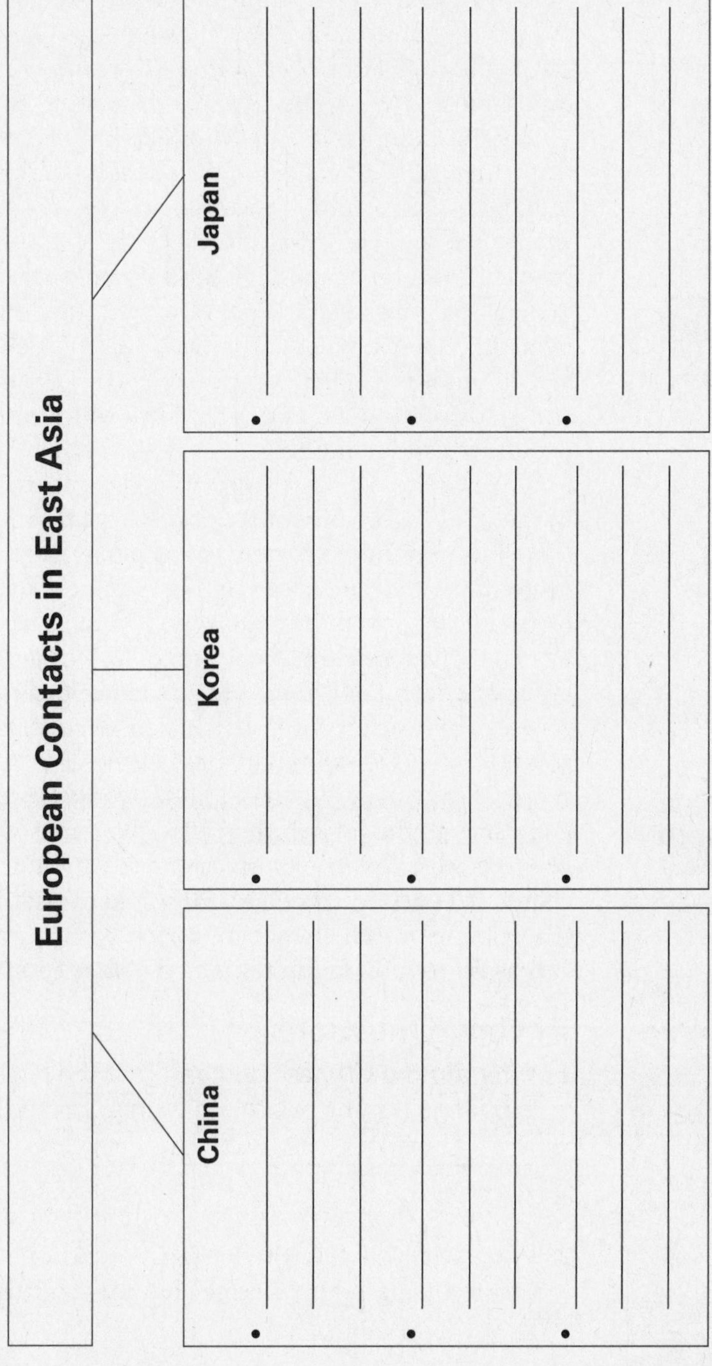

Name________________________ Class____________ Date______

CHAPTER 2 SECTION 4

Section Summary

ENCOUNTERS IN EAST ASIA

When Portuguese traders reached China in 1514, they wanted Chinese silks and porcelains. The European textiles and metalwork they had to offer in exchange, however, were inferior to Chinese products. The Chinese, therefore, demanded payment in gold or silver. The Ming rulers eventually allowed the Portuguese and other Europeans a trading post at **Macao,** in present-day **Guangzhou.** With the traders came Portuguese missionaries and, later, the Jesuits. The brilliant Jesuit priest **Matteo Ricci** made a strong impression on the Chinese, who welcomed learning about Renaissance Europe.

By the early 1600s, the Ming dynasty was decaying. In 1644, the **Manchus,** who ruled Manchuria, succeeded in seizing Beijing and making it their capital. They set up a new dynasty called the **Qing.** Two rulers oversaw the most brilliant age of the Qing—Kangxi and his grandson **Qianlong.** Under both emperors, the Chinese economy expanded. Internal trade grew, as did the demand for Chinese goods from all over the world. The Qing maintained the Ming policy of restricting foreign traders, however. In 1793, **Lord Macartney** led a British diplomatic mission to China, but his attempt to negotiate for expanded trade failed.

Like China, Korea also restricted contacts with the outside world. In the 1590s, a Japanese invasion devastated Korea. Then in 1636, the Manchus conquered Korea. In response, the Koreans chose isolation, excluding all foreigners except the Chinese and a few Japanese. Korea became known in the West as the "Hermit Kingdom."

The Japanese at first welcomed Westerners. Traders arrived in Japan at a turbulent time, when warrior lords were struggling for power. The warrior lords quickly adopted Western firearms. Jesuit priests converted many Japanese to the Christian faith. The Tokugawa shoguns, however, worried that Japanese Christians owed their allegiance to the pope rather than to Japanese leaders. In response, the shoguns expelled foreign missionaries and barred all European merchants. To keep informed about world events, however, they permitted just one or two Dutch ships each year to trade at a small island in **Nagasaki** harbor. Japan remained isolated for more than 200 years.

READING CHECK

Who conquered the Ming dynasty in 1644?

____

____

____

VOCABULARY STRATEGY

What does the word *allegiance* mean in the underlined sentence? Think about your prior knowledge of this word. Ask yourself: To what do I owe my allegiance? Use your prior knowledge to help you figure out what *allegiance* means.

READING SKILL

Identify Effects Describe the effect of the Japanese and Manchu invasions on Korea.

____

____

____

Review Questions

1. Why did the Chinese demand that the Portuguese traders pay for Chinese silks and porcelain with gold or silver?

____

____

2. What suggests that the Ming were curious about Europe and wanted to gain knowledge about its culture?

____

____

Name_______________ Class_______________ Date_______

CHAPTER 3 SECTION 1

Note Taking Study Guide

CONQUEST IN THE AMERICAS

Focus Question: How did a small number of Spanish conquistadors conquer huge Native American empires?

As you read this section of your textbook, fill in the chart below to help you record the sequence of events that led to European empires in the Americas.

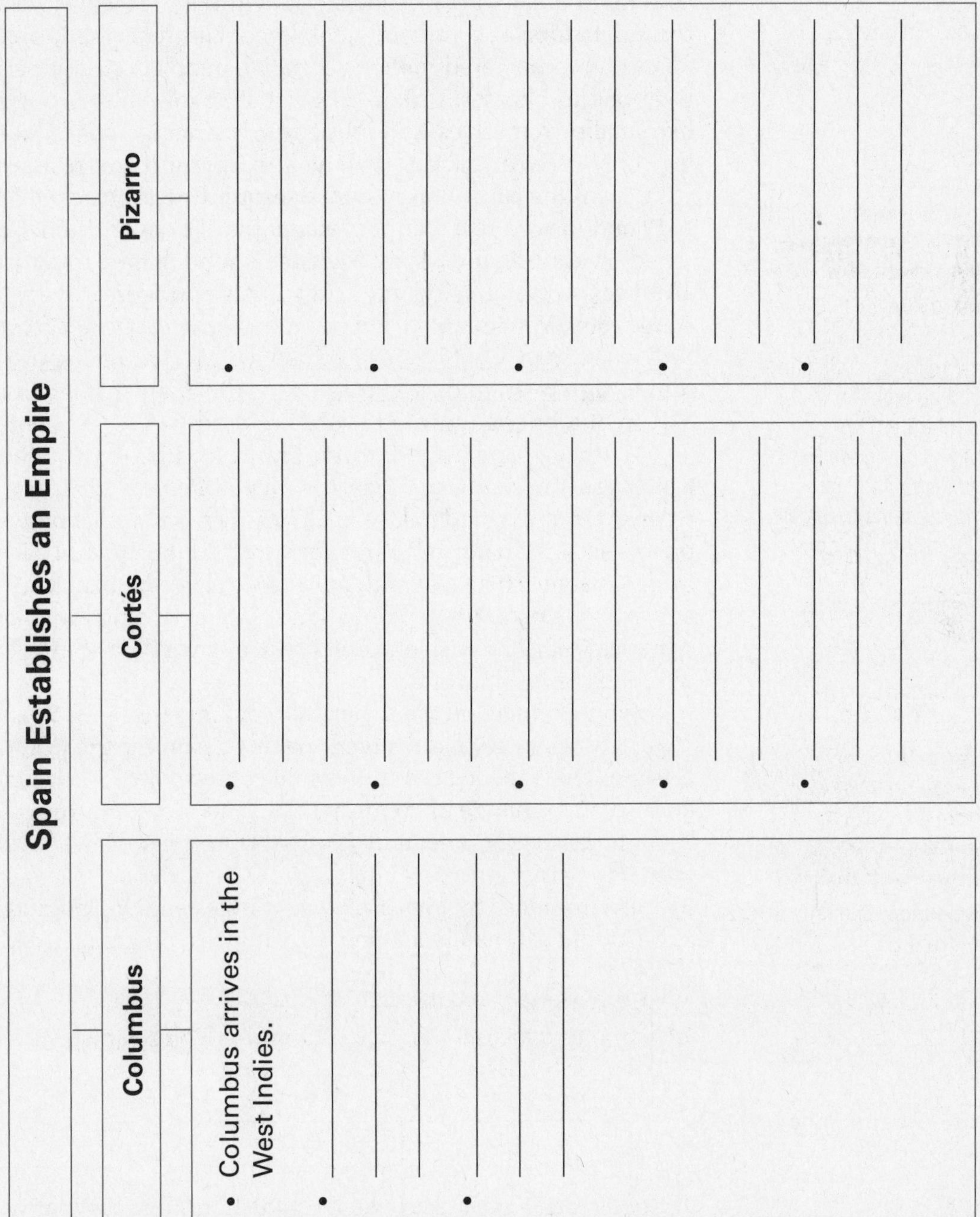

Name________________________ Class___________ Date______

CHAPTER 3 SECTION 1

Section Summary

CONQUEST IN THE AMERICAS

In 1492, Christopher Columbus reached the Caribbean islands now called the West Indies. Columbus' first meeting with Native Americans there began a recurring cycle of encounter, conquest, and death across the Western Hemisphere.

Columbus first encountered the Taíno people and claimed their land for Spain, taking prisoners back with him. A wave of Spanish **conquistadors,** or conquerors, followed. Ultimately, hundreds of Spanish overpowered millions of native people, using superior weapons and horses. Unknowingly, the Spanish also brought diseases like smallpox, measles, and influenza. This wiped out village after village of Native Americans, who had no **immunity,** or resistance.

One of the earliest explorers, **Hernán Cortés,** reached Mexico in 1519 and moved toward the Aztec capital, **Tenochtitlán.** Cortés was aided by an Indian woman, **Malinche,** who helped him form **alliances** with native peoples previously conquered by the Aztecs. Aztec ruler **Moctezuma** tried but failed to keep Cortés from coming to Tenochtitlán. Cortés later imprisoned Moctezuma and compelled him to sign over lands and treasure to the Spanish. Cortés was driven out, but he returned in 1521 and destroyed Tenochtitlán.

Another Spanish adventurer, **Francisco Pizarro,** sought riches from Peru's Inca empire. Pizarro reached Peru in 1532. The Inca ruler, Atahualpa, had just won a **civil war,** or conflict between people of the same nation. Pizarro captured Atahualpa and demanded a huge ransom. This was paid, but Pizarro had the Inca ruler killed anyway. Spanish forces overran Inca lands, adding much of South America to the Spanish empire. Pizarro was killed a few years later by a rival Spanish group.

Spain's impact on the Americas was immense. The Spanish took vast fortunes in gold and silver, making Spain the greatest power of Europe. They opened sea routes that connected two hemispheres and opened an exchange of goods, people, and ideas. However, they also brought disease and death to Native Americans. Many survivors converted to Christianity, seeking hope. Others, like the Maya, resisted Spanish influence by preserving their own religion, language, and culture, and ultimately leaving their imprint on Latin America.

Review Questions

1. Name two factors that helped hundreds of Spanish soldiers conquer millions of Native Americans.

____

____

2. Some native peoples resisted Spanish influence. What was one such group and how did it resist?

____

____

READING CHECK

How did Malinche aid Cortés?

____

____

____

VOCABULARY STRATEGY

Find the word *compelled* in the underlined sentence. What clues to its meaning can you find in the surrounding words, phrases, or sentences? For example, what does the phrase "relations grew strained" suggest about the relations between the two men? Circle other context clues in the paragraph that could help you figure out what *compelled* means.

READING SKILL

Recognize Sequence Sequence the following events:

____ Spanish forces take over Inca lands.

____ Pizarro arrives in Peru.

____ Columbus takes the Taínos as prisoners.

____ Cortés captures Tenochtitlán.

Name____________________ Class________________ Date________

CHAPTER 3 SECTION 2

Note Taking Study Guide

SPANISH AND PORTUGUESE COLONIES IN THE AMERICAS

Focus Question: How did Spain and Portugal build colonies in the Americas?

A. *As you read "Ruling the Spanish Empire," fill in the chart below to record the steps the Spanish took to establish an empire in America.*

Governing the empire	Catholic Church	Trade	Labor
• Viceroys	• ______	• ______	• ______
• ______	• ______	• ______	• ______
	• ______		• ______

B. *As you read "Colonial Society and Culture" and "Beyond the Spanish Empire," fill in the Venn diagram below to compare and contrast the Spanish and Portuguese empires.*

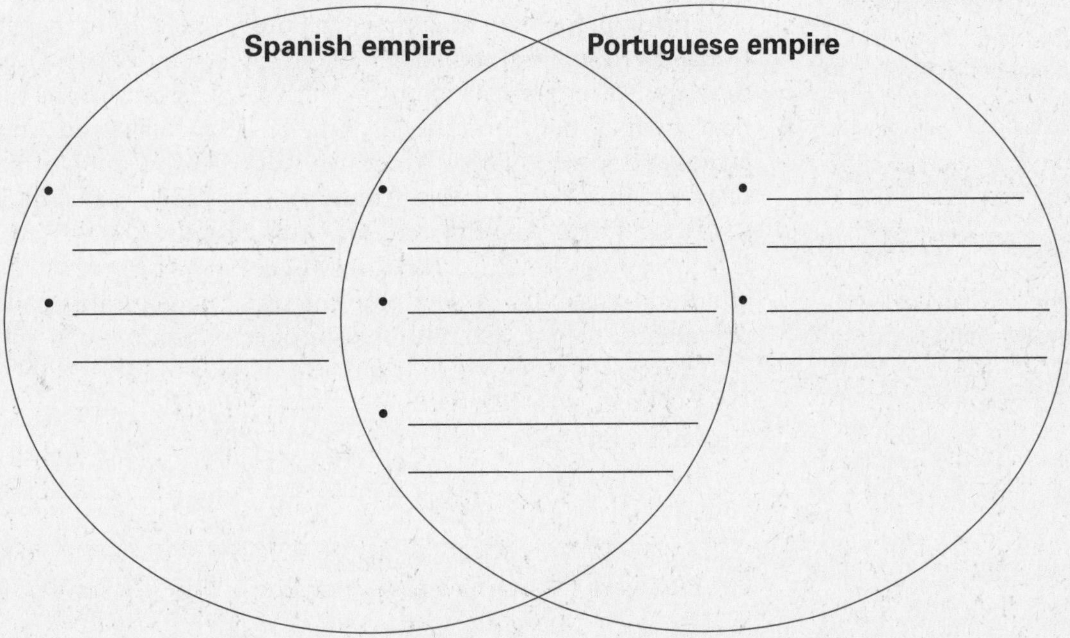

Spanish empire	Both	Portuguese empire
• ______	• ______	• ______
• ______	• ______	• ______
	• ______	

Name________________________ Class____________ Date______

CHAPTER 3 SECTION 2

Section Summary

SPANISH AND PORTUGUESE COLONIES IN THE AMERICAS

Spanish settlers and missionaries followed conquerors into the Americas. They built colonies and created a culture that blended European, Native American, and African traditions. By the mid-1500s, Spain's empire reached from modern California to South America.

The Spanish monarch appointed **viceroys,** or representatives who ruled in his name. They closely monitored Spanish colonies and managed their valuable raw materials. Conquistadors received **encomiendas,** or rights to demand work from Native Americans. Under this system, Native Americans were forced to work under brutal conditions. Disease, starvation, and cruel treatment caused a drastic decline in the Native American population. A priest, **Bartolomé de Las Casas,** begged the Spanish king to end the abuse, and laws were passed in 1542, banning enslavement and mistreatment. But Spain was too far away to enforce the laws. Some landlords forced people to become **peons,** paid workers who labored to repay impossibly high debts created by the landlord. To fill a labor shortage, colonists also brought in millions of Africans as slaves.

Blending of diverse cultures resulted. Native Americans contributed building styles, foods, and arts. The Spanish introduced Christianity and the use of animals, especially horses. Africans contributed farming methods, crops, and arts.

However, society in the colonies was strictly structured. **Peninsulares,** or people born in Spain, filled the highest positions. Next were **creoles,** or American-born descendants of Spanish settlers. Lower groups included **mestizos,** people of Native American and European descent, and **mulattoes,** people of African and European descent. At the bottom were Native Americans and African slaves.

Portugal, too, had an empire in South America, with colonies in Brazil. Portugal granted land to nobles, who sent settlers to develop the area. As in Spanish colonies, Native Americans in Brazil were nearly wiped out from disease. Brazil's rulers also used African slaves and forced Native American labor. A new culture emerged, blending European, Native American, and African traditions.

In the 1500s, wealth from the Americas made Spain and Portugal Europe's most wealthy and powerful countries. Pirates often attacked treasure ships from the colonies. Some pirates, called **privateers,** even did so with the support of their nations' monarchs.

READING CHECK

What was the name of the priest who pleaded with the Spanish king to end the abuse of Native Americans?

____

____

____

VOCABULARY STRATEGY

In the underlined sentence, what do you think the word *drastic* means? Try to determine the meaning based on the context, or how and where it is used. Circle any nearby words or phrases that help you figure out the meaning of *drastic.*

READING SKILL

Recognize Sequence Circle the event that happened first.

- Spanish colonies are closely monitored.
- The king of Spain appoints viceroys.
- Laws are passed banning enslavement of workers.

Review Questions

1. What were encomiendas?

____

____

2. How were the Spanish and Portuguese colonies similar?

____

____

Name____________________________ Class______________________ Date________

CHAPTER 3 SECTION 3

Note Taking Study Guide

STRUGGLE FOR NORTH AMERICA

Focus Question: How did European struggles for power shape the North American continent?

As you read this section of your textbook, complete the following timeline to show the sequence of events in the struggle for North America.

Name____________________ Class__________ Date______

CHAPTER 3 SECTION 3

Section Summary

STRUGGLE FOR NORTH AMERICA

READING CHECK

What was the name of the agreement written by the Pilgrims to set the guidelines for governing their new colony?

____

____

____

VOCABULARY STRATEGY

Find the word *prevailed* in the first underlined sentence. What do you think *prevailed* means? Read the second underlined sentence to see what happened after England *prevailed.* Use this information to help you come up with another definition, in your own words, for *prevailed.*

READING SKILL

Recognize Sequence What happened after the signing of the Treaty of Paris in 1763?

____

____

____

In the 1600s, the French, Dutch, English, and Spanish competed for lands in North America. By 1700, France and England dominated large parts of the continent. Their colonies differed from one another in terms of language, government, resources, and society.

In 1534, Jacques Cartier explored and claimed for the French much of eastern Canada, called **New France.** Eventually, France's empire stretched from Quebec to the Great Lakes and down the Mississippi River to Louisiana. However, a permanent French settlement was not established until 1608 in Quebec. Harsh Canadian winters discouraged settlers, and many abandoned farming for more profitable fur trapping and fishing. In the late 1600s, the French king Louis XIV wanted greater **revenue,** or income from taxes. He appointed officials to manage economic activities in North America and sent soldiers and more settlers.

In the early 1700s, while New France's population remained small, English colonies expanded along the Atlantic coast. Jamestown in Virginia, the first permanent English colony, was established in 1607. In 1620, **Pilgrims,** or English Protestants who rejected the Church of England, landed at what became Plymouth, Massachusetts. They wrote a **compact,** or agreement, called the Mayflower Compact. It set guidelines for governing their colony. In the 1600s and 1700s, the English created 13 colonies in all. Some were commercial ventures or havens for religious groups. Some were primarily agricultural. English monarchs exercised control through royal governors. Yet, English colonists enjoyed a greater degree of self-government than did French and Spanish colonists. They had their own representative assemblies that could advise the governor and decide local issues.

During the 1700s, England and France emerged as powerful rivals. In 1754, the **French and Indian War** erupted in North America and then spread to other parts of the world by 1756, where it is known as the Seven Years' War. British and colonial troops eventually captured New France's capital city, Quebec. <u>Although the war dragged on, the British ultimately prevailed.</u> <u>The 1763 **Treaty of Paris** ended this worldwide conflict.</u> France surrendered Canada and other North American possessions to Britain, while retaining its territory in the central region of North America.

Review Questions

1. How did Canadian winters affect French settlement?

____

____

2. In what way did English colonists have a greater degree of self-government than did French or Spanish colonists?

____

____

Name________________ Class________________ Date________

CHAPTER 3 SECTION 4

Note Taking Study Guide

THE ATLANTIC SLAVE TRADE

Focus Question: How did the Atlantic slave trade shape the lives and economies of Africans and Europeans?

As you read this section in your textbook, complete the following flowchart to record the sequence of events that led to millions of Africans being brought to the Americas.

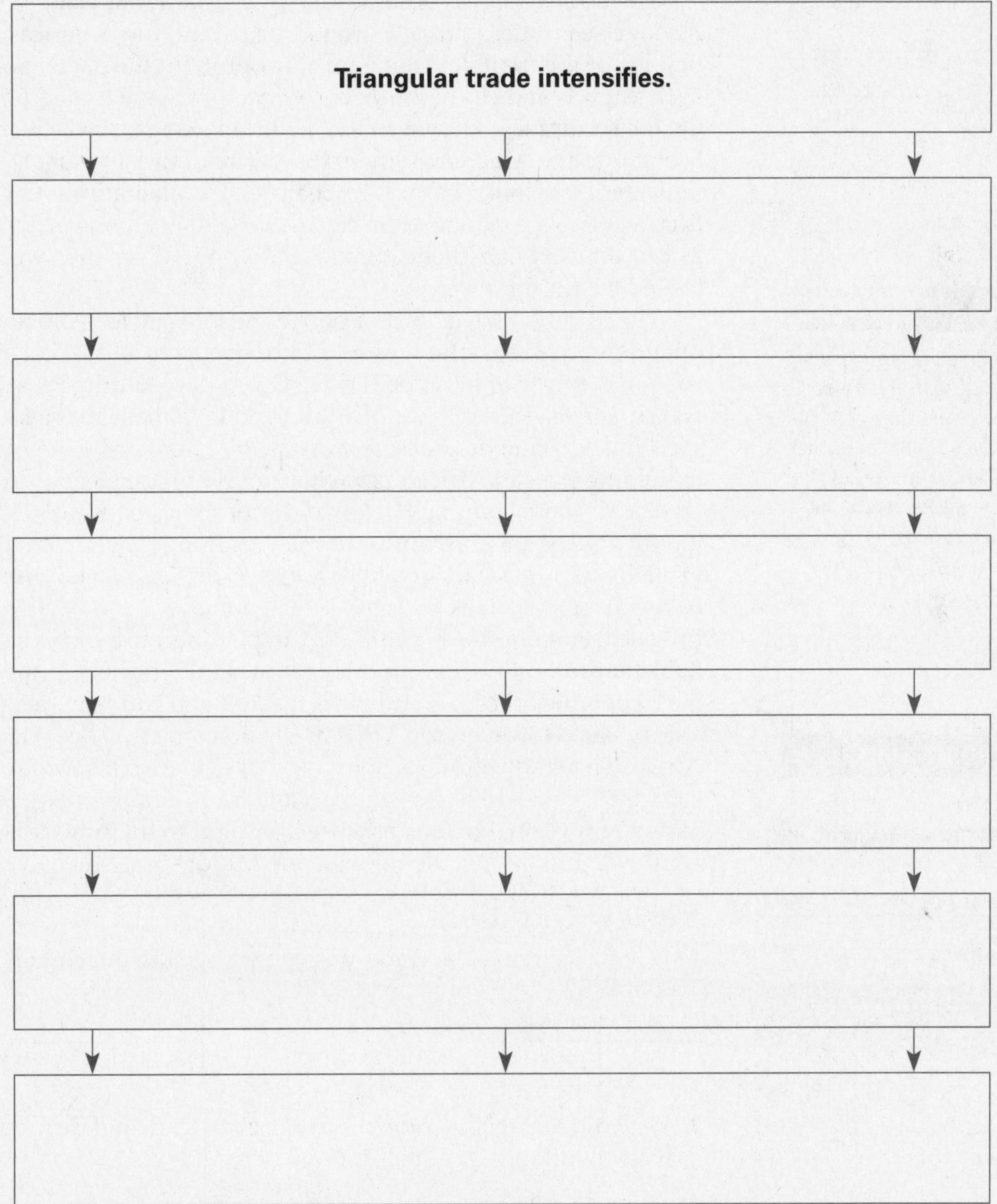

Name____________________ Class__________ Date_____

CHAPTER 3 SECTION 4

Section Summary

THE ATLANTIC SLAVE TRADE

Empires grew in the 1500s, and trade increased between the Americas and other parts of the world. Spain was the first major power to import slaves into its South American colonies, but slave trade grew as other European powers established colonies. Slave labor became a way to gain greater profits, but at the expense of millions of lives.

The trade of slaves became known as **triangular trade,** a series of Atlantic sea routes joining Europe, Africa, and the Americas. On the first leg of the triangle, merchant ships brought European goods, such as guns and cloth, to Africa, where they were traded for slaves. On the second leg, known as the **Middle Passage,** slaves were brought to the Americas, where they were traded for sugar, molasses, and cotton from European-owned plantations. On the final leg, these products were traded for other colonial goods, such as furs and salt fish, then shipped to Europe, where they were traded for European goods.

The Middle Passage was a horrifying journey for Africans. **Olaudah Equiano,** who was sold into slavery as an 11-year-old in the 1750s, wrote of his experiences. During the Middle Passage, slaves were captured, bound, and forced to walk as much as a thousand miles. Many died on the way. <u>Those who lived were restrained in holding pens in African port cities until European ships arrived.</u> Hundreds were crammed below deck for the three-week to three-month voyages. Some committed suicide. Many died from disease, brutality, or other dangers, like storms, pirate raids, and **mutinies,** or revolts, by captives trying to return home.

The triangular trade continued, in part, because it was so profitable. It brought riches to merchants and traders, helped the colonial economies succeed, and helped European and American port cities grow. However, for Africans the outcome was devastating. African societies were torn apart, and lives were cut short or brutalized. By the mid-1800s, when the slave trade finally ended, an estimated 11 million Africans had been brought to the Americas, and another 2 million had died during the Middle Passage.

Review Questions

1. What was triangular trade, and what were the three main areas it linked?

____

____

2. Why did triangular trade continue, even though it devastated the lives of millions of people?

____

____

READING CHECK

Which European power was the first to begin importing slaves to its colonies in the Americas?

____

____

____

VOCABULARY STRATEGY

In the underlined sentence, what does the word *restrained* mean? Think about where these people were *restrained.* What does that suggest? Use the answer to this question to help you figure out what *restrained* means.

READING SKILL

Recognize Sequence List the three "legs" of the triangular trade.

____

____

____

Name______________________ Class__________________ Date________

CHAPTER 3 SECTION 5

Note Taking Study Guide

EFFECTS OF GLOBAL CONTACT

Focus Question: How did the voyages of European explorers lead to new economic systems in Europe and its colonies?

A. *As you read "The Columbian Exchange," complete the following flowchart to record the sequence of events that led to the Columbian Exchange, as well as the effects.*

Causes	Columbian Exchange	Effects
• ______	• ______	• ______
• ______	• ______	• ______
• ______	• ______	• ______
		• ______
		• ______
		• ______

B. *As you read "A Commercial Revolution," complete the following flowchart to record the sequence of events that led to new global economic systems, as well as the effects.*

Causes	New Economic Systems	Effects
• ______	• Capitalism	• ______
• ______	• ______	• ______
• ______	• ______	• ______
		• ______
		• ______

Name____________________ Class__________ Date______

CHAPTER 3 SECTION 5

Section Summary

EFFECTS OF GLOBAL CONTACT

READING CHECK

What is the name for the vast global interchange begun by Columbus' first voyage?

____

____

____

VOCABULARY STRATEGY

In the underlined sentence, what does the word *dispersal* mean? Study the surrounding words, phrases, or sentences. Circle any context clues that help you decide on the meaning of *dispersal.*

READING SKILL

Recognize Sequence What happened in the 1500s that led to inflation in Europe?

____

____

____

Exploration in the 1500s and 1600s led to European domination of the globe. By the 1700s, worldwide contact brought major changes to people in Europe, the Americas, Asia, and Africa.

When Columbus returned to Europe in 1493, he brought back American plants and animals. Later, he carried European plants, animals, and settlers back to the Americas. This began a vast global interchange named for Columbus, the **Columbian Exchange.** Sharing different foodstuffs and livestock helped people around the world. The dispersal of new crops from the Americas also contributed to worldwide population growth by the 1700s. Additionally, the Columbian Exchange started a migration to the Americas, the forcible transfer of millions of slaves, and brought death to millions of Native Americans from European diseases.

Another effect of global contact was great economic change. In the 1500s, the pace of **inflation** increased in Europe, fueled by silver and gold flowing in from the Americas. Inflation is a rise in prices linked to sharp increases in the money supply. This period of rapid inflation in Europe is known as the **price revolution.** Out of this change came **capitalism,** an economic system of private business ownership. The key to capitalism was **entrepreneurs,** or people who take financial risks for profits. European entrepreneurs hired workers, paid production costs, joined investors in overseas ventures, and ultimately helped convert local economies into international trading economies. Fierce competition for trade and empires led to a new economic system called **mercantilism,** which measured wealth by a nation's gold and silver. Mercantilists believed the nation must export more than it imports. They also pushed governments to impose **tariffs,** or taxes on foreign goods, giving an advantage to local goods over now costlier imports.

Economic changes, however, took centuries to affect most Europeans, who were still peasants. But by the 1700s, many social changes had taken place, too. Nobles, whose wealth was in land, were hurt by the price revolution. Merchants who invested in overseas ventures grew wealthy, and skilled workers in Europe's growing cities thrived. A thriving middle class developed.

Review Questions

1. Why did mercantilists push governments to impose tariffs?

____

____

2. By the 1700s, what groups were benefiting most from economic change?

____

____

Name________________________ Class____________________ Date________

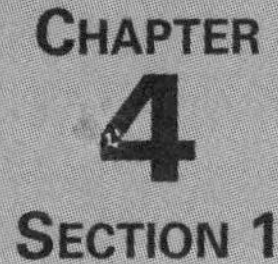

Chapter 4 Section 1

Note Taking Study Guide

SPANISH POWER GROWS

Focus Questions: How did Philip II extend Spain's power and help establish a golden age?

As you read this section in your textbook, use the outline to identify main ideas and supporting details about Spain's power.

I. Charles V Inherits Two Crowns

- **A.** Ruling the Hapsburg empire
  - **1.** Spain
  - **2.** Holy Roman Empire and Netherlands
- **B.** Charles V abdicates
  - **1.** ____________________
  - **2.** ____________________
  - **3.** ____________________

II. ____________________

- **A.** ____________________
  - **1.** ____________________
  - **2.** ____________________
- **B.** ____________________
  - **1.** ____________________
  - **2.** ____________________
- **C.** ____________________
  - **1.** ____________________
  - **2.** ____________________
- **D.** ____________________
  - **1.** ____________________
  - **2.** ____________________
  - **3.** ____________________
  - **4.** ____________________
  - **5.** ____________________

(Outline continues on next page.)

Name__________ Class__________ Date______

Chapter 4 Section 1

Note Taking Study Guide

SPANISH POWER GROWS

(Continued from page 63)

III. __________

A. __________

B. __________

C. __________

D. __________

E. __________

Name________________________ Class___________ Date______

CHAPTER 4 SECTION 1

Section Summary

SPANISH POWER GROWS

In 1519, **Charles V,** the king of Spain and ruler of the Spanish colonies in the Americas, inherited the **Hapsburg empire.** This included the Holy Roman Empire and the Netherlands. Ruling two empires involved Charles in constant religious warfare. Additionally, the empire's vast territory became too cumbersome for Charles to rule effectively. His demanding responsibilities led him to abdicate the throne and divide his kingdom between his brother Ferdinand and his son Philip.

Under **Philip II,** Spanish power increased. He was successful in expanding Spanish influence, strengthening the Catholic Church, and making his own power absolute. Philip reigned as an **absolute monarch**—a ruler with complete authority over the government and the lives of the people. He also declared that he ruled by **divine right.** This meant he believed that his authority to rule came directly from God. Philip was determined to defend the Catholic Church against the Protestant Reformation in Europe. He fought many battles in the Mediterranean and the Netherlands to advance or preserve Spanish Catholic power.

To expand his empire, Philip II needed to eliminate his rivals. He saw Elizabeth I of England as his chief Protestant enemy. Philip prepared a huge **armada,** or fleet, to carry an invasion force to England. However, the English ships were faster and easier to maneuver than Spanish ships. Several disasters led to the defeat of this powerful Spanish fleet.

This defeat marked the beginning of a decline in Spanish power. Wars were costly and contributed to Spain's economic problems. However, while Spain's strength and wealth decreased, art and learning took on new importance. Philip was a supporter of the arts and founded academies of science and mathematics. The arts flourished between 1550 and 1650, a time known as Spain's *Siglo de Oro,* or "golden century." Among the outstanding artists of this period was a painter called **El Greco.** Famous for his religious paintings and portraits of Spanish nobles, his use of vibrant color influenced many other artists. This period also produced several remarkable writers. One of the most significant was **Miguel de Cervantes.** His *Don Quixote,* which mocks medieval tales of chivalry, is considered Europe's first modern novel.

Review Questions

1. What territories were included in the Hapsburg empire?

____

____

2. In what ways was Philip II an absolute monarch?

____

____

READING CHECK

Who wrote Europe's first modern novel?

____

____

____

VOCABULARY STRATEGY

What does the word *cumbersome* mean in the underlined sentence? Circle context clues in the nearby words and phrases to help you figure out the meaning of *cumbersome.*

READING SKILL

Identify Main Ideas and Supporting Details What details support the main idea that the period from 1550 to 1650 was a "golden century" in Spain?

____

____

____

Name____________________________ Class______________________ Date_________

CHAPTER 4 SECTION 2

Note Taking Study Guide

FRANCE UNDER LOUIS XIV

Focus Question: How did France become the leading power of Europe under the absolute rule of Louis XIV?

As you read this section in your textbook, complete the concept web to identify supporting details about the rule of Louis XIV.

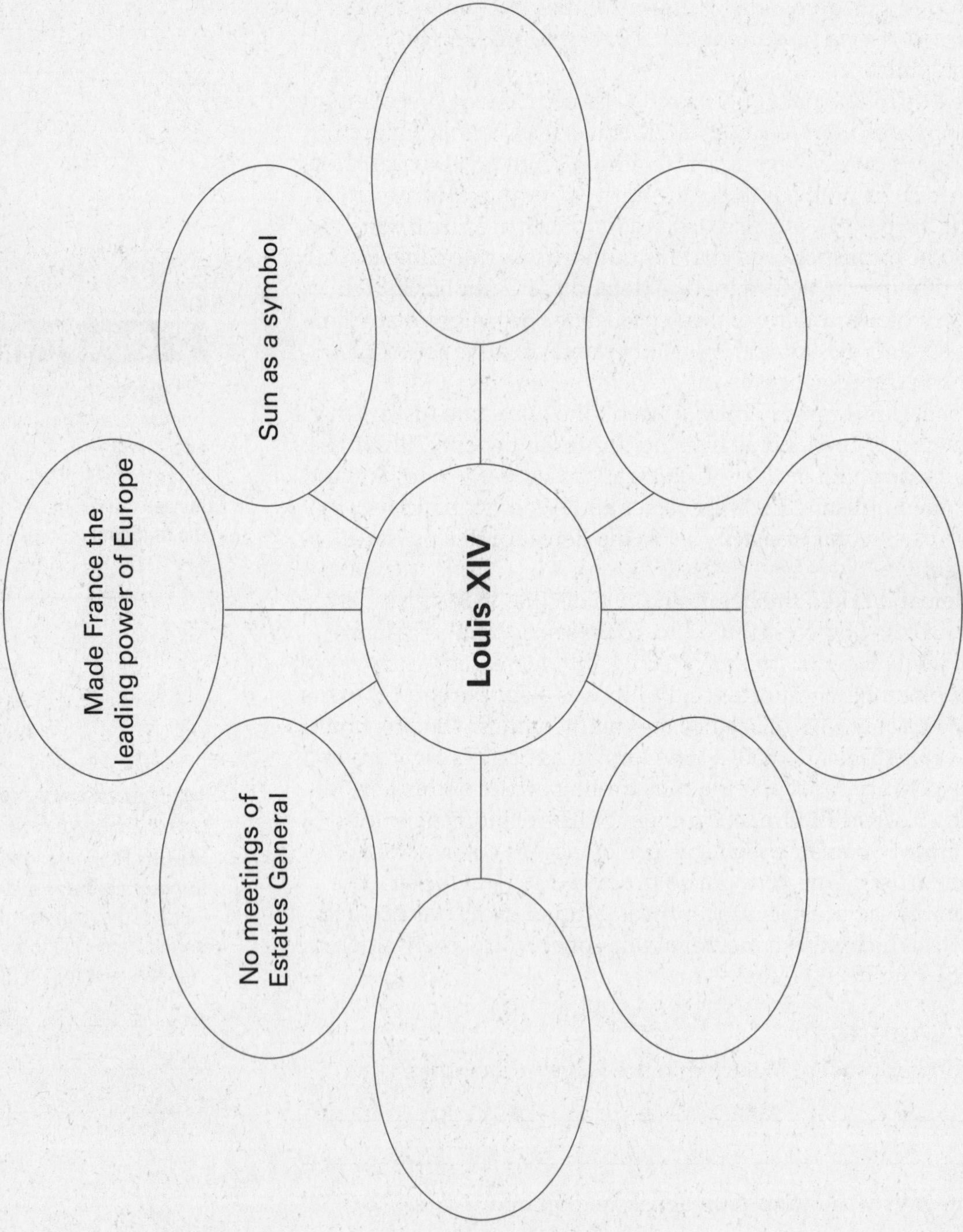

Name________________________ Class____________ Date______

CHAPTER 4 SECTION 2

Section Summary

FRANCE UNDER LOUIS XIV

In the late 1500s, France was torn apart by religious conflict between French Protestants, called **Huguenots,** and Catholics. In an event called the St. Bartholomew's Day Massacre, thousands of Huguenots were slaughtered. In 1598, King **Henry IV** issued the **Edict of Nantes** to protect Protestants. This granted the Huguenots religious toleration and other freedoms.

After Henry's assassination in 1610, his nine-year-old son, Louis XIII, inherited the throne. Louis appointed **Cardinal Richelieu** as his chief minister. Richelieu sought to strengthen royal power by crushing any groups that did not bow to royal authority. In 1643, five-year-old **Louis XIV** inherited the French throne. When his chief minister died, Louis XIV resolved to take complete control of the government. He believed in his divine right to rule and even called himself the Sun King to symbolize his vital role within the nation.

Louis XIV expanded the royal government and appointed **intendants**—royal officials who collected taxes, recruited soldiers, and carried out his policies in the provinces. To fuel the country's economy, Louis's finance minister, **Jean Baptiste Colbert,** expanded commerce and trade. Taxes helped finance the king's extravagant lifestyle.

Outside Paris, Louis XIV transformed a royal hunting lodge into the grand palace of **Versailles.** The palace represented the king's great power and wealth. Elaborate court ceremonies were held to emphasize the king's importance. For example, during the ritual known as the ***levée,*** or rising, high-ranking nobles would compete for the honor of handing the king his shoes. The purpose was to keep the nobles in Versailles to gain their support and prevent them from getting too powerful.

Under Louis XIV, France became the strongest state in Europe. <u>However, the country's prosperity began to erode.</u> This loss of wealth was caused by some of Louis's decisions. He fought costly wars to extend French borders, but rival rulers resisted in order to maintain the **balance of power.** Louis also revoked the Edict of Nantes, driving over 100,000 hard-working and prosperous Huguenots out of France.

Review Questions

1. How did Henry IV end religious conflict?

____

____

2. What was the purpose of intendants?

____

____

READING CHECK

What were the main reasons why France lost economic strength?

____

____

____

VOCABULARY STRATEGY

What does the word *erode* mean in the underlined sentence? Do you know what *erosion* is? Use any prior knowledge you might have about the word *erosion* to help you figure out the meaning of *erode.*

READING SKILL

Identify Supporting Details How did Louis XIV strengthen the French monarchy? Identify key details that contributed to France's becoming the leading power of Europe.

____

____

____

Name________________________ Class__________________ Date________

CHAPTER 4
SECTION 3

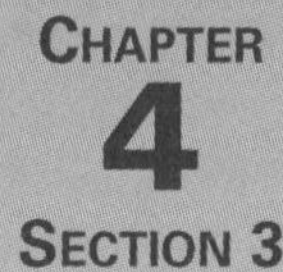

Note Taking Study Guide

PARLIAMENT TRIUMPHS IN ENGLAND

Focus Question: How did the British Parliament assert its rights against royal claims to absolute power in the 1600s?

As you read this section in your textbook, complete the flowchart to identify supporting details about the evolution of Parliament.

Tudors consult with and control Parliament.

Name____________________ Class__________ Date______

CHAPTER 4 SECTION 3

Section Summary

PARLIAMENT TRIUMPHS IN ENGLAND

From 1485 to 1603, England was ruled by the Tudors. While believing in divine right, the Tudors also recognized the value of good relations with Parliament.

This was not the view of the first Stuart king, **James I.** He inherited the throne after Elizabeth I died childless in 1603. He claimed absolute power. Parliament, however, resisted the king's claim. James clashed often with Parliament over money. James was also at odds with **dissenters**—Protestants who disagreed with the Church of England. One such group, the **Puritans,** wanted simpler services and a more democratic church with no bishops.

In 1625, **Charles I** inherited the throne. He too behaved like an absolute monarch. Tensions between Charles and Parliament escalated into civil war. The English Civil War lasted from 1642 to 1651. Supporters of Charles were called Cavaliers. The supporters of Parliament were known as Roundheads. **Oliver Cromwell,** the leader of the Parliament forces, guided them to victory. In January 1649, Charles I was beheaded.

The House of Commons abolished the monarchy and declared England a republic under Cromwell, called the Commonwealth. Many new laws reflected Puritan beliefs. <u>Cromwell did not tolerate open worship for Catholics; however, he did respect the beliefs of other Protestants and welcomed Jews back to England.</u> Eventually people tired of the strict Puritan ways. Cromwell died in 1658. Two years later, Parliament invited Charles II to return to England as king.

Charles II's successor, James II, was forced from the English throne in 1688. Protestants feared that he planned to restore the Roman Catholic Church to power in England. Parliament offered the crown to James's Protestant daughter Mary and her husband William. However, William and Mary had to accept the **English Bill of Rights.** This helped establish a **limited monarchy.** This bloodless overthrow of James II was known as the Glorious Revolution.

During the next century, Britain's government became a **constitutional government,** whose power was defined and limited by law. A **cabinet,** or group of parliamentary advisors who set policies, developed. In essence, British government was now an **oligarchy**—a government that was run by a powerful few.

Review Questions

1. How did the English government change under Cromwell's leadership?

____

____

2. Why was James II forced from the throne?

____

____

READING CHECK

What was the Glorious Revolution?

____

____

____

VOCABULARY STRATEGY

What does the word *tolerate* mean in the underlined sentence? Look for an alternative meaning of *tolerate* later in the same sentence. Use this context clue to figure out what *tolerate* means.

READING SKILL

Identify Supporting Details Find two details in this Summary that support the statement, "Parliament triumphs in England."

____

____

____

Name________________________ Class____________________ Date________

CHAPTER 4
SECTION 4

Note Taking Study Guide

RISE OF AUSTRIA AND PRUSSIA

Focus Question: How did the two great empires of Austria and Prussia emerge from the Thirty Years' War and subsequent events?

As you read this section in your textbook, use the table to identify supporting details about the emergence of Austria and Prussia as European powers.

Rise of Austria	Rise of Prussia
• Austrian ruler keeps title of Holy Roman Emperor.	• Hohenzollern rulers take over German states.
•	•
•	•
•	

Name________________________ Class___________ Date______

CHAPTER 4 SECTION 4

Section Summary

RISE OF AUSTRIA AND PRUSSIA

By the seventeenth century, the Holy Roman Empire had become a mix of several hundred small, separate states. Theoretically, the Holy Roman emperor, who was chosen by seven leading German princes called **electors,** ruled these states. Yet, the emperor had little power over the numerous princes. This power vacuum led to a series of brutal wars that are together called the Thirty Years' War. It began when **Ferdinand,** the Catholic Hapsburg king of Bohemia, wanted to suppress Protestants and declare royal power over nobles. This led to several revolts and then a widespread European war.

The war devastated the German states. **Mercenaries,** or soldiers for hire, burned villages, destroyed crops, and murdered and tortured villagers. This led to famine and disease, which caused severe **depopulation,** or reduction in population.

It was not until 1648 that a series of treaties known as the **Peace of Westphalia** were established. <u>These treaties aspired to bring peace to Europe and also settle other international problems.</u>

While Austria was becoming a strong Catholic state, a region within the German states called **Prussia** emerged as a new Protestant power. The Prussian ruler **Frederick William I** came to power in 1713. He created a new bureaucracy and placed great emphasis on military values.

In Austria, **Maria Theresa** became empress after her father's death in 1740. That same year, **Frederick II** of Prussia seized the Hapsburg province of Silesia. This action sparked the eight-year **War of the Austrian Succession.** Despite tireless efforts, Maria Theresa did not succeed in forcing Frederick out of Silesia. However, she did preserve her empire and won the support of most of her people. She also strengthened Hapsburg power by reorganizing the bureaucracy and improving tax collection.

At his father's insistence, Frederick II endured harsh military training at a early age. After becoming king, he used his military education brilliantly, making Prussia a leading power. By 1750, the great European powers included Austria, Prussia, France, Britain, and Russia. These nations formed various alliances to maintain the balance of power. Often, Austria and Prussia were rivals.

Review Questions

1. What started the Thirty Years' War?

____

____

2. What caused the depopulation in the German states?

____

____

READING CHECK

What was the Peace of Westphalia supposed to accomplish?

____

____

____

VOCABULARY STRATEGY

What does the word *aspired* mean in the underlined sentence? The word *strived* is a synonym for *aspired.* Apply what you already know about *strived* to help you understand the meaning of *aspired.*

READING SKILL

Identify Supporting Details List details to support the statement: The Thirty Years' War had a terrible effect on German states.

____

____

____

Name______________________ Class__________________ Date________

CHAPTER 4 SECTION 5

Note Taking Study Guide

ABSOLUTE MONARCHY IN RUSSIA

Focus Questions: How did Peter the Great and Catherine the Great strengthen Russia and expand its territory?

As you read this section in your textbook, complete the Venn diagram to identify the main ideas about the reigns of Peter the Great and Catherine the Great.

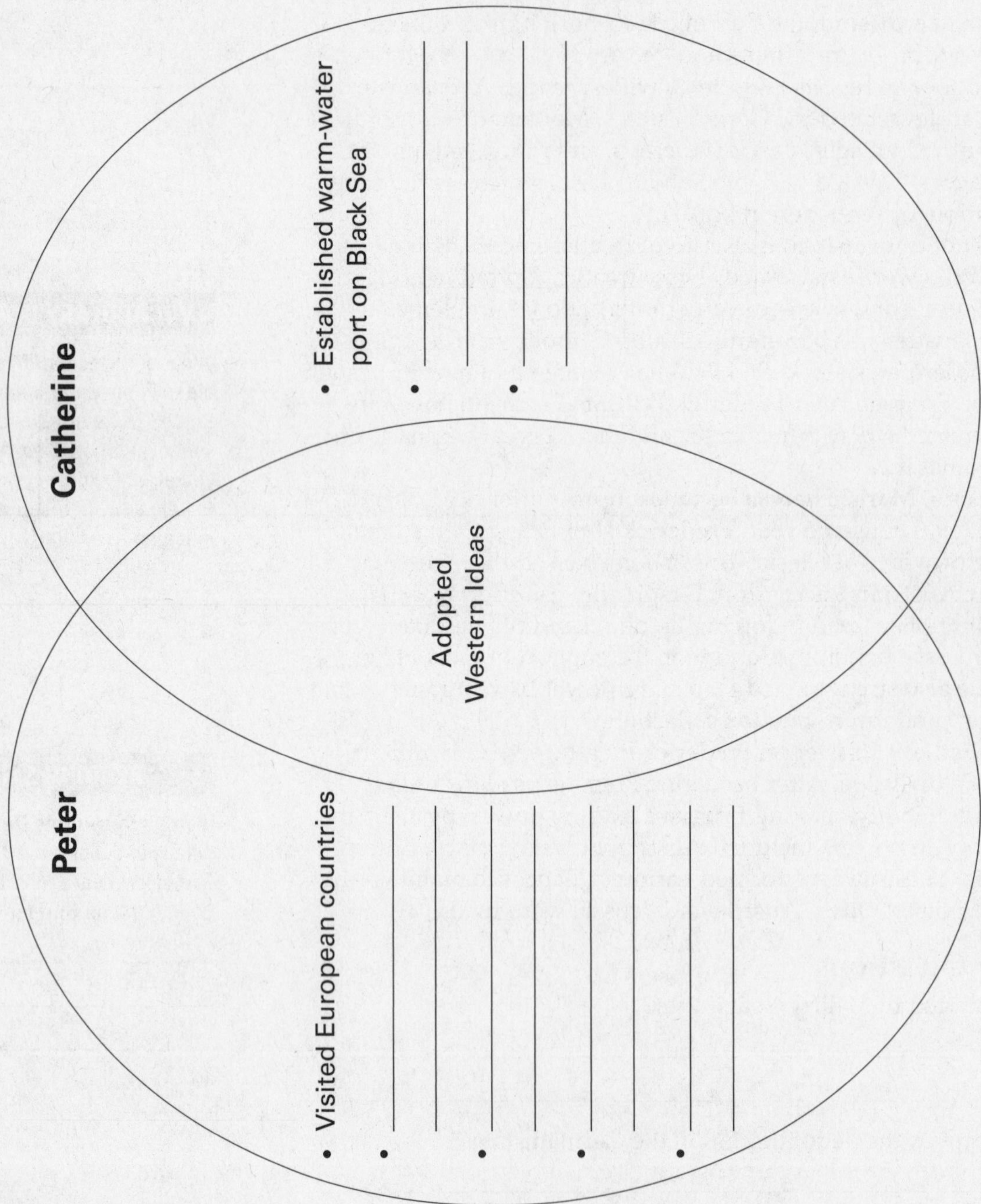

Name________________________ Class____________ Date______

CHAPTER 4 SECTION 5

Section Summary

ABSOLUTE MONARCHY IN RUSSIA

In the early 1600s, Russia was isolated from Western Europe and had remained a medieval state. It was not until the end of that century that a new tsar, **Peter the Great,** transformed Russia into a leading power.

To modernize Russia, Peter began a new policy of **westernization**—the adoption of Western ideas, technologies, and culture. Many resisted change. To enforce his new policy, Peter became an **autocratic** monarch—one who ruled with unlimited authority.

All Russian institutions were under Peter the Great's control. He executed anyone who resisted the new order. He forced the **boyars**—landowning nobles—to serve the state in civilian or military positions. Peter also stipulated that they shave their beards and wear Western-style clothes.

Peter pushed through social and economic reforms. He also increased Russia's military power and extended its borders. However, Russia still needed a **warm-water port.** This would increase Russia's trade with the West. The nearest port of this kind to Russia was on the Black Sea, but Peter could not defeat the Ottoman empire, which controlled the region.

Determined to expand Russia's territory, Peter also waged a long war against Sweden to win territory along the Baltic Sea. On this territory, he built a new capital city, **St. Petersburg.** It became the symbol of modern Russia. When Peter died in 1725, he left a mixed legacy. Although he had modernized Russia, he had used terror to enforce his absolute power.

In 1762, **Catherine the Great** ruled as an absolute monarch. She followed Peter's lead in embracing Western ideas and expanding Russia's borders. She was an efficient and energetic empress. Under her rule, laws were codified and state-supported education began for both boys and girls. After waging war, she defeated the Ottoman empire and finally won the warm-water port on the Black Sea.

In the 1770s, Russia, Prussia, and Austria each wanted Poland as part of their territory. In order to avoid war, the three kingdoms agreed to **partition,** or divide up, Poland. In 1772, Russia gained part of eastern Poland, while Prussia and Austria took over the West. Poland vanished from the map.

Review Questions

1. What did Peter the Great do to modernize Russia?

____

____

2. What were two achievements of Catherine the Great?

____

____

READING CHECK

Where was St. Petersburg built?

____

____

____

VOCABULARY STRATEGY

What does *stipulated* mean in the underlined sentence? It comes from a Latin word that means "to bargain." Use this word-origins clue to help you figure out the meaning of *stipulated.*

READING SKILL

Identify Main Ideas Write a new title for this Summary that identifies its main idea.

____

____

____

Name________________________ Class____________________ Date________

Note Taking Study Guide

PHILOSOPHY IN THE AGE OF REASON

Focus Question: What effects did Enlightenment philosophers have on government and society?

As you read this section in your textbook, complete the following table to summarize each thinker's works and ideas.

Thinkers' Works and Ideas	
Hobbes	• *Leviathan* • ________________
Locke	• ________________ • ________________ • ________________
Montesquieu	• ________________ • ________________ • ________________
	• ________________ • ________________ • ________________
	• ________________ • ________________ • ________________ • ________________
	• ________________ • ________________
	• ________________ • ________________ • ________________

Name________________________ Class__________ Date______

CHAPTER 5 SECTION 1

Section Summary

PHILOSOPHY IN THE AGE OF REASON

In the 1500s and 1600s, the Scientific Revolution introduced reason and scientific method as the basis of knowledge, changing the way people looked at the world. In the 1700s, scientific successes, such as a vaccine against smallpox, convinced educated Europeans of the power of human reason. **Natural law**—rules discovered by reason—could be used to study human behavior and solve society's problems. In this way, the Scientific Revolution sparked another revolution in thinking, known as the Enlightenment.

The ideas of **Thomas Hobbes** and **John Locke,** two seventeenth-century English thinkers, were key to the Enlightenment. Hobbes argued that people are "brutish" by nature, and therefore need to be controlled by an absolute monarchy. According to Hobbes, people enter into a **social contract** with their government, giving up their freedom in exchange for an organized society. In contrast, Locke thought that people are basically reasonable and moral. He also believed that people have certain **natural rights,** including the right to life, liberty, and property. Locke rejected absolute monarchy, believing that the best kind of government had limited power. In fact, Locke felt that people could overthrow a government if it violated their natural rights.

In France, Enlightenment thinkers called ***philosophes*** believed that the use of reason could lead to reforms in government, law, and society. Baron de **Montesquieu** proposed the ideas of separation of powers and of checks and balances as a way to protect liberty. His ideas would deeply affect the Framers of the United States Constitution. With his biting wit, **Voltaire** exposed abuses of power and defended the principle of freedom of speech. Denis **Diderot** edited a 28-volume *Encyclopedia.* This work included articles on human knowledge, explaining new ideas on topics such as government, philosophy, and religion. **Jean-Jacques Rousseau** believed that the good of the community should be placed above individual interests. However, the Enlightenment slogan "free and equal" did not apply to women.

Other thinkers, including **Adam Smith,** focused on using natural laws for economic reform. They rejected government regulation of the economy and instead urged the policy of **laissez faire.**

Review Questions

1. How did the Scientific Revolution lead to the Enlightenment?

____

____

2. Identify three major ideas developed by Enlightenment thinkers.

____

____

READING CHECK

Who were the *philosophes* and what did they believe?

____

____

____

VOCABULARY STRATEGY

What does the word *philosophy* mean in the underlined sentence? It comes from a Greek word that means "love of wisdom." Use this word-orgins clue to help you figure out what *philosophy* means.

READING SKILL

Summarize What ideas did Thomas Hobbes and John Locke have about human nature and the role of government?

____

____

____

Name______________________ Class________________ Date________

CHAPTER 5 SECTION 2

Note Taking Study Guide

ENLIGHTENMENT IDEAS SPREAD

Focus Question: As Enlightenment ideas spread across Europe, what cultural and political changes took place?

A. *As you read "New Ideas Challenge Society" and "Arts and Literature Reflect New Ideas," complete the following concept web to categorize how Enlightenment ideas spread.*

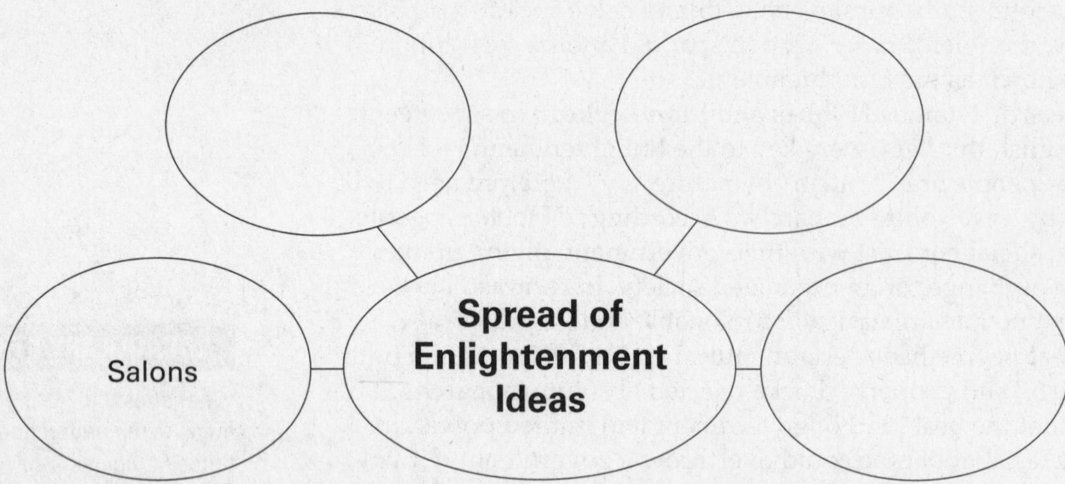

B. *As you read "Enlightened Despots Embrace New Ideas" and "Lives of the Majority Change Slowly," complete the following concept web to summarize information about enlightened despots and their contributions.*

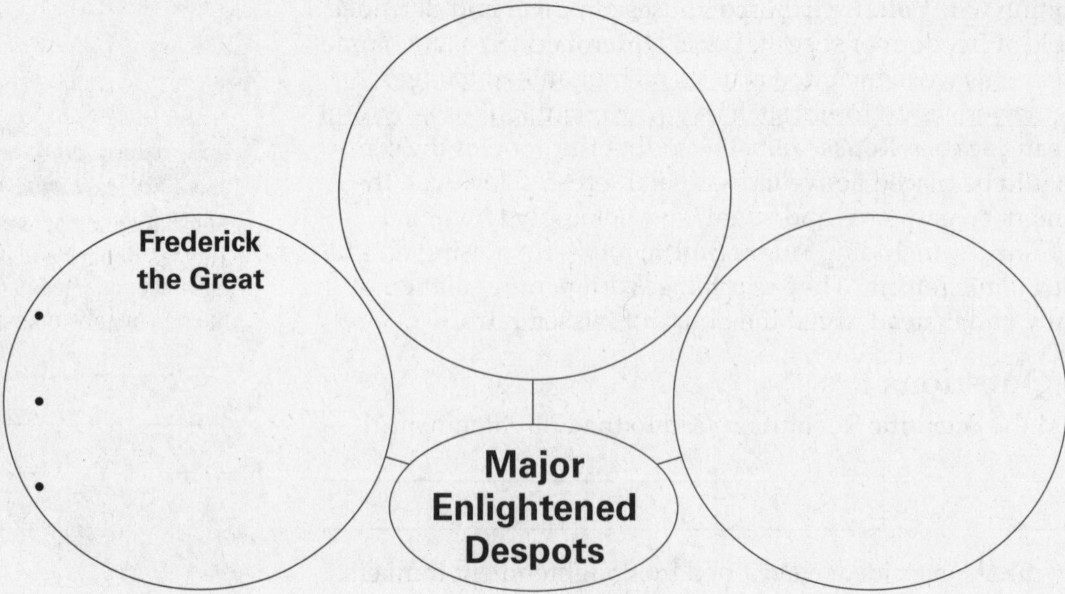

Name________________ Class__________ Date______

CHAPTER 5 SECTION 2

Section Summary

ENLIGHTENMENT IDEAS SPREAD

Enlightenment ideas flowed from France, across Europe and beyond. Before the Enlightenment, most Europeans had accepted a society based on divine-right rule, a strict class system, and a belief in a heavenly reward for earthly suffering. The ideas of the Enlightenment, found in books such as Diderot's *Encyclopedia*, challenged those traditional beliefs and customs. In response, most government and church authorities waged a war of **censorship.** They banned and burned books, and imprisoned writers. Censorship, however, did not stop the spread of ideas. *Philosophes* and others disguised their ideas in works of fiction. Ideas continued to spread in **salons,** where people gathered to discuss new concepts in literature, the arts, science, and philosophy.

In the 1600s and 1700s, the arts evolved to meet changing tastes and reflect new Enlightenment ideals. In visual art and in music there was a transition from the heavier splendor of the **baroque** style to the lighter, more charming style of **rococo.** Ballets and operas—plays set to music—were performed at royal courts. Opera houses sprang up in Europe. Composers later created elegant works in a style known as classical. A growing audience of middle-class readers also led to the rise of a new type of literature—a prose form called the novel. Daniel Defoe's *Robinson Crusoe* was written at this time.

The courts of Europe were also affected by the Enlightenment as *philosophes* tried to persuade European rulers to make reforms. A few European monarchs did accept Enlightenment ideas, but retained their absolute control. These **enlightened despots** used their power to bring about some political and social changes. In Prussia, **Frederick the Great** kept tight control over his subjects yet allowed a free press and religious tolerance. **Catherine the Great** of Russia abolished torture and criticized the institution of serfdom. In Austria, **Joseph II** traveled in disguise among his subjects to learn of their problems. Despite the spread of Enlightenment ideas, however, the lives of most regular Europeans changed slowly.

Review Questions

1. How did most government and church authorities try to stop the spread of Enlightenment ideas?

____

____

2. What effect did Enlightenment ideas have on art, music, and literature?

____

____

READING CHECK

What traditional beliefs and customs did the ideas of the Enlightenment challenge?

____

____

____

VOCABULARY STRATEGY

What does the word *evolved* mean in the underlined sentence? What clues can you find in the surrounding words, phrases, or sentences? Circle the context clues in the paragraph that could help you learn what *evolved* means.

READING SKILL

Summarize How did enlightened despots contribute to the Enlightenment?

____

____

____

Name______________________ Class__________________ Date________

CHAPTER 5 SECTION 3

Note Taking Study Guide

BIRTH OF THE AMERICAN REPUBLIC

Focus Question: How did ideas of the Enlightenment lead to the independence and founding of the United States of America?

As you read this section in your textbook, complete the following timeline with the dates of important events that led to the formation of the United States.

1760

1763 — French and Indian War ends.

Name________________________ Class____________ Date______

CHAPTER 5 SECTION 3

Section Summary

BIRTH OF THE AMERICAN REPUBLIC

In the mid-1700s, Britain was a formidable global power. Key reasons for this status included its location, support of commerce, and huge gains in territory around the world. Furthermore, the new king, **George III,** began to assert his leadership and royal power.

Britain's growing empire included 13 prosperous colonies on the east coast of North America. The colonists shared many values. These included an increasing sense of their own destiny separate from Britain. In some cases, Britain neglected to enforce laws dealing with colonial trade and manufacturing.

Tensions between the colonists and Britain grew as Parliament passed laws, such as the **Stamp Act,** that increased colonists' taxes. The colonists protested what they saw as "taxation without representation." A series of violent clashes with British soldiers intensified the colonists' anger. Finally, representatives from each colony, including **George Washington** of Virginia, met in the Continental Congress to decide what to do. Then in April 1775, colonists fought British soldiers at Lexington and Concord, and the American Revolution began.

On July 4, 1776, the Second Continental Congress adopted the Declaration of Independence. Written primarily by **Thomas Jefferson,** it reflects John Locke's ideas about the rights to "life, liberty, and property." It also details the colonists' grievances and emphasizes the Enlightenment idea of **popular sovereignty.**

At first, chances for American success looked bleak. The colonists struggled against Britain's trained soldiers, huge fleet, and greater resources. When the colonists won the Battle of Saratoga, other European nations, such as France, joined the American side. With the help of the French fleet, Washington forced the British to surrender at **Yorktown, Virginia,** in 1781. Two years later American, British, and French diplomats signed the **Treaty of Paris,** ending the war.

By 1789, leaders of the new United States, such as **James Madison** and **Benjamin Franklin,** had established a **federal republic** under the Constitution. The new government was based on the separation of powers, an idea borrowed directly from Montesquieu. The Bill of Rights, the first ten amendments to the Constitution, protected basic rights. The United States Constitution put Enlightenment ideas into practice and has become an important symbol of freedom.

Review Questions

1. What first caused tensions to rise between the colonists and Britain?

____

____

2. What are some Enlightenment ideas found in the Declaration of Independence?

____

____

READING CHECK

How did France help the Americans win the Revolution?

____

____

____

VOCABULARY STRATEGY

What does the word *assert* mean in the underlined sentence? What context clues can you find in the surrounding words, phrases, or sentences that hint at its meaning? Circle the word below that is a synonym for *assert.*

1. declare
2. deny

READING SKILL

Recognize Sequence Place the events leading to the American Revolution in the correct order.

____

____

____

Name______________________ Class______________________ Date________

CHAPTER 6
SECTION 1

Note Taking Study Guide

ON THE EVE OF REVOLUTION

Focus Question: What led to the storming of the Bastille, and therefore, to the start of the French Revolution?

As you read this section in your textbook, complete the following chart by identifying the multiple causes of the French Revolution.

Name________________________ Class____________ Date______

CHAPTER 6
SECTION 1

Section Summary

ON THE EVE OF REVOLUTION

Under France's **ancien régime**, there were three social classes, or **estates**. The First Estate was the clergy, who enjoyed great wealth and privilege. The Second Estate was the titled nobility. They held top jobs in government, the army, and the courts. The vast majority of the population, including the **bourgeoisie,** or middle class, formed the Third Estate. The bulk of the Third Estate consisted of rural peasants. The poorest members of the Third Estate were urban workers.

Members of the Third Estate resented the privileges enjoyed by their social "betters." The First and Second Estates, for example, were exempt from most taxes, while peasants paid taxes on many things, including necessities. Then Enlightenment ideas led people to question the inequalities of the old social structure. The Third Estate demanded that the privileged classes pay their share.

Economic troubles added to the social unrest. **Deficit spending** had left France deeply in debt. In the 1780s, bad harvests sent food prices soaring. **Louis XVI** chose **Jacques Necker** as an economic advisor. Later, the king was forced to dismiss Necker for proposing to tax the First and Second Estates. The crisis deepened. Powerful nobles and clergy called for a meeting of the **Estates-General** to try to control reform. Louis XVI finally set a meeting at Versailles. Beforehand, the king asked all three estates to prepare **cahiers** listing their grievances. Some lists demonstrated the high level of resentment among the classes.

The Estates-General met in May 1789. After weeks of stalemate, delegates of the Third Estate abandoned the Estates-General and formed the National Assembly. Later, when they were locked out of their meeting place, the members of the new legislature took their famous **Tennis Court Oath.** They swore never to separate until they had established a just constitution.

On July 14, 1789, the streets of Paris buzzed with rumors that royal troops were going to occupy the city. More than 800 Parisians assembled outside the **Bastille,** demanding weaponry stored there. When the commander refused, the enraged mob stormed the Bastille, sparking the French Revolution.

Review Questions

1. How was society structured under France's *ancien régime?*

____

____

2. What economic troubles did France face in the 1780s?

____

____

READING CHECK

Which group paid the most taxes?

____

____

____

VOCABULARY STRATEGY

What does the word *urban* mean in the underlined sentence? Notice that the word *rural* appears in the previous sentence. *Rural* is an antonym of *urban.* Use the meaning of the antonym to help you figure out what *urban* means.

READING SKILL

Recognize Multiple Causes Identify three causes of the French Revolution.

____

____

____

Name______________________ Class__________________ Date________

CHAPTER 6 SECTION 2

Note Taking Study Guide

THE FRENCH REVOLUTION UNFOLDS

Focus Question: What political and social reforms did the National Assembly institute in the first stage of the French Revolution?

As you read this section in your textbook, complete the following outline by identifying the main ideas and supporting details in this section.

I. Political crisis leads to revolt

A. The Great Fear

1. Inflamed by famine and rumors
2. ______________________

B. ______________________

1. ______________________
2. ______________________

II. ______________________

A. ______________________

1. ______________________
2. ______________________

B. ______________________

1. ______________________
2. ______________________

C. ______________________

1. ______________________
2. ______________________

III. ______________________

A. ______________________

1. ______________________
2. ______________________

B. ______________________

1. ______________________
2. ______________________

C. ______________________

1. ______________________
2. ______________________

(Outline continues on the next page.)

CHAPTER 6 SECTION 2

Note Taking Study Guide

THE FRENCH REVOLUTION UNFOLDS

(Continued from page 82)

IV. ______________________________

A. ______________________________

1. ______________________________

2. ______________________________

B. ______________________________

1. ______________________________

2. ______________________________

C. ______________________________

1. ______________________________

2. ______________________________

D. ______________________________

1. ______________________________

2. ______________________________

Name____________ Class__________ Date______

CHAPTER 6 SECTION 2

Section Summary

THE FRENCH REVOLUTION UNFOLDS

READING CHECK

Who were the sans-culottes?

____

____

____

VOCABULARY STRATEGY

What do you think the word *proclaimed* means in the underlined sentence? The words *proclamation, declaration,* and *announcement* are all synonyms for *proclaimed.* Use what you know about these synonyms to figure out the meaning of *proclaimed.*

READING SKILL

Identify Supporting Details Identify two aspects of the Constitution of 1791 that reflect Enlightenment goals.

____

____

____

In France, the political crisis of 1789 coincided with a terrible famine. Peasants were starving and unemployed. In such desperate times, rumors ran wild. Inflamed by famine and fear, peasants unleashed their fury on the nobles. Meanwhile, a variety of **factions** in Paris competed to gain power. Moderates looked to the **Marquis de Lafayette** for leadership. However, a more radical group, the Paris Commune, replaced the city's royalist government.

The storming of the Bastille and the peasant uprisings pushed the National Assembly into action. In late August, the Assembly issued the Declaration of the Rights of Man and the Citizen. <u>It proclaimed that all male citizens were equal before the law.</u> Upset that women did not have equal rights, journalist **Olympe de Gouges** wrote a declaration that provided for this. The Assembly did not adopt it, however. Nor was King Louis XVI willing to accept reforms. Much anger was directed at the queen, **Marie Antoinette,** who lived a life of great extravagance.

The National Assembly produced the Constitution of 1791. This document reflected Enlightenment goals, set up a limited monarchy, ensured equality before the law for all male citizens, and ended Church interference in government.

Events in France stirred debate all over Europe. Some applauded the reforms of the National Assembly. Rulers of other nations, however, denounced the French Revolution. Horror stories were told by **émigrés** who had fled France. Rulers of neighboring monarchies increased border patrols to stop the spread of the "French plague" of revolution.

In October 1791, the newly elected Legislative Assembly took office, but falling currency values, rising prices, and food shortages renewed turmoil. Working-class men and women, called **sans-culottes,** pushed the revolution in a more radical direction, and demanded a **republic.** The sans-culottes found support among other radicals, especially the **Jacobins.** The radicals soon held the upper hand in the Legislative Assembly. Eager to spread the revolution, they declared war against Austria and other European monarchies.

Review Questions

1. What was the Declaration of the Rights of Man and the Citizen? Why were some people dissatisfied with it?

____

____

2. How did rulers of European monarchies react to the French Revolution?

____

____

Name____________________ Class________________ Date______

CHAPTER 6
SECTION 3

Note Taking Study Guide

RADICAL DAYS OF THE REVOLUTION

Focus Question: What events occurred during the radical phase of the French Revolution?

As you read this section in your textbook, complete the following timeline to show the sequence of events that took place during the radical phase of the French Revolution.

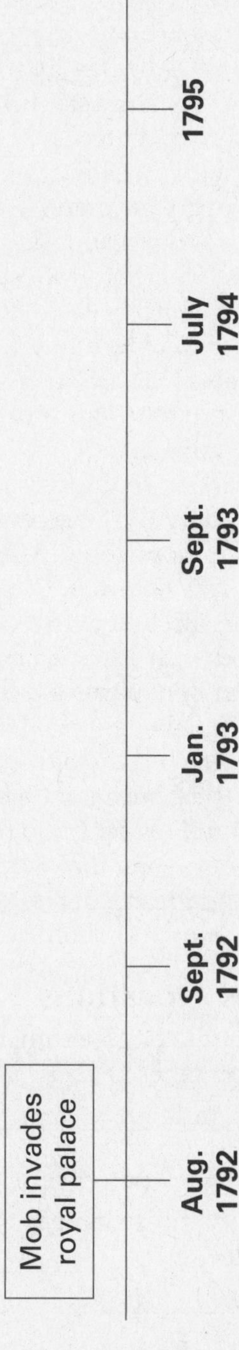

Name______________________ Class__________ Date______

CHAPTER 6
SECTION 3

Section Summary

RADICAL DAYS OF THE REVOLUTION

In 1793, the revolution entered a frightening and bloody phase. The war with Austria was not going well for France. Some felt the king was in league with France's enemies. Others wanted to restore the king's power. On August 10, 1792, a mob stormed the royal palace. Radicals then took control of the Assembly and called for the election of a new legislative body called the National Convention. **Suffrage** was to be extended to all male citizens, not just to those who owned property. The Convention that met in September 1792 was a more radical body than earlier assemblies. It voted to abolish the monarchy and establish the French Republic. Louis XVI and his queen were executed.

War with other European nations and internal rebellions concerned the government. The Convention created the Committee of Public Safety to deal with these issues. It had almost absolute power. Jacobin Maximilien **Robespierre** led the Committee. He was one of the chief architects of the **Reign of Terror,** which lasted from September 1793 to July 1794. During that time, courts conducted hasty trials for those suspected of resisting the revolution. Many people were the victims of false accusations. About 17,000 were executed by **guillotine.**

In reaction to the Terror, the revolution entered a third stage, dominated by the bourgeoisie. It moved away from the excesses of the Convention, and moderates created the Constitution of 1795. This set up a five-man Directory to rule, and a two-house legislature. However, discontent grew because of corrupt leaders. Also, war continued with Austria and Britain. Politicians planned to use **Napoleon** Bonaparte, a popular military hero, to advance their goals.

By 1799, the French Revolution had dramatically changed France. It had dislodged the old social order, overthrown the monarchy, and brought the Church under state control. **Nationalism** spread throughout France. From the city of **Marseilles,** troops marched to a rousing new song that would become the French national anthem. Revolutionaries also made social reforms. They set up systems to help the poor and abolished slavery in France's Caribbean colonies.

READING CHECK

Who was Robespierre?

____

____

____

VOCABULARY STRATEGY

What do you think *radical* means in the underlined sentence? Notice that the word *more* appears before *radical.* Use the word *more* and your prior knowledge to help you figure out what *radical* means.

READING SKILL

Recognize Sequence What occurred after the radicals took control of the Assembly in 1792?

____

____

____

Review Questions

1. What type of government did the National Convention establish in September 1792?

____

____

2. Identify three changes that the French Revolution brought to France.

____

____

Name________________________ Class__________________ Date________

CHAPTER 6 SECTION 4

Note Taking Study Guide

THE AGE OF NAPOLEON

Focus Question: Explain Napoleon's rise to power in Europe, his subsequent defeat, and how the outcome still affects Europe today.

As you read this section in your textbook, complete the flowchart to list the main ideas about Napoleon's rise to power and his defeat.

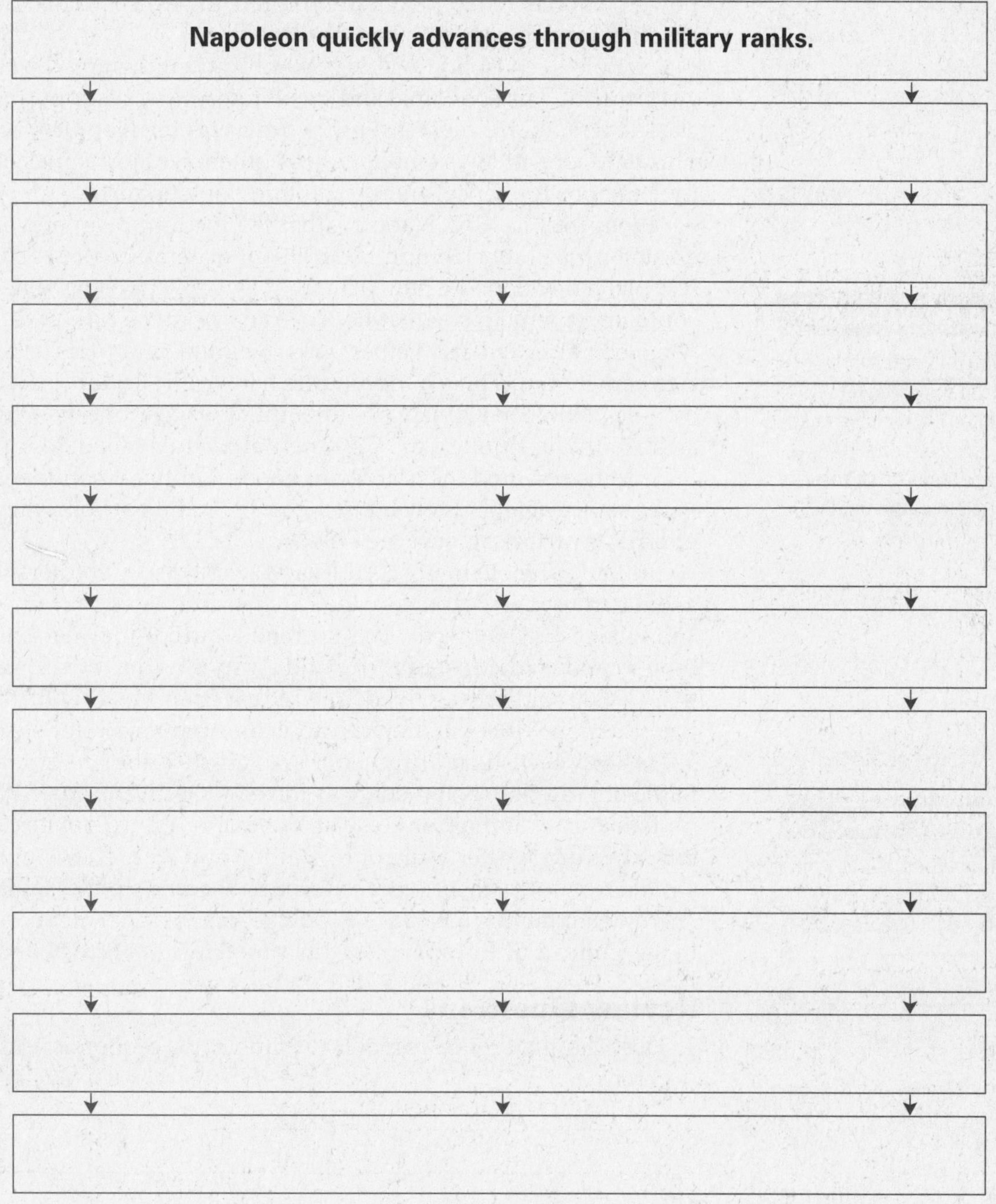

Name________________________ Class__________ Date______

CHAPTER 6
SECTION 4

Section Summary

THE AGE OF NAPOLEON

READING CHECK

What was the Napoleonic Code?

____

____

____

VOCABULARY STRATEGY

What do you think the word *anticipate* means in the underlined sentence? What clues can you find in the surrounding words and phrases? Use these context clues to figure out the meaning of *anticipate*.

READING SKILL

Identify Main Ideas Write a new title for this section Summary to express the main idea in another way.

____

____

____

The final phase of the revolution is known as the Age of Napoleon. When the revolution first broke out, Napoleon Bonaparte was a young lieutenant. Battle victories fueled his ambitions and his rise through army ranks. By 1804, Napoleon had acquired enough power to assume the title Emperor of the French. At each step on his rise to power, Napoleon had held a **plebiscite.** However, he still had absolute power, although he was elected.

Napoleon consolidated his power by strengthening the central government. His economic and social reforms won support across classes. Among his most lasting reforms was the **Napoleonic Code.** This new code of laws embodied Enlightenment principles of equality, religious tolerance, and the abolition of feudalism.

From 1804 to 1812, Napoleon battled the European powers and created a vast French empire. A brilliant general, before each battle Napoleon developed a new plan. In this way, opposing generals could never anticipate what he would do next. He rarely lost. Napoleon **annexed** the Netherlands, Belgium, and parts of Italy and Germany to build his Grand Empire. However, Britain remained outside Napoleon's grasp. His attempt to wage economic warfare against Britain through the **Continental System** failed. Many Europeans resented the scarcity of goods. Growing nationalism led to resistance against French influence. In Spain, patriots waged **guerrilla warfare** against the French.

In 1812, Napoleon invaded Russia with 600,000 soldiers. To avoid battles with Napoleon, the Russians retreated, burning crops and villages as they went. This **scorched-earth policy** left the French hungry and cold. Most of the Grand Army was destroyed. Fewer than 20,000 soldiers survived. The retreat from Moscow through the long Russian winter shattered Napoleon's reputation for success.

In 1815, British and Prussian forces crushed the French at the Battle of Waterloo. Napoleon was forced to **abdicate.** After Waterloo, diplomats met at the **Congress of Vienna** to restore stability and order in Europe after years of revolution and war. The Congress strived to create a lasting peace through the principle of **legitimacy** and by maintaining a balance of power. Leaders also met periodically in the **Concert of Europe** to discuss problems that threatened peace.

Review Questions

1. How did the French respond to Napoleon's economic and social reforms?

____

____

2. Why did Napoleon's invasion of Russia fail?

____

____

Name______________________ Class______________ Date________

CHAPTER 7 SECTION 1

Note Taking Study Guide

DAWN OF THE INDUSTRIAL AGE

Focus Question: What events helped bring about the Industrial Revolution?

As you read this section in your textbook, complete the following flowchart to list multiple causes of the Industrial Revolution.

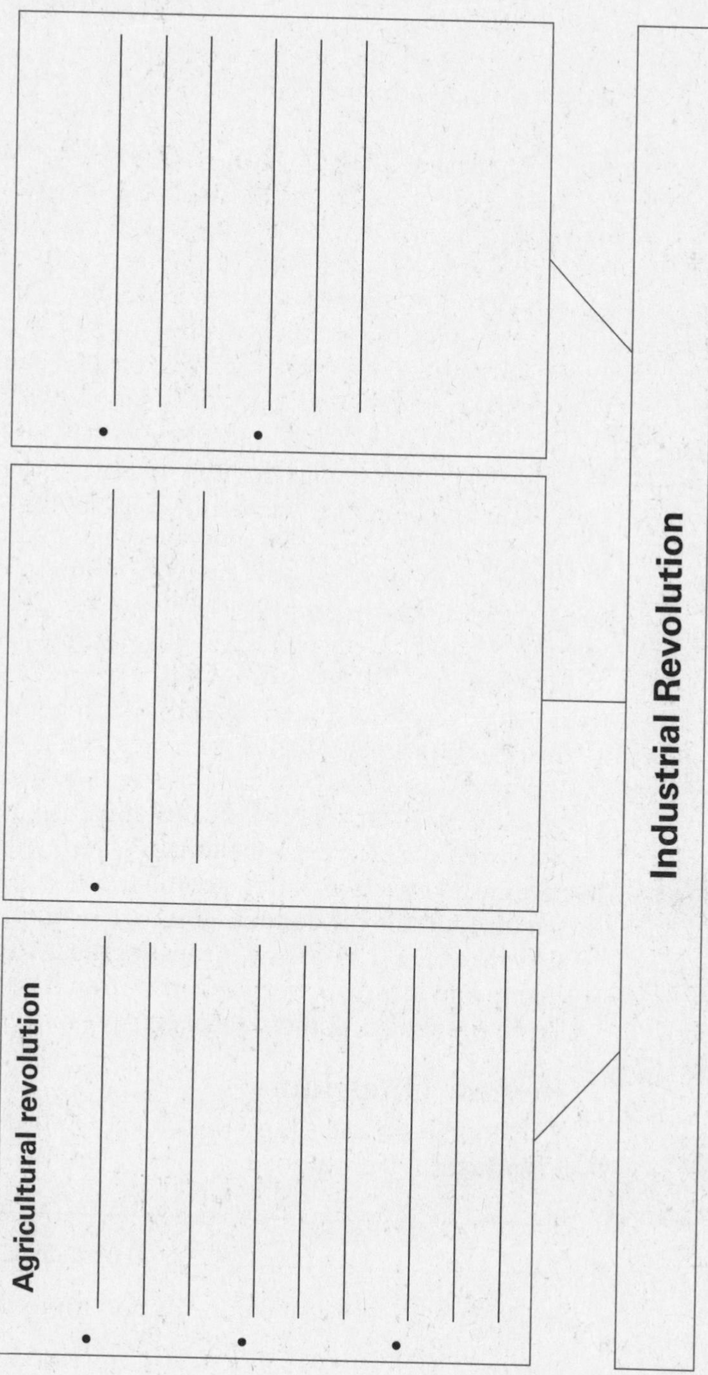

Name________________________ Class____________ Date______

CHAPTER 7 SECTION 1

Section Summary

DAWN OF THE INDUSTRIAL AGE

READING CHECK

Who formed the growing labor force for the Industrial Revolution?

____

____

____

VOCABULARY STRATEGY

What does the word *statistics* mean in the underlined sentence? What prior knowledge do you have of this word? For example, think of where you may have seen statistics before. Use your prior knowledge and context clues in the sentence to help you learn what *statistics* means.

READING SKILL

Recognize Multiple Causes Identify three events in the agricultural revolution that caused population and industry to grow.

____

____

____

The Industrial Revolution started in Britain. In 1750, most people worked the land, using handmade tools. They made their own clothing and grew their own food. With the onset of the Industrial Revolution, the rural way of life in Britain began to disappear. By the 1850s, many country villages had grown into industrial towns and cities. New inventions and scientific "firsts" appeared each year. Between 1830 and 1855, for example, an American dentist first used an **anesthetic** during surgery and a French physicist measured the speed of light.

A series of related causes helped spark the Industrial Revolution. It was made possible, in part, by another revolution—in agriculture—that greatly improved the quality and quantity of food. Farmers mixed different kinds of soils and tried out new methods of crop rotation to get higher yields. Meanwhile, rich landowners pushed ahead with **enclosure,** the process of taking over and consolidating land formerly shared by peasant farmers. As millions of acres were enclosed, farm output and profits rose. The agricultural revolution created a surplus of food, so fewer people died from starvation. <u>Statistics show that the agricultural revolution contributed to a rapid growth in population.</u>

Agricultural progress, however, had a human cost. Many farm laborers were thrown out of work. In time, jobless farm workers migrated to towns and cities. There, they formed a growing labor force that would soon operate the machines of the Industrial Revolution.

Another factor that helped trigger the Industrial Revolution was the development of new technology, aided by new sources of energy and new materials. One vital power source was coal, used to develop the steam engine. In 1764, Scottish engineer **James Watt** improved the steam engine to make it more efficient. Watt's engine became a key power source of the Industrial Revolution. Coal was also used in the production of iron, a material needed for the construction of machines and steam engines. In 1709, Adam Darby used coal to **smelt** iron, or separate iron from its ore. Darby's experiments led to the production of less-expensive and better-quality iron.

Review Questions

1. How did people's lifestyles change in Britain with the start of the Industrial Revolution?

____

____

2. Why was the steam engine important to the Industrial Revolution?

____

____

Name____________________ Class________________ Date________

CHAPTER 7 SECTION 2

Note Taking Study Guide

BRITAIN LEADS THE WAY

Focus Question: What key factors allowed Britain to lead the way in the Industrial Revolution?

As you read this section in your textbook, complete the following concept webs to identify causes and effects of Britain's early lead in industrialization. Fill in the first concept web with causes. Fill in the second concept web with effects.

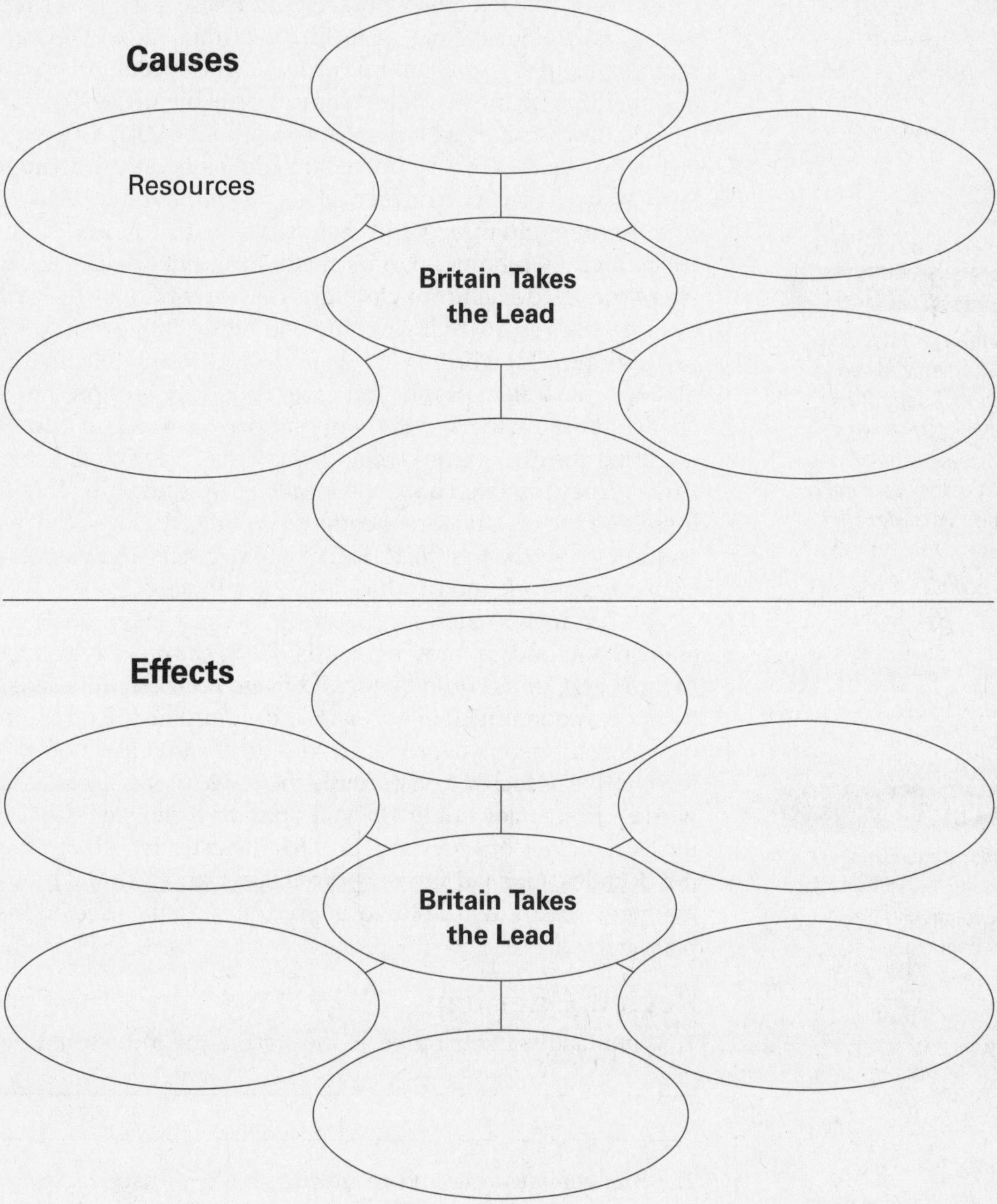

Name____________________ Class__________ Date______

CHAPTER 7 SECTION 2

Section Summary

BRITAIN LEADS THE WAY

The start of the Industrial Revolution in Britain can be attributed to many factors, including population growth and plentiful natural resources. The growing population and ready workforce boosted demand for goods. To increase production to meet the demand, however, another key ingredient was needed—money to start businesses. Beginning with the slave trade, the business class accumulated **capital** to invest in enterprises. An **enterprise** is a business in areas such as shipping, mining, or factories. Britain had a stable government that supported economic growth. **Entrepreneurs** managed and assumed the financial risks of starting new businesses.

The Industrial Revolution first took hold in Britain's largest industry—textiles. British merchants developed the **putting-out system,** in which raw cotton was distributed to peasant families. They spun it into thread and then wove the thread into cloth, working in their own homes. Under the putting-out system, production was slow. As demand for cloth grew, inventors came up with new devices, such as the flying shuttle and the spinning jenny, which revolutionized the British textile industry. Meanwhile, in the United States, these faster spinning and weaving machines presented a challenge—how to produce enough cotton to keep up with Britain. Cleaning the raw cotton by hand was time-consuming. To solve this, **Eli Whitney** invented a machine called the cotton gin. This greatly increased the production of cotton. To house these machines, manufacturers built the first factories, where spinners and weavers came each day to work and produce large quantities of goods.

As production increased, entrepreneurs needed faster and cheaper methods of moving goods. Some capitalists invested in **turnpikes.** Goods could be moved faster on these toll roads, and turnpikes soon linked every part of Britain. The great revolution in transportation, however, occurred with the invention of the steam locomotive, which made possible the growth of railroads. The world's first major rail line began operating between the British industrial cities of **Liverpool** and **Manchester** in 1830. In the following decades, railroad travel became faster and railroad building boomed. The Industrial Revolution dramatically affected the way people lived.

READING CHECK

What machine did Eli Whitney invent?

____

____

____

VOCABULARY STRATEGY

What does the word *decades* mean in the underlined sentence? The word *decades* comes from the Greek word *deka,* which means "ten." Use the meaning of the word *deka* to help you learn what *decades* means.

READING SKILL

Identify Causes and Effects Identify causes and effects of the great revolution in transportation in England.

____

____

____

Review Questions

1. What factors contributed to the start of the Industrial Revolution?

____

____

2. What changes revolutionized the textile industry?

____

____

Name____________________ Class__________ Date______

CHAPTER 8 SECTION 1

Section Summary

AN AGE OF IDEOLOGIES

After the Congress of Vienna, people with opposing **ideologies** plunged Europe into decades of turmoil. Conservatives, including monarchs, nobles, and church leaders, favored a return to the social order that had existed before 1789. They decided to work together in an agreement called the Concert of Europe. They wanted to restore the royal families that Napoleon had deposed. They supported a social hierarchy in which lower classes respected and obeyed their social superiors. They also backed established churches and opposed constitutional governments. Conservative leaders such as Prince Metternich of Austria sought to suppress revolutionary ideas.

Inspired by the Enlightenment and the French Revolution, liberals and nationalists challenged conservatives. Liberals included business owners, bankers, lawyers, politicians, and writers. They wanted governments based on written constitutions. They opposed established churches and divine-right monarchies. They believed that liberty, equality, and property were natural rights. They saw government's role as limited to protecting basic rights, such as freedom of thought, speech, and religion. Only later in the century did liberals come to support **universal manhood suffrage,** giving all men the right to vote. Liberals also strongly supported laissez-faire economics.

Nationalism gave people with a common heritage a sense of identity and the goal of creating their own homeland. In the 1800s, national groups within the Austrian and Ottoman empires set out to create their own states. Rebellions erupted in the Balkans, where there were people of various religions and ethnic groups. The Serbs were the first to revolt. By 1830, Russian support helped the Serbs win **autonomy,** or self-rule, within the Ottoman empire. In 1821, the Greeks revolted, and by 1830, Greece was independent from the Ottomans. Revolts spread to Spain, Portugal, and Italy. Metternich urged conservative rulers to crush the uprisings. In response, French and Austrian troops smashed rebellions in Spain and Italy.

In the next decades, sparks of rebellion would flare anew. Added to liberal and nationalist demands were the goals of the new industrial working class. <u>By the mid-1800s, social reformers and agitators were urging workers to support socialism or other ways of reorganizing property ownership.</u>

Review Questions

1. How did government views of conservatives and liberals differ?

____

____

2. Why did French and Austrian troops stop revolts in Spain and Italy?

____

____

READING CHECK

What is universal manhood suffrage?

____

____

____

VOCABULARY STRATEGY

What does the word *agitators* mean in the underlined sentence? Review the surrounding words and phrases to look for clues to its meaning. Use these context clues to help you understand what an *agitator* is.

READING SKILL

Identify Main Ideas What two groups generally struggled for political control during the early nineteenth century?

____

____

____

Name_______________________ Class__________________ Date________

CHAPTER 8
SECTION 2

Note Taking Study Guide

REVOLUTIONS OF 1830 AND 1848

Focus Question: What were the causes and effects of the revolutions in Europe in 1830 and 1848?

As you read this section, fill in the table below with a country, date, and main idea for each revolution of 1830 and 1848.

Revolutions of 1830 and 1848		
France	1830	Radicals force king to abdicate.

Name________________________ Class___________ Date______

CHAPTER 8 SECTION 2

Section Summary

REVOLUTIONS OF 1830 AND 1848

When Louis XVIII died in 1824, Charles X inherited the French throne. In 1830, Charles suspended the legislature, limited the right to vote, and restricted the press. Angry citizens, led by liberals and **radicals,** rebelled and soon controlled Paris. Charles X abdicated. Radicals hoped to set up a republic, but liberals insisted on a constitutional monarchy. **Louis Philippe** was chosen king. As the "citizen king," Louis favored the bourgeoisie, or middle class, over the workers.

The Paris revolts inspired uprisings elsewhere in Europe. Most failed, but the revolutions frightened rulers and encouraged reforms. One notable success was in Belgium, which achieved its independence from Holland in 1831. Nationalists also revolted in Poland in 1830, but they failed to win widespread support. Russian forces crushed the rebels.

In the 1840s, discontent began to grow again in France. Radicals, socialists, and liberals denounced Louis Philippe's government. Discontent was heightened by a **recession.** People lost their jobs, and poor harvests caused bread prices to rise. When the government tried to silence critics, angry crowds took to the streets in February 1848. The turmoil spread, and Louis Philippe abdicated. A group of liberals, radicals, and socialists proclaimed the Second Republic. By June, the upper and middle classes had won control of the government. Workers again took to the streets of Paris. At least 1,500 people were killed before the government crushed the rebellion. By the end of 1848, the National Assembly issued a constitution for the Second Republic, giving the right to vote to all adult men. When the election for president was held, Louis Napoleon, the nephew of Napoleon Bonaparte, won. However, by 1852 he had proclaimed himself Emperor **Napoleon III.** This ended the Second Republic.

The revolts in Paris in 1848 again led to revolutions across Europe, especially in the Austrian empire. Revolts broke out in Vienna, and Metternich resigned. In Budapest, Hungarian nationalists led by **Louis Kossuth** demanded an independent government. In Prague, the Czechs made similar demands. The Italian states also revolted, and the German states demanded national unity. While the rebellions had some short-term success, most of them had failed by 1850.

Review Questions

1. What caused the rebellion in France in 1830?

____

____

2. In what parts of Europe did revolts take place following the Paris revolts of 1848?

____

____

READING CHECK

What brought the Second Republic to an end?

____

____

____

VOCABULARY STRATEGY

What does the word *denounced* mean in the underlined sentence? Reread the sentences before and after the underlined sentence. Were the French people happy or unhappy with Louis Philippe's government? Note that the government "tried to silence critics." Use these context clues to help you understand the meaning of *denounce.*

READING SKILL

Identify Main Ideas What is the main idea of the last paragraph in the Summary?

____

____

____

Name________________________ Class____________________ Date________

CHAPTER 8
SECTION 3

Note Taking Study Guide

REVOLTS IN LATIN AMERICA

Focus Question: Who were the key revolutionaries to lead the movements for independence in Latin America, and what were their accomplishments?

As you read this section, fill in the table below with a country, a date, and a main idea for each of the revolts in Latin America.

Revolts in Latin America		
Haiti	1791	Toussaint L'Ouverture leads an army of former slaves and ends slavery there.

Name________________________ Class____________ Date______

CHAPTER 8 SECTION 3

Section Summary

REVOLTS IN LATIN AMERICA

By the late 1700s, revolutionary fever had spread to Latin America, where the social system had led to discontent. Spanish-born ***peninsulares,*** the highest social class, dominated the government and the Church. Many **creoles**—Latin Americans of European descent who owned the haciendas, ranches, and mines—resented their second-class status. **Mestizos,** people of Native American and European descent, and **mulattoes,** people of African and European descent, were angry at being denied the status, wealth, and power that the other groups enjoyed. The Enlightenment and the French and American revolutions inspired creoles, but they were reluctant to act. However, when Napoleon invaded Spain in 1808, Latin American leaders decided to demand independence from Spain.

Revolution had already erupted in Hispaniola in 1791 when **Toussaint L'Ouverture** led a slave rebellion there. The fighting cost many lives, but the rebels achieved their goal of abolishing slavery and taking control of the island. Napoleon's army tried to reconquer the island but failed. In 1804, the island declared itself independent under the name Haiti.

In 1810, a creole priest, **Father Miguel Hidalgo,** called Mexicans to fight for independence. After some successes, he was captured and executed. **Father José Morelos** tried to carry the revolution forward, but he too was captured and killed. Success finally came in 1821 when revolutionaries led by Agustín de Iturbide overthrew the Spanish viceroy and declared independence. Central American colonies soon declared independence, too.

In the early 1800s, discontent spread across South America. **Simón Bolívar** led an uprising in Venezuela. Conservative forces toppled his new republic, but Bolívar did not give up. In a grueling campaign, he marched his army across the Andes, swooping down into Bogotá and taking the city from the surprised Spanish. Then he moved south to free Ecuador, Peru, and Bolivia. There, he joined forces with another great leader, **José de San Martín.** San Martín helped Argentina and Chile win freedom from Spain. The wars of independence ended in 1824, but power struggles among South American leaders led to destructive civil wars. In Brazil, **Dom Pedro,** the son of the Portuguese king, became emperor and proclaimed independence for Brazil in 1822.

Review Questions

1. Why were creoles ready to revolt by 1808?

____

____

2. How did Brazil gain its independence?

____

____

READING CHECK

What two leaders helped free much of South America?

____

____

____

VOCABULARY STRATEGY

What does the word *proclaimed* mean in the underlined sentence? *Proclaim* comes from the Latin word *proclamare.* The prefix *pro-* means "before," and *clamare* means "to cry out" or "shout." Use these word-origin clues to help you to figure out the meaning of *proclaimed.*

READING SKILL

Identify Main Ideas In the first paragraph of the Summary, most of the sentences are supporting details. Which sentence states the main idea of that paragraph?

____

____

____

Name____________________ Class________________ Date________

CHAPTER 9 SECTION 1

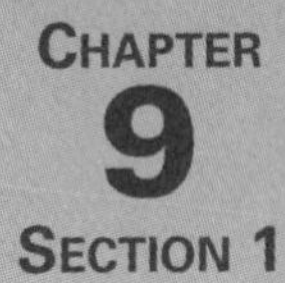

Note Taking Study Guide

THE INDUSTRIAL REVOLUTION SPREADS

Focus Question: How did science, technology, and big business promote industrial growth?

As you read this section in your textbook, complete the following chart to identify main ideas about the major developments of the Industrial Revolution.

The Second Industrial Revolution		
	Transportation/ Communication	• • •
	Industry/Business	• • • • • •
	New Powers	• • •

Name________________________ Class____________ Date______

CHAPTER 9
SECTION 1

Section Summary

THE INDUSTRIAL REVOLUTION SPREADS

During the early Industrial Revolution, Britain was the world's industrial giant. Later, two new industrial powers emerged—Germany and the United States. These nations had more abundant supplies of coal, iron, and other resources than Britain. This helped them become the new industrial leaders. These nations also had the advantage of being able to follow Britain's lead, borrowing its experts and technology. The demands of an industrial society brought about many social, economic, and political changes.

Technology sparked industrial and economic growth. **Henry Bessemer** patented the process for making steel from iron. Steel became so important that industrialized countries measured their success in steel output. **Alfred Nobel** earned enough money from his invention of dynamite to fund today's Nobel prizes. Electricity replaced steam as the dominant industrial energy source. **Michael Faraday** created the first simple electric motor, as well as the first **dynamo.** In the 1870s, **Thomas Edison** made the first electric light bulb. Soon, electricity lit entire cities, the pace of city life quickened, and factories continued to operate after dark. **Interchangeable parts** and the **assembly line** made production faster and cheaper.

Technology also transformed transportation and communication. Steamships replaced sailing ships. Railroads connected cities, seaports, and industrial centers. The invention of the internal combustion engine sparked the automobile age. In the early 1900s, Henry Ford developed an assembly line to produce cars, making the United States a leader in the automobile industry. The air age began when **Orville and Wilbur Wright** flew their plane for a few seconds in 1904. Communication advances included the telegraph and telephone. **Guglielmo Marconi's** radio became the cornerstone of today's global communication network.

New technologies needed investments of large amounts of money. To get the money, owners sold **stock** to investors, growing businesses into giant **corporations.** <u>By the late 1800s, what we call "big business" came to dominate industry.</u> Corporations formed **cartels** to control markets.

Review Questions

1. What advantages did the new industrial powers have?

____

____

2. How did the development of electricity change life in cities?

____

____

READING CHECK

What two new industrial powers emerged in the mid-1800s?

____

____

____

VOCABULARY STRATEGY

What does the word *dominate* mean in the underlined sentence? It comes from a Latin word that means "lord" or "master." Use this information about the word's origin to help you figure out what *dominate* means.

READING SKILL

Identify Main Ideas How was transportation transformed during the Industrial Revolution?

____

____

____

Name________________________ Class__________________ Date________

Note Taking Study Guide

THE RISE OF THE CITIES

Focus Question: How did the Industrial Revolution change life in the cities?

As you read this section in your textbook, complete the following outline to identify main ideas and supporting details about how the Industrial Revolution changed life in the cities.

I. Medicine and the population explosion

A. The fight against disease

1. ______________________

2. ______________________

B. ______________________

1. ______________________

2. ______________________

II. ______________________

A. ______________________

1. ______________________

2. ______________________

B. ______________________

1. ______________________

2. ______________________

C. ______________________

1. ______________________

2. ______________________

D. ______________________

1. ______________________

2. ______________________

III. ______________________

A. ______________________

1. ______________________

2. ______________________

B. ______________________

1. ______________________

2. ______________________

Name________________________ Class___________ Date______

CHAPTER 9 SECTION 2

Section Summary

THE RISE OF THE CITIES

Between 1800 and 1900, the population of Europe more than doubled. Advances in medicine slowed death rates and caused a population explosion. In the fight against disease, scientists speculated about a **germ theory**. They believed that certain germs might cause specific diseases. In 1870, French chemist **Louis Pasteur** showed that this link is real. Ten years later, German doctor **Robert Koch** identified the bacteria that causes tuberculosis, a deadly respiratory disease. As people began to understand how germs cause diseases, they practiced better hygiene. This helped decrease the number of deaths from disease. Better hygiene also led to improvements in hospital care. British nurse and reformer **Florence Nightingale** introduced sanitary measures in hospitals. The English surgeon **Joseph Lister** discovered how antiseptics prevent infection.

As industrialization progressed, city life underwent dramatic changes in Europe and the United States. The most extensive **urban renewal** took place in Paris in the 1850s. Wide boulevards, paved streets, and splendid public buildings replaced old streets full of tenement housing. Architects used steel to build soaring buildings called skyscrapers. <u>Electric streetlights illuminated the night, increasing safety.</u> Massive new sewage systems in London and Paris provided cleaner water and better sanitation, sharply cutting death rates from disease.

Despite these efforts, urban life remained difficult for the poor. In the worst tenements, whole families were often crammed into a single room. Slums remained a fact of city life. Still, millions of people were attracted to cities because of the promise of work, entertainment, and educational opportunities.

However, industrialization and urban improvements did not improve conditions for workers. Most experienced low wages, long hours, unsafe environments, and the constant threat of unemployment. Workers protested these terrible conditions. They formed **mutual-aid societies** and organized unions. Pressured by unions, reformers, and working-class voters, governments passed laws to regulate working conditions. Wages varied, but overall, the **standard of living** for most workers did rise.

Review Questions

1. How did advances in medicine cause a population explosion?

____

____

2. What two changes in the 1800s made city life safer and healthier?

____

____

READING CHECK

What did Louis Pasteur do in 1870?

____

____

____

VOCABULARY STRATEGY

What does the word *illuminated* mean in the underlined sentence? The root of this word is from *lumen*, which is Latin for "light." How can you use the root of *illuminated* to help you figure out its meaning?

READING SKILL

Identify Supporting Details In what ways were working conditions difficult for most industrial workers?

____

____

____

Name________________________ Class____________________ Date________

CHAPTER 9 SECTION 3

Note Taking Study Guide

CHANGING ATTITUDES AND VALUES

Focus Question: How did the Industrial Revolution change the old social order and long-held traditions in the Western world?

As you read this section in your textbook, complete the following table. List new issues that caused change in the first column and identify two supporting details for each in the second column.

Changes in Social Order and Values	
Issue	**Change**
• New social order	• Upper class: old nobility, new industrialists, business families • •
• Rights for women	• •
•	• •
•	• •
•	• •

Name________________________ Class____________ Date______

CHAPTER 9
SECTION 3

Section Summary

CHANGING ATTITUDES AND VALUES

In the late 1800s, the social order in the Western world slowly changed. Instead of nobles and peasants, a more complex social structure emerged, made up of three classes. The new upper class included very rich business families. Below this tiny elite were a growing middle class and a struggling lower middle class. Workers and peasants were at the bottom of the social ladder.

The middle class developed its own values and way of life, which included a strict code of rules that dictated behavior for every occasion. A **cult of domesticity** also emerged that idealized women and the home.

Demands for women's rights also challenged the traditional social order. Across Europe and the United States, many women campaigned for fairness in marriage, divorce, and property laws. Many women's groups also supported the **temperance movement.** In the United States, reformers such as **Elizabeth Cady Stanton** and **Sojourner Truth** were dedicated to achieving **women's suffrage.**

Industrialized societies recognized the need for a literate workforce. Reformers persuaded many governments to require basic education for all children and to set up public schools. More and more children attended school, and public education improved.

At the same time, new ideas in science challenged long-held beliefs. **John Dalton** developed the modern atomic theory. The most controversial new idea, however, came from the British naturalist **Charles Darwin.** His ideas upset those who debated the validity of his conclusions. Darwin argued that all forms of life had evolved over millions of years. His theory of natural selection explained the long, slow process of evolution. In natural selection, members of each species compete to survive. Unfortunately, some people applied Darwin's theory of natural selection to encourage **racism.** Others applied his ideas to economic competition.

Religion continued to be a major force in Western society. The grim realities of industrial life stirred feelings of compassion and charity. For example, the **social gospel** urged Christians to push for reforms in housing, healthcare, and education.

Review Questions

1. How did the social structure change in the late 1800s?

____

____

2. For what rights did women in Europe and the United States campaign?

____

____

READING CHECK

What new scientific theory did Charles Darwin promote to explain evolution?

____

____

____

VOCABULARY STRATEGY

What does the word *controversial* mean in the underlined sentence? Use context clues, or surrounding words and sentences, to figure out what *controversial* means.

READING SKILL

Identify Supporting Details What changes in education were brought about by the Industrial Revolution?

____

____

____

Name______________________ Class__________________ Date________

Note Taking Study Guide

ARTS IN THE INDUSTRIAL AGE

Focus Question: What artistic movements emerged in reaction to the Industrial Revolution?

As you read this section in your textbook, complete the following table. Identify supporting details about the major features of the artistic movements of the 1800s.

Major Artistic Movements of the 1800s		
Movement	**Goals/Characteristics**	**Major Figures**
Romanticism	• Rebellion against reason • • • • •	• William Wordsworth • • • • • • •
Realism	• • • • •	• • • • •
Impressionism	• •	• •
	•	• • •

Name________________________ Class____________ Date______

CHAPTER 9 SECTION 4

Section Summary

ARTS IN THE INDUSTRIAL AGE

From about 1750 to 1850, a cultural movement called **romanticism** emerged in Western art and literature. The movement was a reaction against the rationality and restraint of the Enlightenment. Romanticism emphasized imagination, freedom, and emotion. <u>In contrast to Enlightenment literature, the works of romantic writers included direct language, intense feelings, and a glorification of nature.</u>

Poets **William Wordsworth, William Blake,** and **Lord Byron** were among the major figures of the romantic movement. Romantic novelists, such as **Victor Hugo,** were inspired by history, legend, and folklore. Romantic composers also tried to stir deep emotions. The passionate music of **Ludwig van Beethoven** combined classical forms with a stirring range of sound. Painters, too, broke free from the formal styles of the Enlightenment. They sought to capture the beauty and power of nature with bold brush strokes and colors.

By the mid-1800s, another new artistic movement, **realism,** took hold in the West. Realists sought to represent the world as it was, without romantic sentiment. Their works made people aware of the grim conditions of the Industrial Age. Many realists wanted to improve the lives of those they depicted. **Charles Dickens,** for example, vividly portrayed in his novels the lives of slum dwellers and factory workers. Some of his novels shocked middle-class readers with images of poverty, mistreatment of children, and urban crime. Painters such as **Gustave Courbet** also portrayed the realities of the time.

By the 1840s, a new art form, photography, emerged. **Louis Daguerre** produced some of the first successful photographs. Some artists questioned the effectiveness of realism when a camera could make such exact images. By the 1870s, one group had started a new art movement, **impressionism**. Impressionists, such as **Claude Monet,** sought to capture the first fleeting impression made by a scene or object on the viewer's eye. By concentrating on visual impressions, rather than realism, artists created a fresh view of familiar subjects. Later painters, called postimpressionists, developed a variety of styles. **Vincent van Gogh,** for example, experimented with sharp brush lines and bright colors.

Review Questions

1. How did the romantic movement differ from the Enlightenment?

____

____

2. What was the goal of the impressionist artists?

____

____

READING CHECK

Against what was the romantic movement a reaction?

____

____

____

VOCABULARY STRATEGY

What does the word *intense* mean in the underlined sentence? What clues can you find in the surrounding words, phrases, or sentences that might have a similar meaning? Use these context clues to help you learn what *intense* means.

READING SKILL

Identify Supporting Details Identify two supporting details for the following main idea: The artists of the realism movement made people more aware of the harsh conditions of life in the Industrial Age.

____

____

____

Name______________________ Class__________________ Date________

Chapter 10 Section 1

Note Taking Study Guide

BUILDING A GERMAN NATION

Focus Question: How did Otto von Bismarck, the chancellor of Prussia, lead the drive for German unity?

As you read this section in your textbook, complete the following chart to record the sequence of events that led to German unification.

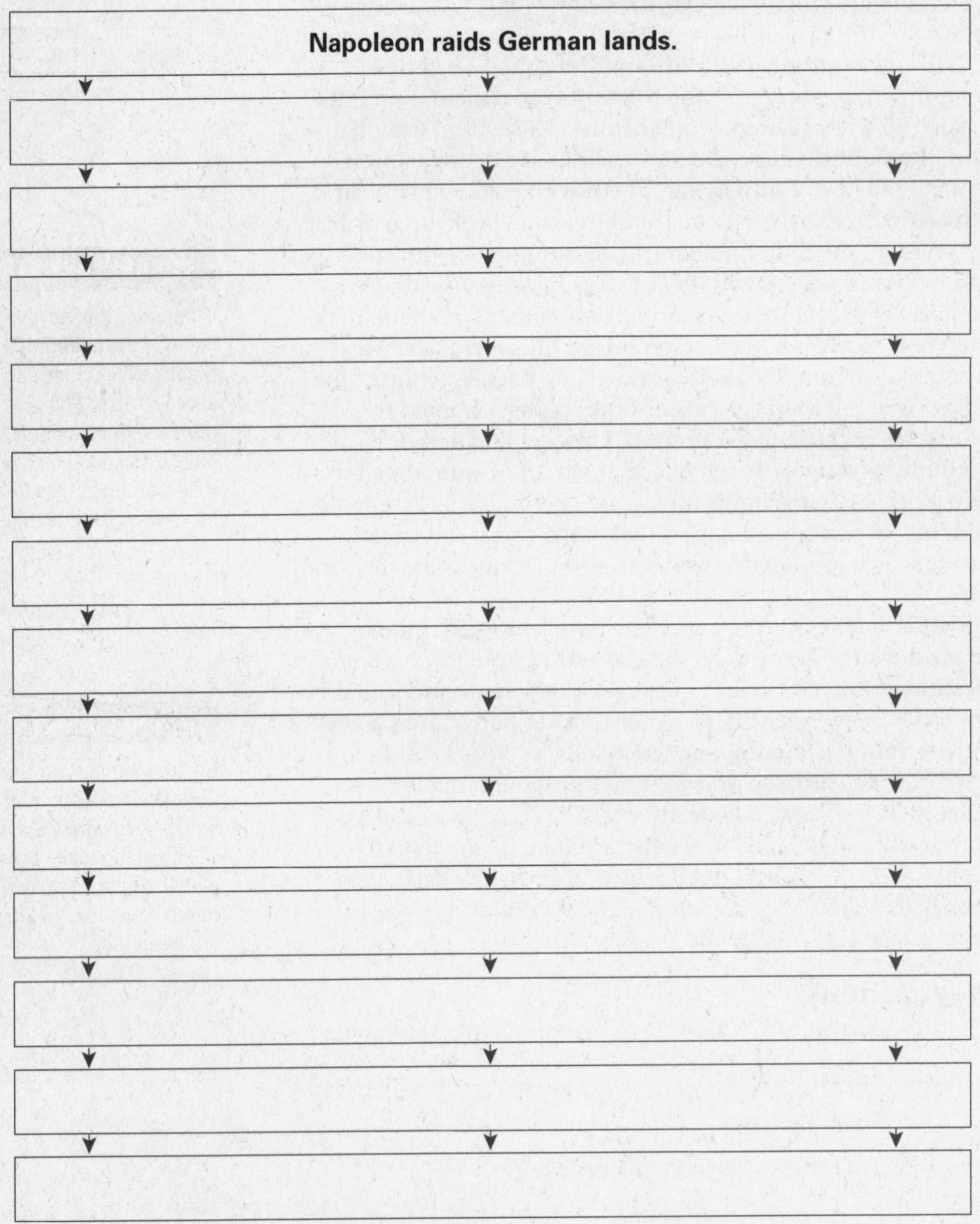

Name________________________ Class___________ Date______

CHAPTER 10 SECTION 1

Section Summary

BUILDING A GERMAN NATION

In the early 1800s, German-speaking people lived in a number of German states. Many also lived in Prussia and the Austrian empire. There was no unified German nation. However, events unfolded in the mid-nineteenth century that eventually led to the formation of one Germany. Between 1806 and 1812, Napoleon invaded these lands. He organized a number of German states into the Rhine Confederation. After Napoleon's defeat, the Congress of Vienna created the German Confederation. This was a weak alliance of German states headed by Austria. In the 1830s, Prussia created an economic union called the *Zollverein.* This union removed tariff barriers between many German states, yet they remained politically fragmented.

Otto von Bismarck, the **chancellor** of Prussia, led the drive to unite the German states—but under Prussian rule. Bismarck was a master of **Realpolitik,** or realistic politics based on the needs of the state. After creating a powerful military, he was ready to pursue an aggressive foreign policy. Over the next decade, Bismarck led Prussia into three wars. Each war increased Prussian power and paved the way for German unity.

In 1866, Bismarck created an excuse to attack Austria. The Austro-Prussian War lasted only seven weeks. Afterwards, Prussia **annexed** several north German states. In France, the Prussian victory angered Napoleon III. A growing rivalry between the two nations led to the Franco-Prussian War of 1870. Bismarck worsened the crisis by rewriting and releasing to the press a telegram that reported on a meeting between William I of Prussia and the French ambassador. Bismarck's editing of the telegram made it seem that William I had insulted the Frenchman. Furious, Napoleon III declared war on Prussia, as Bismarck had hoped. The Prussian army quickly defeated the French.

Delighted by the victory, German princes persuaded William I to take the title **kaiser** of Germany. In January 1871, German nationalists celebrated the birth of the Second **Reich.** Bismarck drafted a constitution that created a two-house legislature. Even so, the real power was in the hands of the kaiser and Bismarck.

Review Questions

1. What events occurred in the early 1800s that helped promote German unity?

____

____

2. How did Bismarck use war to create a united Germany under Prussian rule?

____

____

READING CHECK

What was Realpolitik?

____

____

____

VOCABULARY STRATEGY

What does the word *editing* mean in the underlined sentence? Circle the context clues in the paragraph that could help you figure out what *editing* means.

READING SKILL

Recognize Sequence What events led Napoleon III to declare war on Prussia?

____

____

____

Name________________________ Class__________________ Date________

CHAPTER 10 SECTION 2

Note Taking Study Guide

GERMANY STRENGTHENS

Focus Question: How did Germany increase its power after unifying in 1871?

As you read this section in your textbook, complete the following chart to record the causes and effects of a strong German nation.

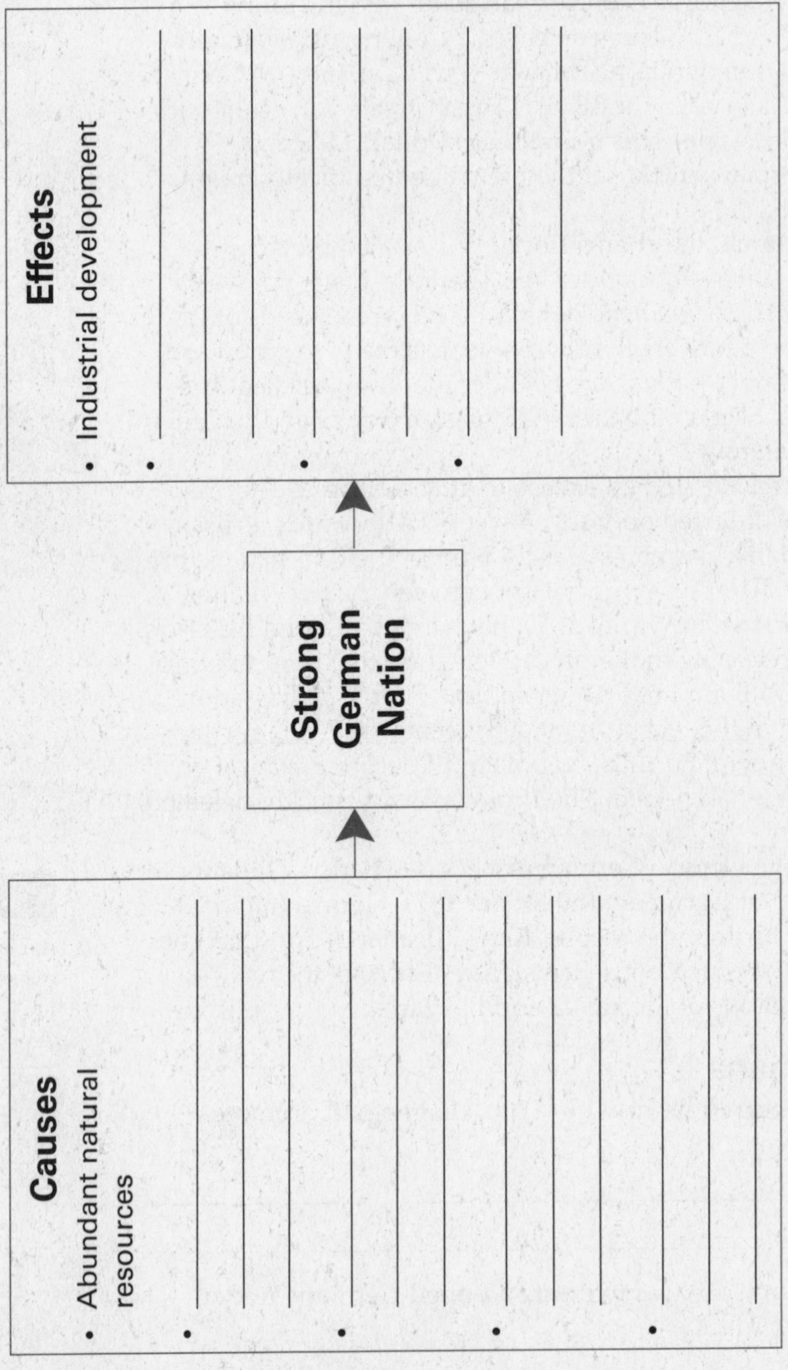

Name______________________ Class___________ Date______

CHAPTER 10 SECTION 2

Section Summary

GERMANY STRENGTHENS

After unification in 1871, the new German empire emerged as an industrial giant. Several factors made industrialization in Germany possible, such as ample iron and coal resources. These are the basic ingredients for industrial development. A disciplined and educated workforce also helped the economy grow. The German middle class created a productive and efficient society that prided itself on its sense of responsibility. Additionally, a growing population provided a huge home market for goods and a large supply of industrial workers.

German industrialists recognized the value of applied science in developing new products, such as synthetic chemicals and dyes. Both industrialists and the government supported scientific research and development. The government also promoted economic development. It issued a single form of currency for Germany and reorganized the banking system. The leaders of the new empire were determined to maintain economic strength as well as military power.

Bismarck pursued several foreign-policy goals. He wanted to keep France weak and build strong links with Austria and Russia. On the domestic front, Bismarck, called "the Iron Chancellor," targeted the Catholic Church and the Socialists. He believed these groups posed a threat to the new German state. He thought Catholics would be more loyal to the Church than to Germany. He also worried that Socialists would undermine the loyalty of workers and turn them toward revolution. Bismarck tried to repress both groups, but his efforts failed. For example, the ***Kulturkampf*** was a set of laws intended to weaken the role of the Church. Instead, the faithful rallied to support the Church. When repressing the Socialists failed to work, Bismarck changed course and pioneered social reform.

In 1888, **William II** became the kaiser. He believed that his right to rule came from God, and he shocked Europe by asking Bismarck to resign. Not surprisingly, William II resisted efforts to introduce democratic reforms. However, his government provided many **social welfare** programs to help certain groups of people. The government also provided services such as cheap transportation and electricity.

Review Questions

1. What did the German government do to promote economic development?

____

____

2. Why did Bismarck believe Catholics posed a threat to the new German state?

____

____

READING CHECK

What two ingredients are basic for industrial development?

____

____

____

VOCABULARY STRATEGY

What does the word *synthetic* mean in the underlined sentence? Notice that these chemicals and dyes did not appear in nature, but were developed. Using this clue, write a definition for *synthetic*.

READING SKILL

Recognize Sequence Correctly number the following events:

___ William II becomes Kaiser.

___ Germany unifies in 1871.

___ Government reorganizes the banking system.

___ Bismarck is asked to resign.

Name________________________ Class__________________ Date________

CHAPTER 10 SECTION 3

Note Taking Study Guide

UNIFYING ITALY

Focus Question: How did influential leaders help create a unified Italy?

As you read this section in your textbook, complete the following timeline to show the sequence of events that led to Italian unification.

1870

1850

1831 Mazzini founds Young Italy.

1830

Name________________________ Class____________ Date______

CHAPTER 10 SECTION 3

Section Summary

UNIFYING ITALY

The peoples of the Italian peninsula had not been unified since Roman times. By the early 1800s, however, patriots were determined to build a new, united Italy. As in Germany, Napoleon's invasions had sparked dreams of nationalism.

In the 1830s, the nationalist leader Giuseppe Mazzini founded Young Italy. The goal of this secret society was "to constitute Italy, one, free, independent, republican nation." To nationalists like Mazzini, establishing a unified Italy made sense because of geography and a common language and history. It also made economic sense because it would end trade barriers among Italian states. Unification would stimulate industry, too.

Victor Emmanuel II, the constitutional monarch of Sardinia, hoped to join other states with his own and increase his power. In 1852, he made Count **Camillo Cavour** his prime minister. Cavour's long-term goal was to end Austrian power in Italy. With help from France, Sardinia defeated Austria and annexed Lombardy. Meanwhile, nationalist groups overthrew Austrian-backed leaders in other northern Italian states. In the south, **Giuseppe Garibaldi** had recruited a force of 1,000 red-shirted volunteers. He and his "Red Shirts" quickly won control of Sicily. Then they crossed to the mainland and marched triumphantly to Naples. Garibaldi turned over both regions to Victor Emmanuel. In 1861, Victor Emmanuel II was crowned king of Italy. Only Rome and Venetia remained outside the nation. During the Franco-Prussian War, however, France was forced to withdraw its troops from Rome. Additionally, Italy acquired Venetia in a deal with Bismarck after the Austro-Prussian War. For the first time since the fall of the Roman empire, Italy was a united land.

However, Italy faced many problems as **anarchists** and radicals struggled against the conservative government. Tensions grew between the north and south. The north was richer and had more cities. The south was poor and rural. Still, Italy developed economically and the population grew. For many, however, **emigration** offered a chance to improve their lives. Large numbers of Italians left for the United States, Canada, and Latin America.

Review Questions

1. Why did nationalists feel that a unified Italy made sense?

____

____

2. Why did tensions between the north and south grow after unification?

____

____

READING CHECK

What was Camillo Cavour's long-term goal as prime minister?

____

____

____

VOCABULARY STRATEGY

What does the word *constitute* mean in the first underlined sentence? Note that the word is a verb, which means it describes an action. Read the second underlined sentence to find out what action the nationalists wanted to take. Use this information to help you figure out what *constitute* means.

READING SKILL

Recognize Sequence What events took place between Garibaldi's recruitment of the "Red Shirts" and Victor Emmanuel II's crowning as king of Italy?

____

____

____

Name________________________ Class____________________ Date________

CHAPTER 10 SECTION 4

Note Taking Study Guide

NATIONALISM THREATENS OLD EMPIRES

Focus Question: How did the desire for national independence among ethnic groups weaken and ultimately destroy the Austrian and Ottoman empires?

As you read this section in your textbook, complete the following table to record some major events in Austrian history during the 1800s.

Events in Austrian History	
1840	
1848	
1859	
1866	
1867	

Name________________________ Class___________ Date______

CHAPTER 10 SECTION 4

Section Summary

NATIONALISM THREATENS OLD EMPIRES

In 1800, the Hapsburgs of Austria, the oldest ruling house in Europe, presided over a multinational empire. The emperor, Francis I, upheld conservative goals against growing liberal forces. He could not, however, hold back the changes that were happening throughout Europe. By the 1840s, Austria was facing the problems of industrial life, including growth of cities, worker discontent, and socialism. Nationalists were threatening the old order. The Hapsburgs ignored these demands for change and crushed revolts. Amid the turmoil, 18-year-old **Francis Joseph** inherited the Hapsburg throne. He granted some limited reforms, such as adopting a constitution. The reforms, however, satisfied only the German-speaking Austrians, but none of the other ethnic groups.

Austria's defeat in the 1866 war with Prussia brought even more pressure for change, especially from Hungarians within the empire. **Ferenc Deák** helped work out a compromise known as the **Dual Monarchy** of Austria-Hungary. Under this agreement, Austria and Hungary became separate states. Each had its own constitution, but Francis Joseph ruled both—as emperor of Austria and king of Hungary. However, other groups within the empire resented this arrangement. Restlessness increased among various Slavic groups. Some nationalist leaders called on Slavs to unite in "fraternal solidarity." By the early 1900s, nationalist unrest left the government paralyzed in the face of pressing political and social problems.

Like the Hapsburgs, the Ottomans ruled a multinational empire. It stretched from Eastern Europe and the Balkans to the Middle East and North Africa. As in Austria, nationalist demands tore at the fabric of the Ottoman empire. During the 1800s, various peoples revolted, hoping to set up their own independent states. With the empire weakened, European powers scrambled to divide up Ottoman lands. A complex web of competing interests led to a series of crises and wars in the Balkans. Russia fought several wars against the Ottomans. France and Britain sometimes joined the Russians, and sometimes the Ottomans. By the early 1900s, observers were referring to the region as the "Balkan powder keg." The "explosion" came in 1914 and helped set off World War I.

Review Questions

1. What problems threatened the Hapsburg empire in the 1840s?

____

____

2. What effect did nationalist unrest have on the Ottoman empire?

____

____

READING CHECK

What new political entity did Ferenc Deák help create?

____

____

____

VOCABULARY STRATEGY

What does the word *fraternal* mean in the underlined sentence? The word derives from the Latin word *frater,* which means "brother." Use this information about the word's origin to help you figure out what *fraternal* means.

READING SKILL

Recognize Sequence What are two events that led to the decline of the Austrian empire in the late 1800s?

1. _______________________

____

2. _______________________

____

Name________________________ Class____________________ Date________

CHAPTER 10 SECTION 5

Note Taking Study Guide

RUSSIA: REFORM AND REACTION

Focus Question: Why did industrialization and reform come more slowly to Russia than to Western Europe?

As you read this section in your textbook, complete the following timeline to show the sequence of events in Russia during the late 1800s and early 1900s.

Name________________________ Class___________ Date______

CHAPTER 10 SECTION 5

Section Summary

RUSSIA: REFORM AND REACTION

By 1815, Russia was the largest, most populous nation in Europe. The Russian **colossus** had immense natural resources. Reformers hoped to free Russia from autocratic rule, economic backwardness, and social injustice. One of the obstacles to progress was the rigid social structure. Another was that, for centuries, tsars had ruled with absolute power, while the majority of Russians were poor serfs.

Alexander II became tsar in 1855 during the **Crimean War.** Events in his reign represent the pattern of reform and repression of previous tsars. The war, which ended in a Russian defeat, revealed the country's backwardness and inefficient bureaucracy. People demanded changes, so Alexander II agreed to some reforms. He ordered the **emancipation** of the serfs. He also set up a system of local, elected assemblies called **zemstvos.** Then he introduced legal reforms, such as trial by jury. These reforms, however, failed to satisfy many Russians. Radicals pressed for even greater changes and more reforms. The tsar then backed away from reform and moved toward repression. This sparked anger among radicals and, in 1881, terrorists assassinated Alexander II. In response to his father's death, Alexander III revived harsh, repressive policies. He also suppressed the cultures of non-Russian peoples, which led to their persecution. Official persecution encouraged **pogroms,** or violent mob attacks on Jewish people. Many left Russia and became **refugees.**

Russia began to industrialize under Alexander III and his son Nicholas II. However, this just increased political and social problems because nobles and peasants feared the changes industrialization brought. News of military disasters added to the unrest. On Sunday, January 22, 1905, a peaceful protest calling for reforms turned deadly when the tsar's troops killed and wounded hundreds of people. In the months that followed this "Bloody Sunday," discontent exploded across Russia. Nicholas was forced to make sweeping reforms. He agreed to summon a **Duma.** He then appointed a new prime minister, **Peter Stolypin.** Stolypin soon realized Russia needed reform, not just repression. Unfortunately, the changes he introduced were too limited. By 1914, Russia was still an autocracy, but the nation was simmering with discontent.

Review Questions

1. What effect did the Crimean War have on Russia?

____

____

2. What happened on January 22, 1905?

____

____

READING CHECK

What were zemstvos?

____

____

____

VOCABULARY STRATEGY

What does the word *radicals* mean in the underlined sentence? Think about why these people were dissatisfied with Alexander II's reforms. Circle the words in the underlined sentence that help you figure out what *radical* means.

READING SKILL

Recognize Sequence What happened between Alexander II's becoming tsar and his assassination in 1881?

____

____

____

Name________________________ Class__________________ Date__________

CHAPTER 11 SECTION 1

Note Taking Study Guide

DEMOCRATIC REFORM IN BRITAIN

Focus Question: How did political reform gradually expand suffrage and make the British Parliament more democratic during the 1800s?

As you read this section in your textbook, complete the outline below to identify the main ideas in the section.

I. Reforming Parliament

A. Reformers press for change.

1. ______________________________

2. ______________________________

B. ______________________________

1. ______________________________

2. ______________________________

3. ______________________________

C. ______________________________

1. ______________________________

2. ______________________________

II. ______________________________

A. ______________________________

1. ______________________________

2. ______________________________

B. ______________________________

1. ______________________________

2. ______________________________

III. ______________________________

A. ______________________________

1. ______________________________

2. ______________________________

3. ______________________________

B. ______________________________

1. ______________________________

2. ______________________________

Name____________________ Class__________ Date______

CHAPTER 11 SECTION 1

Section Summary

DEMOCRATIC REFORM IN BRITAIN

In 1815, Britain was governed by a constitutional monarchy with a Parliament and two political parties. However, it was far from democratic. The House of Commons, although elected, was controlled by wealthy nobles and squires. The House of Lords could veto any bill passed by the House of Commons. Catholics and non-Church of England Protestants could not vote. **Rotten boroughs,** rural towns that had lost most of their voters during the Industrial Revolution, still sent members to Parliament. At the same time, new industrial cities had no seats allocated in Parliament.

The Great Reform Act of 1832 redistributed seats in the House of Commons, giving representation to new cities and eliminating rotten boroughs. It enlarged the **electorate** but kept a property requirement for voting. Protesters known as the Chartists demanded universal male suffrage, annual parliamentary elections, salaries for members of Parliament, and a **secret ballot.** In time, most of the reforms they proposed were passed by Parliament.

From 1837 to 1901, the great symbol in British life was **Queen Victoria.** She set the tone for the Victorian age that was named for her. She embodied the values of duty, thrift, honesty, hard work, and respectability. Under Victoria, the middle class felt confident. That confidence grew as the British empire expanded.

In the 1860s, a new era dawned in British politics. **Benjamin Disraeli** forged the Tories into the modern Conservative Party. The Whigs, led by **William Gladstone,** evolved into the Liberal Party. Disraeli and Gladstone alternated as prime minister and fought for important reforms. The Conservative Party pushed through the Reform Bill of 1867, which gave the vote to many working-class men. In the 1880s, the Liberals got the vote extended to farm workers and most other men.

By century's end, Britain had truly transformed from a constitutional monarchy to a **parliamentary democracy.** In this form of government, executive leaders are chosen by and responsible to the parliament, and they are members of it. In 1911, measures were passed that restricted the power of the House of Lords, and it eventually became a largely ceremonial body.

Review Questions

1. What was the result of the Great Reform Act of 1832?

____

____

2. How is a parliamentary democracy organized?

____

____

READING CHECK

What are rotten boroughs?

____

____

____

VOCABULARY STRATEGY

What does the word *allocated* mean in the underlined sentence? Note that the Great Reform Act of 1832 corrected the problem described in this sentence by "redistributing" seats in the House of Commons. Use this context clue to help you understand the meaning of the word *allocated.*

READING SKILL

Identify Main Ideas What is the main idea in the first paragraph of the Summary?

____

____

____

Name____________________ Class______________ Date________

CHAPTER 11 SECTION 2

Note Taking Study Guide

SOCIAL AND ECONOMIC REFORM IN BRITAIN

Focus Question: What social and economic reforms were passed by the British Parliament during the 1800s and early 1900s?

As you read this section in your textbook, complete the chart below by listing reforms in Britain during the 1800s and early 1900s.

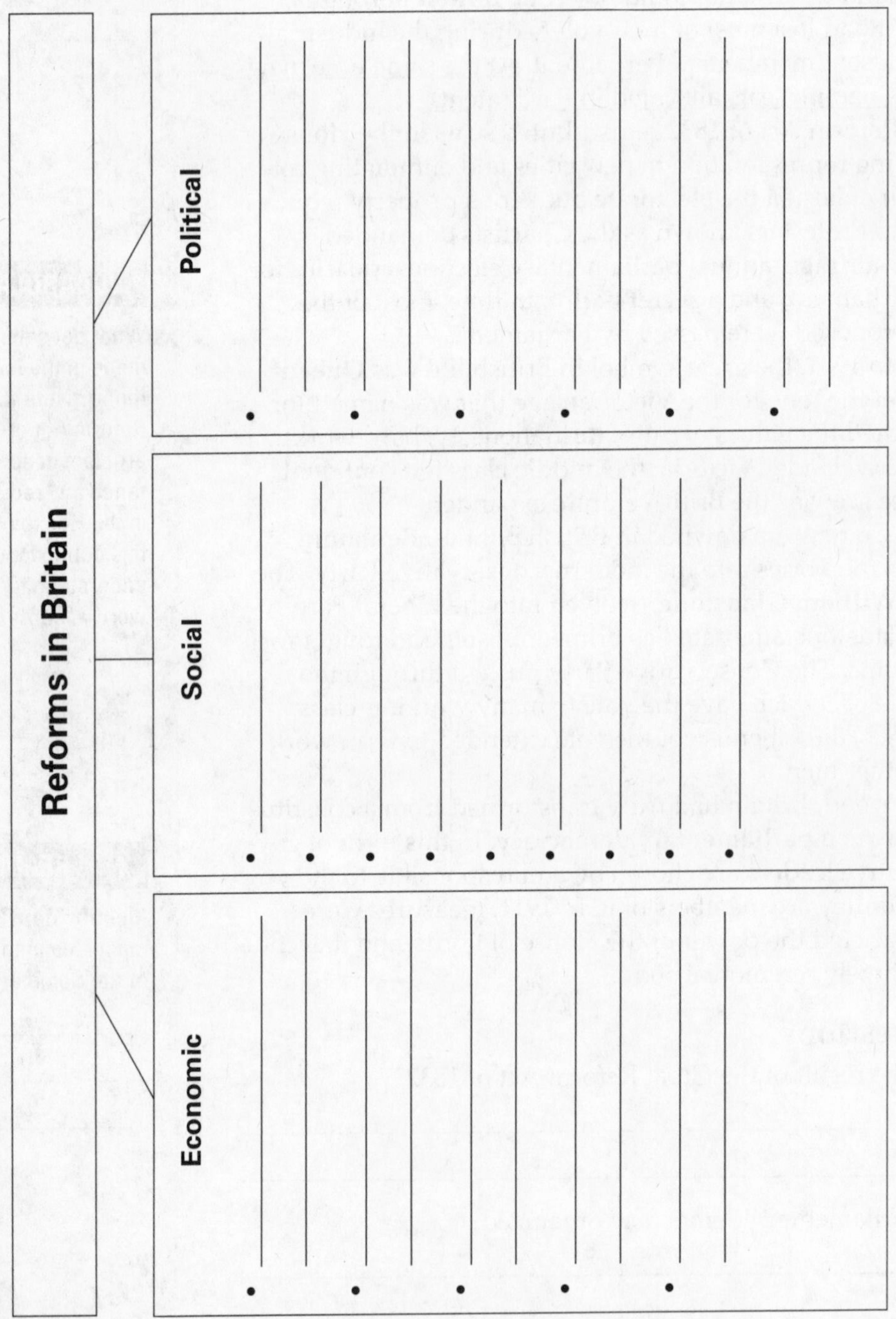

Name________________________ Class____________ Date______

CHAPTER 11 SECTION 2

Section Summary

SOCIAL AND ECONOMIC REFORM IN BRITAIN

During the 1800s, the British Parliament passed important laws. One issue was **free trade,** or trade without restrictions between countries. The Corn Laws caused fierce debate. These laws imposed high tariffs on imported grain. Farmers and landowners benefited, but the tariffs made bread more expensive. In 1846, Parliament **repealed** the Corn Laws. Another important reform, brought about by the **abolition movement,** was the end of the slave trade in 1807. By 1833, Parliament had banned slavery in all British colonies. Other reforms reduced the number of **capital offenses,** or crimes punishable by death. Instead of being put to death, many petty criminals were transported to **penal colonies** in Australia and New Zealand.

Working conditions in the industrial age were grim and often dangerous. Gradually, Parliament passed laws to regulate conditions in factories and mines. Other laws set minimum wages and maximum hours of work. Trade unions became legal in 1825 and worked to improve the lives of their members. Both the Liberal and Conservative parties enacted reforms to benefit workers, including free elementary education. The Labour Party, formed in 1900, soon became one of Britain's major parties. In the early 1900s, Parliament passed laws to protect workers with old-age pensions and accident, health, and unemployment insurance.

During this time, women struggled for the right to vote. When mass meetings and other peaceful efforts brought no results, Emmeline Pankhurst and other suffragists turned to more drastic, violent protest. They smashed windows, burned buildings, and went on hunger strikes. Not until 1918 did Parliament finally grant suffrage to women over 30.

Throughout the 1800s, Britain faced the "Irish Question." The Irish resented British rule. Many Irish peasants lived in poverty while paying high rents to **absentee landlords** living in England. Irish Catholics also had to pay tithes to the Church of England. The potato famine made problems worse. Charles Stewart Parnell and other Irish leaders argued for **home rule,** or self-government, but this was debated for decades. Under Gladstone, the government finally ended the use of Irish tithes to support the Church of England and passed laws to protect the rights of Irish tenant farmers.

READING CHECK

What are capital offenses?

____

____

____

VOCABULARY STRATEGY

What does the word *drastic* mean in the underlined sentence? Note that the suffragists first tried "peaceful efforts" before turning to "more *drastic,* violent protest." The next sentence describes this. Use these context clues to help you understand what *drastic* means.

READING SKILL

Categorize Sort the laws that were passed to help workers into three categories.

____

____

____

Review Questions

1. Why did the Corn Laws cause fierce debate in Britain?

____

____

2. How did the government under Gladstone help improve conditions in Ireland?

____

____

Name________________________ Class____________________ Date________

Chapter 11
Section 3

Note Taking Study Guide

DIVISION AND DEMOCRACY IN FRANCE

Focus Question: What democratic reforms were made in France during the Third Republic?

As you read this section in your textbook, complete the timeline below by labeling the main events described in this section.

Name________________________ Class____________ Date________

CHAPTER 11 SECTION 3

Section Summary

DIVISION AND DEMOCRACY IN FRANCE

After the revolution of 1848, **Napoleon III** established the Second Empire in France. At first, he ruled like a dictator. In the 1860s, however, he lifted some censorship and gave the legislature more power. He promoted investment in industry and ventures such as railroad building. During this period, a French entrepreneur organized the building of the **Suez Canal** in Egypt.

However, Napoleon III had major failures in foreign affairs. He tried to put the Austrian archduke Maximilian on the throne of Mexico, but Maximilian was overthrown and killed. France and Britain won the Crimean War, but France suffered terrible losses and few gains. The Franco-Prussian War was a disaster, and the Prussians captured Napoleon. He died a few years later in England.

Following Napoleon's capture, republicans established a **provisional,** or temporary, government. In 1871, an uprising broke out in Paris, and rebels set up the Paris Commune. Its goal was to save the Republic from royalists. When the rebels did not disband, the government sent troops and 20, 000 rebels were killed.

The provisional government soon became the Third Republic. Although the legislature elected a president, the **premier** had the real power. There were many political parties, and none could take control. Because of this, parties had to form **coalitions,** or alliances, to rule. Coalition governments are often unstable, and France had 50 different coalition governments in the first 10 years of the Third Republic.

A series of political scandals in the 1880s and 1890s shook public trust in the government. The most divisive scandal was the **Dreyfus affair.** Alfred Dreyfus was a Jewish army officer wrongly accused of spying for Germany. Author Émile Zola was convicted of **libel** when he charged the army and government with suppressing the truth. The affair revealed strong anti-Semitic feelings in France and led Theodor Herzl to launch modern **Zionism.**

France achieved serious reforms in the early 1900s, however. It passed labor laws regulating wages, hours, and safety conditions. Free public elementary schools were established. France tried to repress Church involvement in government. In 1905, it passed a law to separate church and state. Women made some gains, but they did not win the right to vote until after World War II.

Review Questions

1. What failures in foreign affairs took place under Napoleon III?

____

____

2. Why did French governments have to form coalitions to rule?

____

____

READING CHECK

What did the Dreyfus affair reveal about France?

____

____

____

VOCABULARY STRATEGY

What does the word *repress* mean in the underlined sentence? Reread the sentence after the underlined sentence. What did France do to *repress* Church involvement in government? Use this context clue to help you understand the meaning of *repress.*

READING SKILL

Recognize Sequence List, in chronological order, the three French governments described in this section.

____

____

____

Name______________________ Class______________ Date________

Note Taking Study Guide

EXPANSION OF THE UNITED STATES

Focus Question: How did the United States develop during the 1800s?

As you read this section in your textbook, complete the chart below by listing key events under the appropriate headings.

Civil War	
Before	**After**
• Western expansion • ______________ • ______________ • ______________	• Fifteenth Amendment extends voting rights to all adult male citizens. • ______________ • ______________ • ______________ • ______________ • ______________ • ______________ • ______________

Name________________________ Class__________ Date______

CHAPTER 11 SECTION 4

Section Summary

EXPANSION OF THE UNITED STATES

In the 1800s, the United States followed a policy of **expansionism,** or extending the nation's boundaries. In 1803, the **Louisiana Purchase** nearly doubled the size of the country. More territory was soon added in the West and South. Americans believed in **Manifest Destiny,** or the idea that their nation was destined to spread across the entire continent.

Voting, slavery, and women's rights were important issues at this time. In 1800, only white men who owned property could vote. By the 1830s, most white men had the right to vote. William Lloyd Garrison, Frederick Douglass, and other abolitionists called for an end to slavery. Lucretia Mott, Elizabeth Cady Stanton, Susan B. Anthony, and others began to seek equality.

Economic differences, as well as slavery, divided the country into the North and the South. When Abraham Lincoln was elected in 1860, most Southern states **seceded,** or withdrew, from the Union. The American Civil War soon began. Southerners fought fiercely, but the North had more people, more industry, and more resources. The South finally surrendered in 1865.

During the war, Lincoln issued the Emancipation Proclamation, which declared that the slaves in the South were free. After the war, slavery was banned throughout the nation, and African Americans were granted some political rights. However, African Americans still faced restrictions, including **segregation,** or legal separation, in public places. Some state laws prevented African Americans from voting.

After the Civil War, the United States became the world leader in industrial and agricultural production. By 1900, giant monopolies controlled whole industries. For example, John D. Rockefeller's Standard Oil Company dominated the world's petroleum industry. Big business enjoyed huge profits, but not everyone shared in the prosperity. Reformers tried to address this problem. Unions sought better wages and working conditions for factory workers. Farmers and city workers formed the Populist Party to seek changes. Progressives sought to ban child labor, limit working hours, regulate monopolies, and give voters more power. Progressives also worked to get women the right to vote, which they did in 1920.

READING CHECK

What is Manifest Destiny?

____

____

____

VOCABULARY STRATEGY

What does the word *dominated* mean in the underlined sentence? Reread the sentence that precedes the underlined sentence. The Standard Oil Company was an example of the giant monopolies that "controlled" whole industries. Use this context clue to help you understand the meaning of the word *dominated.*

READING SKILL

Categorize Categorize the reforms discussed in this Summary by the group that did or would benefit from them.

____

____

____

Review Questions

1. Why did the North win the Civil War?

____

____

2. How were African Americans deprived of equality after the Civil War?

____

____

Name________________________ Class________________ Date________

CHAPTER 12 SECTION 1

Note Taking Study Guide

BUILDING OVERSEAS EMPIRES

Focus Question: How did Western nations come to dominate much of the world in the late 1800s?

As you read this section in your textbook, complete the chart below with the multiple causes of imperialism in the 1800s.

Name________ Class______ Date______

CHAPTER 12 SECTION 1

Section Summary

BUILDING OVERSEAS EMPIRES

Many western countries built overseas empires in the late 1800s. This expansion, referred to as **imperialism,** is the domination by one country of the political, economic, or cultural life of another country or region. In the 1800s, Europeans embarked on a path of aggressive expansion called the "new imperialism." There were several causes. The Industrial Revolution was one. Manufacturers wanted access to natural resources, as well as markets for their goods. Colonies also were an outlet for Europe's growing population. Leaders claimed that colonies were needed for national security. Industrial nations seized overseas islands and harbors as bases to supply their ships.

Nationalism played an important role, too. When one European country claimed an area, rival nations would move in and claim nearby areas. Europeans felt that ruling a global empire increased a nation's prestige. Missionaries, doctors, and colonial officials believed that they had a duty to spread Western civilization. Behind the idea of the West's civilizing mission was a growing sense of racial superiority. Many Westerners used Social Darwinism to justify their domination of non-Western societies. As a result, millions of non-Westerners were robbed of their cultural heritage.

Europeans had the advantages of strong economies, well-organized governments, and powerful armies and navies. Superior technology, such as riverboats, the telegraph, and the Maxim machine gun enhanced European power. Africans and Asians tried to resist Western expansion. Some people fought the invaders. Others tried to strengthen their societies by reforming their traditions. Many organized nationalist movements to expel the imperialists.

The leading imperial powers developed several systems to control colonies. The French practiced direct rule. They sent officials and soldiers from France to run the colony. Their goal was to impose French culture on the natives. The British, by contrast, relied on indirect rule. To govern their colonies, they used local rulers. In a **protectorate,** local rulers were left in place but were expected to follow the advice of European advisors on issues such as trade or missionary activity. In a **sphere of influence,** an outside power claimed exclusive investment or trading privileges, but did not rule the area.

Review Questions

1. Which aspect of the new imperialism led to non-Westerners being robbed of their cultural heritage?

____

____

2. What is the difference between a protectorate and a sphere of influence?

____

____

READING CHECK

How did Africans and Asians resist Western expansion?

____

____

____

VOCABULARY STRATEGY

What does the word *prestige* mean in the underlined sentence? Notice that the word *increased* appears in the same sentence. What would ruling a global empire *increase* for a European nation? Use this context clue to help you figure out the meaning of *prestige.*

READING SKILL

Multiple Causes List the multiple causes of imperialism mentioned in this summary.

____

____

____

Name________________________ Class__________________ Date________

CHAPTER 12
SECTION 2

Note Taking Study Guide

THE PARTITION OF AFRICA

Focus Question: How did imperialist European powers claim control over most of Africa by the end of the 1800s?

As you read this section in your textbook, complete the chart below by identifying the causes and effects of the partition of Africa by European nations.

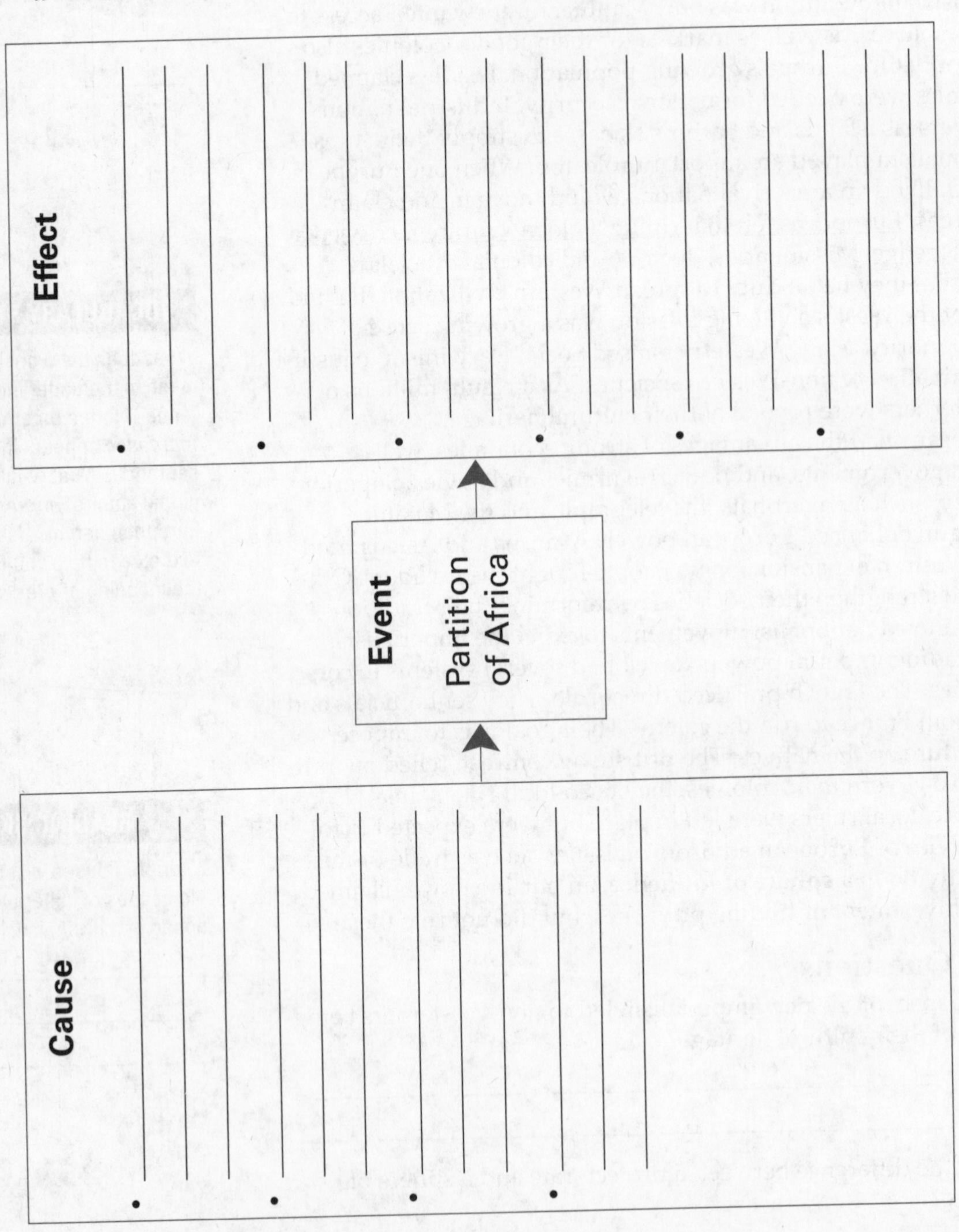

Name________________________ Class___________ Date______

CHAPTER 12 SECTION 2

Section Summary

THE PARTITION OF AFRICA

Before the scramble for colonies began in the 1800s, North Africa was under the rule of the declining Ottoman empire. West Africa experienced an Islamic revival inspired by **Usman dan Fodio.** In East Africa, port cities carried on a profitable trade. Zulus were a major force in southern Africa. A brilliant Zulu leader, **Shaka,** conquered nearby peoples. Groups driven from their homelands by the Zulus migrated north, conquering other peoples and creating powerful states.

For many years, Europeans had been trading along the African coasts. In the 1800s, contact increased as European explorers began pushing into the interior of Africa. One of the best-known was the missionary explorer **Dr. David Livingstone.** In 1869, the journalist **Henry Stanley** trekked into Africa to find Livingstone, who had not been heard from for years. Other missionaries followed explorers such as Livingstone. They built schools, churches, and medical clinics, often taking a **paternalistic** view of Africans.

About 1871, **King Leopold II** of Belgium hired Stanley to arrange trade treaties with African leaders. Leopold's action prompted Britain, France, and Germany to join in a scramble for African land. Eventually, without consulting any Africans, European leaders met in Berlin to divide the continent of Africa among themselves. In the following years, Europeans expanded further into Africa, often exploiting African people and resources. In southern Africa, the **Boer War** began when Britain wanted to claim Boer land. The Boers were descendants of Dutch farmers. The British wanted the land because gold and diamonds had been discovered there.

Africans fought back against European imperialism. In West Africa, **Samori Touré** fought French forces. **Yaa Asantewaa** was an Asante queen who led the fight against the British in West Africa. Another female leader was **Nehanda** of the Shona in Zimbabwe. In most cases resistance was not successful. However, Ethiopia was able to keep its independence. <u>Earlier, Ethiopia had been divided up among a number of rival princes who then ruled their own domains.</u> **Menelik II** modernized his country and trained an army, successfully resisting Italian invaders.

The Age of Imperialism caused a Western-educated African **elite** to emerge. Some admired Western ways. Others sought independence through nationalist movements.

Review Questions

1. Who ruled North Africa before the 1800s?

____

____

2. What set off a European scramble for African territories?

____

____

READING CHECK

Which African country was able to resist European conquest and maintain its independence?

____

____

____

VOCABULARY STRATEGY

What does the word *domains* mean in the underlined sentence? Use context clues. Think about what a prince rules. What would have been divided? Use these context clues to help you figure out the meaning of *domains.*

READING SKILL

Cause and Effect What caused groups of Africans in southern Africa to migrate north? What was the effect of this?

____

____

____

Name____________________ Class______________ Date________

CHAPTER 12 SECTION 3

Note Taking Study Guide

EUROPEAN CLAIMS IN MUSLIM REGIONS

Focus Question: How did European nations extend their power into Muslim regions of the world?

As you read this section in your textbook, complete the concept web below to understand the effects of European imperialism on Muslim regions of the world.

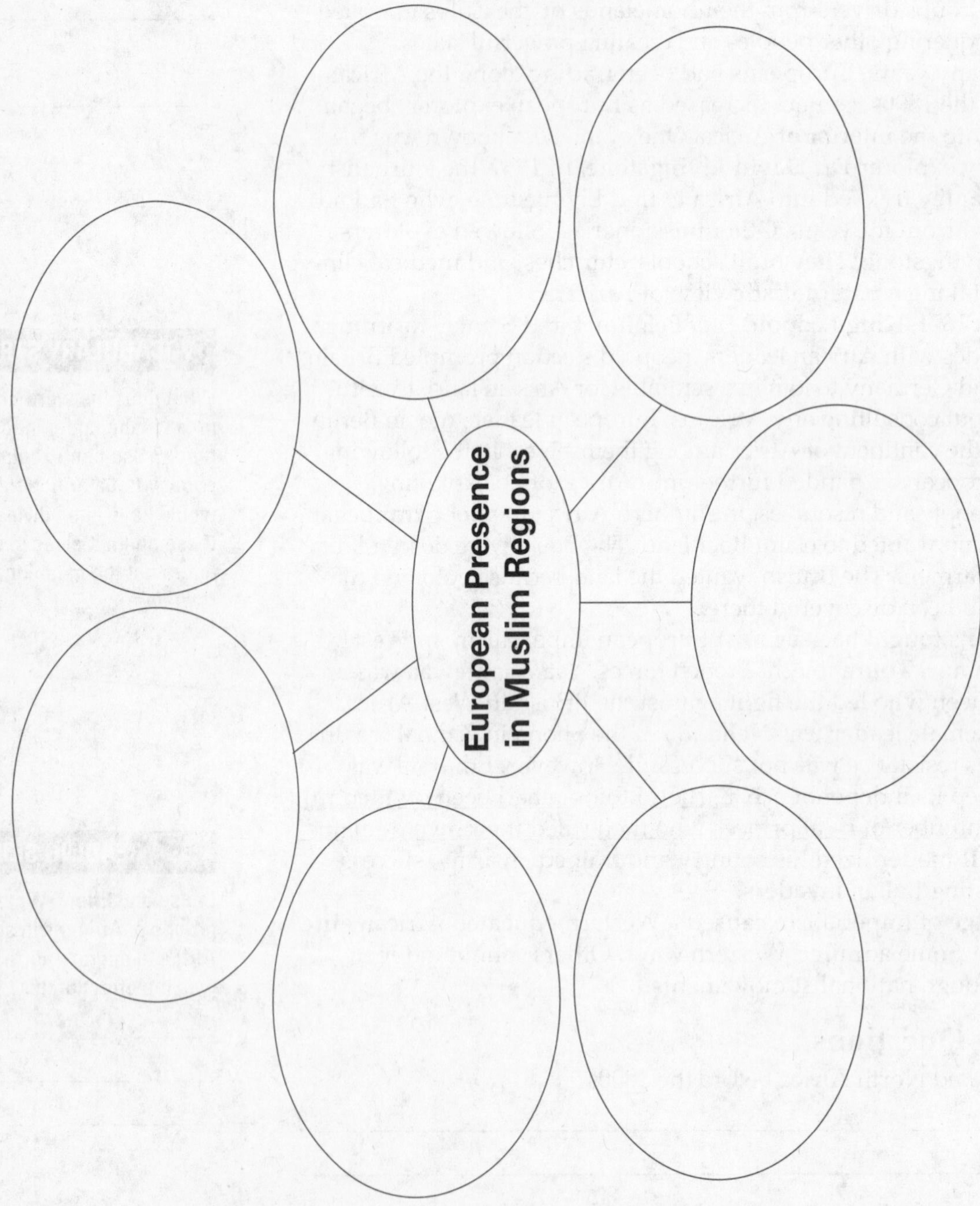

Name________________________ Class____________ Date______

CHAPTER 12 SECTION 3

Section Summary

EUROPEAN CLAIMS IN MUSLIM REGIONS

In the 1500s, three giant Muslim empires ruled large areas of the world—the Ottomans in the Middle East, the Safavids in Persia, and the Mughals in India. By the 1700s, all three Muslim empires were in decline, in part because of corruption and discontent. Reform movements arose, stressing religious piety and strict rules of behavior. For example, in the Sudan, **Muhammad Ahmad** announced that he was the **Mahdi,** the long-awaited savior of the faith. The Mahdi and his followers fiercely resisted British expansion into the region.

At its height, the Ottoman empire extended across North Africa, Southeastern Europe, and parts of the Middle East. Ambitious **pashas** and economic problems added to the Ottoman decline. As ideas of nationalism spread from Western Europe, internal revolts by subject peoples weakened the empire. European states took advantage of this weakness to grab Ottoman territory. Some Ottoman leaders saw the need for reform. They looked to the West for ideas on reorganizing the government and its rigid rules. In the early 1700s, they reorganized the bureaucracy and system of tax collection. However, **sultans** usually rejected reform, adding to the tension. Tension between Ottoman Turkish nationalists and minority groups led to a brutal **genocide** of Christian Armenians. Turks accused Christian Armenians of supporting Russia against the Ottoman empire.

In the early 1800s, Egypt was a semi-independent province of the Ottoman empire. **Muhammad Ali** is sometimes called the "father of modern Egypt" because he introduced a number of political and economic reforms. He also conquered the neighboring lands of Arabia, Syria, and Sudan. Before he died in 1849, he had set Egypt on the road to becoming a major Middle Eastern power. His successors were less skilled, however, and in 1882 Egypt became a protectorate of Britain.

Like the Ottoman empire, Persia—now Iran—faced major challenges. The Qajar shahs exercised absolute power. Foreign nations, especially Russia and Britain, wanted to control Iran's oil fields. They were granted **concessions** and sent troops to protect their interests. These actions outraged Iranian nationalists.

Review Questions

1. What was the extent of the Ottoman empire?

____

____

2. Why is Muhammad Ali sometimes called the "father of modern Egypt"?

____

____

READING CHECK

What were the three great Muslim empires in the 1500s?

____

____

____

VOCABULARY STRATEGY

What does the word *bureaucracy* mean in the underlined sentence? *Bureau* is a French word that means "office." The suffix *-cracy* means "type of government." Use these word-origin clues to help you figure out what *bureaucracy* means.

READING SKILL

Understanding Effects What was the effect of the concessions granted to Britain and Russia in Iran?

____

____

____

Name ____________ Class ____________ Date ________

CHAPTER 12 SECTION 4

Note Taking Study Guide

THE BRITISH TAKE OVER INDIA

Focus Question: How did Britain gradually extend its control over most of India despite opposition?

As you read this section in your textbook, complete the flowchart below to identify the causes and effects of British colonial rule in India.

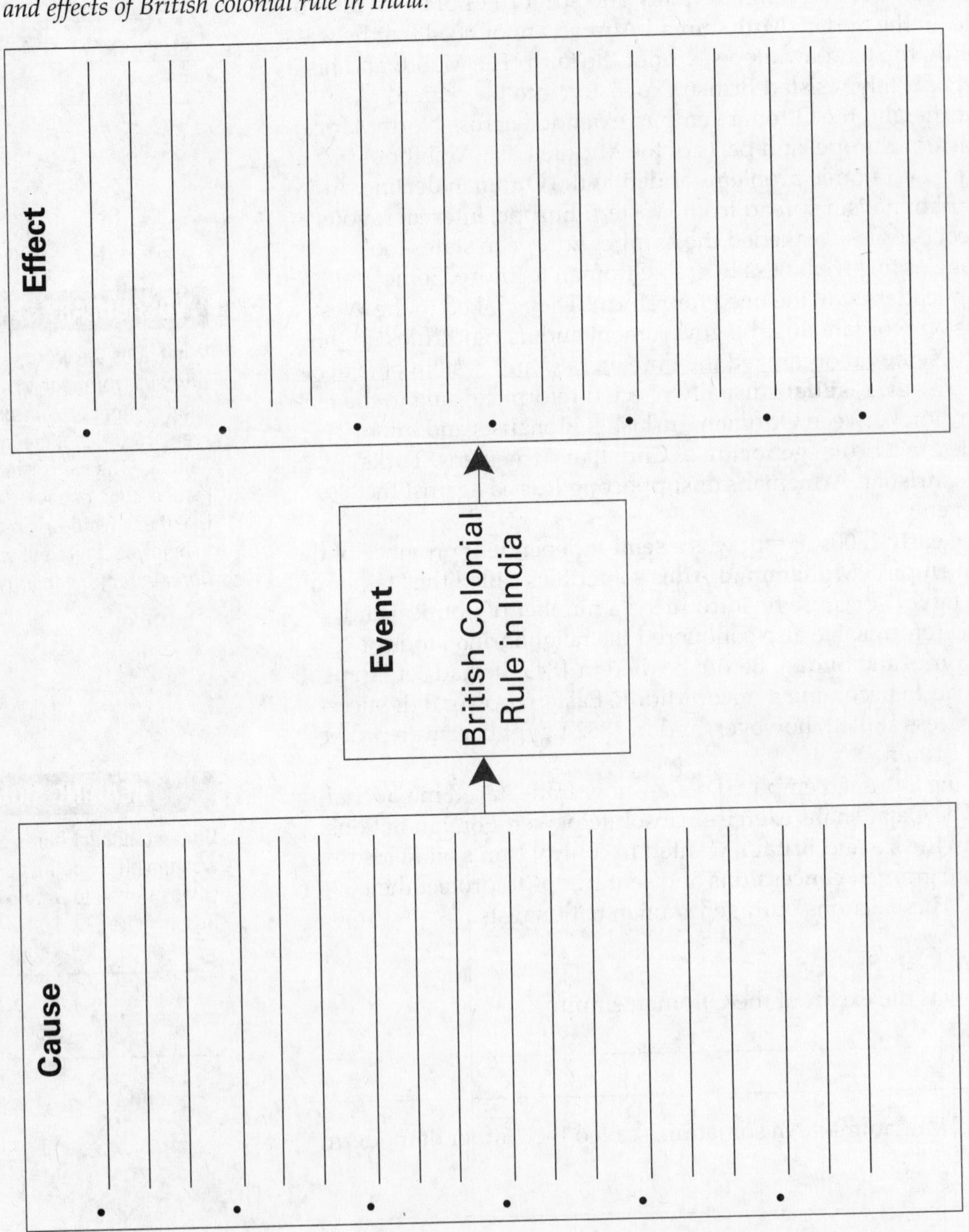

Name________________________ Class____________ Date______

CHAPTER 12 SECTION 4

Section Summary

THE BRITISH TAKE OVER INDIA

Mughal rulers governed a powerful Muslim empire in India. The British East India Company had trading rights on the fringes of the Mughal empire. The main goal of the East India Company was to make money. As Mughal power declined, the East India Company extended its power. By the mid-1800s, it controlled three-fifths of India. The British were able to conquer India by exploiting its diversity, and by encouraging competition and disunity among rival princes. When necessary, the British also used force. However, British officials worked to end slavery and the caste system. They banned **sati,** a custom that called for a widow to throw herself on her husband's funeral fire. In the 1850s, the East India Company made several unpopular moves. The most serious brought about the Sepoy Rebellion. Indian soldiers, or **sepoys,** were told to bite off the tips of their rifle cartridges. This order caused a rebellion because the cartridges were greased with animal fat, violating local religious beliefs. The British crushed the revolt, killing thousands of unarmed Indians. The rebellion left a legacy of mistrust on both sides.

After the rebellion, Parliament ended the rule of the East India Company. Instead, a British **viceroy** governed India in the name of the monarch. <u>In this way, all of Britain could benefit from trade with India as Britain incorporated India into the overall British economy.</u> However, it remained an unequal partnership, favoring the British. Although the British built railroads and telegraph lines, they destroyed India's hand-weaving industry. Encouraging Indian farmers to grow cash crops led to massive **deforestation** and famines.

Some educated Indians urged India to follow a Western model of progress. Others felt they should keep to their own Hindu or Muslim cultures. In the early 1800s, **Ram Mohun Roy** combined both views. Roy condemned rigid caste distinctions, child marriage, sati, and **purdah,** or the isolation of women in separate quarters. He also set up educational societies to help revive pride in Indian culture. Most British disdained Indian culture and felt that Western-educated Indians would support British rule. Instead, Indians dreamed of ending British control. In 1885, Indian nationalists formed the Indian National Congress and began pressing for self-rule.

Review Questions

1. How were the British able to conquer India?

____

____

2. How did India benefit from Western technology?

____

____

READING CHECK

What was sati?

____

____

____

VOCABULARY STRATEGY

What does the word *overall* mean in the underlined sentence? Notice that it is a compound word. A compound word is made from two separate words. Use the two words that make up *overall* to help you figure out what it means.

READING SKILL

Identify Causes and Effects What caused the sepoys to rebel? What were two effects of the rebellion?

____

____

____

Name________________________ Class________________ Date________

CHAPTER 12 SECTION 5

Note Taking Study Guide

CHINA AND THE NEW IMPERIALISM

Focus Question: How did Western powers use diplomacy and war to gain power in Qing China?

As you read this section in your textbook, complete the chart below by listing the multiple causes that led to the decline of Qing China.

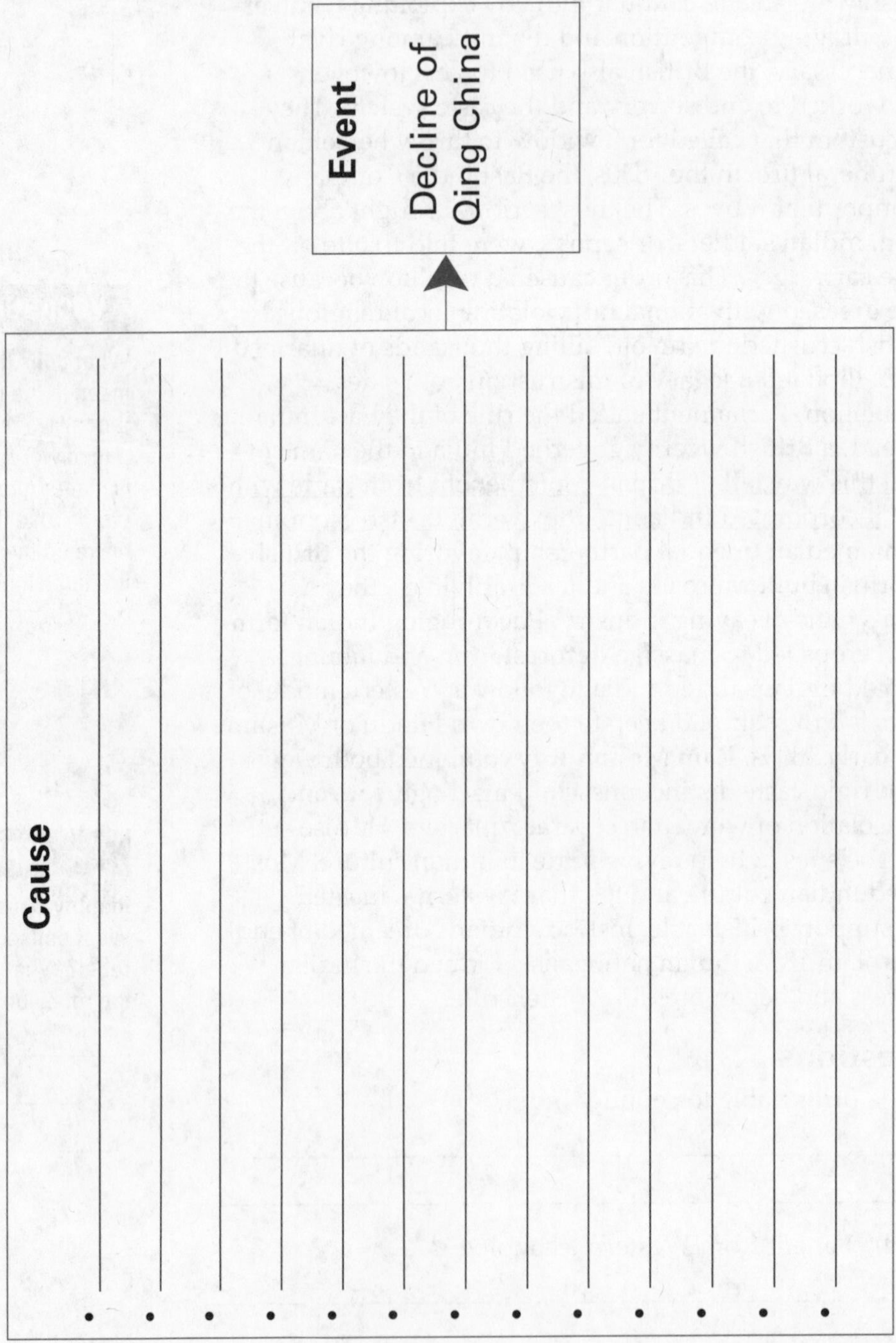

Name__________ Class__________ Date__________

CHAPTER 12
SECTION 5

Section Summary

CHINA AND THE NEW IMPERIALISM

For centuries, China had a favorable **balance of trade,** because of a **trade surplus.** Westerners had a **trade deficit** with China, buying more from the Chinese than they sold to them. This changed in the late 1700s when the British began trading opium grown in India in exchange for Chinese tea. The Chinese government outlawed opium and called on Britain to stop this drug trade. The British refused, leading to the **Opium War** in 1839. With outdated weapons and fighting methods, the Chinese were easily defeated. Under the Treaty of Nanjing, which ended the war, Britain received a huge **indemnity** and British citizens gained the right of **extraterritoriality.** About a decade later China lost another war. France, Russia, and the United States then each made specific demands on China. China was pressured to sign treaties stipulating the opening of more ports and allowing Christian missionaries in China.

China also faced internal problems. Peasants hated the Qing government because of corruption. The resulting **Taiping Rebellion** against this government led to an estimated 20 million to 30 million deaths. However, the Qing government survived. In addition, the Chinese were divided over the need to adopt Western ways. Some felt Western ideas and technology threatened Confucianism. Reformers who wanted to adopt Western ways in the "self-strengthening movement" did not have government support.

Meanwhile, China's defeat in the **Sino-Japanese War** of 1894 encouraged European nations to carve out spheres of influence in China. The United States feared that American merchants might be shut out. Eventually, without consulting the Chinese, the United States insisted that Chinese trade should be open to everyone on an equal basis as part of an **Open Door Policy.** Chinese reformers blamed conservatives for not modernizing China. In 1898, the emperor, **Guang Xu,** launched the Hundred Days of Reform. Conservatives opposed this reform effort and the emperor was imprisoned.

Many Chinese, including a secret society known to Westerners as the Boxers, were angry about the presence of foreigners. Antiforeign feeling exploded in the **Boxer Uprising** in 1900. Although the Boxers failed, nationalism increased. Reformers called for a republic. One of them, **Sun Yixian,** became president of the new Chinese republic when the Qing dynasty fell in 1911.

Review Questions

1. What were the results of the Opium War?

____

____

2. Why was the Qing government so hated?

____

____

READING CHECK

Who was the Chinese reformer who became president of China in 1911?

____

____

____

VOCABULARY STRATEGY

What does the word *stipulating* mean in the underlined sentence? What clues can you find in the surrounding words, phrases, or sentences? Use these context clues to help you figure out what *stipulating* means.

READING SKILL

Recognize Multiple Causes What brought about the Open Door Policy in China?

____

____

____

Name________________________ Class________________ Date__________

CHAPTER 13 SECTION 1

Note Taking Study Guide

JAPAN MODERNIZES

Focus Question: How did Japan become a modern industrial power, and what did it do with its new strength?

As you read this section in your textbook, complete the chart below to identify causes and effects of the Meiji Restoration.

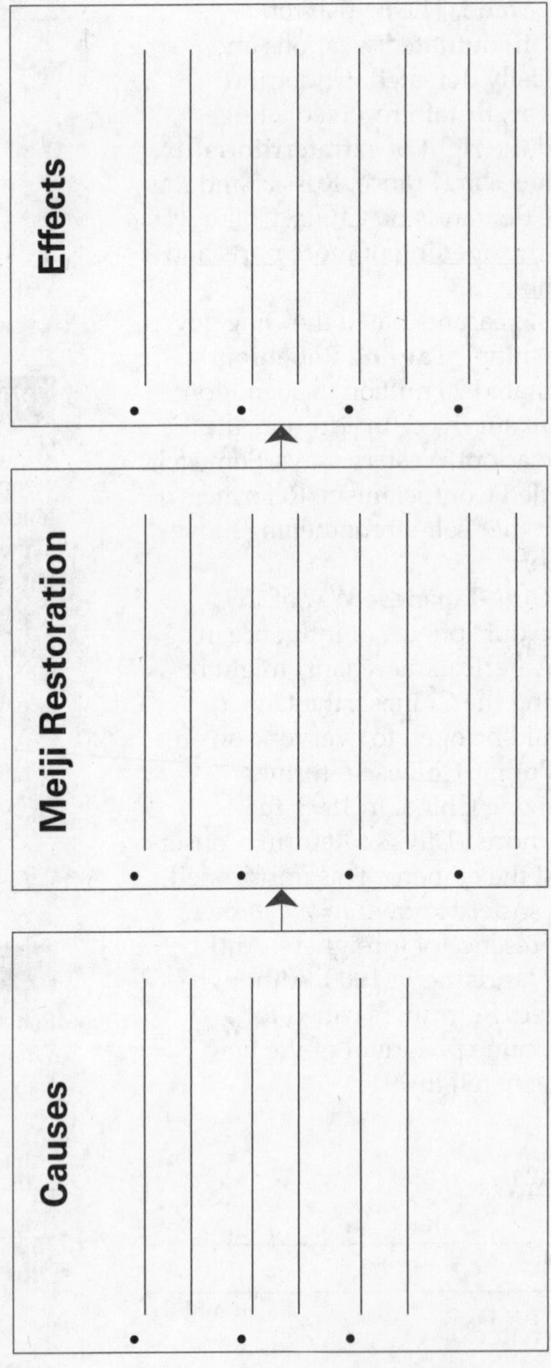

Name________________________ Class____________ Date______

CHAPTER 13 SECTION 1

Section Summary

JAPAN MODERNIZES

In 1603, the Tokugawa shoguns seized power in Japan and closed it to foreigners. For more than 200 years, Japan was isolated from other nations. Over time, unrest grew among many Japanese as they suffered financial hardship and lack of political power. The government responded by trying to revive old ways, emphasizing farming over commerce. These efforts had little success, and the shoguns' power weakened.

Then, in 1853, a fleet of well-armed U.S. ships led by Commodore **Matthew Perry** arrived. He demanded that Japan open its ports. Unable to defend itself, Japan was forced to sign treaties giving the United States trading and other rights. Humiliated by the terms of these unequal treaties, discontented daimyo and samurai led a revolt that unseated the shogun and placed the emperor Mutsuhito in power. Mutsuhito moved to the shogun's palace in the city of Edo, which was renamed **Tokyo,** and began a long reign known as the **Meiji Restoration.** This was a turning point in Japan's history.

The Meiji reformers wanted to create a new political and social system and build a modern industrial economy. The Meiji constitution gave all citizens equality before the law. A legislature, or **Diet,** was formed, but the emperor held absolute power. With government support, powerful banking and industrial families, known as **zaibatsu,** soon ruled over industrial empires. By the 1890s, industry was booming. Japan, a **homogeneous society,** modernized with amazing speed, partly due to its strong sense of identity.

As a small island nation, Japan lacked many resources essential for industry. Spurred by the need for natural resources and a strong ambition to equal the western imperial nations, Japan sought to build an empire. In 1876, Japan forced Korea to open its ports to Japanese trade. In 1894, competition between Japan and China in Korea led to the **First Sino-Japanese War,** which Japan easily won. Japan gained ports in China, won control over Taiwan, and joined the West in the race for empire. Ten years later, Japan successfully fought Russia in the **Russo-Japanese War.** By the early 1900s, Japan was the strongest power in Asia.

Review Questions

1. How did the Japanese respond to the unequal treaties signed with the United States?

____

____

2. How did the Meiji reformers try to modernize Japan?

____

____

READING CHECK

What helped to create a strong sense of identity in Japanese society?

____

____

____

VOCABULARY STRATEGY

What does the word *emphasizing* mean in the underlined sentence? Look for context clues to its meaning in the surrounding words. Use the context clues to help you figure out what *emphasizing* means.

READING SKILL

Identify Causes and Effects What were the causes and effects of the Meiji Restoration?

____

____

____

Name________________ Class________________ Date________

CHAPTER 13 SECTION 2

Note Taking Study Guide

IMPERIALISM IN SOUTHEAST ASIA AND THE PACIFIC

Focus Question: How did industrialized powers divide up Southeast Asia, and how did the colonized peoples react?

As you read this section, complete the flowchart below to identify causes, events, and effects of imperialism in Southeast Asia and the Pacific.

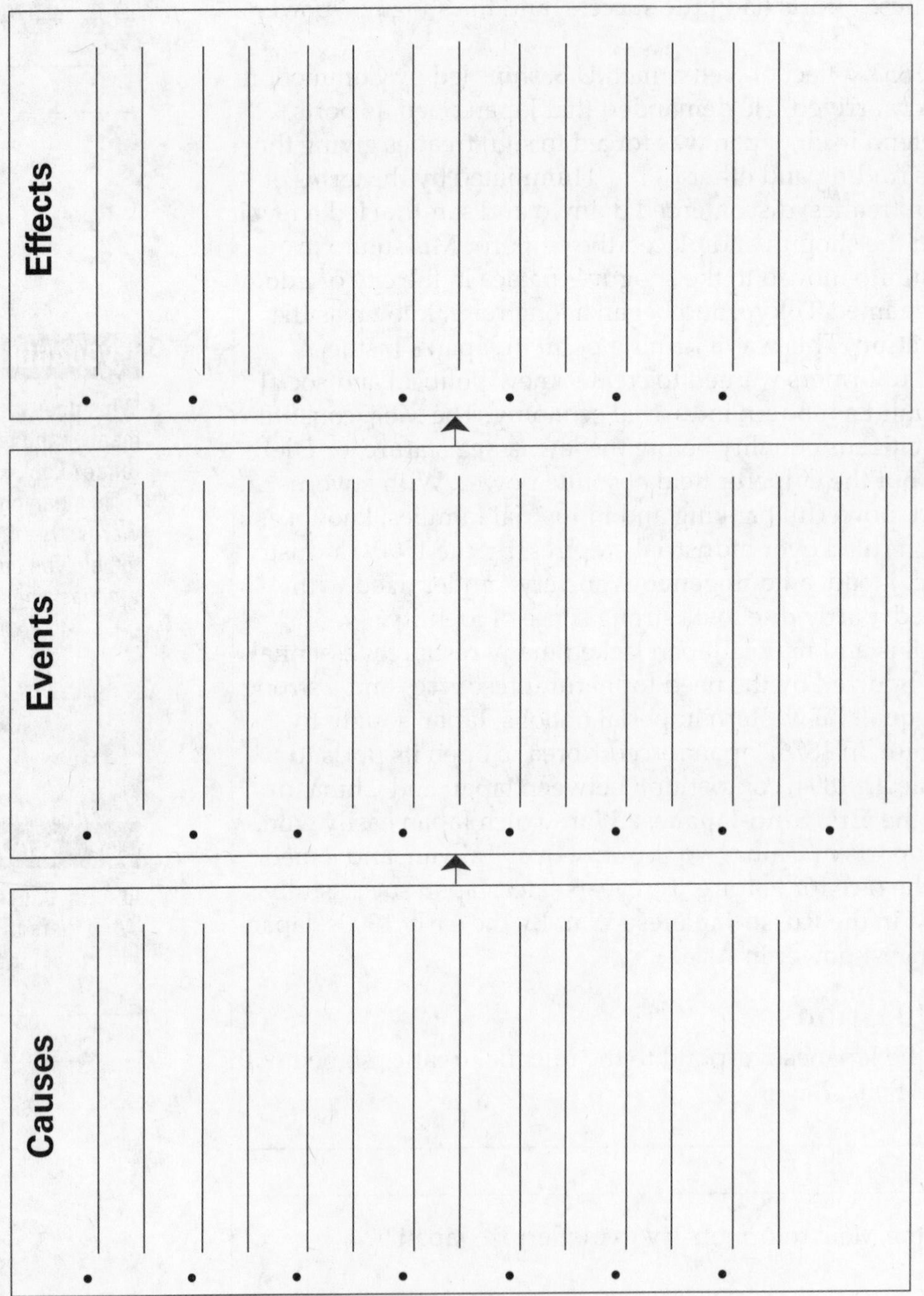

Name________________________ Class____________ Date______

CHAPTER 13 SECTION 2

Section Summary

IMPERIALISM IN SOUTHEAST ASIA AND THE PACIFIC

By the 1700s, European merchants had gained footholds in Southeast Asia, but most of the area was still independent. In the 1800s, however, Westerners colonized much of Southeast Asia. The Dutch, for example, expanded to dominate the Dutch East Indies (now Indonesia). The British expanded from India into Burma and Malaya.

The Burmese resisted British rule and annexation but suffered disastrous defeats. The French invaded Vietnam, seeking more influence and trade markets. The Vietnamese fought fiercely but lost to superior European firepower. The French eventually took over all of Vietnam, Laos, and Cambodia and referred to these holdings as **French Indochina.** Meanwhile, the king of Siam, **Mongkut,** accepted some unequal treaties to keep Siam from becoming a European colony. By the 1890s, Europeans controlled most of Southeast Asia, where they introduced modern technology and expanded commerce and industry.

The Philippines had been under Spanish rule since the 1500s. In 1898, the **Spanish-American War** broke out. During the war, U.S. battleships destroyed the Spanish fleet stationed in the Philippines. Filipino rebel leaders declared independence and joined the Americans against Spain. In return for their help, the Filipino rebels expected the United States to recognize their independence. Instead, in the treaty that ended the war, the United States gave Spain $20 million in exchange for control of the Philippines. Bitterly disappointed, Filipinos renewed their struggle for independence, but the United States crushed the rebellion. <u>The United States, however, did promise Filipinos a gradual transition to self-rule sometime in the future.</u>

In the 1800s, the industrialized powers also began to take an interest in the Pacific islands. American sugar growers, for example, pressed for power in the Hawaiian Islands. When the Hawaiian queen **Liliuokalani** tried to reduce foreign influence, American planters overthrew her. In 1898, the United States annexed Hawaii. Supporters of annexation argued that if the United States did not take Hawaii, Britain or Japan might. By 1900, the United States, Britain, France, or Germany had claimed nearly every island in the Pacific.

Review Questions

1. How did the people of Burma and Vietnam respond to European attempts to colonize them?

____

____

2. Why did Filipino rebels renew their struggle for independence after the Spanish-American War?

____

____

READING CHECK

Which countries made up French Indochina?

____

____

____

VOCABULARY STRATEGY

What does the word *transition* mean in the underlined sentence? Note that the word begins with the prefix *trans-*, which means "across or through." Use this knowledge to help you learn what the word *transition* means.

READING SKILL

Identify Causes and Effects Identify the causes and effects of Liliuokalani's attempts to reduce foreign influence in Hawaii.

____

____

____

Name________________________ Class________________ Date__________

CHAPTER 13
SECTION 3

Note Taking Study Guide

SELF-RULE FOR CANADA, AUSTRALIA, AND NEW ZEALAND

Focus Question: How were the British colonies of Canada, Australia, and New Zealand settled, and how did they win self-rule?

As you read this section, complete the chart below to identify the causes and effects of events in the British colonies of Canada, Australia, and New Zealand.

Cause	Event	Effect
Loyalist Americans flee to Canada.	Up to 30,000 loyalists settle in Canada.	Ethnic tensions arise between English- and French-speaking Canadians.

Name______________________ Class__________ Date______

CHAPTER 13 SECTION 3

Section Summary

SELF-RULE FOR CANADA, AUSTRALIA, AND NEW ZEALAND

In Canada, Britain created two provinces: English-speaking Upper Canada and French-speaking Lower Canada. When unrest grew in both colonies, the British sent Lord Durham to compile a report on the causes of the unrest. In response to his report, Parliament joined the two Canadas into one colony in 1840.

As the country grew, Canadian leaders urged **confederation** of Britain's North American colonies. They felt that confederation would strengthen the new nation against the United States' ambitions and help Canada's economic development. Britain finally agreed, and Parliament passed a law that created the Dominion of Canada. As a **dominion,** Canada had its own parliament. As the growing country expanded westward, the way of life of Native Americans was destroyed. People of French and Native American descent, called **métis,** resisted in two revolts. However, government troops put down both uprisings.

In 1770, Captain James Cook claimed Australia for Britain. Like most regions claimed by imperialist powers, Australia had already long been inhabited. The **indigenous** people there are called Aborigines. When white settlers arrived in Australia, the Aborigines suffered. Britain made Australia into a **penal colony** to fill a need for prisons. Then, Britain encouraged free citizens to emigrate to Australia by offering them land and tools. As the newcomers settled in, they thrust aside or killed the Aborigines. Like Canada, Australia was made up of separate colonies scattered around the continent. To counter possible interference from other European powers and to boost development, Britain agreed to Australian demands for self-rule. In 1901, the colonies united into the independent Commonwealth of Australia.

Captain James Cook also claimed New Zealand for Britain. The indigenous people of New Zealand are the **Maori.** The Maori were determined to defend their land. In 1840, Britain annexed New Zealand. As colonists poured in, they took more and more land, leading to fierce wars with the Maori. Many Maori died in the struggle. By the 1870s, resistance crumbled. Like settlers in Australia and Canada, white New Zealanders sought self-rule. In 1907, New Zealand won independence.

Review Questions

1. Why did Britain agree to create the Dominion of Canada?

____

____

2. Why did Britain agree to demands for self-rule in Australia?

____

____

READING CHECK

What happened to the Aborigines when white settlers arrived in Australia?

____

____

____

VOCABULARY STRATEGY

What does the word *compile* mean in the underlined sentence? Think about research reports you have written for school. What process did you go through to create a report? Use your prior knowledge to help you learn what *compile* means.

READING SKILL

Identify Causes and Effects Identify the causes and effects of the Maori fight against New Zealand colonists.

____

____

____

Name________________________ Class________________ Date________

CHAPTER 13 SECTION 4

Note Taking Study Guide

ECONOMIC IMPERIALISM IN LATIN AMERICA

Focus Question: How did Latin American nations struggle for stability, and how did industrialized nations affect them?

A. *As you read this section, complete the chart below to identify multiple causes of instability in Latin America. Then, give an example of how each cause affected Mexico.*

Instability in Latin America	
Causes	**Mexican Example**

B. *As you read "The Economics of Dependence" and "The Influence of the United States," complete the chart below to identify effects of foreign influence on Latin America.*

Effects of Foreign Influence		

Name________________________ Class____________ Date______

CHAPTER 13 SECTION 4

Section Summary

ECONOMIC IMPERIALISM IN LATIN AMERICA

Many factors undermined democracy in the newly independent nations of Latin America. Constitutions in these nations guaranteed equality before the law, but inequalities remained. With no tradition of unity, **regionalism** also weakened the new nations. Local strongmen, called ***caudillos,*** assembled private armies to resist the central government. Power remained in the hands of a privileged few.

Mexico is an example of the challenges faced by many Latin American nations. Large landowners, army leaders, and the Catholic Church dominated Mexican politics. The ruling elite was divided between conservatives and liberals. Conservatives defended the traditional social order. Liberals saw themselves as enlightened supporters of progress. Bitter battles between these two groups led to revolts and the rise of dictators. When **Benito Juárez** and other liberals gained power, they began an era of reform known as **La Reforma.** Juárez offered hope to the oppressed people of Mexico. After Juárez died, however, General Porfirio Díaz ruled as a harsh dictator. Many Indians and mestizos fell into **peonage** to their employers.

Under colonial rule, Latin America was economically dependent on Spain and Portugal, which had prevented the colonies from developing their own economies. After independence, the new Latin American republics did adopt free trade, but Britain and the United States replaced Spain as Latin America's chief trading partners.

As nations like Mexico tried to build stable governments, the United States expanded across North America. To discourage any new European colonization of the Americas, the United States issued the **Monroe Doctrine.** The United States then issued a series of policies claiming "international police power" in the Western Hemisphere. Under these policies, U.S. companies continued to invest in the countries of Latin America. To protect these investments, the United States sent troops to many of these countries, which made the United States a target of increasing resentment and rebellion. When the United States built the **Panama Canal** across Central America, it was an engineering marvel that boosted trade and shipping worldwide. To people in Latin America, however, the canal was another example of "Yankee imperialism."

Review Questions

1. What limited democracy in the independent nations of Latin America?

____

____

2. Why did the new Latin American republics remain economically dependent after independence?

____

____

READING CHECK

Which Mexican leader offered hope to the oppressed people of Mexico?

____

____

____

VOCABULARY STRATEGY

What does the word *enlightened* mean in the underlined sentence? Break the word into its word parts. Circle the root word, or the word part without the prefix and suffixes. Use the meaning of the root word to help you figure out what *enlightened* means.

READING SKILL

Identify Causes and Effects Identify what caused the United States to issue the Monroe Doctrine and what its effects were on Latin America.

____

____

____

Name________________________ Class______________ Date________

CHAPTER 14 SECTION 1

Note Taking Study Guide

THE GREAT WAR BEGINS

Focus Question: Why and how did World War I begin in 1914?

As you read this section in your textbook, complete the following chart to summarize the events that led to the outbreak of World War I.

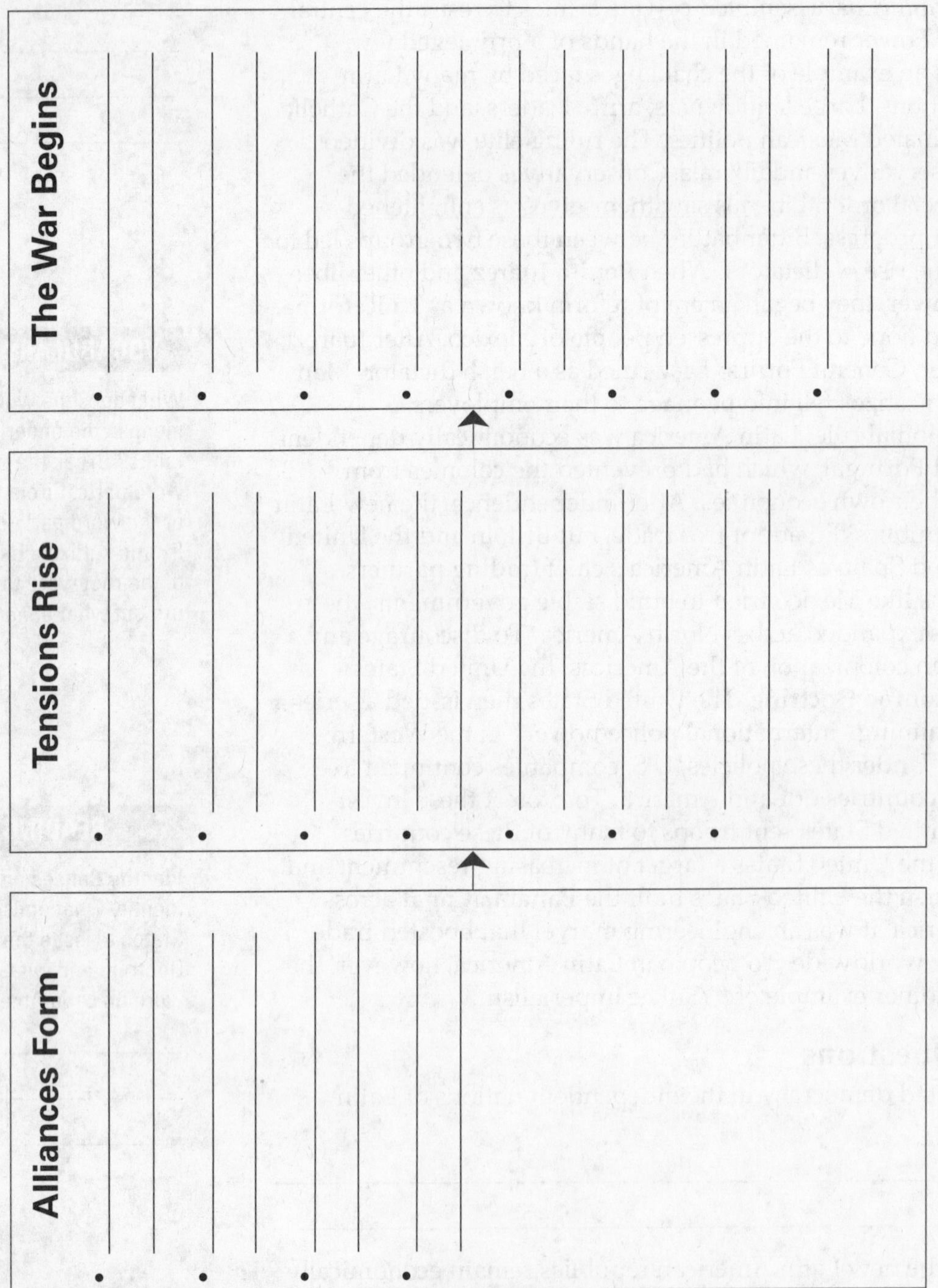

Name________________________ Class____________ Date______

CHAPTER 14 SECTION 1

Section Summary

THE GREAT WAR BEGINS

Although powerful forces were pushing Europe towards war, the great powers had formed alliances signing non-binding agreements, called **ententes,** to try to keep the peace. The Triple Alliance included Germany, Austria-Hungary, and Italy. Russia and France, and later Britain, formed the Triple Entente. During World War I, Germany and Austria fought together as the Central Powers. At that time, Russia, France, and Britain became known as the Allies.

In the decades before 1914, European powers competed to protect their status. Overseas rivalries divided them, as they fought for new colonies in Africa and elsewhere. They began to build up their armies and navies. The rise of **militarism** helped to feed this arms race. At the same time, sensational journalism stirred the public against rival nations.

Nationalism also increased tensions. Germans were proud of their military and economic might. The French yearned for the return of **Alsace and Lorraine.** Russia supported a powerful form of nationalism called Pan-Slavism. This led Russia to support nationalists in Serbia. Austria-Hungary worried that nationalism might lead to rebellions within its empire, while Ottoman Turkey felt threatened by nearby new nations in the Balkans, such as Serbia and Greece. Serbia's dreams of a South Slav state could take land away from both Austria-Hungary and Turkey. Soon, unrest made the Balkans a "powder keg." Then, in 1914, a Serbian nationalist assassinated the heir to the Austrian throne at Sarajevo, Bosnia.

Some Austrian leaders saw this as an opportunity to crush Serbian nationalism. They sent Serbia an **ultimatum,** which Serbia refused to meet completely. Austria, with the full support of Germany, declared war on Serbia in July 1914.

Soon, the network of alliances drew other great powers into the conflict. Russia, in support of Serbia, began to **mobilize** its army. Germany declared war on Russia. France claimed it would honor its treaty with Russia, so Germany declared war on France, too. When the Germans violated Belgian **neutrality** to reach France, Britain declared war on Germany. World War I had begun.

Review Questions

1. How did the network of European alliances cause World War I to develop?

____

____

2. What act caused Britain to declare war?

____

____

READING CHECK

Which countries made up the Central Powers?

____

____

____

VOCABULARY STRATEGY

What does the word *overseas* mean in the underlined sentence? What clues can you find in the surrounding words, phrases, or sentences? Circle the words in the paragraph that could help you learn what *overseas* means.

READING SKILL

Summarize Describe the events that led Austria to declare war on Serbia.

____

____

____

Name______________________ Class__________________ Date________

CHAPTER 14 SECTION 2

Note Taking Study Guide

A NEW KIND OF WAR

Focus Question: How and where was World War I fought?

A. *As you read "Stalemate on the Western Front," "Battle on Other European Fronts," and "War Around the World," complete the following flowchart with important details about each battlefront of World War I.*

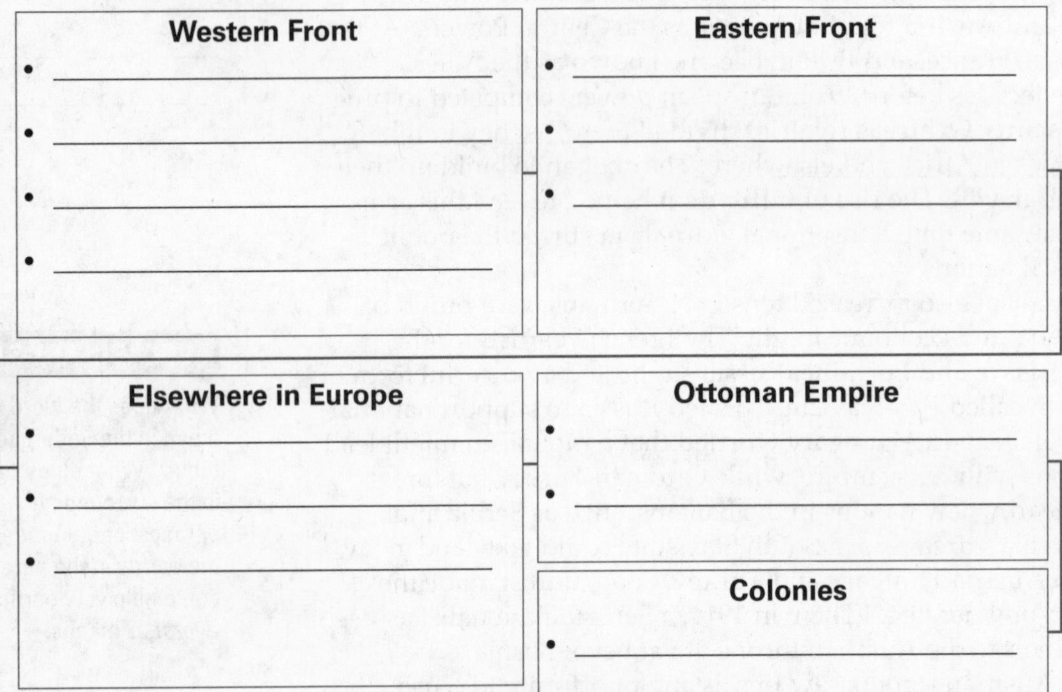

B. *As you read "Technology of Modern Warfare," complete the following concept web to summarize information about the technology of World War I. Add ovals as needed.*

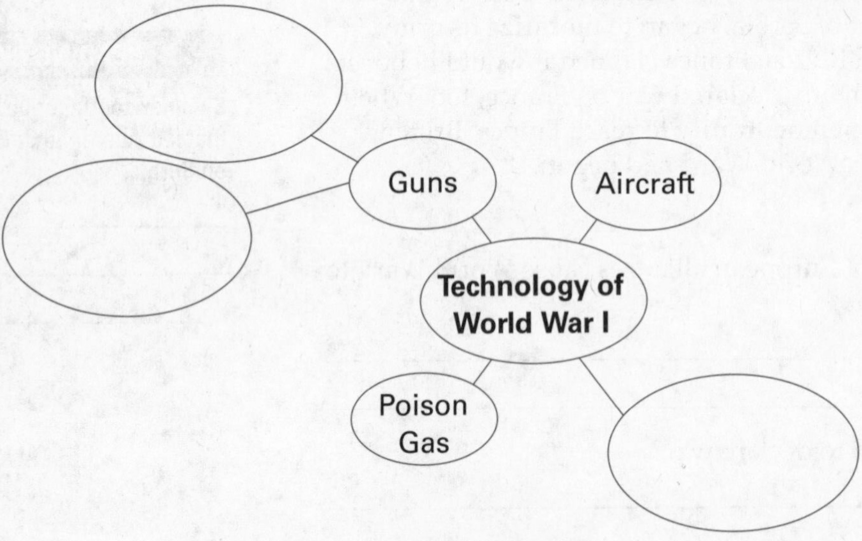

Name________________________ Class____________ Date______

CHAPTER 14 SECTION 2

Section Summary

A NEW KIND OF WAR

The Great War was the largest conflict in history up to that time. Millions of French, British, Russian, and German soldiers mobilized for battle. German forces fought their way toward France, but Belgian resistance foiled Germany's plans for a quick victory. Both sides dug deep trenches along the battlefront to protect their armies from enemy fire. The fighting on this Western Front turned into a long, deadly **stalemate,** a deadlock that neither side could break.

Technology made World War I different from earlier wars. Modern weapons caused high casualties. In 1915, first Germany then the Allies began using poison gas. Advances in technology brought about the introduction of tanks, airplanes, and modern submarines. Germany used **zeppelins** to bomb the English coast. Both sides equipped airplanes with machine guns. Pilots known as "flying aces" confronted each other in the skies, but these "dog fights" had little effect on the ground war. German submarines, called **U-boats,** did tremendous damage to the Allied shipping. To defend against them, the Allies organized **convoys,** or groups of merchant ships protected by warships.

On Europe's Eastern Front, battle lines shifted back and forth, sometimes over large areas. Casualties rose higher than on the Western Front. Russia was ill-prepared and suffered a disastrous defeat when pushing into eastern Germany. In 1915, Italy declared war on Austria-Hungary and Germany. In 1917, the Austrians and Germans launched a major offensive against the Italians.

Although most of the fighting took place in Europe, World War I was a global conflict. Japan used the war to seize German outposts in China and islands in the Pacific. The Ottoman empire joined the Central Powers. Its strategic location enabled it to cut off Allied supply lines to Russia through the **Dardanelles,** a vital strait.. The Ottoman Turks were hard hit in the Middle East, however. Arab nationalists revolted against Ottoman rule. The British sent **T.E. Lawrence,** or Lawrence of Arabia, to aid the Arabs. European colonies in Africa and Asia were also drawn into the war.

Review Questions

1. Why did a stalemate develop on the Western Front?

____

____

2. How did technology make World War I different from earlier wars?

____

____

READING CHECK

What were the two battlefronts in Europe called?

____

____

____

VOCABULARY STRATEGY

What does the word *confronted* mean in the underlined sentence? What clues or examples can you find in the surrounding words that hint at its meaning? Think about what the goal of these pilots was. Circle the words in the underlined sentence that could help you learn what *confronted* means.

READING SKILL

Identify Supporting Details Identify important details that show the differences between the course of the war on the Western Front and on the Eastern Front.

____

____

____

Name________________________ Class____________________ Date________

CHAPTER 14 SECTION 3

Note Taking Study Guide

WINNING THE WAR

Focus Question: How did the Allies win World War I?

As you read this section in your textbook, complete the following outline to summarize the content of this section.

I. **Waging total war**
   A. Economies committed to war production.
      1. Conscription
      2. Rationing
      3. Price controls
   B. Economic warfare
      1. ____________________
      2. ____________________
      3. ____________________
   C. ____________________
      1. ____________________
      2. ____________________
      3. ____________________
   D. ____________________
      1. ____________________
      2. ____________________
      3. ____________________

II. ____________________
   A. ____________________
      1. ____________________
      2. ____________________
      3. ____________________
   B. ____________________
      1. ____________________
      2. ____________________
      3. ____________________

(Outline continues on the next page.)

Name________________________ Class______________________ Date__________

CHAPTER 14 SECTION 3

Note Taking Study Guide

WINNING THE WAR

(Continued from page 152)

III. ____

A. ____

1. ____
2. ____
3. ____

B. ____

1. ____
2. ____
3. ____

C. ____

1. ____
2. ____
3. ____

IV. ____

A. ____

B. ____

C. ____

Name________________________ Class____________ Date________

CHAPTER 14 SECTION 3

Note Taking Study Guide

WINNING THE WAR

READING CHECK

Why did women take on new jobs during the war?

____

____

____

VOCABULARY STRATEGY

What does the word *eroded* mean in the underlined sentence? What clues or examples can you find in the surrounding words, phrases, or sentences that hint at its meaning? Circle the words in the paragraph that could help you learn what *eroded* means.

READING SKILL

Summarize Describe what made World War I a total war.

____

____

____

World War I was a **total war,** in which the participants channeled all their resources into the war effort. Both sides set up systems to recruit, arm, transport, and supply their armies. Nations imposed universal military **conscription,** or "the draft," requiring all young men to be ready to fight. Women also played a critical role. As millions of men left to fight, women took over their jobs and kept national economies going.

International law allowed wartime blockades to confiscate **contraband,** but British blockades kept ships from carrying other supplies, such as food, in and out of Germany. In retaliation, German U-boats torpedoed the British passenger liner ***Lusitania.*** Both sides used **propaganda** to control public opinion, circulating tales of **atrocities,** some true and others completely made up.

As time passed, war fatigue set in. Long casualty lists, food shortages, and the failure to win led to calls for peace. The morale of both troops and civilians plunged. <u>In Russia, stories of incompetent generals and corruption eroded public confidence and led to revolution.</u>

Until 1917, the United States had been neutral, but in that year it declared war on Germany. Many factors contributed to this decision, including Germany's unrestricted submarine warfare. Also, many Americans supported the Allies because of cultural ties with Britain and sympathy for its fellow democracy, France. By 1918, about two million fresh American soldiers had joined the war-weary Allied troops on the Western Front. In that year, President Wilson also issued his **Fourteen Points,** his terms for resolving this and future wars. Among the most important was **self-determination** for peoples in Eastern Europe.

A final showdown on the Western Front began in March 1918. With American troops, the Allies drove back German forces. In September, German generals told the kaiser that the war could not be won. The kaiser stepped down and the new German government sought an **armistice** with the Allies. At 11 A.M. on November 11, 1918, the Great War at last came to an end.

Review Questions

1. What caused the morale of troops and civilians to plunge?

____

____

2. What are two factors that caused the United States to enter the war?

____

____

Name________________________ Class____________________ Date__________

CHAPTER 14 SECTION 4

Note Taking Study Guide

MAKING THE PEACE

Focus Question: What factors influenced the peace treaties that ended World War I, and how did people react to the treaties?

A. *As you read "The Costs of War," complete this concept web to summarize the costs of World War I.*

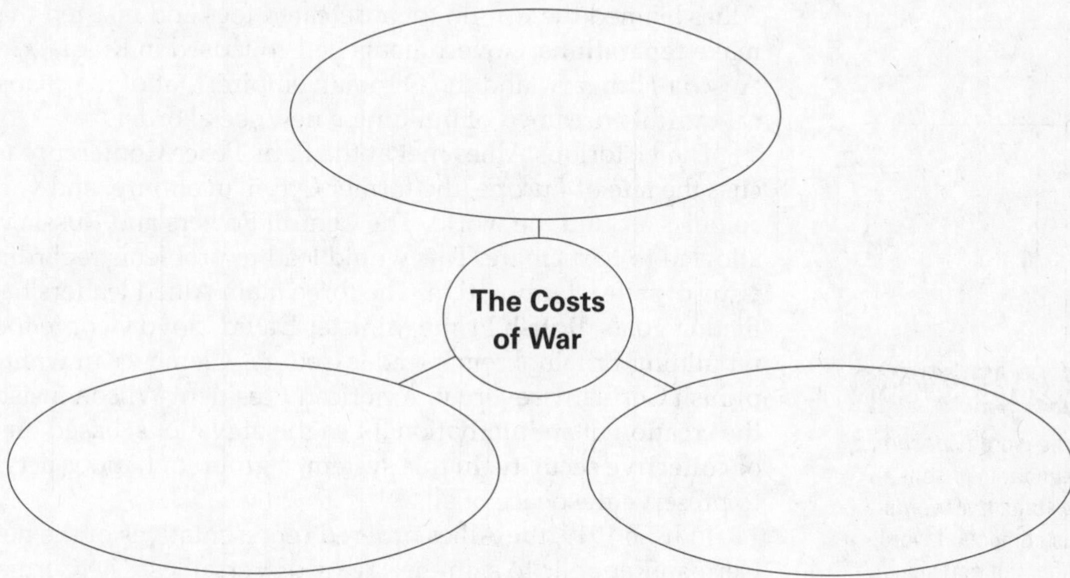

B. *As you read "The Paris Peace Conference," "The Treaty of Versailles," and "Outcome of the Peace Settlements," complete this table to categorize issues and problems that resulted from agreements made after the war.*

Issue	Treaty Settlement	Problems
War Debt		
Fear of German Strength		
Nationalism		
Colonies and Other Non-European Territories		
League of Nations		

Name________________________ Class____________ Date______

CHAPTER 14 SECTION 4

Section Summary

MAKING THE PEACE

The human, material, and political costs of World War I were staggering. The huge loss of life was made even worse in 1918 by a deadly **pandemic** of influenza. From France to Russia, homes, farms, factories, and roads had been bombed into rubble. Reconstruction costs and war debts would burden an already battered world. The Allies blamed the war on their defeated foes and insisted that they make **reparations.** Governments had collapsed in Russia, Germany, Austria-Hungary, and the Ottoman empire. Out of the chaos, political **radicals** dreamed of building a new social order.

The victorious Allies met at the Paris Peace Conference to discuss the fate of Europe, the former Ottoman empire, and various colonies around the world. The Central Powers and Russia were not allowed to participate. This would lead to problems regarding the issue of self-determination. The three main Allied leaders had conflicting goals. British Prime Minister David Lloyd George focused on rebuilding Britain. French leader Georges Clemenceau wanted to punish Germany severely. American President Wilson insisted on the creation of an international League of Nations, based on the idea of **collective security.** In this system, a group of nations acts as one to preserve the peace of all.

In June 1919, the Allies ordered representatives of the new German Republic to sign the Treaty of Versailles. The German delegates were horrified. The treaty forced Germany to assume full blame for the war. The treaty also imposed huge reparations that would burden an already damaged German economy and limited the size of Germany's military.

The Allies drew up treaties with the other Central Powers. <u>Like the Treaty of Versailles, these treaties left widespread dissatisfaction, especially among many colonies that had hoped for an end to imperial rule.</u> Many nations felt betrayed by the peacemakers. As a result of these treaties, new nations emerged where the German, Austrian, and Russian empires had once ruled. Outside Europe, the Allies added to their overseas empires. The treaties also created a system of **mandates.** The one ray of hope was the establishment of the League of Nations. The failure of the United States to support the League, however, weakened the League's power.

Review Questions

1. What were some of the human, material, and political costs of the war?

____

____

2. Why were German representatives at Versailles horrified?

____

____

READING CHECK

Which three main Allied leaders negotiated the terms of the Treaty of Versailles?

____

____

____

VOCABULARY STRATEGY

What does the word *widespread* mean in the underlined sentence? Look at the two words that form this compound word, and think about their meanings. Use what you know about the parts of this compound word to figure out its meaning.

READING SKILL

Summarize How did the goals of the three main leaders at the Paris Peace Conference differ?

____

____

____

Name________________________ Class________________________ Date________

CHAPTER 14 SECTION 5

Note Taking Study Guide

REVOLUTION AND CIVIL WAR IN RUSSIA

Focus Question: How did two revolutions and a civil war bring about Communist control of Russia?

As you read the section, fill in the following timeline with dates and facts about the series of events that led to Communist control of Russia. Then write two sentences summarizing the information in the timeline.

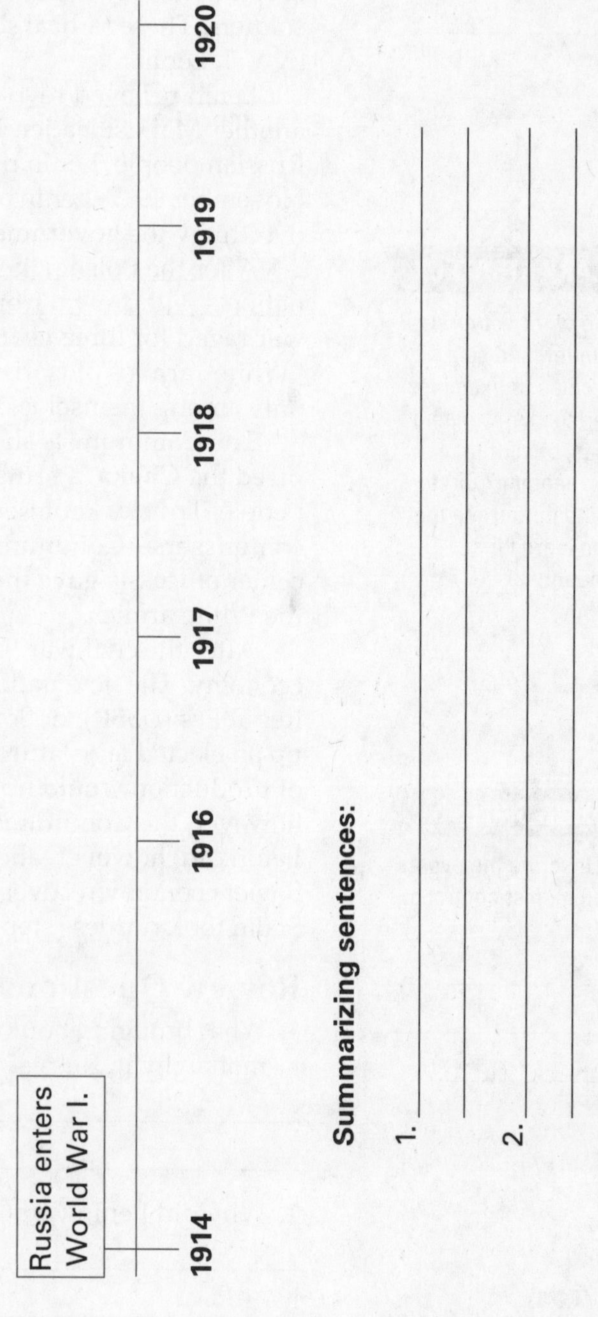

Name________________________ Class____________ Date______

CHAPTER 14 SECTION 5

Section Summary

REVOLUTION AND CIVIL WAR IN RUSSIA

READING CHECK

What was the name of the new Communist nation?

____

____

____

VOCABULARY STRATEGY

What does the word *withdrawal* mean in the underlined sentence? What clues or examples can you find in the surrounding words, phrases, or sentences that hint at its meaning? Circle the words in the paragraph that could help you learn what *withdrawal* means.

READING SKILL

Summarize Describe the events that led to Communist control of Russia.

____

____

____

At the beginning of the 1900s, Russia had many political, economic, and social problems. Tsar Nicholas II resisted change. Marxists tried to ignite revolution among the **proletariat.** World War I quickly strained Russian resources. By March 1917, disasters on the battlefield and shortages at home brought the monarchy to collapse, and the tsar abdicated. While politicians set up a temporary government, revolutionary socialists set up **soviets,** or councils of workers and soldiers. These radical socialists were called Bolsheviks and were led by V. I. Lenin.

Lenin believed revolution could bring change. Leon Trotsky, another Marxist leader, helped Lenin lead the fight. To the weary Russian people, Lenin promised "Peace, Land, and Bread." In November 1917, Lenin and the Bolsheviks, renamed Communists, overthrew the government and seized power.

After the Bolshevik Revolution, events in Russia led to the nation's withdrawal from World War I. After the withdrawal, civil war raged for three years between the Communist "Reds" and the "White" armies of tsarist imperial officers. The Russians now fought only among themselves.

The Communists shot the former tsar and his family. They organized the **Cheka,** a brutal secret police force, to control their own people. Trotsky kept Red Army officers under the close watch of **commissars**—Communist Party officials. The Reds' position in the center of Russia gave them a strategic advantage, and they defeated the White armies.

After the civil war, Lenin had to rebuild a shattered state and economy. The new nation was called the Union of Soviet Socialist Republics (USSR), or Soviet Union. The Communist constitution set up an elected legislature. All political power, resources, and means of production would now belong to workers and peasants. In reality, however, the Communist Party, not the people, had all the power. Lenin did, however, allow some capitalist ventures that helped the Soviet economy recover. After Lenin's death, party leader Joseph Stalin took ruthless steps to win total control of the nation.

Review Questions

1. What brought about the tsar's abdication and the end of the monarchy in Russia?

____

____

2. Why did Lenin want revolution?

____

____

Name________________________ Class__________________ Date________

CHAPTER 15 SECTION 1

Note Taking Study Guide

STRUGGLE IN LATIN AMERICA

Focus Question: How did Latin Americans struggle for change in the early 1900s?

A. *As you read the "The Mexican Revolution" and "Revolution Leads to Change," complete the chart by listing the causes and effects of the Mexican Revolution.*

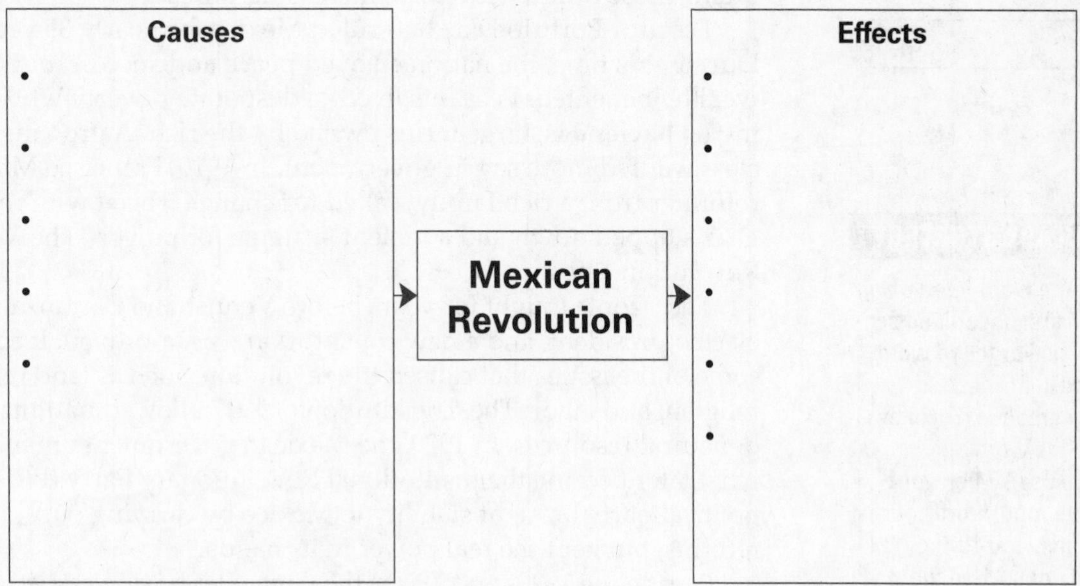

B. *As you read "Nationalism at Work in Latin America," complete the following chart as you list the effects of nationalism in Latin America.*

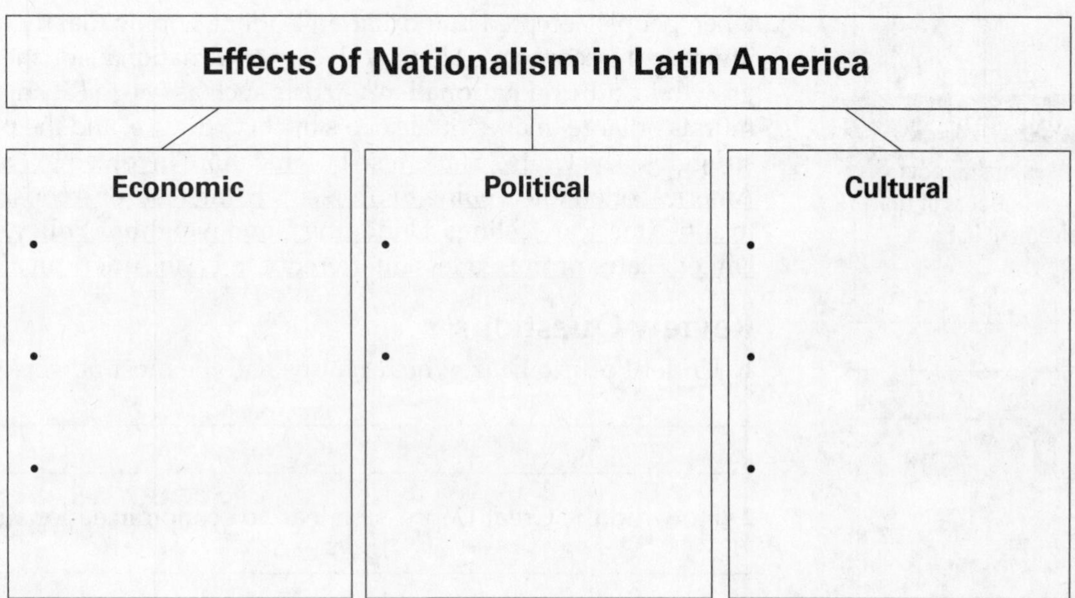

Name________________ Class____________ Date______

CHAPTER 15 SECTION 1

Section Summary

STRUGGLE IN LATIN AMERICA

In the early 1900s, exports kept Latin America's economy booming. Even though foreign investors controlled much of the natural resources, stable governments helped keep economies strong. Yet turmoil brewed because military leaders and wealthy landowners held most of the power. Workers and peasants had no say in government. These differences led to increasing unrest.

Dictator Porfirio Díaz had ruled Mexico for nearly 35 years. During this time, the nation enjoyed peace and success, but only the wealthy benefited. Peasants lived in desperate poverty while working on **haciendas,** large farms owned by the rich. A growing middle class wanted more say in government. In 1910, Francisco Madero, a reformer from a rich family, called for change. Faced with rebellion, Díaz stepped down and a violent struggle for power—the Mexican Revolution—began.

The people fought for years before Venustiano Carranza was elected president, and a new constitution was approved. It addressed some of the issues that caused the revolution, such as land reform, religion, and labor. The Constitution of 1917 allowed **nationalization** of natural resources. In 1929, the Mexican government organized what later became the Institutional Revolutionary Party (PRI). This political party brought stability to Mexico by carrying out some reforms, but kept the real power in its hands.

During the 1920s and 1930s, the Great Depression caused Latin American exports to drop and import prices to rise. As a result, **economic nationalism** became popular. Latin Americans wanted to develop their own industries. Some Latin American nations took over foreign-owned companies. The government became more powerful when people accepted authoritarian leaders, hoping that they could improve the economy. Along with economic nationalism, there was a growth in **cultural nationalism.** Artists such as Diego Rivera painted murals or large images of Mexico's history, culture, and the people's struggles. The United States also became more involved in Latin America, often intervening to protect U.S. interests or troops. This led to anti-American feelings. Under the **Good Neighbor Policy,** the United States promised less interference in Latin American affairs.

Review Questions

1. Under Porfirio Díaz, which groups had the most power?

____

____

2. How did the Great Depression lead to economic nationalism?

____

____

READING CHECK

What was the PRI, and what was its impact on Mexico?

____

____

____

VOCABULARY STRATEGY

What does the word *intervening* mean in the first underlined sentence? It is similar to the word *interference* in the second underlined sentence. You may have heard the word *interference* used when you watch sports. Both words begin with the prefix *inter-*, which means "between." Use the meaning of *inter-* and the context clues to help you figure out what *intervening* means.

READING SKILL

Identify Causes and Effects What were two effects of United States involvement in Latin America?

____

____

____

Name____________________ Class________________ Date__________

CHAPTER 15
SECTION 2

Note Taking Study Guide

NATIONALISM IN AFRICA AND THE MIDDLE EAST

Focus Question: How did nationalism contribute to changes in Africa and the Middle East following World War I?

As you read this section in your textbook, complete the following table to identify the causes and effects of the rise of nationalism.

Rise of Nationalism

Region	Reasons for Rise	Effects
Africa	• • •	• • •
Turkey and Persia	• • •	• • •
Middle East	• • •	• • •

Name________________________ Class___________ Date______

CHAPTER 15 SECTION 2

Section Summary

NATIONALISM IN AFRICA AND THE MIDDLE EAST

READING CHECK

What was the négritude movement?

____

____

____

Europe ruled over most of Africa during the early 1900s. Improved farming methods meant more exports; however, this mostly benefited colonial rulers. Europeans kept the best lands, and African farmers were forced to grow cash crops instead of food. They also were forced to work in mines and then pay taxes to the colonial governments. Many Africans began criticizing imperial rule, but their freedoms only eroded further. An example was the system of **apartheid** in South Africa. Under this policy, black Africans were denied many of their previous rights, such as the right to vote.

During the 1920s, the **Pan-Africanism** movement called for the unity of Africans and people of African descent around the world. During the first Pan-African Congress, delegates asked world leaders at the Paris Peace Conference to approve a charter of rights for Africans. Their request was ignored. The members of the **négritude movement** in West Africa and the Caribbean protested colonial rule while expressing pride in African culture. These movements, however, brought about little real change.

VOCABULARY STRATEGY

What does the word *advocated* mean in the underlined sentence? What clues can you find in the surrounding sentences? Think about why Britain issued the Balfour Declaration. Use this information to help you understand the meaning of *advocated.*

In **Asia Minor,** Mustafa Kemal overthrew the Ottoman ruler and established the republic of Turkey. Also referred to as Atatürk (father of the Turks), his government promoted industrial expansion by building factories and railroads. Inspired by Atatürk's successes, Reza Khan overthrew the shah of Persia. Khan sought to turn Persia into a modern country. He, too, built factories and railroads. Khan also demanded a bigger portion of profits for Persia from British-controlled oil companies. Both leaders pushed aside Islamic traditions, replacing them with Western alternatives.

Pan-Arabism was a movement based on a shared history of Arabs living from the Arabian Peninsula to North Africa. Leaders of Arab nations and territories had hoped to gain independence after World War I, but felt betrayed when France and Britain were given control over their lands. In Palestine, Arab nationalists faced Zionists, or Jewish nationalists. To win the support of European Jews, Britain issued the **Balfour Declaration.** In it, the British advocated for a "national home for the Jewish people" in Palestine. Arabs felt the declaration favored the Jews. As a result, an ongoing conflict developed in the Middle East.

READING SKILL

Identify Causes and Effects What was one effect of the Balfour Declaration?

____

____

____

Review Questions

1. How did colonial rule hurt Africans?

____

____

2. How did Reza Khan change Persia?

____

____

Name________________________ Class____________________ Date________

CHAPTER 15 SECTION 3

Note Taking Study Guide

INDIA SEEKS SELF-RULE

Focus Question: How did Gandhi and the Congress party work for independence in India?

As you read this section in your textbook, complete the following chart by recording the causes and effects of Gandhi's leadership on India's independence movement.

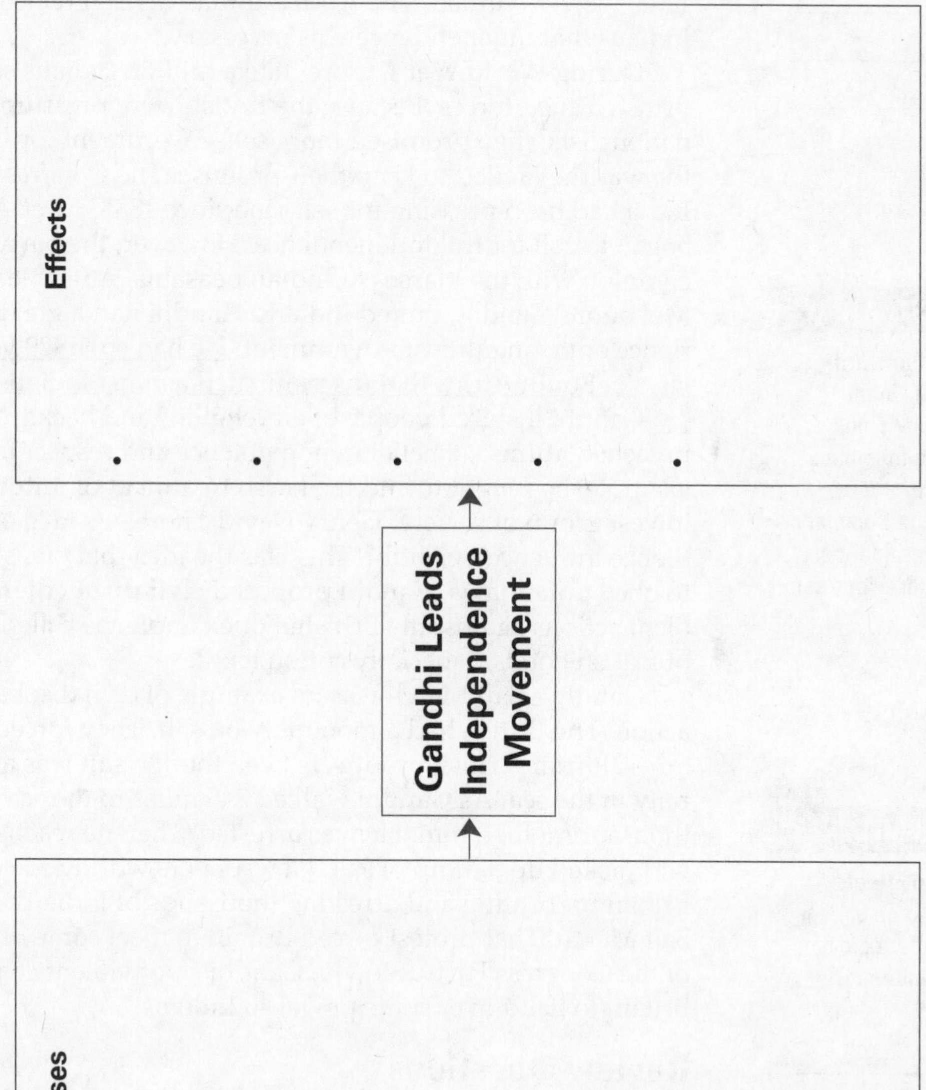

Name______________________ Class____________ Date______

CHAPTER 15 SECTION 3

Section Summary

INDIA SEEKS SELF-RULE

In 1919, Indian protests against colonial rule led to riots and attacks on British residents. The British then banned public meetings. On April 13, 1919, a peaceful crowd of Indians gathered in an enclosed field in Amritsar. As Indian leaders spoke, British soldiers fired on the unarmed crowd. Nearly 400 people were killed and more than 1,100 were wounded. The **Amritsar massacre** convinced many Indians that independence was necessary.

During World War I, more than a million Indians served in the British armed forces. Because the British were pressured by Indian nationalists, they promised more self-government for India. After the war they failed to keep their promise. The Congress Party of India had been pressing for self-rule since 1885. After Amritsar it began to call for full independence. However, the party had little in common with the masses of Indian peasants. A new leader, Mohandas Gandhi, united Indians. Gandhi had a great deal of experience opposing unjust government. He had spent 20 years fighting laws in South Africa that discriminated against Indians.

Gandhi inspired people of all religions and backgrounds. He preached **ahimsa,** a belief in nonviolence and respect for all life. For example, he fought to end the harsh treatment of **untouchables,** the lowest group of society. Henry David Thoreau's idea of civil disobedience influenced Gandhi. This was the idea that one should refuse to obey unfair laws. Gandhi proposed **civil disobedience** and nonviolent actions against the British. For example, he called for a **boycott** of British goods, especially cotton textiles.

Gandhi's Salt March was an example of civil disobedience in action. The British had a monopoly on salt. They forced Indians to buy salt from British producers even though salt was available naturally in the sea. As Gandhi walked 240 miles to the sea to collect salt, thousands joined him. He was arrested when he reached the water and picked up a lump of salt. Newspapers worldwide criticized Britain for beating and arresting thousands of Indians during the Salt March. That protest forced Britain to meet some of the demands of the Congress Party. Slowly, Gandhi's nonviolent campaign forced Britain to hand over some power to Indians.

READING CHECK

What had Gandhi done before becoming a leader for Indian independence?

____

____

____

VOCABULARY STRATEGY

What do you think the word *discriminated* means in the underlined sentence? Think about why Gandhi would have been fighting laws in South Africa. Note what the Summary says about the government of South Africa in the previous sentence.

READING SKILL

Identify Causes and Effects What caused the Amritsar massacre? What effect did it have on the independence movement?

Cause:______________________

____

Effect:______________________

____

Review Questions

1. Why did the Congress party fail to unite all Indians?

____

____

2. What was the significance of the Salt March?

____

____

Name________________________ Class____________________ Date________

CHAPTER 15 SECTION 4

Note Taking Study Guide

UPHEAVALS IN CHINA

Focus Question: How did China cope with internal division and foreign invasion in the early 1900s?

A. *As you read "The Chinese Republic in Trouble," complete the following chart by listing the multiple causes of upheaval in the Chinese Republic.*

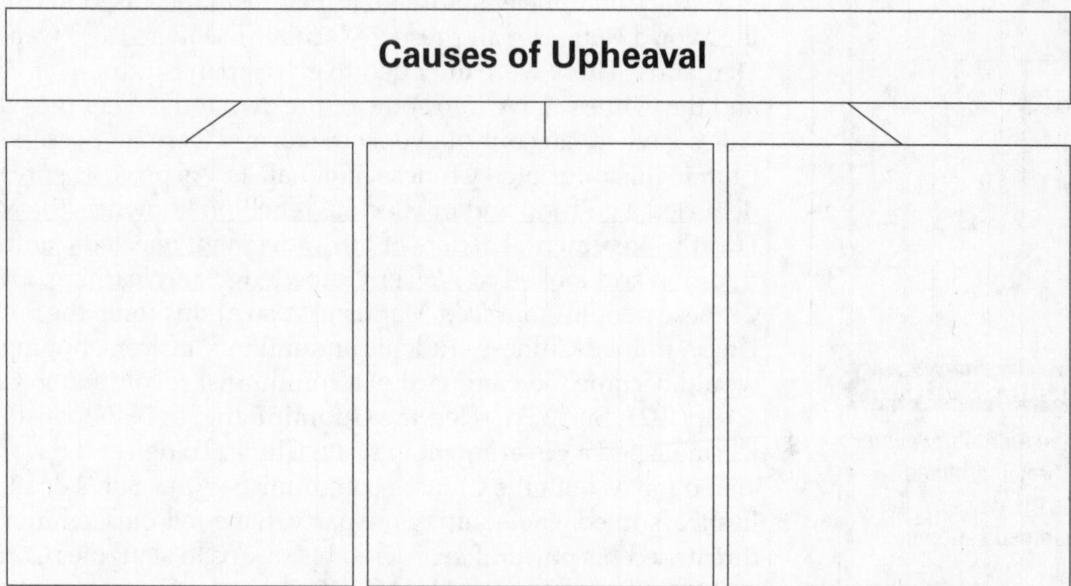

B. *As you read "Struggle for a New China" and "Japanese Invasion," complete the chart to sequence the fighting among the Guomindang, the warlords, the Chinese Communists, and the Japanese.*

1926 • Guomindang and Communists defeat warlords. →	→	

Name____________________ Class__________ Date______

CHAPTER 15 SECTION 4

Section Summary

UPHEAVALS IN CHINA

READING CHECK

What group of people spearheaded the May Fourth Movement?

____

____

____

VOCABULARY STRATEGY

What does the word *intellectual* mean in the first underlined sentence? Circle the words in the second underlined sentence that could help you figure out what *intellectual* means.

READING SKILL

Recognize Multiple Causes Why did Chinese peasants support the Communists?

____

____

____

When the Qing dynasty collapsed in 1911, Sun Yixian became president of China's new republic. He hoped to rebuild China, but he made little progress. The country fell into chaos when local warlords seized power and the economy fell apart. Millions of peasants suffered severe hardships. Sun Yixian stepped down as president in 1912.

Amid the upheaval, foreign imperialism increased in China. During World War I, Japan presented Chinese leaders the **Twenty-One Demands.** These were intended to give Japan control over China, and the Chinese gave into some of the demands. After the war, the Allies gave Japan control over some former German possessions in China. This infuriated Chinese nationalists. As protests spread, students led a cultural and intellectual rebellion known as the **May Fourth Movement.** Leaders of this movement rejected Confucian tradition and looked to Western knowledge and learning. Other Chinese people embraced Marxism. Also at this time, the Soviet Union trained Chinese students and military officers, hoping they would become the **vanguard** of a communist revolution in China.

In 1921, Sun Yixian led the **Guomindang,** or Nationalist party, as it established a government in south China. To defeat the warlords he joined forces with the Chinese communists. After Sun's death, Jiang Jieshi assumed leadership of the party. Jiang felt the Communists threatened his power. He ordered his troops to slaughter Communists and their supporters. Led by Mao Zedong, the Communist army escaped north in what became known as the **Long March.** During the March, Mao's soldiers fought back using guerrilla tactics. Along the way, Mao's soldiers treated the peasants kindly. They paid for the goods they needed and were careful not to destroy crops. Many peasants had suffered because of the Guomindang, so they supported the Communists.

While Jiang pursued the Communists across China, the Japanese invaded Manchuria, adding it to their growing empire. Then, in 1937, Japanese planes bombed Chinese cities and Japanese soldiers marched into Nanjing, killing hundreds of thousands of people. In response, Jiang and Mao formed an alliance to fight the invaders. The alliance held up until the end of the war with Japan.

Review Questions

1. How did Japan gain territory and control of areas of China during World War I?

____

____

2. Why did Jiang and Mao form an alliance?

____

____

Name______________________ Class__________________ Date________

CHAPTER 15 SECTION 5

Note Taking Study Guide

CONFLICTING FORCES IN JAPAN

Focus Question: How did Japan change in the 1920s and 1930s?

As you read this section in your textbook, complete the table by listing the effects of liberalism and militarism in Japan during the 1920s and 1930s.

Conflicting Forces in Japan

Liberalism in the 1920s	Militarism in the 1930s
•	•
•	•
•	•
•	•

Name_________________________ Class____________ Date______

CHAPTER 15 SECTION 5

Section Summary

CONFLICTING FORCES IN JAPAN

READING CHECK

Who became emperor of Japan in 1926?

____

____

____

VOCABULARY STRATEGY

What does the word *manipulated* mean in the underlined sentence? Think about the Latin root *manus*, which means "hand" or "to handle." How did the zaibatsu "handle" politicians? Use this information about the word's root to help you understand what *manipulated* means.

READING SKILL

Understand Effects What effect did the Great Depression have on Japanese politics?

____

____

____

The Japanese economy grew during World War I, based on the export of goods to the Allies and increased production. At this time, Japan also expanded its influence throughout East Asia and sought further rights in China. Additionally, Japan gained control of some former German possessions in China after the war. **Hirohito** became emperor of Japan in 1926, and during his reign, the country experienced both success and tragedy

In the 1920s, the Japanese government moved toward greater democracy. All adult men gained the right to vote, regardless of social class. Despite greater democratic freedoms, however, the zaibatsu, a group of powerful business leaders, manipulated politicians. By donating to political parties, the zaibatsu were able to push for policies that favored their interests.

Peasants and factory workers did not share in the nation's prosperity. Young Japanese rejected tradition and family authority. There was tension between the government and the military. The Great Depression fed the discontent of the military and the extreme nationalists, or **ultranationalists.** They resented Western limits on the expansion of Japan's empire. As the economic crisis worsened, the ultranationalists set their sights on **Manchuria** in northern China. In 1931, a group of Japanese army officers set explosives to blow up railroad tracks in Manchuria. They blamed it on the Chinese and used it as an excuse to invade. Without consulting government leaders, the military conquered Manchuria. Politicians objected to the army's actions, but the people sided with the military. When the League of Nations condemned the invasion, Japan withdrew from the organization.

Militarists and ultranationalists increased their power in the 1930s. Extremists killed some politicians and business leaders who opposed expansion. To please the ultranationalists, the government suppressed most democratic freedoms. Japan planned to take advantage of China's civil war and conquer the country. In 1939, however, World War II broke out in Europe. The fighting quickly spread to Asia. Earlier, Japan had formed an alliance with Germany and Italy. In September 1940, Japan's leaders signed the Tripartite Pact linking the three nations. Together, the three nations formed the Axis Powers.

Review Questions

1. Describe the economic success of Japan in the 1920s.

____

____

2. How did militarists and ultranationalists increase their power in the 1930s?

____

____

Name________________________ Class____________________ Date________

CHAPTER 16 SECTION 1

Note Taking Study Guide

POSTWAR SOCIAL CHANGES

Focus Question: What changes did Western society and culture experience after World War I?

As you read this section in your textbook, complete the concept web below to identify supporting details related to "Changes to Society" and "Cultural Changes."

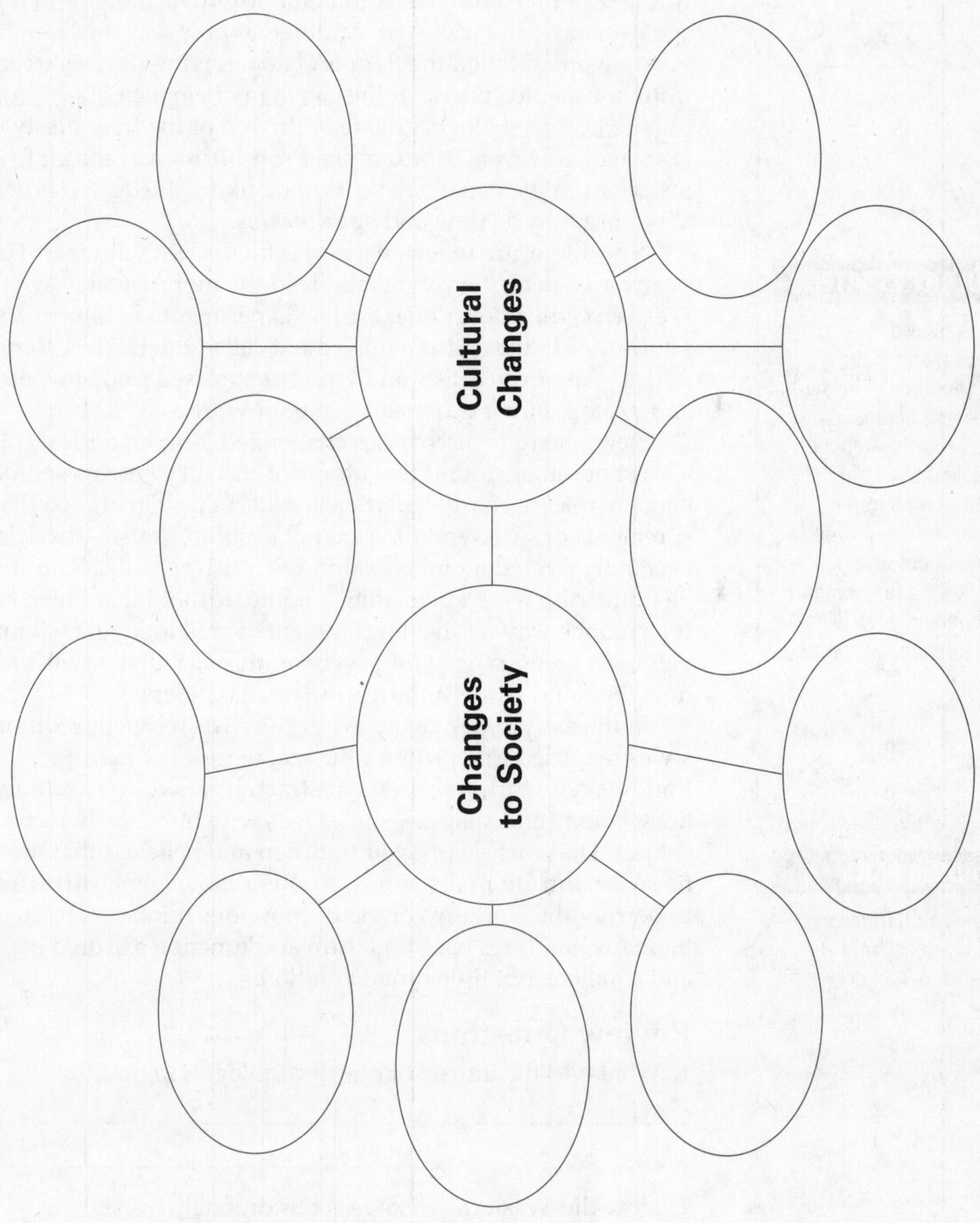

Name______________________ Class__________ Date______

CHAPTER 16 SECTION 1

Section Summary

POSTWAR SOCIAL CHANGES

READING CHECK

What were two symbols of American culture in the 1920s?

____

____

____

VOCABULARY STRATEGY

What does the word *emancipation* mean in the underlined sentence? The sentence containing *emancipation* follows two sentences about women. Think about what flappers were like compared to young women who had lived before. Think about what labor-saving devices did for women. Use these context clues to figure out what *emancipation* means.

READING SKILL

Identify Supporting Details What were three aspects of postwar literature?

____

____

____

In reaction to World War I, society and culture in the United States and elsewhere underwent rapid changes. During the 1920s, new technologies helped create a mass culture, and to connect people around the world. American culture was characterized by a greater freedom and willingness to experiment. One symbol of this new age was jazz, with its original sound and improvisations, and it gave the age its name—the Jazz Age. Another symbol was the liberated young woman called the **flapper.** Labor-saving devices freed women from household chores. In this new era of emancipation, women pursued careers. Not everyone approved of the freer lifestyle of the Jazz Age, however. For example, **Prohibition** was meant to keep people from the negative effects of drinking. Instead, it brought about organized crime and **speakeasies.**

New literature reflected a powerful disgust with war. To some postwar writers, the war symbolized the moral breakdown of Western civilization. Other writers experimented with stream of consciousness. In the cultural movement called the **Harlem Renaissance,** African American artists and writers expressed pride in their culture and explored their experiences in their work.

New scientific discoveries challenged long-held ideas. Marie Curie and others found that atoms of certain elements spontaneously release charged particles. Albert Einstein argued that measurements of space and time are not absolute. Italian physicist Enrico Fermi discovered atomic fission. A Scottish scientist, Alexander Fleming, discovered penicillin, a nontoxic mold that killed bacteria. It paved the way for the development of antibiotics to treat infections. Sigmund Freud pioneered **psychoanalysis,** a method of studying how the mind works and treating mental illness.

In the early 1900s, many Western artists rejected traditional styles that tried to reproduce the real world. For example, Vasily Kandinsky's work was called **abstract.** It was composed only of lines, colors, and shapes—sometimes with no visually recognizable subject. **Dada** artists rejected tradition and believed that there was no sense or truth in the world. Another movement, **surrealism,** tried to portray the workings of the unconscious mind. In architecture, Bauhaus buildings based on form and function featured glass, steel, and concrete, but little ornamentation.

Review Questions

1. What was the impact of new technologies in the 1920s?

____

____

2. How did Western artists reject traditional styles?

____

____

Name________________________ Class____________________ Date________

CHAPTER 16 SECTION 2

Note Taking Study Guide

THE WESTERN DEMOCRACIES STUMBLE

Focus Question: What political and economic challenges did the leading democracies face in the 1920s and 1930s?

A. *As you read "Politics in the Postwar World," Postwar Foreign Policy," and "Postwar Economics," complete the chart below to identify the main ideas under each heading.*

Postwar Issues			
Country	**Politics**	**Foreign Policy**	**Economics**

B. *As you read "The Great Depression," and "The Democracies React to the Depression," complete the chart below to identify the main ideas on the causes, effects, and reactions related to the Great Depression.*

The Great Depression		
Causes	**Effects**	**Reactions**
•	•	•
•	•	•
•	•	•
•		
•		

Name____________________ Class__________ Date______

CHAPTER 16 SECTION 2

Section Summary

THE WESTERN DEMOCRACIES STUMBLE

READING CHECK

How did Britain and France pay back their war loans to the United States?

____

____

____

VOCABULARY STRATEGY

What does the word *affluent* mean in the underlined sentence? *Affluent* comes from a Latin word that means "to flow." Ask yourself what people have a lot of if they are *affluent*. Use these clues to help you figure out the meaning of *affluent*.

READING SKILL

Identify Main Ideas Write a sentence that summarizes the main idea of this Summary.

____

____

____

In 1919, after World War I, Britain, France, and the United States appeared powerful. However, postwar Europe faced grave problems. The most pressing issues were finding jobs for veterans and rebuilding war-ravaged lands. These problems made radical ideas more popular. Britain had to deal with growing socialism and the "Irish question." Fear of radicals set off a "Red Scare" in the United States.

The three democracies also faced international issues. Concern about a strong Germany led France to build the **Maginot Line** and insist on strict enforcement of the Versailles treaty. Many nations signed the **Kellogg-Briand Pact** promising to "renounce war as an instrument of national policy." In this optimistic spirit, the great powers pursued **disarmament.** Unfortunately, neither the Kellogg-Briand Pact nor the League of Nations had the power to stop aggression. Ambitious dictators in Europe noted this weakness.

The war affected economies all over the world. Both Britain and France owed huge war debts to the United States and relied on reparation payments from Germany to pay their loans. Britain was deeply in debt, with high unemployment and low wages. In 1926, a **general strike** lasted nine days and involved three million workers. On the other hand, the French economy recovered fairly quickly, and the United States emerged as the world's top economic power. <u>In the affluent 1920s, middle-class Americans enjoyed the benefits of capitalism, buying cars, radios, and refrigerators.</u>

However, better technologies allowed factories to make more products faster, leading to **overproduction** in the United States. Factories then cut back, and many workers lost their jobs. A crisis in **finance** led the **Federal Reserve** to raise interest rates. This made people even more nervous about the economy. In the autumn of 1929, financial panic set in. Stock prices crashed. The United States economy entered the **Great Depression,** which soon spread around the world.

Governments searched for solutions. In the United States, President **Franklin D. Roosevelt** introduced the programs of the **New Deal.** Although the New Deal failed to end the Depression, it did ease much suffering. However, as the Depression wore on, it created fertile ground for extremists.

Review Questions

1. After the war, what international agreement was intended to ensure peace?

____

____

2. What economic problems did Britain face after the war?

____

____

Name________________________ Class__________________ Date________

CHAPTER 16 SECTION 3

Note Taking Study Guide

FASCISM IN ITALY

Focus Question: How and why did fascism rise in Italy?

A. *As you read "Mussolini's Rise to Power" and Mussolini's Rule," complete the flowchart below as you identify the main ideas under each heading.*

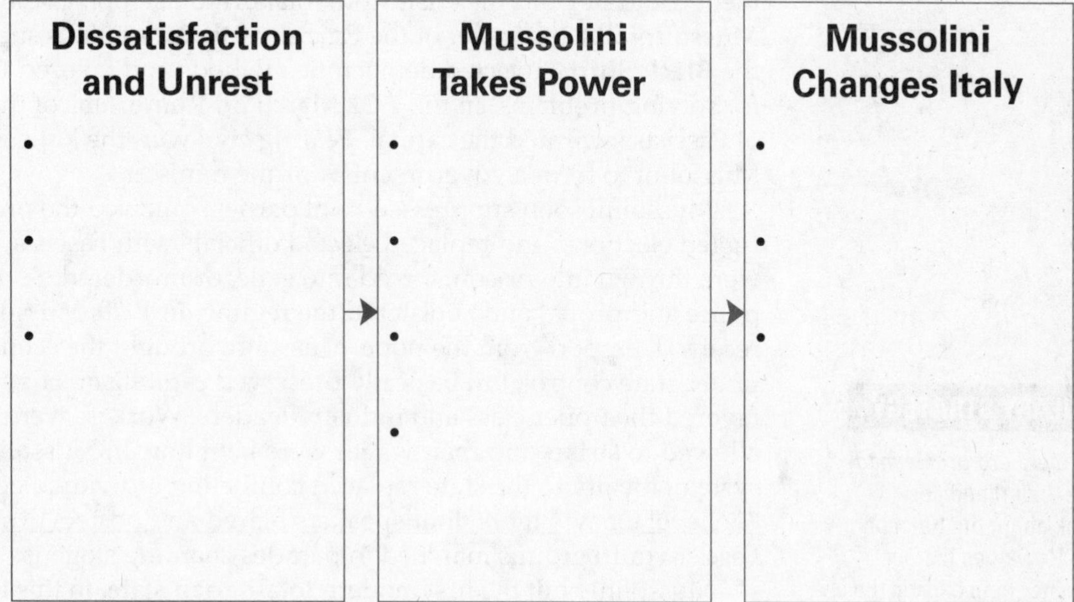

B. *As you read "The Nature of Fascism," use the table below to identify the main ideas for each heading.*

What Is Fascism?	
Values	
Characteristics	
Differences from Communism	
Similarities to Communism	

Name______________________ Class__________ Date______

CHAPTER 16 SECTION 3

Section Summary

FASCISM IN ITALY

READING CHECK

Who were the Black Shirts?

____

____

____

VOCABULARY STRATEGY

What does the word *proclaimed* mean in the underlined sentence? Think about the function of a poster. How does the purpose of a poster help explain the meaning of *proclaimed*?

READING SKILL

Identify Main Ideas How did Mussolini's Fascists take over Italy?

____

____

____

After World War I, Italian nationalists were outraged when Italy received just some of the territories promised by the Allies. Chaos ensued as peasants seized land, workers went on strike, veterans faced unemployment, trade declined, and taxes rose. The government could not end the crisis. Into this turmoil stepped **Benito Mussolini,** the organizer of the Fascist party. Mussolini's supporters, the **Black Shirts,** rejected democratic methods and favored violence for solving problems. In the 1922 **March on Rome,** tens of thousands of Fascists swarmed the capital. Fearing civil war, the king asked Mussolini to form a government as prime minister.

Mussolini soon suppressed rival parties, muzzled the press, rigged elections, and replaced elected officials with Fascists. Critics were thrown into prison, forced into exile, or murdered. Secret police and propaganda bolstered the regime. In 1929, Mussolini also received support from the pope. Mussolini brought the economy under state control, but basically preserved capitalism. His system favored the upper class and industry leaders. Workers were not allowed to strike, and their wages were kept low. In Mussolini's new system, loyalty to the state replaced conflicting individual goals. "Believe! Obey! Fight!" loudspeakers blared and posters proclaimed. Fascist youth groups marched in parades chanting slogans.

Mussolini built the first modern **totalitarian state.** In this form of government, a one-party dictatorship attempts to control every aspect of the lives of its citizens. Today, we usually use the term **fascism** to describe the underlying ideology of any centralized, authoritarian governmental system that is not communist. Fascism is rooted in extreme nationalism. Fascists believe in action, violence, discipline, and blind loyalty to the state. They praise warfare. They are antidemocratic, rejecting equality and liberty. Fascists oppose communists on important issues. Communists favor international action and the creation of a classless society. Fascists are nationalists who support a society with defined classes. Both base their power on blind devotion to a leader or the state. Both flourish during economic hard times.

Fascism appealed to Italians because it restored national pride, provided stability, and ended the political feuding that had paralyzed democracy in Italy.

Review Questions

1. What was the result of the March on Rome?

____

____

2. How are communism and fascism similar?

____

____

Name______________________ Class________________ Date________

CHAPTER 16 SECTION 4

Note Taking Study Guide

THE SOVIET UNION UNDER STALIN

Focus Question: How did Stalin transform the Soviet Union into a totalitarian state?

As you read this section in your textbook, complete the chart below by identifying the main ideas about the Soviet Union under Stalin for each heading.

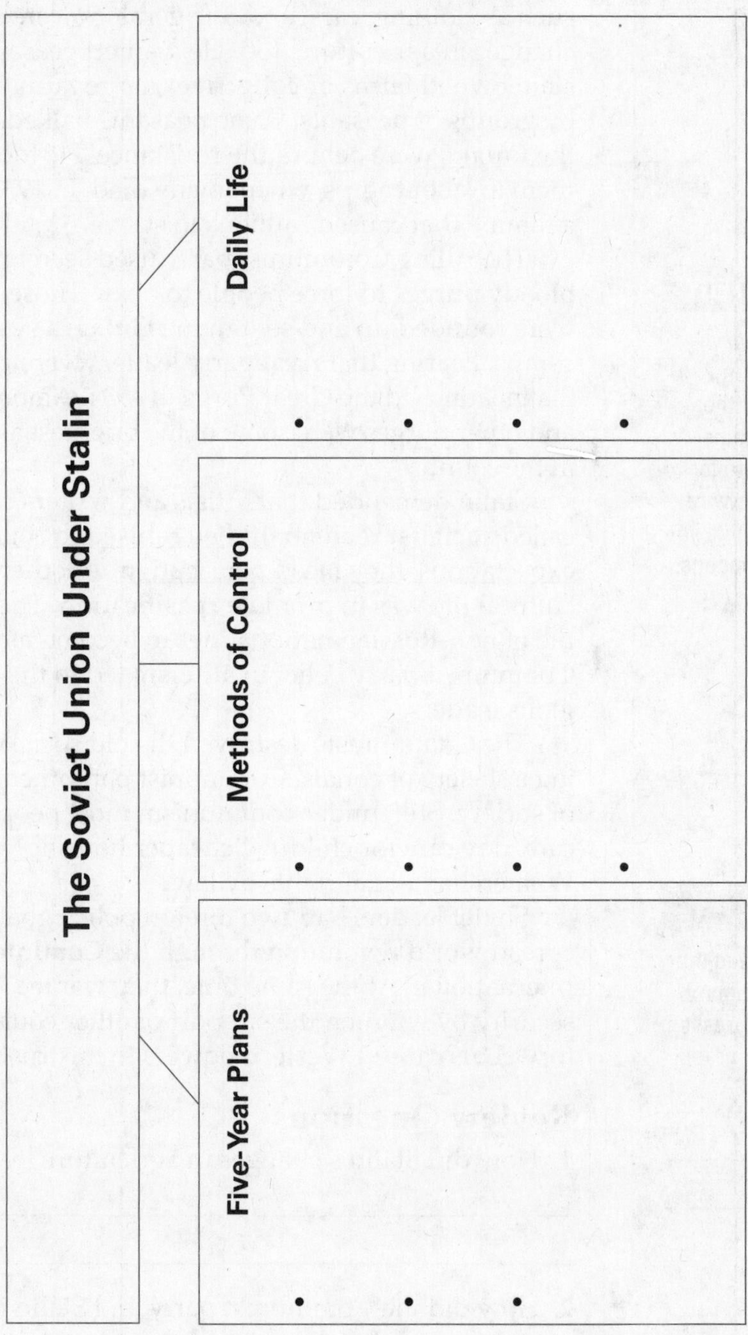

Name____________________ Class__________ Date______

CHAPTER 16 SECTION 4

Section Summary

THE SOVIET UNION UNDER STALIN

Under Joseph Stalin, the Soviet Union grew into a totalitarian state, controlling all aspects of life, including agriculture, culture, art, and religion. The state also developed a **command economy,** in which it made all economic decisions. Stalin's five-year plans set high production goals. Despite great progress in some sectors, products such as clothing, cars, and refrigerators were scarce. Stalin forced changes in agriculture, too. He wanted peasants to farm on either state-owned farms or **collectives,** large farms owned and operated by groups of peasants. Some peasants balked. Stalin believed that the **kulaks** were behind the resistance. He took their land and sent them to labor camps, where many died. In 1932, Stalin's policies led to a famine that caused millions to starve.

The ruling Communist party used secret police, torture, and bloody purges to force people to obey. Those who opposed Stalin were rounded up and sent to the **Gulag,** a system of brutal labor camps. Fearing that rival party leaders were plotting against him, Stalin launched the Great Purge in 1934. Among the victims of this and other purges were some of the brightest and most talented people in the country.

Stalin demanded that artists and writers create works in a style called **socialist realism.** <u>If they refused to conform to government expectations, they faced persecution.</u> Another way Stalin controlled cultural life was to promote **russification.** The goal was to force people of non-Russian nationalities to become more Russian. The official Communist party belief in **atheism** led to the cruel treatment of religious leaders.

The Communists destroyed the old social order. Instead of creating a society of equals, Communist party members became the heads of society. Still, under communism most people enjoyed free medical care, day care for children, cheaper housing, and public recreation. Women had equal rights by law.

Soviet leaders had two foreign policy goals. They hoped to spread world revolution through the **Comintern,** or Communist International. At the same time, they wanted to ensure their nation's security by winning the support of other countries. These contradictory goals caused Western powers to mistrust the Soviet Union.

Review Questions

1. How did Stalin's changes in agriculture lead to a famine?

____

____

2. How did the Communist party and Stalin force people to obey?

____

____

READING CHECK

What is a command economy?

____

____

____

VOCABULARY STRATEGY

What does the word *conform* mean in the underlined sentence? Circle the letter of the word set below that contains words you could substitute for *to conform.* Use the correct word set and context clues to help you figure out what *conform* means.

a. to go along with

b. to disagree with

READING SKILL

Identify Main Ideas Reread the last paragraph in the Summary. Write a sentence that expresses the main idea of that paragraph.

____

____

____

Name________________________ Class____________________ Date________

CHAPTER 16 SECTION 5

Note Taking Study Guide

HITLER AND THE RISE OF NAZI GERMANY

Focus Question: How did Hitler and the Nazi Party establish and maintain a totalitarian government in Germany?

As you read this section in your textbook, complete the flowchart below to identify the main ideas about Hitler and the rise of Nazi Germany for each heading.

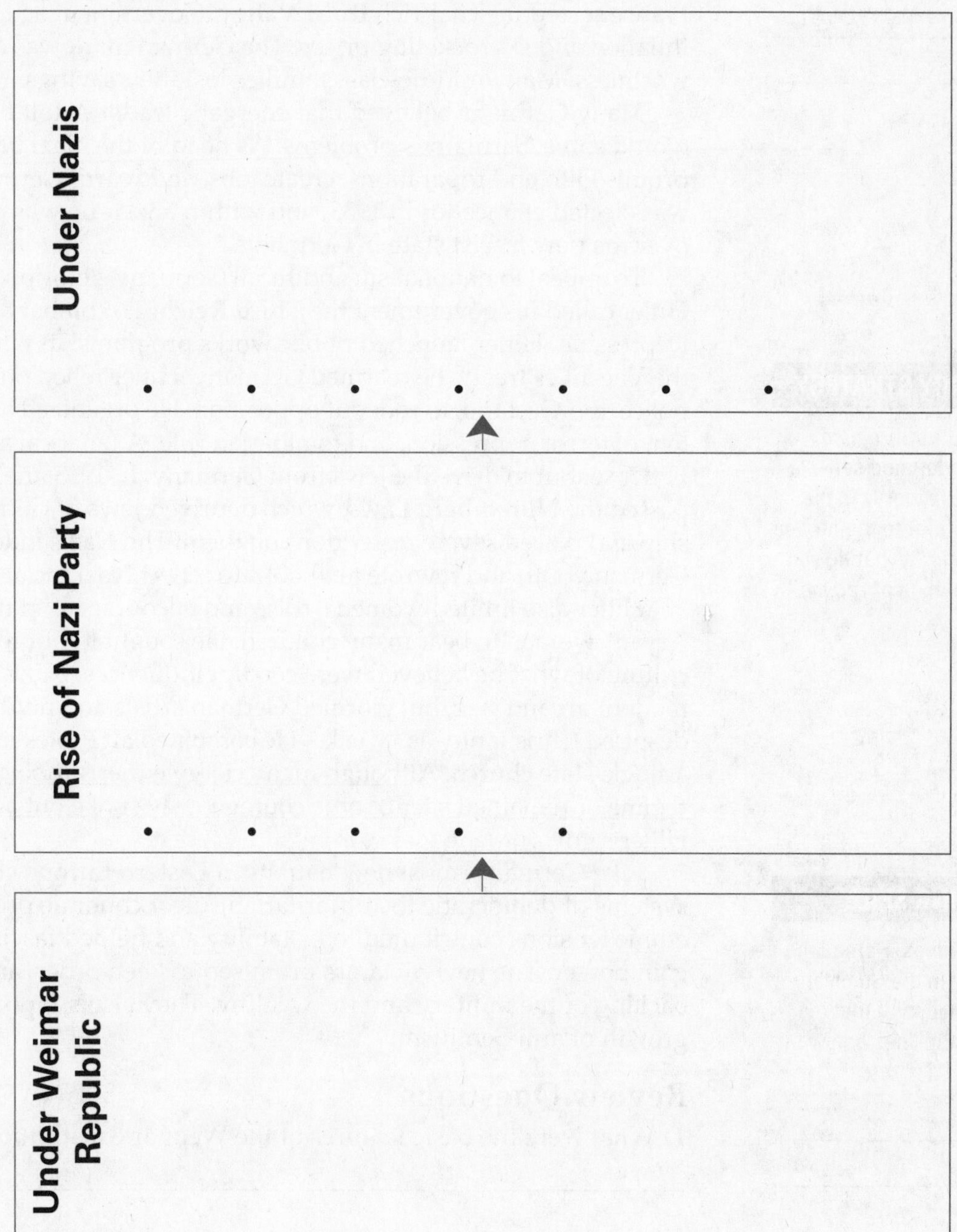

Name________________________ Class____________ Date______

CHAPTER 16 SECTION 5

Section Summary

HITLER AND THE RISE OF NAZI GERMANY

After World War I, German leaders set up a democratic government known as the Weimar Republic. The Weimar constitution established a parliamentary system led by a **chancellor.** It gave women the right to vote and included a bill of rights. However, the new republic faced severe problems. When Germany could not make its war reparations France seized the coal-rich **Ruhr Valley.** Government actions led to inflation and skyrocketing prices. The German mark was almost worthless. Many middle-class families lost their savings.

Many Germans believed that energetic leader Adolf Hitler would solve Germany's problems. As head of the Nazi party, Hitler promised to end reparations, create jobs, and rearm Germany. He was elected chancellor in 1933, and within a year he was dictator over the new fascist state in Germany.

To appeal to nationalism and recall Germany's glorious past, Hitler called his government the **Third Reich.** To combat the Depression, Hitler launched public works programs. In violation of the Versailles treaty, he rearmed Germany. Hitler relied on his secret police, the **Gestapo,** to root out opposition. He organized a brutal system of terror, repression, and totalitarian rule. A fanatical anti-Semite, Hitler set out to drive the Jews from Germany. In 1935, the Nazis passed the **Nuremberg Laws,** which deprived Jews of German citizenship and placed severe restrictions on them. The Nazis indoctrinated German youth and rewrote textbooks to reflect Nazi racial views.

Hitler also limited women's roles and encouraged "pure-blooded Aryan" women to bear many children. He sought to purge German culture of what he believed were corrupt influences. Nazis denounced modern art and jazz, but glorified German artists and myths. Hitler despised Christianity as "weak." He combined all Protestant sects into a single state church. Although many clergy either supported the new regime or remained silent, some courageously spoke out against Hitler's government.

Like Germany, most new nations in Eastern Europe slid from systems of democratic to authoritarian rule. Economic problems and ethnic tensions contributed to instability and helped fascist rulers to gain power. The new dictators promised to keep order, and won the backing of the military and the wealthy. They also supported the growth of anti-Semitism.

Review Questions

1. What were the basic features of the Weimar constitution?

____

____

2. Why did many Germans support Hitler?

____

____

READING CHECK

What was the purpose of the Nuremberg Laws?

____

____

____

VOCABULARY STRATEGY

What does the word *regime* mean in the underlined sentence? Circle the words in the sentence that refer to the phrase "the new *regime*." What do you think is the meaning of *regime?*

READING SKILL

Identify Main Ideas Reread the last paragraph in the Summary. Write the main idea of that paragraph on the lines below.

____

____

____

Name________________ Class________________ Date________

CHAPTER 17 SECTION 1

Note Taking Study Guide

FROM APPEASEMENT TO WAR

Focus Question: What events unfolded between Chamberlain's declaration of "peace in our time" and the outbreak of a world war?

A. *As you read "Aggression Goes Unchecked" and "Spain Collapses into Civil War," complete the chart below to record the sequence of events that led to the outbreak of World War II.*

Acts of Aggression	
Japan	• ________________ • ________________
Italy	• ________________
Germany	• ________________ • ________________
Spain	•

B. *As you read "German Aggression Continues" and "Europe Plunges Toward War," complete the timetable below to recognize the sequence of German aggression.*

German Aggression	
March 1938	
September 1938	
March 1939	
September 1939	

Name________________________ Class___________ Date______

CHAPTER 17 SECTION 1

Section Summary

FROM APPEASEMENT TO WAR

READING CHECK

Who were the members of the Axis powers?

____

____

____

VOCABULARY STRATEGY

What does the word *sanctions* mean in the underlined sentence? Look at the words, phrases, and sentences surrounding the word. Use the context clues you find to help you figure out the meaning of *sanctions.*

READING SKILL

Recognize Sequence What happened in Spain before Francisco Franco started a civil war there?

____

____

____

Throughout the 1930s, dictators took aggressive action. Yet, they met only verbal protests and pleas for peace from Western powers. For example, when the League of Nations condemned Japan's invasion of Manchuria in 1931, Japan simply withdrew from the League. A few years later, Japanese armies invaded China, starting the Second Sino-Japanese War. Meanwhile, Mussolini invaded Ethiopia in 1935. The League of Nations voted sanctions against Italy, but the League had no power to enforce its punishment of Mussolini. Hitler, too, defied the Western democracies by building up the German military and sending troops into the "demilitarized" Rhineland. This went against the Treaty of Versailles. The Western democracies denounced Hitler but adopted a policy of **appeasement.** Appeasement developed for a number of reasons, including widespread **pacifism**. The United States responded with a series of **Neutrality Acts.** The goal was to avoid involvement in a war, rather than to prevent one. While the Western democracies sought to avoid war, Germany, Italy, and Japan formed an alliance. It became known as the **Axis powers.**

In Spain, a new, more liberal government passed reforms that upset conservatives. General **Francisco Franco,** who was opposed to the new government, started a civil war. Hitler and Mussolini supported Franco, their fellow fascist. The Soviet Union sent troops to support the anti-Fascists, or Loyalists. The governments of Britain, France, and the United States remained neutral, although individuals from these countries fought with the Loyalists. By 1939, Franco had triumphed.

German aggression continued. In 1938, Hitler forced the **Anschluss,** or union with Austria. Next, Hitler set his sights on the **Sudentenland.** This was a part of Czechoslovakia where three million Germans lived. At the Munich Conference, which was held to discuss the situation, British and French leaders chose appeasement and allowed Hitler to annex the territory.

In March 1939, Hitler took over the rest of Czechoslovakia. Months later, Hitler and Stalin signed the **Nazi-Soviet Pact.** They agreed not to fight if the other went to war. This paved the way for Germany's invasion of Poland in September of 1939, which set off World War II.

Review Questions

1. How did the United States respond to the aggressive action of dictators in the 1930s?

____

____

2. What was the result of the Munich Conference?

____

____

Name________________________ Class____________________ Date__________

CHAPTER 17 SECTION 2

Note Taking Study Guide

THE AXIS ADVANCES

Focus Question: Which regions were attacked and occupied by the Axis powers, and what was life like under their occupation?

A. *As you read "The Axis Attacks," "Germany Invades the Soviet Union," and "Japan Attacks the United States," use the chart below to record the sequence of events.*

B. *As you read "Life Under Nazi and Japanese Occupation," use the concept web to identify supporting details about the occupations.*

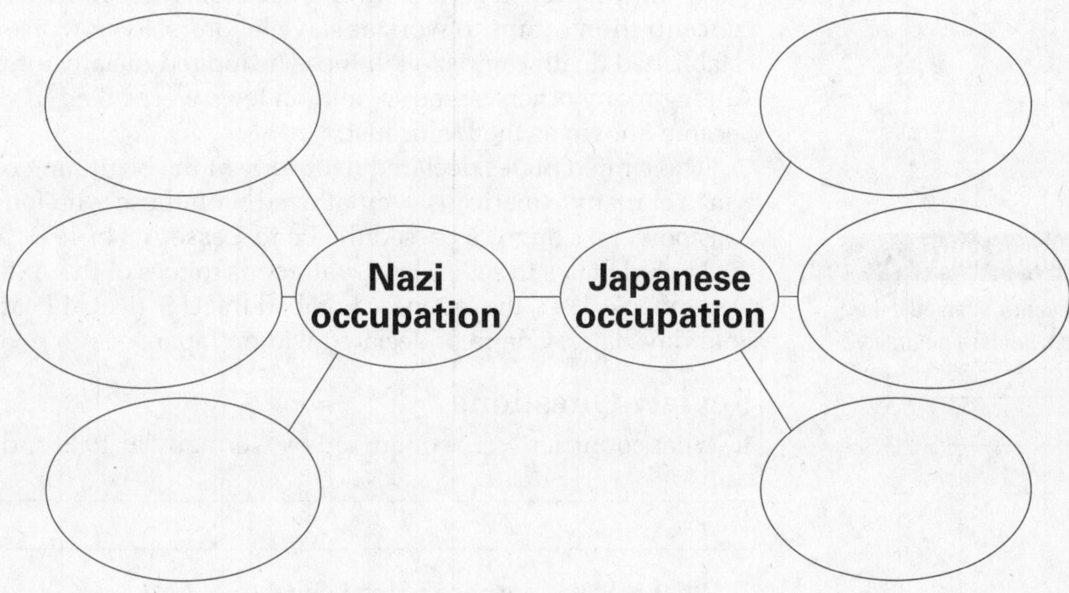

Name________________________ Class____________ Date______

CHAPTER 17 SECTION 2

Section Summary

THE AXIS ADVANCES

READING CHECK

What was the name of the German government in southern France?

____

____

____

In September 1939, Nazi forces launched a **blitzkrieg** against Poland. First the **Luftwaffe,** the German air force, bombed. Then, tanks and troops pushed their way in. At the same time, Stalin invaded from the east, grabbing land. Within a month, Poland ceased to exist.

Then, in early 1940, Hitler conquered Norway, Denmark, the Netherlands, and Belgium. By May, German forces had bypassed France's Maginot Line. British forces that had been sent to help the French were trapped. In a desperate scheme, the British rescued their troops from **Dunkirk.** However, in June, the French were forced to surrender. Germany occupied northern France and set up a puppet state, the **Vichy** government, in the south.

The British, led by Winston Churchill, remained defiant against Hitler. In response, Hitler launched bombing raids over British cities that lasted from September 1940 until June 1941. Despite this blitz, Hitler was not able to take Britain. Meanwhile, Hitler sent one of his best commanders, **General Erwin Rommel,** to North Africa. Rommel had a string of successes there. In the Balkans, German and Italian forces added Greece and Yugoslavia to the growing Axis territory. At the same time, the Japanese were occupying lands in Asia and the Pacific.

VOCABULARY STRATEGY

Find the word *nullified* in the underlined sentence. In math class you might have learned that there is nothing, or zero, in the null set. Use this clue about related words to help you figure out the meaning of *nullified.*

<u>In June 1941, Hitler nullified the Nazi-Soviet Pact by invading the Soviet Union.</u> Stalin was unprepared, and the Soviet army suffered great losses. The Germans advanced toward Moscow and Leningrad. During a lengthy siege of Leningrad, more than a million Russians died. The severe Russian winter finally slowed the German army.

As they marched across Europe, the Nazis sent millions to **concentration camps** to work as slave laborers. Even worse, Hitler established death camps to kill those he judged racially inferior. Among many others, some six million Jews were killed in what became known as the **Holocaust.**

READING SKILL

Sequence Events When did the United States declare neutrality?

____

____

____

The United States declared neutrality at the beginning of the war. Yet many Americans sympathized with those who fought the Axis powers. Congress passed the **Lend-Lease Act** of 1941, allowing the United States to sell or lend war goods to foes of the Axis. On December 7, 1941, the Japanese bombed the U.S. fleet at Pearl Harbor. Four days later, Congress declared war on Japan.

Review Questions

1. What countries were conquered by Germany in 1939 and 1940?

____

____

2. What was the purpose of the Lend-Lease Act?

____

____

Name______________________ Class______________________ Date__________

CHAPTER 17 SECTION 3

Note Taking Study Guide

THE ALLIES TURN THE TIDE

Focus Question: How did the Allies begin to push back the Axis powers?

As you read this section in your textbook, complete the chart below to record the sequence of events that turned the tide of the war in favor of the Allies.

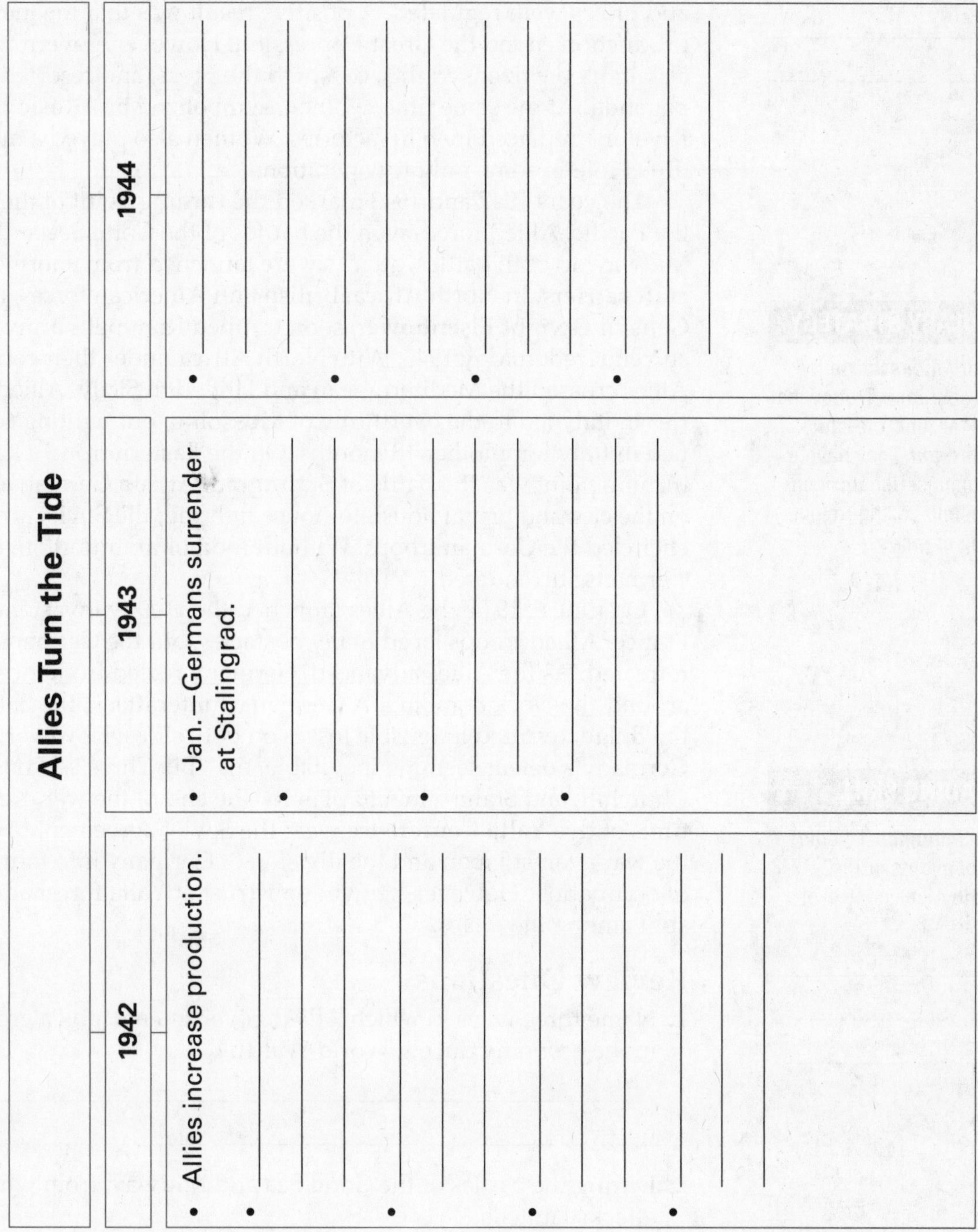

Name________________________ Class____________ Date______

CHAPTER 17 SECTION 3

Section Summary

THE ALLIES TURN THE TIDE

READING CHECK

Who were the "Big Three"?

____

____

____

VOCABULARY STRATEGY

Find the word *incessant* in the underlined sentence. Notice that the phrase "around-the-clock" follows *incessant*. They have similar meanings. Use this context clue to help you figure out the meaning of *incessant*.

READING SKILL

Recognize Sequence List the sequence of events in 1942–1943 that gave the Allies control of North Africa.

____

____

____

To defeat the Axis powers in World War II, the Allies devoted all their resources to the war effort. Governments took a greater role in the economy. For example, governments ordered factories to make tanks instead of cars. Consumer goods were rationed, and wages and prices were regulated. A positive result was that the increase in production ended the Great Depression. However, governments also limited citizens' rights, censored the press, and resorted to propaganda. At the same time, women, symbolized by **"Rosie the Riveter,"** replaced men in factories. Women also played a more direct role in some military operations.

The years 1942 and 1943 marked the turning point of the war. In the Pacific, Allied forces won the battles of the Coral Sea and Midway. In both battles, attacks were launched from enormous **aircraft carriers.** In North Africa, British and American forces, led by General **Dwight Eisenhower,** soon trapped Rommel's army, and he surrendered in May 1943. With North Africa under their control, the Allies crossed the Mediterranean and landed in Sicily. Allied victories in Italy led to the overthrow of Mussolini, but fighting continued in Italy for another 18 months. On the Eastern front, a key turning point was the Battle of **Stalingrad.** After a German advance on the city and brutal house-to-house fighting, the Soviet army encircled the German troops. Without food or ammunition, the Germans surrendered.

On June 6, 1944, the Allies launched the **D-Day** invasion of France. Allied troops faced many obstacles, but the Germans finally retreated. <u>As the Allies advanced, Germany reeled from incessant, around-the-clock bombing.</u> A German counterattack, the Battle of the Bulge, resulted in terrible losses on both sides. However, with Germany's defeat seeming inevitable, the "Big Three"—Roosevelt, Churchill, and Stalin—met to plan for the end of the war. Key features of this **Yalta Conference** were the Soviet agreement to enter the war against Japan and the division of Germany into four zones of occupation. However, growing mistrust at Yalta foreshadowed a split among the Allies.

Review Questions

1. Name three ways in which Allied governments took a greater role in the economy during World War II.

____

____

2. During the battles of the Coral Sea and Midway, from where were attacks launched?

____

____

Name________________________ Class____________________ Date________

CHAPTER 17 SECTION 4

Note Taking Study Guide

VICTORY IN EUROPE AND THE PACIFIC

Focus Question: How did the Allies finally defeat the Axis powers?

As you read this section in your textbook, complete the timeline below to sequence the events that led to the defeat of the Axis powers.

Name________________________ Class____________ Date______

CHAPTER 17 SECTION 4

Section Summary

VICTORY IN EUROPE AND THE PACIFIC

In Europe, World War II officially ended on May 8, 1945, or **V-E Day.** The Allies were able to defeat the Axis powers for many reasons. Because of their location, the Axis powers had to fight on several fronts at the same time. Hitler also made some poor military decisions. For example, he underestimated the Soviet Union's ability to fight. The huge productive capacity of the United States was another factor. At the same time, Allied bombing hindered German production and caused oil to become scarce. This nearly grounded the Luftwaffe.

Although Germany was defeated, the Allies still had to defeat the Japanese in the Pacific. By May 1942, the Japanese had gained control of the Philippines, killing thousands during the **Bataan Death March.** However, after the battles of Midway and the Coral Sea, the United States took the offensive. General **Douglas MacArthur** began an **"island-hopping"** campaign to recapture islands from the Japanese. The captured islands served as stepping-stones to the next objective—Japan. The Americans gradually moved north and were able to blockade Japan. Bombers pounded Japanese cities and industries. At the same time, the British pushed Japanese forces back into the jungles of Burma and Malaya.

In early 1945, bloody battles on Iwo Jima and Okinawa showed that the Japanese would fight to the death rather than surrender. Some young Japanese became **kamikaze** pilots who flew their planes purposefully into U.S. ships. While Allied military leaders planned to invade, scientists offered another way to end the war. They had conducted research, code-named the **Manhattan Project,** that led to the building of an atomic bomb for the United States. The new U.S. president, Harry Truman, decided that dropping the bomb would save American lives. The Allies first issued a warning to the Japanese to surrender or face "utter and complete destruction," but the warning was ignored. On August 6, 1945, a U.S. plane dropped an atomic bomb on the city of **Hiroshima,** instantly killing more than 70,000 people. Many more died from radiation sickness. When the Japanese did not surrender, another bomb was dropped on **Nagasaki** on August 9. The next day, Japan finally surrendered, ending World War II.

READING CHECK

What was the "island-hopping" campaign?

____

____

____

VOCABULARY STRATEGY

What does the word *objective* mean in the underlined sentence? Say the sentence aloud and omit *objective.* Think about other words that might complete the sentence. Use this strategy to help you figure out the meaning of *objective.*

READING SKILL

Recognize Sequence Create a timeline of the events that took place in Japan from August 6 to August 10, 1945.

____

____

____

Review Questions

1. What were two reasons why the Allies were able to defeat the Axis powers?

____

____

2. Why did Truman decide to drop the atomic bomb on Japan?

____

____

Name______________________ Class__________________ Date________

CHAPTER 17 SECTION 5

Note Taking Study Guide

THE END OF WORLD WAR II

Focus Question: What issues arose in the aftermath of World War II and how did new tensions develop?

As you read this section in your textbook, sequence the events following World War II by completing the outline below.

I. The War's Aftermath
- **A.** Devastation
  - **1.** As many as 50 million are dead.
  - **2.** ______________________
- **B.** ______________________
  - **1.** ______________________
  - **2.** ______________________
  - **3.** ______________________
- **C.** ______________________
  - **1.** ______________________
  - **2.** ______________________

II. ______________________
- **A.** ______________________
  - **1.** ______________________
- **B.** ______________________
  - **1.** ______________________
  - **2.** ______________________
- **C.** ______________________
  - **1.** ______________________
  - **2.** ______________________

III. ______________________
- **A.** ______________________
  - **1.** ______________________
  - **2.** ______________________
- **B.** ______________________
  - **1.** ______________________
  - **2.** ______________________

(Outline continues on the next page.)

Name______________________ Class__________________ Date________

CHAPTER 17 SECTION 5

Note Taking Study Guide

THE END OF WORLD WAR II

(Continued from page 187)

3. ______________________________

IV. ______________________________

A. ______________________________

1. ______________________________
2. ______________________________
3. ______________________________

B. ______________________________

1. ______________________________
2. ______________________________
3. ______________________________

C. ______________________________

1. ______________________________
2. ______________________________
3. ______________________________
4. ______________________________

D. ______________________________

1. ______________________________
2. ______________________________
3. ______________________________

E. ______________________________

1. ______________________________
2. ______________________________

F. ______________________________

1. ______________________________
2. ______________________________

Name________________________ Class___________ Date______

CHAPTER 17 SECTION 5

Section Summary

THE END OF WORLD WAR II

While the Allies enjoyed their victory, the huge costs of World War II began to emerge. As many as 50 million people had been killed. The Allies also learned the full extent of the horrors of the Holocaust. War crimes trials, such as those at **Nuremberg** in Germany, held leaders accountable for their wartime actions. To ensure tolerance and peace, the Western Allies set up democratic governments in Japan and Germany.

In 1945, delegates from 50 nations convened to form the **United Nations.** Under the UN Charter, each member nation has one vote in the General Assembly. A smaller Security Council has greater power. It has five permanent members: the United States, the Soviet Union (today Russia), Britain, France, and China. Each has the right to veto any council decision. UN agencies have tackled many world problems, from disease to helping refugees.

However, conflicting ideologies soon led to a **Cold War.** This refers to the state of tension and hostility between the United States and the Soviet Union from 1946 to 1990. Soviet leader Stalin wanted to spread communism into Eastern Europe. He also wanted to create a buffer zone of friendly countries as a defense against Germany. By 1948, pro-Soviet communist governments were in place throughout Eastern Europe.

When Stalin began to threaten Greece and Turkey, the United States outlined a policy called the **Truman Doctrine.** This policy meant that the United States would resist the spread of communism throughout the world. To strengthen democracies in Europe, the United States offered a massive aid package, called the **Marshall Plan.** Western attempts to rebuild Germany triggered a crisis over the city of Berlin. The Soviets controlled East Germany, which surrounded Berlin. To force the Western Allies out of Berlin, the Soviets blockaded West Berlin, but a yearlong airlift forced them to end the blockade.

However, tensions continued to mount. In 1949, the United States and nine other nations formed a new military alliance called the **North Atlantic Treaty Organization (NATO).** The Soviets responded by forming the **Warsaw Pact,** which included the Soviet Union and seven Eastern European nations.

Review Questions

1. What was the purpose of the post-World War II war crimes trials?

____

____

2. Why did the United States offer aid under the Marshall Plan to European countries?

____

____

READING CHECK

What was the Cold War?

____

____

____

VOCABULARY STRATEGY

What does the word *convened* mean in the underlined sentence? The word *convene* comes from the Latin *convenire.* In Latin, *con-* means "together" and *venire* means "to come." Use this word-origins clue to help you figure out the meaning of *convened.*

READING SKILL

Recognize Sequence List the sequence of events that led to the Berlin airlift.

____

____

____

Name________________________ Class__________________ Date________

CHAPTER 18 SECTION 1

Note Taking Study Guide

THE COLD WAR UNFOLDS

Focus Question: What were the military and political consequences of the Cold War in the Soviet Union, Europe, and the United States?

As you read this section in your textbook, complete the following chart to summarize the consequences of the Cold War in the Soviet Union, Europe, and the United States.

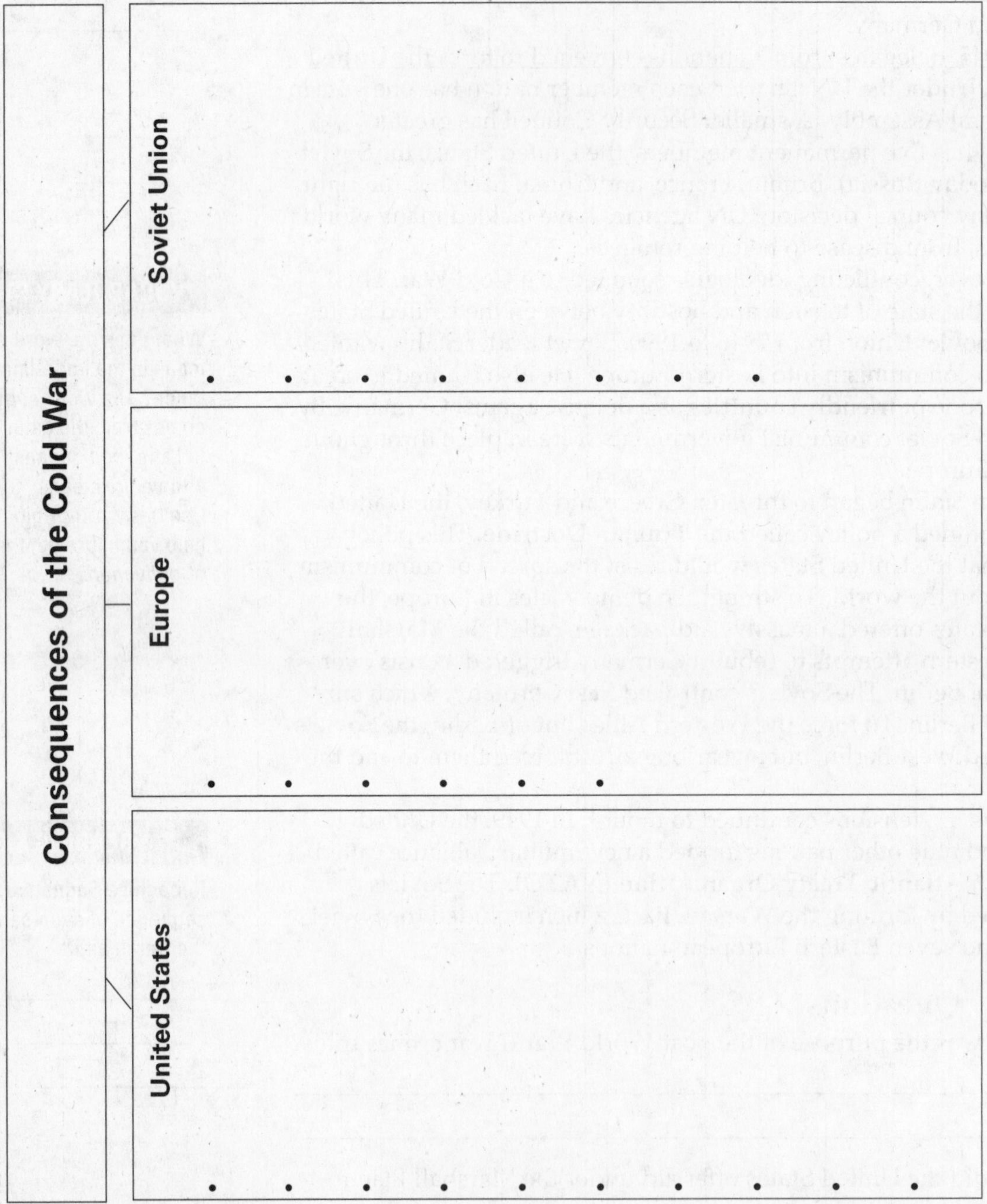

Name________________________ Class___________ Date______

CHAPTER 18 SECTION 1

Section Summary

THE COLD WAR UNFOLDS

After World War II, the United States and the Soviet Union emerged as **superpowers.** They each created military alliances made up of nations they protected or occupied. The United States helped form the North Atlantic Treaty Organization (NATO), which comprised Western European allies. The Soviet Union signed the Warsaw Pact with Eastern European countries. The line between the democratic West and communist East was called the Iron Curtain. Many revolts challenging Soviet domination were extinguished with military force.

The superpowers also engaged in a weapons race—both developed nuclear weapons. To reduce the threat of war, the two sides held several disarmament talks. One agreement was intended to limit the use of **anti-ballistic missiles (ABMs).** These weapons were designed to shoot down missiles launched by hostile nations. The ABMs were considered a threat because they could give one side more protection, which might encourage it to attack. Then during the 1980s, President **Ronald Reagan** proposed a missile defense program called "Star Wars." Other agreements limited the number of nuclear weapons that nations could maintain, which eased Cold War tensions. This period was called the era of **détente.** It ended, however, when the Soviet Union invaded Afghanistan in 1979.

During the 1950s, **Fidel Castro** led a revolution in Cuba and became its leader. To bring down Castro's communist regime, U.S. President **John F. Kennedy** supported an invasion of Cuba, but the attempt failed. One year later, the Soviets sent nuclear missiles to Cuba. Many feared a nuclear war. After the United States blockaded Cuba, Soviet leader **Nikita Khrushchev** agreed to remove the missiles.

The Soviets wanted to spread communist **ideology** around the globe. When Khrushchev came to power, he eased censorship and increased tolerance. However, repression returned under **Leonid Brezhnev.** American leaders followed a policy of **containment.** This was a strategy of keeping communism from spreading to other nations. In addition, a "red scare" in the United States resulted in Senator Joseph McCarthy leading an internal hunt for communists in the government and military. The House Un-American Activities Committee (HUAC) also sought out communist sympathizers.

Review Questions

1. What did the two superpowers do to reduce the threat of war during the Cold War?

____

____

2. What ended the period of détente between the United States and the Soviet Union?

____

____

READING CHECK

Who were the two superpowers during the Cold War?

____

____

____

VOCABULARY STRATEGY

What does the word *comprised* mean in the underlined sentence? What clues can you find in the surrounding words, phrases, or sentences? Use these context clues to help you figure out what *comprised* means.

READING SKILL

Summarize What was the United States policy known as containment?

____

____

____

Name____________ Class____________ Date________

CHAPTER 18 SECTION 2

Note Taking Study Guide

THE INDUSTRIALIZED DEMOCRACIES

Focus Question: How did the United States, Western Europe, and Japan achieve economic prosperity and strengthen democracy during the Cold War years?

As you read this section in your textbook, use the chart below to categorize economic and political changes in the industrialized democracies.

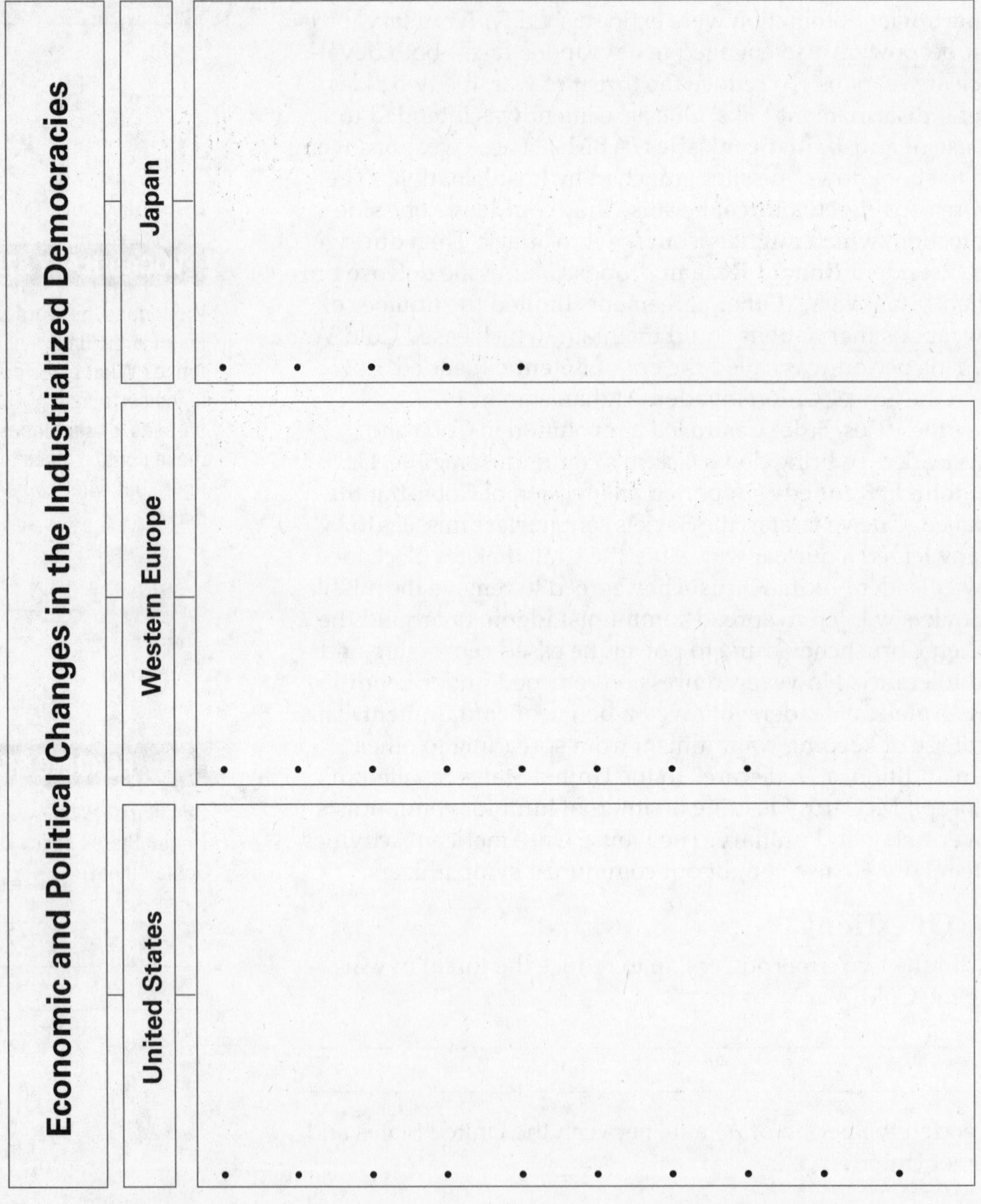

Name________________________ Class___________ Date______

CHAPTER 18 SECTION 2

Section Summary

THE INDUSTRIALIZED DEMOCRACIES

During the postwar period, U.S. businesses expanded into the global marketplace. Other nations needed goods and services to rebuild. This led to a period of economic success that changed life in the United States. During the 1950s and 1960s, **recessions** were brief and mild. As Americans prospered, they left the cities to live in the suburbs. This trend is called **suburbanization.** Also, job opportunities in the Sunbelt attracted many people to that region. By the 1970s, however, a political crisis in the Middle East made Americans aware of their dependence on imported oil. The price of oil and gas rose substantially, which meant that people had less money to buy other products. The decades of prosperity ended in 1974 with a serious recession.

During the period of prosperity, African Americans and other minorities faced **segregation** in housing and education. They suffered from **discrimination** in jobs and voting. **Dr. Martin Luther King, Jr.,** emerged as the main civil rights leader in the 1960s. The U.S. Congress passed some civil rights legislation. Other minority groups were inspired by the movement's successes. For example, the women's rights movement helped to end much gender-based discrimination.

Western Europe rebuilt after World War II. The Marshall Plan helped restore European economies by providing U.S. aid. After the war, Germany was divided between the communist East and the democratic West, but reunited at the end of the Cold War in 1990. Under **Konrad Adenauer,** West Germany's chancellor from 1949 to 1963, Germany built modern cities and re-established trade. European governments also developed programs that increased government responsibility for the needs of people. These **welfare states** required high taxes to pay for their programs. During the 1980s, some leaders, such as Britain's Margaret Thatcher, reduced the role of the government in the economy. Western Europe also moved closer to economic unity with the **European Community**, an organization dedicated to establishing free trade among its members.

Japan also prospered after World War II. Its **gross domestic product (GDP)** soared. Like Germany, Japan built factories. The government protected industries by raising tariffs on imported goods. This helped create a trade surplus for Japan.

Review Questions

1. What caused a U.S. recession in 1974?

____

____

2. Explain how Germany rebuilt its economy after World War II.

____

____

READING CHECK

What is suburbanization?

____

____

____

VOCABULARY STRATEGY

What does the word *prospered* mean in the underlined sentence? The word *decline* is an antonym of *prosper*. It means to "sink," "descend," or "deteriorate." Use these meanings of *decline* to figure out the meaning of *prospered*.

READING SKILL

Categorize In what ways were minorities denied equality and opportunity?

____

____

____

Name____________________ Class________________ Date______

CHAPTER 18 SECTION 3

Note Taking Study Guide

COMMUNISM SPREADS IN EAST ASIA

Focus Question: What did the Communist victory mean for China and the rest of East Asia?

As you read this section in your textbook, complete the flowchart below to help you summarize the effects of the Communist Revolution on China and the impact of the Cold War on China and Korea.

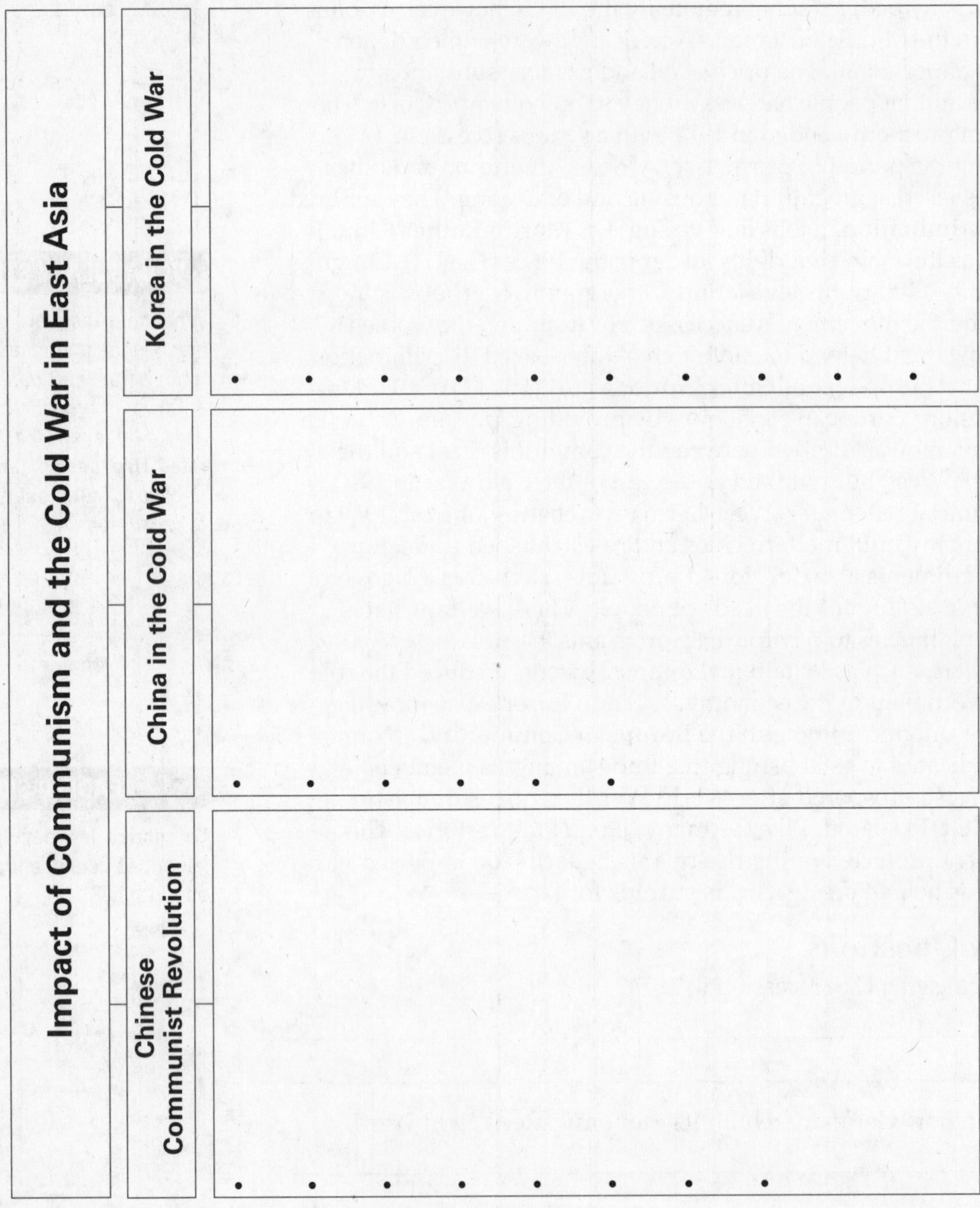

Name________________________ Class____________ Date______

CHAPTER 18 SECTION 3

Section Summary

COMMUNISM SPREADS IN EAST ASIA

After World War II, Mao Zedong led communist forces to victory over Jiang Jieshi's Nationalists, who fled to Taiwan. Then Mao began to reshape China's economy. First, he gave land to peasants, but then called for **collectivization.** Under this system, Mao moved people from their small villages and individual farms into communes of thousands of people on thousands of acres. Known as the **Great Leap Forward,** the program was intended to increase farm and industrial production. Instead, it produced low quality, useless goods and less food. Bad weather also affected crops, and many people starved.

To remove "bourgeois" tendencies from China, Mao began the **Cultural Revolution.** Skilled workers and managers were removed from factories and forced to work on farms or in labor camps. This resulted in a slowed economy and a threat of civil war.

At first, the United States supported the Nationalist government in Taiwan. The West was concerned that the Soviet Union and China would become allies, but border clashes led the Soviets to withdraw aid and advisors from China. U.S. leaders thought that by "playing the China card," or improving relations with the Chinese, they would further isolate the Soviets. In 1979, the United States established diplomatic relations with China.

Korea was an independent nation until Japan invaded it in World War II. After the war, American and Soviet forces agreed to divide the Korean peninsula at the **38th parallel**. **Kim Il Sung**, a communist, ruled the North; and **Syngman Rhee,** allied with the United States, controlled the South. In 1950, North Korean troops attacked South Korea. The United Nations forces stopped them along a line known as the **Pusan Perimeter,** then began advancing north. Mao sent troops to help the North Koreans. UN forces were pushed back south of the 38th parallel.

In 1953, both sides signed an armistice to end the fighting, but troops remained on both sides of the **demilitarized zone (DMZ).** Over time, South Korea enjoyed an economic boom and a rise in living standards, while communist North Korea's economy declined. Kim Il Sung's emphasis on self-reliance kept North Korea isolated and poor.

Review Questions

1. What was the effect of the Cultural Revolution?

____

____

2. How did the North Korean economy differ from the South Korean economy?

____

____

READING CHECK

What is the significance of the 38th parallel?

____

____

____

VOCABULARY STRATEGY

What does the word *commune* mean in the underlined sentence? The terms *group home, community,* and *collective farm* are all synonyms of *commune.* Use the synonyms to help you figure out the meaning of *commune.*

READING SKILL

Summarize Summarize the effects of the Great Leap Forward on the Chinese people.

____

____

____

Name__________________ Class________________ Date________

CHAPTER 18 SECTION 4

Note Taking Study Guide

WAR IN SOUTHEAST ASIA

Focus Question: What were the causes and effects of war in Southeast Asia, and what was the American role in this region?

As you read this section in your textbook, complete the flowchart below to summarize the events in Southeast Asia after World War II.

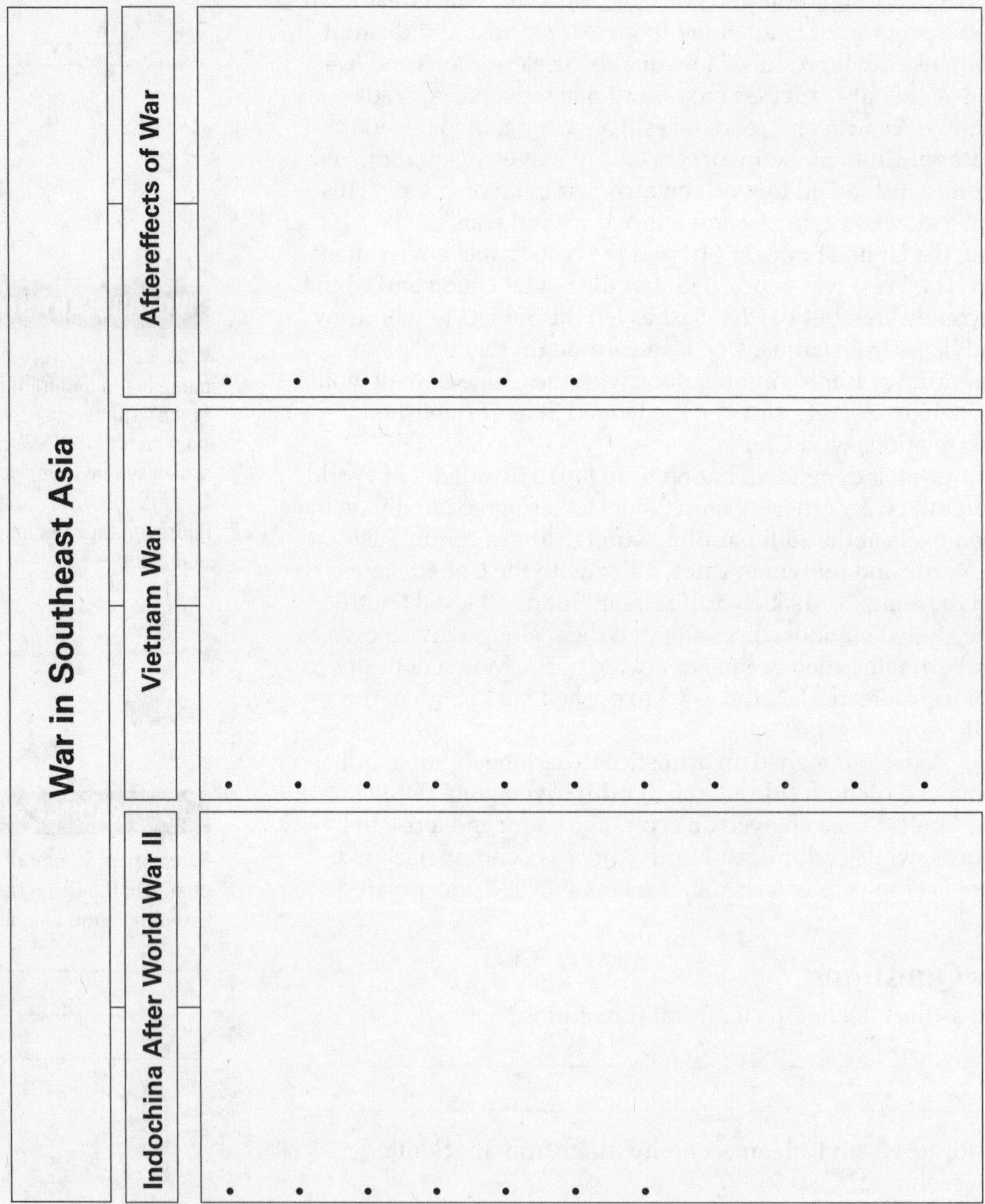

Name________________________ Class____________ Date______

CHAPTER 18 SECTION 4

Section Summary

WAR IN SOUTHEAST ASIA

In the 1800s, the French ruled the area in Southeast Asia called French Indochina. During World War II, Japan invaded that region, but faced resistance from **guerrillas.** After the war, the French tried to reestablish authority in Vietnam. However, forces led by communist leader **Ho Chi Minh** fought the colonialists. The French left Vietnam in 1954, after a Vietnamese victory at **Dienbienphu**. After that, Ho controlled the northern part of Vietnam while the United States supported the noncommunist government in the south.

Ho wanted to unite Vietnam. He provided aid to the National Liberation Front, or **Viet Cong,** a communist guerrilla organization in the south. American leaders saw Vietnam as an extension of the Cold War and developed the **domino theory.** This was the belief that if communists won in South Vietnam, then communism could spread to other governments in Southeast Asia. After a North Vietnamese attack on a U.S. Navy destroyer, Congress authorized the president to take military measures to prevent further communist aggression in Southeast Asia.

Despite massive American support, the South Vietnamese failed to defeat the Viet Cong and their North Vietnamese allies. During the **Tet Offensive,** the North Vietnamese attacked cities all over the south. Even though the communists were not able to hold any cities, it marked a turning point in U.S. public opinion. Upset by civilian deaths from the U.S. bombing of North Vietnam as well as growing American casualties, many Americans began to oppose the war. President Nixon came under increasing pressure to terminate the conflict. The Paris Peace Accord of 1973 established a ceasefire and American troops began to withdraw. Two years later communist North Vietnam conquered South Vietnam.

Neighboring Cambodia and Laos also ended up with communist governments. In Cambodia, guerrillas called the **Khmer Rouge** came to power. Led by the brutal dictator **Pol Pot,** their policies led to a genocide that killed about one third of the population. When Vietnam invaded Cambodia, the genocide ended. Pol Pot and the Khmer Rouge were forced to retreat. Communism did not spread any farther in Southeast Asia.

Review Questions

1. What was the domino theory?

____

____

2. Who were the Khmer Rouge and what role did they play in Cambodia?

____

____

READING CHECK

What was significant about the Tet Offensive?

____

____

____

VOCABULARY STRATEGY

What does the word *terminate* mean in the underlined sentence? Note that the word is a verb. Ask yourself what action President Nixon was being pressured to take. Use this strategy to help you figure out what *terminate* means.

READING SKILL

Summarize Summarize U.S. involvement in Vietnam.

____

____

____

Name_______________ Class_______________ Date_______________

CHAPTER 18 SECTION 5

Note Taking Study Guide

THE END OF THE COLD WAR

Focus Question: What were the causes and effects of the end of the Cold War?

As you read this section in your textbook, complete this flowchart to help you categorize events connected to the end of the Cold War. Some events have been completed for you.

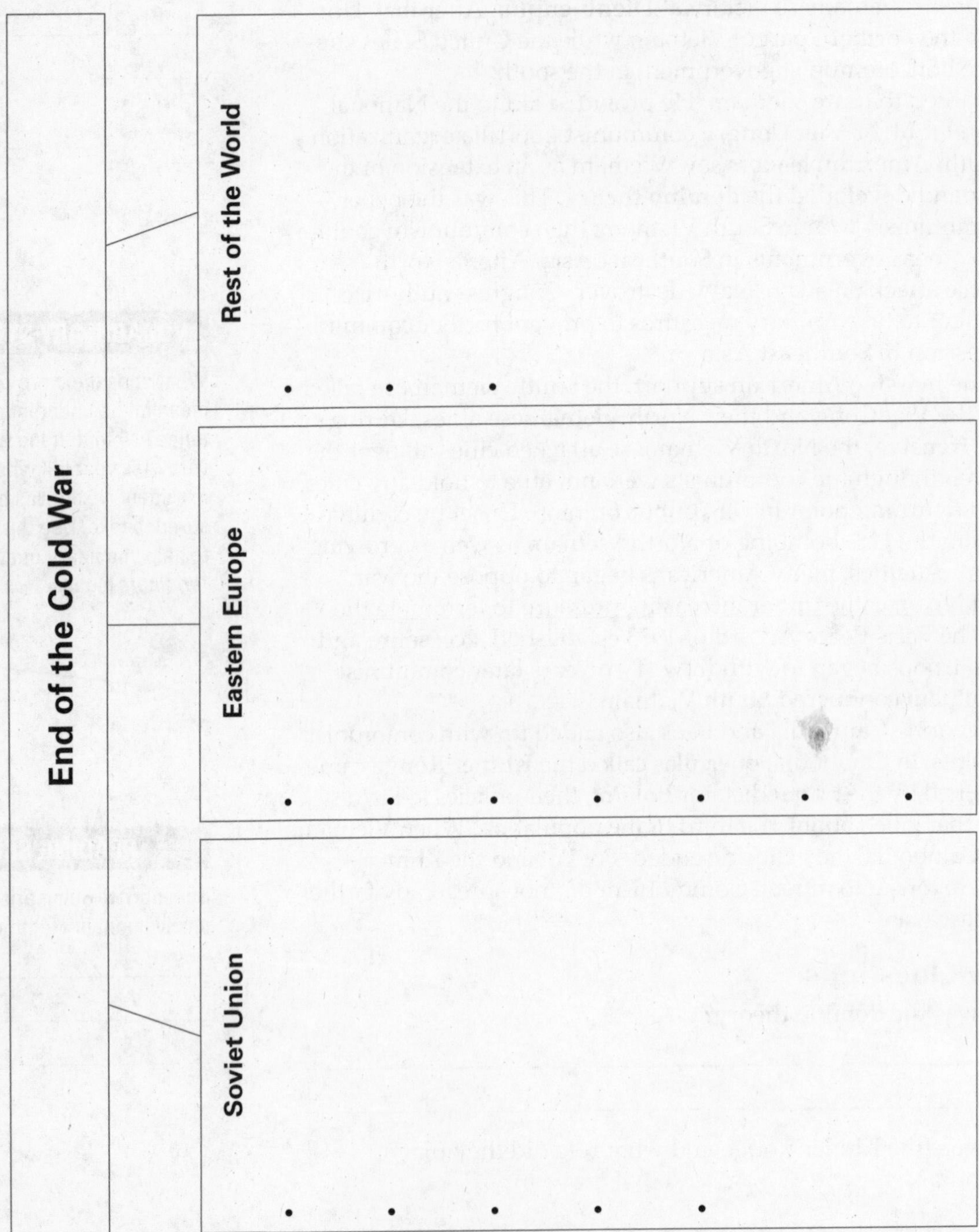

Name________________________ Class___________ Date______

CHAPTER 18 SECTION 5

Section Summary

THE END OF THE COLD WAR

The Soviet Union emerged from World War II as a superpower, with control over many Eastern European countries. For many people, the country's superpower status brought few rewards. Consumer goods were inferior and workers were poorly paid. Because workers had lifetime job security, there was little incentive to produce high-quality goods. Still, there were some important technological successes. One example was *Sputnik I,* the first artificial satellite. Keeping up with the United States in an arms race also strained the economy. Then in 1979, Soviet forces invaded Afghanistan and became involved in a long war. The Soviets had few successes battling the **mujahedin,** or Muslim religious warriors, creating a crisis in morale in the USSR.

Then, new Soviet leader **Mikhail Gorbachev** urged reforms. He called for **glasnost.** He ended censorship and encouraged people to discuss the country's problems. Gorbachev also called for **perestroika,** or a restructuring of the government and economy. His policies, however, fed unrest across the Soviet empire.

Eastern Europeans demanded an end to Soviet rule. Previous attempts to defy the Soviets had failed. When Hungarians and Czechs challenged the communist rulers, military force subdued them. By the end of the 1980s, a powerful democracy movement was sweeping the region. In Poland, **Lech Walesa** led **Solidarity,** an independent, unlawful labor union demanding economic and political changes. When Gorbachev declared he would not interfere in Eastern European reforms, Solidarity was legalized. A year later, Walesa was elected president of Poland.

Meanwhile, East German leaders resisted reform, and thousands of East Germans fled to the West. In Czechoslovakia, **Václav Havel,** a dissident writer, was elected president. One by one, communist governments fell. Most changes happened peacefully, but Romanian dictator **Nicolae Ceausescu** refused to step down and he was executed. The Baltic States regained independence. By the end of 1991, the remaining Soviet republics had all formed independent nations. The Soviet Union ceased to exist after 69 years of communist rule.

In 1992, Czechoslovakia was divided into Slovakia and the Czech Republic. Additionally, some communist governments in Asia, such as China, instituted economic reforms.

Review Questions

1. What kinds of reforms did Gorbachev make?

____

____

2. What happened to the Soviet Union by the end of 1991?

____

____

READING CHECK

How did the arms race affect the Soviet economy?

____

____

____

VOCABULARY STRATEGY

What does the word *incentive* mean in the underlined sentence? The words *motivation* and *reason* are synonyms of *incentive.* Use these synonyms to help you figure out the meaning of *incentive.*

READING SKILL

Categorize Which leaders mentioned in the summary supported reform and which leaders opposed reform?

____

____

____

Name________________ Class________________ Date________

CHAPTER 19 SECTION 1

Note Taking Study Guide

INDEPENDENT NATIONS OF SOUTH ASIA

Focus Question: What were the consequences of independence in South Asia for the region and for the world?

As you read this section in your textbook, fill in the concept web below to identify causes and effects of events in South Asia.

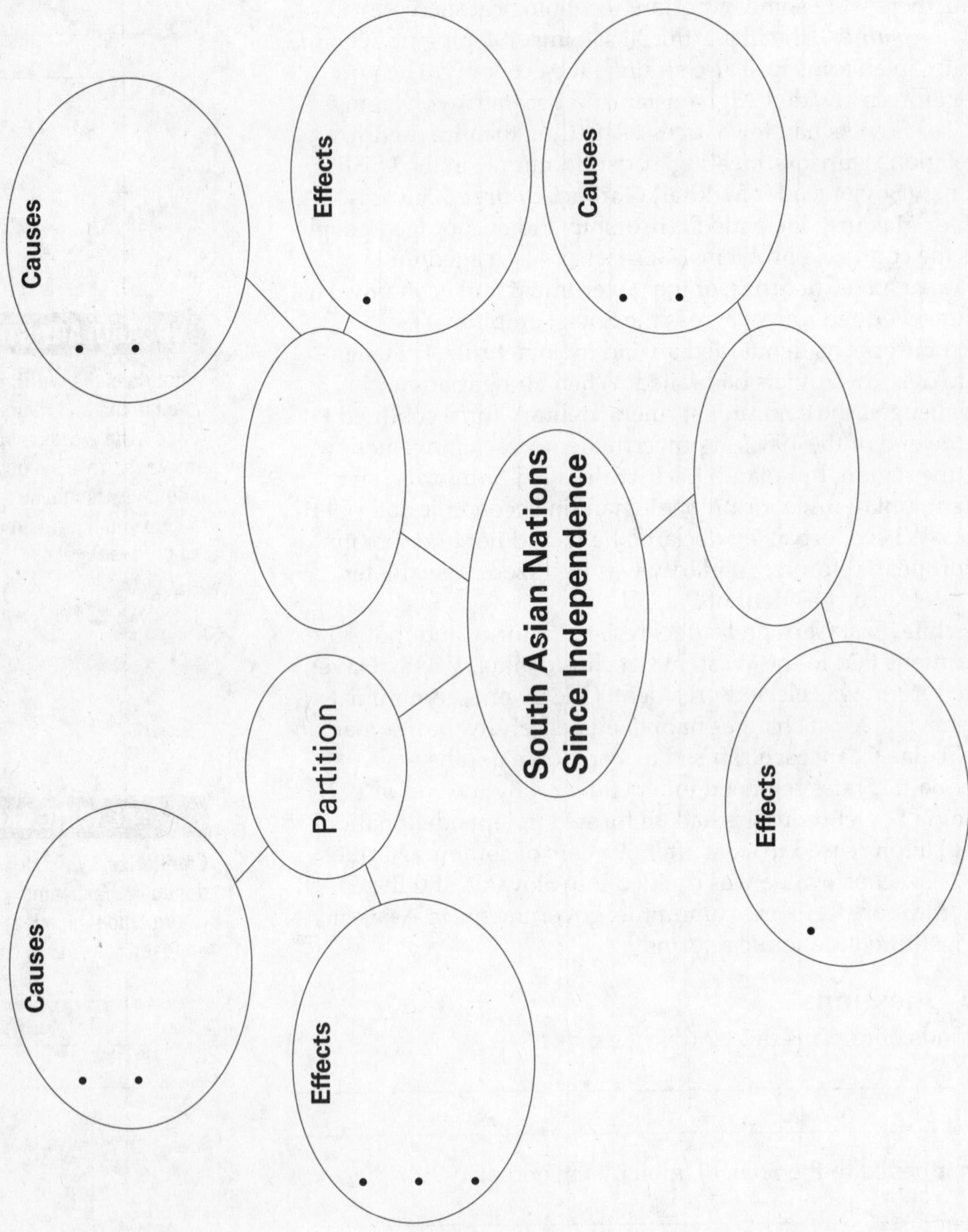

Name____________________ Class__________ Date______

CHAPTER 19 SECTION 1

Section Summary

INDEPENDENT NATIONS OF SOUTH ASIA

In the 1940s, tensions between Hindus and Muslims in India led to violence. The ruling British decided that the only solution was a **partition,** or division, into a Muslim-majority Pakistan and a Hindu-majority India. After Pakistan and India gained their independence in 1947, Hindus in Pakistan fled to India, while Muslims in India fled to Pakistan. As they fled, Muslims, Hindus, and another religious group called **Sikhs** slaughtered one another.

Tensions have continued in the region. India and Pakistan have fought wars over **Kashmir,** a state with Muslim and Hindu populations. When India developed nuclear weapons, Pakistan began its own nuclear weapons program. In the island country of Sri Lanka, a majority are Buddhists. A Tamil-speaking Hindu minority on the island has fought for years for a separate Tamil nation.

In 1947, **Jawaharlal Nehru** became India's first prime minister. He tried to improve living conditions and end discrimination against **dalits,** or outcastes. Nehru's daughter, **Indira Gandhi,** became prime minister in 1966. While she was in office, Sikhs pressed for independence for the state of **Punjab.** In 1984, Sikh separatists occupied the **Golden Temple,** the holiest Sikh shrine. Gandhi sent troops to the temple, and thousands of Sikhs were killed. A few months later, Gandhi's Sikh bodyguards assassinated her.

In 1947, Pakistan was a divided country. A thousand miles separated West Pakistan from East Pakistan. West Pakistan dominated the nation's government. Most people in East Pakistan were Bengalis. They felt their government neglected their region. In 1971, Bengalis declared independence for East Pakistan under the name of **Bangladesh.** <u>Pakistan tried to crush the rebels but was eventually compelled to recognize the independence of Bangladesh.</u>

Pakistan has long lacked political stability. Islamic fundamentalists disagree with those who want a greater separation between religion and government. During the 1980s, the war in Afghanistan drove over a million Afghan refugees into Pakistan. Pakistan's Islamic fundamentalists gained power by forming ties with Afghan refugees.

Despite their differences, India and Pakistan helped organize a conference of newly independent states in 1955. This marked the birth of **nonalignment,** or political and diplomatic independence from the United States or the Soviet Union.

Review Questions

1. Why was Indira Gandhi assassinated?

____

____

2. Why did Bengalis want East Pakistan to be independent?

____

____

READING CHECK

What is nonalignment?

____

____

____

VOCABULARY STRATEGY

What does the word *compelled* mean in the underlined sentence? *Compel* comes from a Latin word that means "to drive." If you substitute the word "driven" for *compelled* in the underlined sentence, it will help you figure out what *compelled* means.

READING SKILL

Identify Causes and Effects What caused the British to partition India? What were some of the effects the partition had on Muslims and Hindus?

____

____

____

Name________________________ Class__________________ Date________

CHAPTER 19 SECTION 2

Note Taking Study Guide

NEW NATIONS OF SOUTHEAST ASIA

Focus Question: What challenges did Southeast Asian nations face after winning independence?

As you read this section in your textbook, fill in the concept web below to understand the effects of recent historical processes in Southeast Asia.

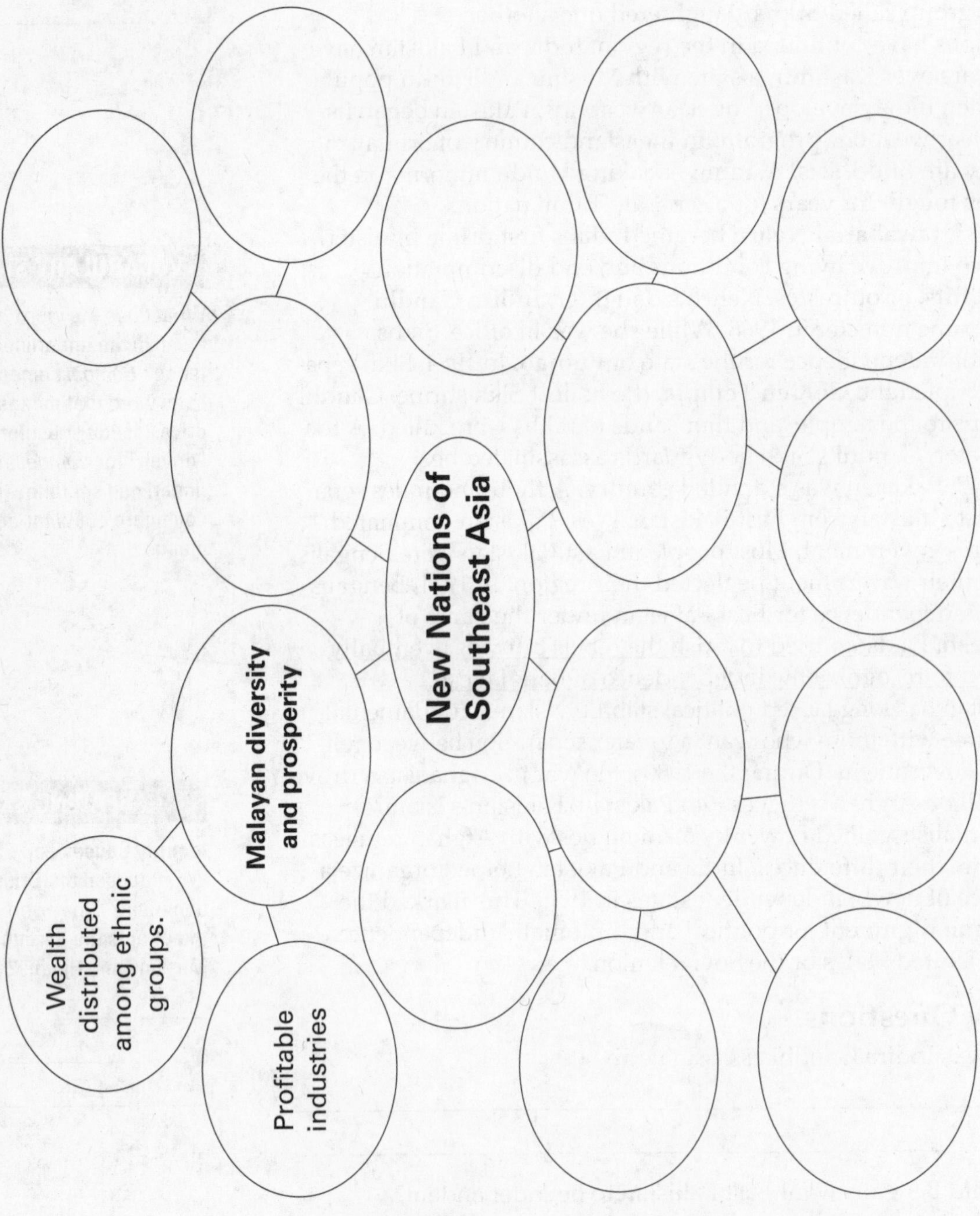

Name______________________ Class___________ Date______

CHAPTER 19 SECTION 2

Section Summary

NEW NATIONS OF SOUTHEAST ASIA

Mainland Southeast Asia is a region of contrasts. Thailand and Malaysia have prospered as market economies. In Malaysia, people of Chinese and Indian descent have made the nation a leader in profitable industries. However, the government has also tried to include the Malay majority in the country's prosperity. By contrast, Myanmar, or Burma, has suffered under an **autocratic** government—a government that has unlimited power. The government has limited foreign trade, and living standards remain low. In 1990, elections were held in Myanmar, and a party that opposed military rule won. It was led by **Aung San Suu Kyi.** However, the military rejected the election results, and Suu Kyi was put under house arrest.

After World War II, Indonesia, formerly the Dutch East Indies, achieved its independence. Indonesia faced many obstacles to its unity. It consists of more than 13,000 islands. Javanese make up almost half of the population, but there are hundreds of ethnic groups. About 90 percent of Indonesians are Muslims, but the population includes Christians, Buddhists, and Hindus. After independence, Indonesia formed a democratic, parliamentary government under its first president, **Sukarno.** In 1966, an army general, **Suharto,** seized power and ruled as a dictator until he was forced to resign in 1998. Religious and ethnic tensions have fueled violence in parts of Indonesia. In 1975, Indonesia seized **East Timor,** a former Portuguese colony. The mostly Catholic East Timorese fought for independence, which they finally achieved in 2002.

In the Philippines, Catholics are the predominant religious group, but there is a Muslim minority in the south. In 1946, the Philippines gained freedom from United States control. Although the Filipino constitution established a democratic government, a wealthy elite controlled politics and the economy. **Ferdinand Marcos,** elected president in 1965, became a dictator and cracked down on basic freedoms. He even had **Benigno Aquino,** a popular rival, murdered. When **Corazon Aquino** was elected in 1986, Marcos tried to deny the results, but the people forced him to resign. Since then, democracy has struggled to survive in the Philippines. Communist and Muslim rebels continue to fight across the country.

Review Questions

1. What happened when Aung San Suu Kyi's party won the 1990 elections in Myanmar?

____

____

2. What are some obstacles to Indonesia's unity?

____

____

READING CHECK

What are the features of the autocratic government in Myanmar?

____

____

____

VOCABULARY STRATEGY

What does *predominant* mean in the underlined sentence? Note that the second part of the sentence mentions another group that is a minority, or a smaller group. Use this context clue to help you figure out the meaning of *predominant.*

READING SKILL

Understand Effects What was the effect of Ferdinand Marcos' denial of the results of the 1986 election?

____

____

____

Name________________ Class________________ Date________

CHAPTER 19 SECTION 3

Note Taking Study Guide

AFRICAN NATIONS GAIN INDEPENDENCE

Focus Question: What challenges did new African nations face?

As you read this section in your textbook, fill in the concept web below to keep track of the causes and effects of independence in Africa.

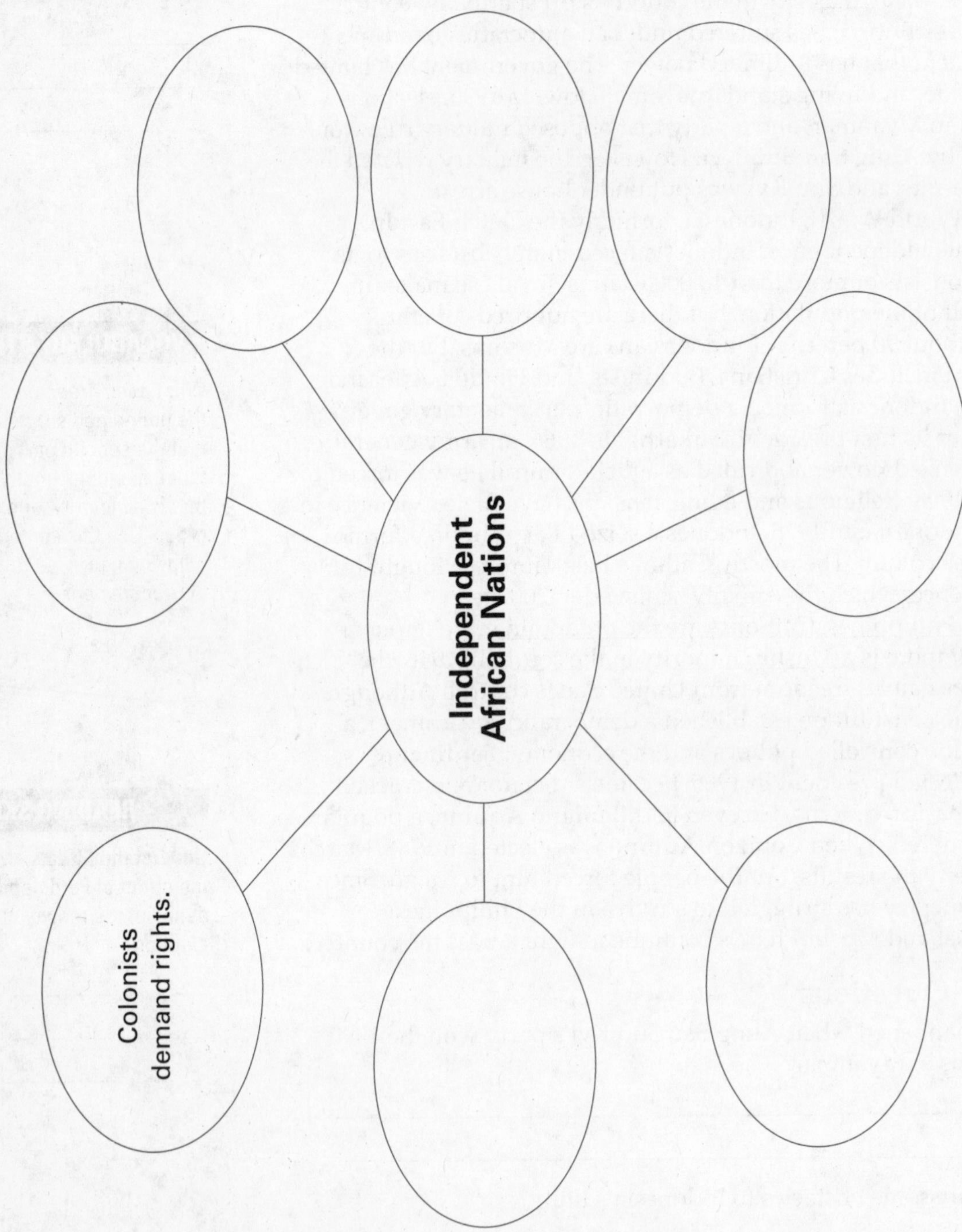

Name__________ Class________ Date______

CHAPTER 19 SECTION 3

Section Summary

AFRICAN NATIONS GAIN INDEPENDENCE

Africa is a diverse continent. Vast **savannas,** or grasslands, cover much of it, but there are also rain forests and deserts. Diversity is reflected in the continent's history, people, languages, and traditions.

After World War II, many Africans demanded freedom from European powers. After gaining independence, some African nations enjoyed peace and democracy. Others faced civil wars, military rule, or corrupt dictators. European powers had drawn colonial boundaries without regard for Africa's ethnic groups. This led to ethnic conflict in many new nations once colonial powers withdrew.

In 1957, Gold Coast gained its freedom from Britain and took the name Ghana. The government of its first president, **Kwame Nkrumah,** eventually became corrupt, and Nkrumah was overthrown in a military **coup d'etat.** Other coups followed, but today Ghana is a democracy.

<u>In Kenya, white settlers had passed laws to ensure their domination of the country.</u> In the 1950s, rebels turned to guerrilla warfare, but the British crushed the rebellion. Kenya finally gained its independence in 1963. **Jomo Kenyatta,** a prominent independence leader, became the first president of the new country. In 2002, Kenya's first fair election removed the ruling party from office.

In Algeria, independence from France came only after a long war but was finally achieved in 1962. A coup in 1965 began a long period of military rule. When the government allowed free elections in 1992, an **Islamist** party won. The military rejected the results, and seven years of civil war followed. Although the fighting has ended, the country remains tense.

After the Congo became independent from Belgium, the copper-rich province of **Katanga** rebelled. The United Nations ended the rebellion in 1963. **Mobutu Sese Seko** ruled as a harsh military dictator from 1965 to 1997. Seven years of civil war ended with a cease-fire in 2003.

Nigeria won its independence in 1960, but regional, ethnic, and religious differences soon led to conflict. In 1966, the Ibo people in the southeast declared independence as the Republic of **Biafra.** After three years of fighting, Nigeria's military ended Biafra's independence. A series of dictators then ruled, but Nigeria returned to democracy in 1999.

Review Questions

1. Why was the first president of Ghana overthrown?

____

____

2. What country did the Ibo people of Nigeria try to establish?

____

____

READING CHECK

What is a coup d'etat?

____

____

____

VOCABULARY STRATEGY

What does the word *ensure* mean in the underlined sentence? The prefix *en-* means to "make" or "cause to be." Think about what the root word, *sure,* means. Use these clues about word parts to help you understand the meaning of *ensure.*

READING SKILL

Identify Causes and Effects How did past decisions made by European powers cause ethnic conflict in many new African nations?

____

____

____

Name________________________ Class__________________ Date________

CHAPTER 19 SECTION 4

Note Taking Study Guide

THE MODERN MIDDLE EAST

Focus Question: What are the main similarities and differences among Middle Eastern nations?

As you read this section in your textbook, fill in the concept web below to identify causes and effects of events in the Middle East since 1945.

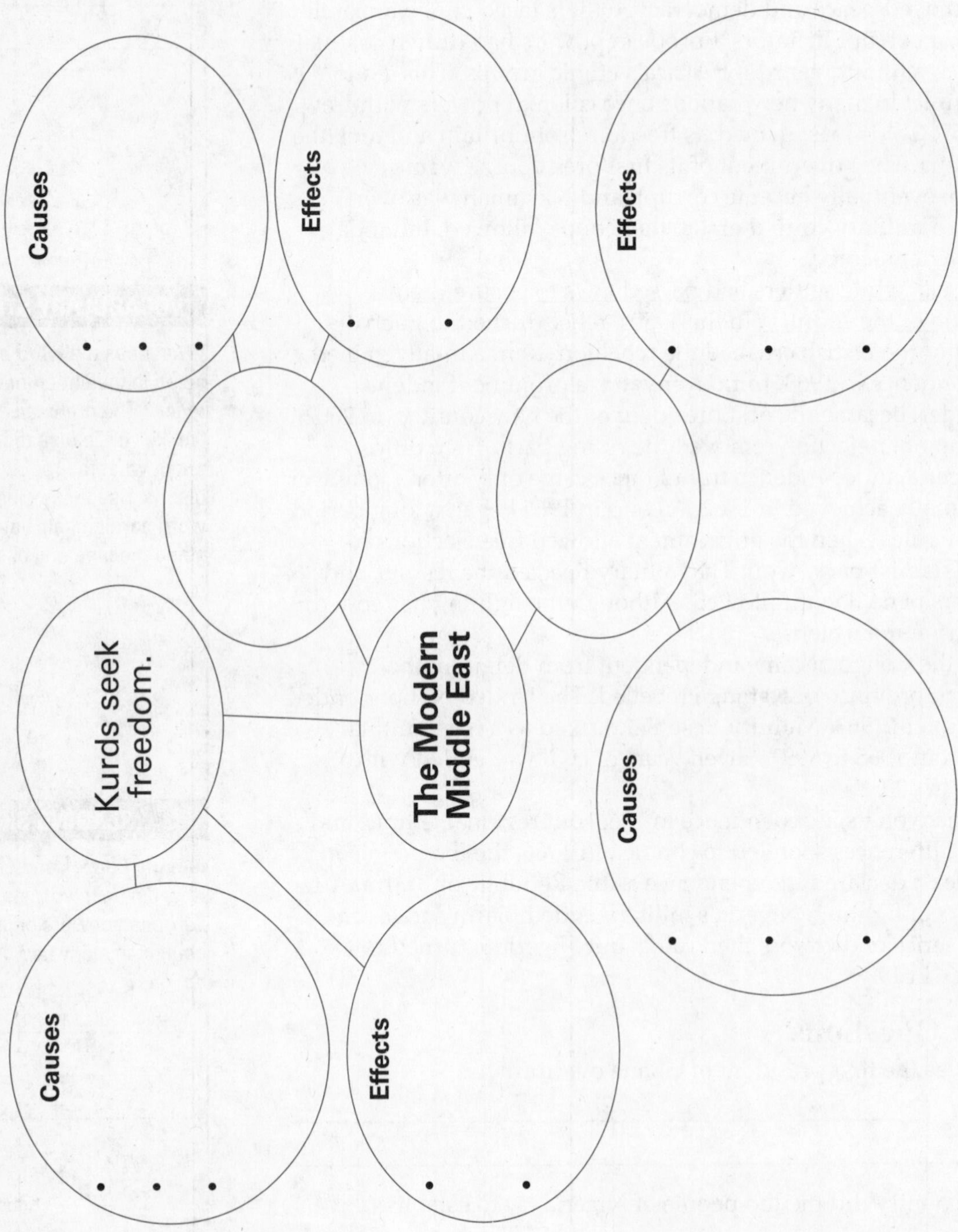

Name________________________ Class____________ Date______

CHAPTER 19 SECTION 4

Section Summary

THE MODERN MIDDLE EAST

Most of the people in the Middle East are Muslims, but there are also Christian communities and the predominantly Jewish nation of Israel. Most countries also have large ethnic or religious minorities. The Kurds are an example of an ethnic minority. They live in Iran, Iraq, Syria, and Turkey and have faced discrimination in each country.

The Holocaust created support for a Jewish homeland after World War II. In 1947, the UN drew up a plan to divide Palestine into an Arab and a Jewish state. In 1948, Jews proclaimed the independent state of Israel. This led to Arab-Israeli conflicts that forced 700,000 Palestinians from their homes. Despite the conflicts, Israel has developed rapidly due to a skilled workforce. Kibbutzim work on what is called a **kibbutz,** or collective farm.

Resources and religion have led to conflicts in the Middle East. The region has the world's largest oil and gas reserves. As a result, it has strategic importance. Some Middle Eastern countries have adopted **secular,** or non-religious, government and laws. However, many Muslim leaders argue that a renewed commitment to Islamic doctrine is needed. In Iran and Saudi Arabia, women are required to wear **hejab,** the traditional Muslim garments.

Egypt, the most populous Arab country, is important because it controls the **Suez Canal.** Under **Gamal Abdel Nasser,** Egypt fought two unsuccessful wars against Israel. His successor, **Anwar Sadat,** made peace with Israel. Islamists were angry about government corruption and the failure to end poverty. In 1981, Sadat was assassinated by Muslim fundamentalists.

In Iran, Shah Mohammad Reza Pahlavi ruled with the support of the United States, which helped oust one of his opponents, **Mohammad Mosaddeq.** The shah's secret police terrorized critics. In the 1970s, the shah's enemies rallied behind Ayatollah **Ruhollah Khomeini.** Protests forced the shah into exile, and Khomeini established an Islamic **theocracy,** or government ruled by religious leaders.

Saudi Arabia has the world's largest oil reserves and is the location of Islam's holy land. Kings from the Sa'ud family have ruled Saudi Arabia since the 1920s. Fundamentalists have criticized the kingdom's close ties to Western nations, and some opponents have adopted violent tactics that threaten to disrupt the Saudi oil industry.

Review Questions

1. What makes the Middle East of strategic importance?

____

____

2. Why have some Islamic fundamentalists criticized the Saudis?

____

____

READING CHECK

What is a theocracy?

____

____

____

VOCABULARY STRATEGY

What does the word *doctrine* mean in the underlined sentence? The words *policy, dogma,* and *tenet* are all synonyms of doctrine. Use what you may know about these synonyms to help you figure out the meaning of the word *doctrine.*

READING SKILL

Identify Causes and Effects What effect did the proclamation of an independent state of Israel have on Palestinians?

____

____

____

Name________________________ Class________________ Date________

CHAPTER 20 SECTION 1 Note Taking Study Guide

CONFLICTS DIVIDE NATIONS

Focus Question: Why have ethnic and religious conflicts divided some nations?

As you read this section in your textbook, fill in the flowchart below to help you recognize the sequence of events that took place in Northern Ireland, Chechnya, and Yugoslavia.

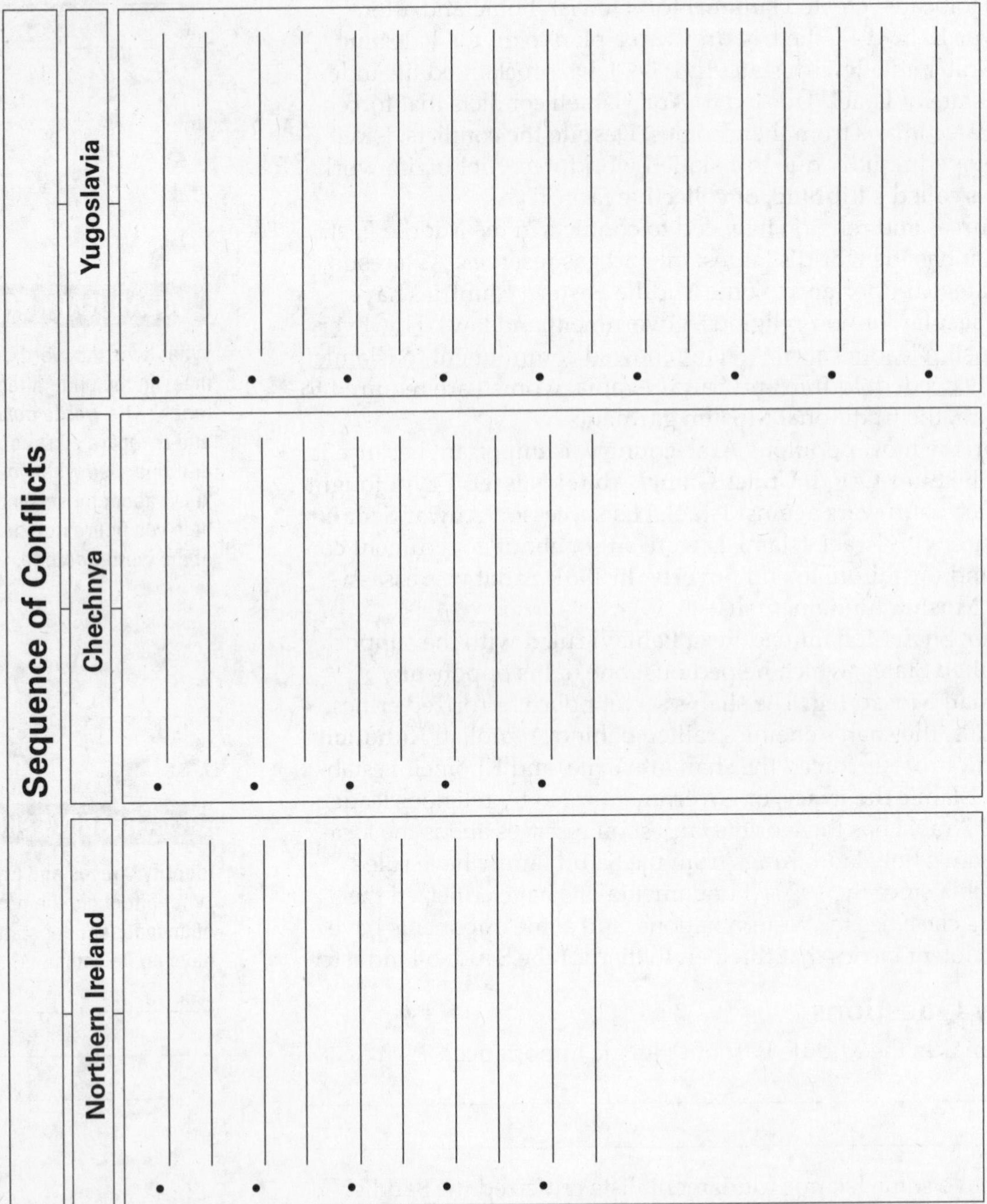

Name__________ Class__________ Date______

CHAPTER 20 SECTION 1

Section Summary

CONFLICTS DIVIDE NATIONS

In recent decades, many wars and conflicts have arisen over ethnic differences. For example, in Sri Lanka, Sinhalese Buddhists are the majority. Sinhalese nationalists forbade the use of the Tamil language and made Sinhalese the official language. This and other policies led to a civil war between the Buddhists and Tamils. Tamils agreed to a ceasefire when the government agreed to negotiations over a separate Tamil government.

In some countries, however, conflicts have been peacefully resolved. In Canada the democratic government helped prevent French-speaking Quebec from seeking independence.

Northern Ireland was the scene of another long-term conflict. In 1922 the Protestant majority in six northern counties voted to remain part of Britain when Ireland became independent. However, many Catholics in those counties wanted to join with Ireland, which has a Catholic majority. Beginning in the 1960s, extremists on both sides turned to violence. Peace talks dragged on for years. Finally, in 1998, Protestants and Catholics signed the **Good Friday Agreement,** a peace accord.

After the fall of the Soviet Union, many minorities in several former republics wanted independence. For example, ethnic Armenians fought for freedom against Azerbaijanis. The fiercest struggle occurred in **Chechnya,** where Muslim Chechen nationalists fought to free Chechnya from Russian control. Russia crushed a Chechen revolt in the mid-1990s. As a result, many civilians were killed. When a 1997 peace treaty failed, some Chechens turned to terrorism.

Ethnic tensions also tore Yugoslavia apart during the 1990s. Before 1991, Yugoslavia was a **multiethnic,** communist country. <u>The Serbs dominated Yugoslavia, which was controlled by the Communist Party.</u> The fall of communism resulted in nationalist unrest and fighting between Serbs and Croats in Croatia. Soon the fighting spread to neighboring Bosnia. During the war, all sides committed atrocities. In Bosnia, the Serbs conducted a vicious campaign of **ethnic cleansing.** In 1995, the war in Bosnia ended. Then, however, another crisis broke out in the Serbian province of **Kosovo.** In 1989 Serbian president **Slobodan Milosevic** began oppressing Kosovar Albanians. Ten years later, NATO launched air strikes against Serbia. UN and NATO forces eventually restored peace.

Review Questions

1. What two groups are in conflict in Sri Lanka?

____

____

2. Why did Chechnya become an area of conflict in Russia?

____

____

READING CHECK

In which country did ethnic tensions not lead to war?

____

____

____

VOCABULARY STRATEGY

What does *dominated* mean in the underlined sentence? What clues can you find in the surrounding words, phrases, or sentences? Use these context clues to help you figure out what *dominated* means.

READING SKILL

Recognize Sequence What happened in Ireland after independence to cause conflict?

____

____

____

Name________________________ Class__________________ Date________

CHAPTER 20 SECTION 2

Note Taking Study Guide

STRUGGLES IN AFRICA

Focus Question: Why have conflicts plagued some African countries?

A. *As you read "South Africa Struggles for Freedom," "South Africa's Neighbors Face Long Conflicts," and "Ethnic Conflicts Kill Millions," record the sequence of events in the conflicts in South Africa and its neighbors.*

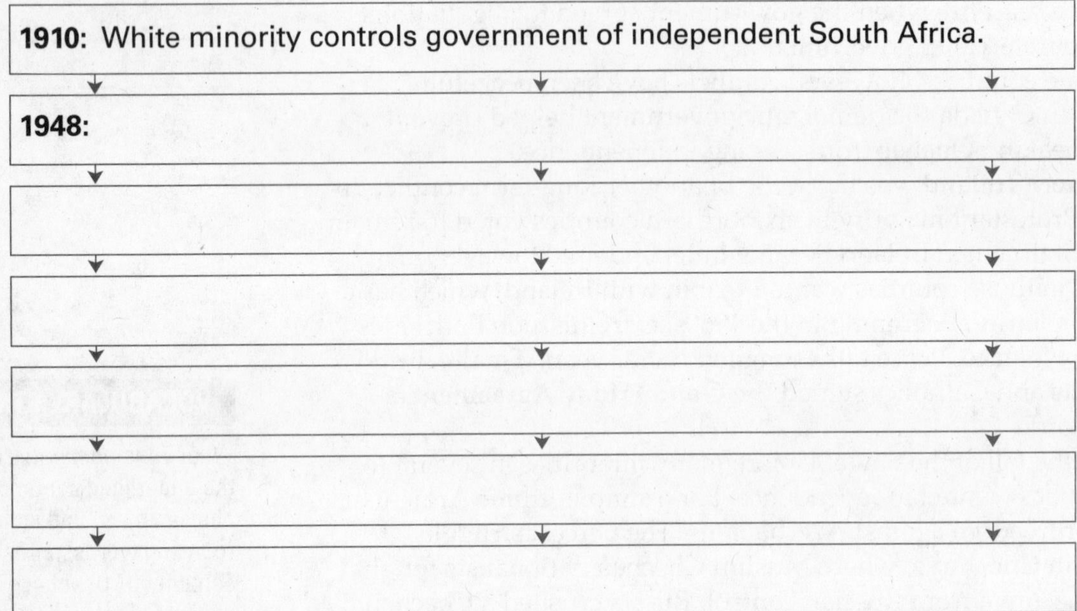

B. *As you read "Ethnic Conflicts Kill Millions," identify the causes and effects of the conflicts in Rwanda, Sudan, Burundi, and Darfur.*

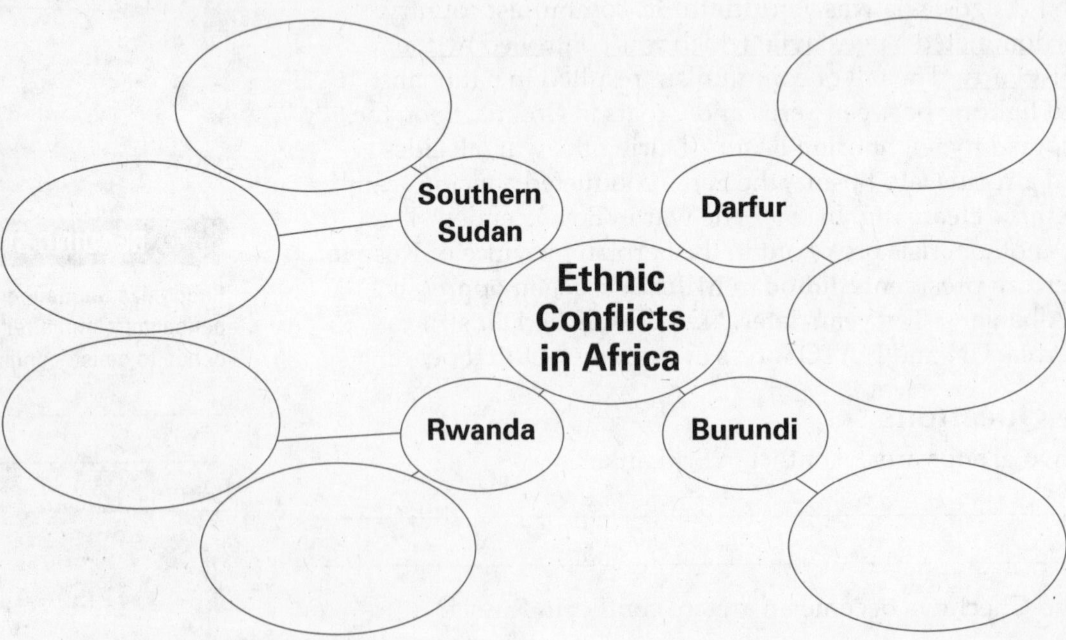

Name________________________ Class___________ Date______

CHAPTER 20 SECTION 2

Section Summary

STRUGGLES IN AFRICA

In the 1950s and 1960s, many new nations won independence in Africa. Several other African nations suffered internal conflicts and civil wars. In 1910, South Africa achieved self-rule from Britain. Most civil rights, however, were limited to white settlers. The black majority had few rights under a legal system of racial segregation called **apartheid.** Under apartheid, nonwhites faced many restrictions. <u>For example, laws banned marriages between races and stipulated segregated restaurants, beaches, and schools.</u>

The **African National Congress (ANC)** opposed apartheid and led the struggle for majority rule. In 1960 police gunned down 69 people during a protest in **Sharpeville,** a black township. The government then outlawed the ANC. **Nelson Mandela,** an ANC leader, was sentenced to life imprisonment.

In the 1980s, international demands for an end to apartheid and for Mandela's release increased. In 1984, Bishop **Desmond Tutu** won the Nobel Peace Prize for his nonviolent opposition to apartheid. In 1990, South African president **F.W. de Klerk** ended apartheid and freed Mandela, who was elected president in 1994.

South Africa's neighbors also experienced long conflicts to attain independence. Portugal granted independence to Angola and Mozambique in 1975. South Africa and the United States saw the new nations as threats because some liberation leaders had ties to the ANC or the Soviet Union.

After independence, ethnic conflicts plagued many nations. Historic resentments divided nations, and regional rivalries fed ethnic violence. In Rwanda, one of Africa's deadliest wars occurred. There, the **Hutus** were the majority, but the minority **Tutsis** dominated the country. In 1994, extremist Hutus slaughtered about 800,000 Tutsis and moderate Hutus. Another 3 million Rwandans lost their homes. In response, world leaders pledged to stop genocide wherever it may occur. Their power to do this, however, was limited. In Sudan, non-Muslim, non-Arab rebels in the south battled Arab Muslims from the north. This war, drought, and famine caused millions of deaths. Finally, southern rebels signed a peace agreement in 2004. In the same year, however, ethnic conflict spread to Darfur in western Sudan. This conflict raised fears of a new genocide.

Review Questions

1. Describe conditions under apartheid in South Africa.

____

____

2. What led to deadly war in Rwanda?

____

____

READING CHECK

Which two African countries gained independence from Portugal?

____

____

____

VOCABULARY STRATEGY

What does the word *stipulated* mean in the underlined sentence? Note that *stipulated* refers to laws. The previous sentence has a reference to restrictions that non-whites faced. Use these context clues to help you understand the meaning of the word *stipulated.*

READING SKILL

Recognize Sequence Did the South African government outlaw the ANC before or after the protest in Sharpeville?

____

____

____

Name________________________ Class________________ Date________

CHAPTER 20 SECTION 3

Note Taking Study Guide

CONFLICTS IN THE MIDDLE EAST

Focus Question: What are the causes of conflict in the Middle East?

As you read the section in your textbook, use the flowchart to record the sequence of events relating to the conflicts in the Middle East.

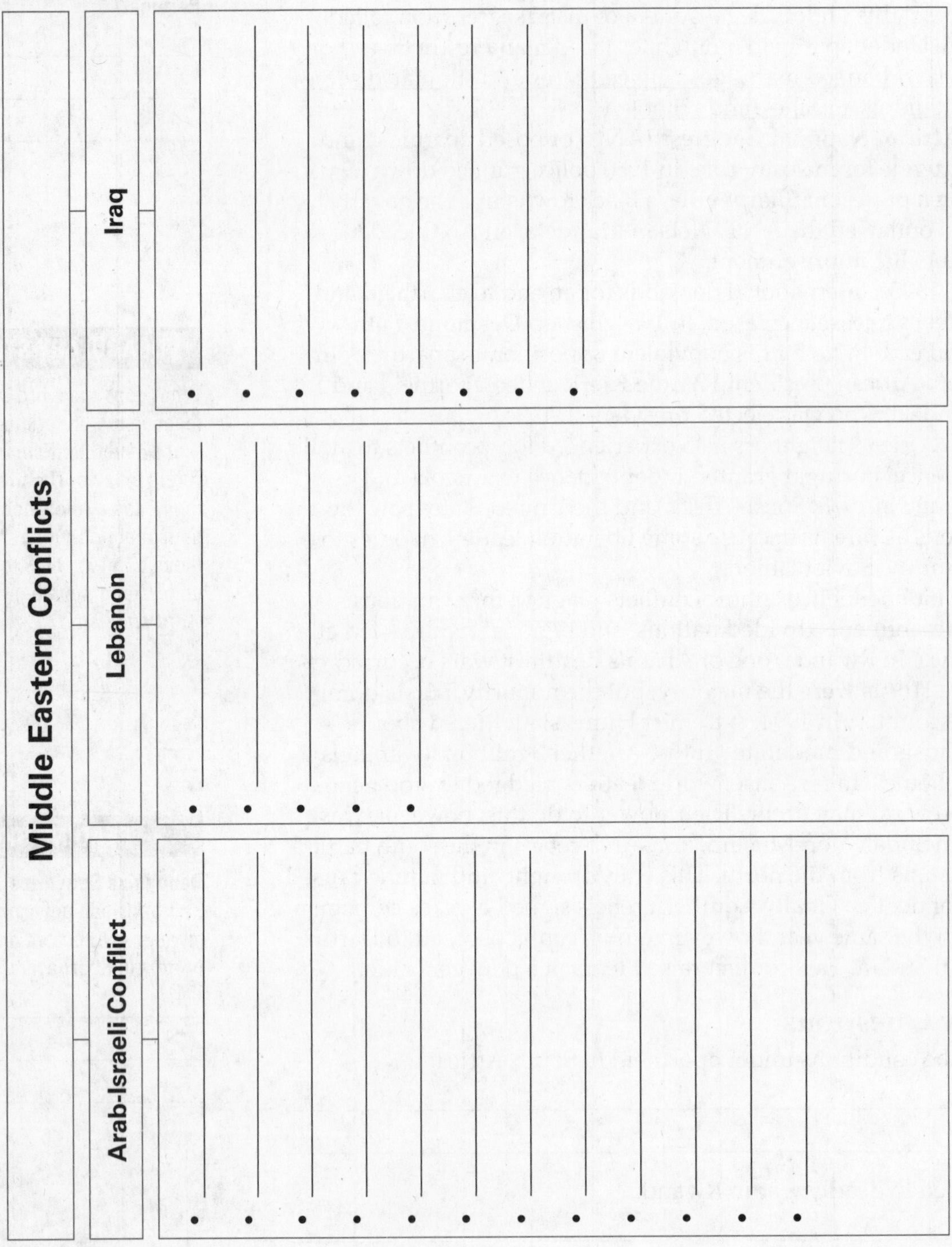

Name________________________ Class___________ Date______

CHAPTER 20 SECTION 3

Section Summary

CONFLICTS IN THE MIDDLE EAST

For decades, the Middle East has been the location of conflict. Modern Israel was created in 1948 on land that had belonged to Palestinian Arabs. As a result, there has been repeated war and violence. In several wars against Egypt and others, Israel gained more land. This is called the **occupied territories.**

The Palestine Liberation Organization, led by **Yasir Arafat,** fought against the Israelis. In the occupied territories, Palestinians launched uprisings called **intifadas.** In addition, suicide bombers spread terror inside Israel. The Israelis responded with armed force, and Palestinian bitterness increased. Leaders, such as Israeli Prime Minister **Yitzhak Rabin,** pushed for peace. There were many stumbling blocks, however, such as disagreements over **Jerusalem,** a city sacred to Jews, Christians, and Muslims. During the early 2000s, new steps toward peace offered some hope, but serious obstacles remained.

Lebanon is home to diverse ethnic and religious groups. The government depended on a delicate balance among Arab Christians, Sunni Muslims, Shiite Muslims, and Druze. In 1975, Christian and Muslim **militias** battled each other, and both Israel and Syria invaded. By 1990, however, peace had been restored.

Conflicts also plagued Iraq. Iraq's Sunni Muslim minority dominated the country for centuries. The Kurdish minority and Shiite Muslim majority were excluded from power. In 1979 **Saddam Hussein** took power as a dictator. He fought a prolonged war against neighboring Iran in the 1980s. In 1990, Iraq invaded Kuwait. In response, the United States led a coalition against that invasion. In the Gulf War that ensued, Kuwait was liberated and Iraqi forces were crushed. Saddam Hussein remained in power and used terror to impose his will. The United States, France, and Britain set up **no-fly zones** to protect the Kurds and Shiites. The UN worked to keep Saddam Hussein from building biological, nuclear, or chemical weapons, called **weapons of mass destruction (WMDs).**

In 2003, the United States led a coalition that invaded Iraq and overthrew Saddam Hussein. Iraqi **insurgents** fought against the occupation that followed. In 2005, national elections were held for the first time.

Review Questions

1. How did Israel come to control the occupied territories?

____

____

2. What were the results of the Gulf War in 1990?

____

____

READING CHECK

Which groups in Iraq were excluded from power?

____

____

____

VOCABULARY STRATEGY

What does the word *diverse* mean in the underlined sentence? Notice how in the next sentence four ethnic groups are mentioned. Use this context clue to help you understand the meaning of *diverse.*

READING SKILL

Recognize Sequence Circle the phrase in the sentence below that signals sequence.

In 1990, Iraq invaded Kuwait. In response, the United States led a coalition against the invasion.

Name________________ Class____________ Date________

CHAPTER 21 SECTION 1

Note Taking Study Guide

THE CHALLENGES OF DEVELOPMENT

Focus Question: How have the nations of the developing world tried to build better lives for their people?

As you read this section in your textbook, complete the chart below with supporting details from the text about economic development and developing countries.

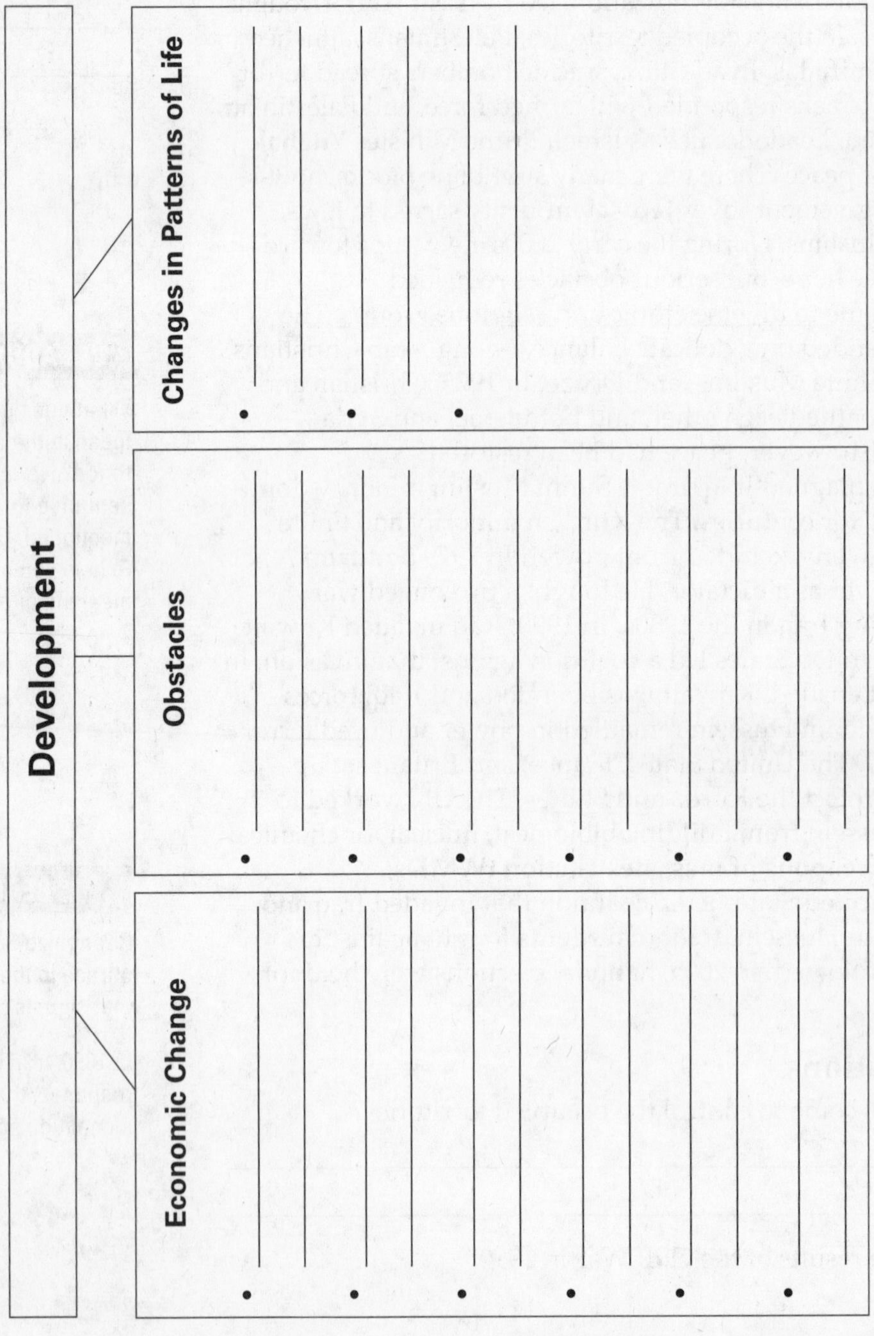

Name________________________ Class___________ Date______

CHAPTER 21 SECTION 1

Section Summary

THE CHALLENGES OF DEVELOPMENT

After World War II, a central goal in Africa, Asia, and Latin America was **development,** or creating a more advanced economy and higher living standards. Nations that are working toward this are referred to as the **developing world.** They are also called the global South, because most of these nations are south of the Tropic of Cancer. Most industrialized nations are north of the Tropic of Cancer, so they are sometimes called the global North. Nations of the global South have tried to develop economically by improving their agriculture and industry. They have also built schools to increase **literacy.**

To pay for development, many countries in the global South procured large loans from industrialized nations. For centuries, most people in the global South had lived and worked in **traditional economies.** After gaining independence from European colonists, some of these countries experimented with government-led command economies. However, when these countries had trouble paying off their loans, lenders from the global North required many of them to change to market economies. Now many developing nations depend on the global North for investment and exports.

Beginning in the 1950s, improved seeds, pesticides, and mechanical equipment led to a **Green Revolution** in many parts of the developing world. This increased agricultural production, feeding many more people. It also benefited large landowners at the expense of small farmers. These farmers sold their land and moved to cities.

The global South still faces many challenges. Some developing nations produce only one export product. If prices for that product drop, their economies suffer. Also, the population in many of these countries has grown rapidly. Many people are caught in a cycle of poverty. When families are forced to move to cities, they often find only low-paying jobs. As a result, many children must work to help support their families. With so many moving to cities, many people are forced to live in crowded and dangerous **shantytowns.**

Economic development has brought great changes to the developing world. In many countries, women have greater equality. However, some religious **fundamentalists** oppose these changes and have called for a return to the basic values of their faiths.

Review Questions

1. What happened when nations in the global South had trouble repaying their loans?

____

____

2. What problems do people in the developing world often face when they move to cities?

____

____

READING CHECK

What is development?

____

____

____

VOCABULARY STRATEGY

What does the word *procured* mean in the underlined sentence? Notice that *procured* refers to loans. Use this clue to help you figure out the meaning of the word *procured.*

READING SKILL

Identify Supporting Details Record details that support this statement: "The global South faces many challenges."

____

____

____

Name________________________ Class__________________ Date________

CHAPTER 21 SECTION 2

Note Taking Study Guide

AFRICA SEEKS A BETTER FUTURE

Focus Question: What challenges have African nations faced in their effort to develop their economies?

As you read this section in your textbook, complete the concept web below to record the main ideas about challenges faced by African nations, and details that support those main ideas.

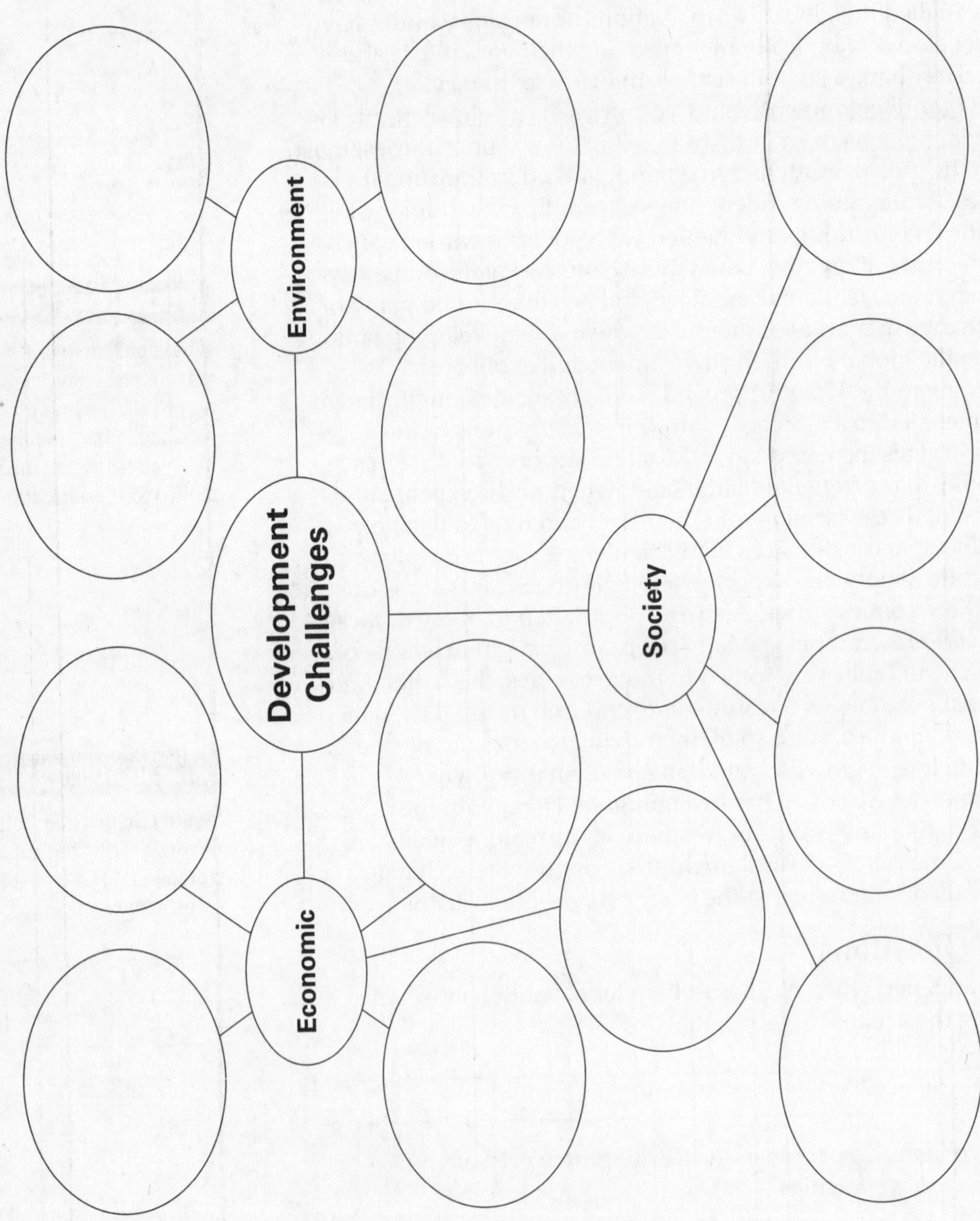

Name________________________ Class___________ Date______

CHAPTER 21 SECTION 2

Section Summary

AFRICA SEEKS A BETTER FUTURE

After World War II, African nations had little capital to invest, so they had to make difficult economic choices. Some nations chose **socialism,** a system in which the government controls parts of the economy. The leaders of these governments hoped to end foreign influence in their countries and to close the gap between the rich and the poor. However, socialism sometimes led to large, inefficient bureaucracies. Other nations relied on capitalism, or market economies. These economies were often more efficient, but foreign owners of businesses took profits out of the country. Some governments tried to fund development by growing crops for export, rather than food crops. However, this forced them to import food to replace the food crops. Governments then had to subsidize part of the cost of importing food from overseas.

African nations faced many obstacles to development. Droughts led to famine in parts of Africa. This was especially true in the Sahel, where overgrazing and farming led to **desertification.** People in African nations also faced the devastating disease AIDS. In the early 2000s, more than 2 million Africans died of the disease each year. **Urbanization** has also created problems in Africa. This shift from rural areas to cities has meant hardship for many and has weakened traditional cultures and ethnic ties. However, in West Africa, the growth of urban markets has increased opportunities for women.

Another concern in Africa is environmental threats. Nearly 70 percent of Africa's animal habitats have been destroyed, causing many animals to become **endangered species.** Other animal species are being killed for their tusks or fur. One environmental activist, **Wangari Maathai,** has fought back by starting the Green Belt Movement. This organization promotes reforestation. It also helps local women with projects of **sustainable development** that aim to provide lasting benefits for future generations.

A close look at Tanzania reveals the problems that many African counties have faced. In the 1960s, the government embraced "African socialism." However, attempts to build on African traditions of cooperation failed to increase agricultural production. In 1985, new leaders introduced economic reforms. However, Tanzania remains poor and has had to rely on foreign loans to avoid economic crisis.

Review Questions

1. Why did some African nations choose socialism?

____

____

2. Why are many animal species in Africa endangered?

____

____

READING CHECK

What is urbanization?

____

____

____

VOCABULARY STRATEGY

What does the word *subsidize* mean in the underlined sentence? *Subsidize* comes from a Latin word that means "aid" or "support." Use this clue to help you figure out the meaning of the word *subsidize.*

READING SKILL

Identify Main Ideas What is the main idea of this Summary?

____

____

____

Name______________________ Class__________________ Date__________

CHAPTER 21 SECTION 3

Note Taking Study Guide

CHINA AND INDIA: TWO GIANTS OF ASIA

Focus Question: How do China and India compare in building strong economies and democratic governments?

As you read this section in your textbook, complete the table below to record the main ideas about reform and change in China and India.

Reform and Change in China and India

Type	China	India
Economic	• Free market • • • • • •	• • • • •
Political	• • •	• • •

Name________________________ Class___________ Date______

CHAPTER 21 SECTION 3

Section Summary

CHINA AND INDIA: TWO GIANTS OF ASIA

After Mao Zedong died, moderate leaders took control of China. **Deng Xiaoping** began a program called the Four Modernizations, which allowed some features of a free-market economy. Some private ownership of property was permitted, and entrepreneurs could set up businesses. Farmers were allowed to sell surplus produce and keep the profits. Foreign investment was also welcomed. These reforms brought a surge of economic growth, although a gap developed between poor farmers and wealthy city dwellers. After 30 years of reforms, China's economic output quadrupled.

Despite these economic reforms, however, Communist leaders refused to allow more political freedom. Demonstrators seeking democratic reforms occupied **Tiananmen Square** in Beijing in May 1989. When the demonstrators refused to disperse, the government sent in troops and tanks. Thousands were killed or wounded.

China continues to face many challenges. Its population is the largest in the world. The government started the **one-child policy** to prevent population growth from hurting economic development. Population growth slowed. Many rural workers have moved to cities, but they often live in poverty there. Pollution and HIV/AIDS are also problems. Critics of the government are jailed, and human rights abuses continue.

By contrast, India is the world's largest democracy. After gaining independence, India's government adopted a command economy, but development was uneven. The Green Revolution in the 1960s improved crop output, but most farmers continued to use traditional methods. In the 1980s, India shifted toward a free-market system. By the 1990s, several Indian industries were expanding rapidly.

Despite these improvements, India's population growth has hurt efforts to improve living conditions. The Indian government backed family planning, but it had limited success. More than one-third of Indians live below the poverty line. Many rural families moved to overcrowded cities like **Kolkata** and **Mumbai.** To help the urban poor, **Mother Teresa** founded the Missionaries of Charity.

Changes in India have brought improvements for India's lowest social castes and women. India's constitution bans discrimination against **dalits**, people in the lowest caste, but prejudice persists. The constitution also grants equal rights to women.

Review Questions

1. What impact have economic reforms had in China?

____

____

2. Name two groups that have benefited from changes in India.

____

____

READING CHECK

Which country, India or China, has had more success in limiting population growth?

____

____

____

VOCABULARY STRATEGY

What does the word *disperse* mean in the underlined sentence? Notice that demonstrators occupied, or gathered in, Tiananmen Square and then refused to *disperse.* Use this clue to help you figure out the meaning of the word *disperse.*

READING SKILL

Identify Main Ideas In your own words, write the main idea of the first paragraph of this Summary.

____

____

____

Name________________ Class________________ Date________

CHAPTER 21 SECTION 4

Note Taking Study Guide

LATIN AMERICA BUILDS DEMOCRACY

Focus Question: What challenges have Latin American nations faced in recent decades in their struggle for democracy and prosperity?

As you read this section in your textbook, complete this outline to identify the main ideas and supporting details about challenges faced by Latin American nations.

I. **Economic and Social Forces**
   A. Society
      1. ________________
      2. ________________
      3. ________________
      4. ________________
   B. ________________
      1. ________________
      2. ________________
      3. ________________
      4. ________________

II. ________________
   A. ________________
      1. ________________
      2. ________________
      3. ________________
   B. ________________
      1. ________________
      2. ________________
   C. ________________
      1. ________________
      2. ________________
      3. ________________
      4. ________________
      5. ________________
      6. ________________
      7. ________________

(Outline continues on the next page.)

Name______________________ Class______________ Date________

CHAPTER 21 SECTION 4

Note Taking Study Guide

LATIN AMERICA BUILDS DEMOCRACY

(Continued from page 220)

D. ______________________________

1. ______________________________

2. ______________________________

E. ______________________________

1. ______________________________

2. ______________________________

III. ______________________________

A. ______________________________

1. ______________________________

2. ______________________________

B. ______________________________

1. ______________________________

2. ______________________________

3. ______________________________

4. ______________________________

5. ______________________________

Name_______________ Class___________ Date______

CHAPTER 21 SECTION 4

Section Summary

LATIN AMERICA BUILDS DEMOCRACY

READING CHECK

What is liberation theology?

____

____

____

VOCABULARY STRATEGY

What does the word *alleged* mean in the underlined sentence? This verb is often used in legal proceedings. The noun form is *allegation.* An *allegation* is "an assertion made without proof." Use these clues to help you understand the meaning of *alleged.*

READING SKILL

Identify Main Ideas and Supporting Details Outline the last paragraph in the Summary on the lines below.

____

____

____

____

____

____

____

In the 1950s and 1960s, many governments in Latin America encouraged industries to manufacture goods that had previously been imported. This is called **import substitution.** More recently, government policies have focused on producing goods for export. Governments have also tried to open more land to farming, but much of the best land belongs to large **agribusinesses.** In many countries, a few people control the land and businesses, and wealth is distributed unevenly. Another problem is population growth, which has contributed to poverty. Many religious leaders have worked for justice and an end to poverty in a movement known as **liberation theology.**

Because of poverty and inequality, democracy has been difficult to achieve in Latin America. Between the 1950s and 1970s, military leaders seized power in Argentina, Brazil, Chile, and other countries. From the 1960s to the 1990s, civil wars shook parts of Central America. In Guatemala, the military targeted the **indigenous** population and slaughtered thousands of Native Americans.

The United States has had a powerful influence in Latin America. It has dominated the **Organization of American States (OAS).** During the Cold War, the United States backed dictators who were anticommunist. When socialist rebels called **Sandinistas** came to power in Nicaragua, the United States supported the **contras,** guerrillas who fought the Sandinistas. The United States has also pressed Latin American governments to help stop the drug trade. Many Latin Americans alleged that the problem was not in Latin America but was based on the demand for drugs in the United States.

By the 1990s, democratic reforms led to free elections in many countries. In Mexico, the Institutional Revolutionary Party (PRI) had dominated the government since the 1920s. However, in 2000, an opposition candidate was elected president. Argentina experienced 50 years of political upheavals beginning in the 1930s. **Juan Perón,** Argentina's president from 1946 to 1955, enjoyed great support from workers but was ousted in a military coup. The military seized control again in 1976 and murdered or kidnapped thousands. Mothers whose sons and daughters were missing protested and became known as the **Mothers of the Plaza de Mayo.** By 1983, the military was forced to allow elections.

Review Questions

1. Why was democracy difficult to achieve in Latin America?

____

____

2. Why did the United States support dictators in Latin America during the Cold War?

____

____

Name______________________ Class__________________ Date________

CHAPTER 22 SECTION 1 Note Taking Study Guide

INDUSTRIALIZED NATIONS AFTER THE COLD WAR

Focus Question: How did the end of the Cold War affect industrialized nations and regions around the world?

As you read this section in your textbook, complete the chart below to compare and contrast developments in industrialized nations after the Cold War.

Asia	• • • • •
Russia/United States	Russia • • • • United States • • • •
Europe	• 1991—Germany is reunified. • • • • •

Name______________________ Class__________ Date______

CHAPTER 22 SECTION 1

Section Summary

INDUSTRIALIZED NATIONS AFTER THE COLD WAR

READING CHECK

Which four Pacific Rim countries are called the "Asian tigers"?

____

____

____

VOCABULARY STRATEGY

What does the word *inflation* mean in the underlined sentence? Think about what happens when you *inflate* a tire. In this sentence, *inflation* refers to prices. If prices are *inflated,* would you expect them to be higher or lower? Use these clues to help you understand the meaning of *inflation.*

READING SKILL

Compare and Contrast Compare and contrast the U.S. economy in the early 1990s with the economy in the early 2000s.

____

____

____

The beginning of a new global economy began with the end of the Cold War. The division between communist Eastern and democratic Western Europe crumbled. Business and travel became easier. At the same time, new challenges emerged, including a rise in unemployment and in immigration from the developing world. One exciting change was the reunification of Germany. However, East Germany's economy was weak and had to be modernized.

In the 1990s, the European Economic Community became the **European Union** (EU). The **euro** soon became the common currency for most of Western Europe. By the early 2000s, more than a dozen countries had joined the EU, including some Eastern European nations. The expanded EU allowed Europe to compete economically with the United States and Japan. However, older members of the EU worried that the weak economies of Eastern European nations might harm the EU. Most Eastern European nations wanted to join NATO, too.

After the breakup of the Soviet Union, Russia struggled to forge a market economy. Unemployment and prices soared, and criminals flourished. In 1998, Russia **defaulted** on much of its foreign debt. <u>High inflation and the collapse of the Russian currency forced banks and businesses to close.</u> When **Vladimir Putin** became president in 2000, he promised to end corruption and strengthen Russia's economy. However, he also increased government power at the expense of civil liberties.

After the Cold War, the United States became the world's only superpower. It waged wars in the Middle East and started peacekeeping operations in Haiti and the former Yugoslavia. An economic boom in the 1990s produced a budget **surplus** in the United States. Within a decade, however, slow economic growth and soaring military expenses led to huge budget **deficits.**

The **Pacific Rim** nations have become a rising force in the global economy. Following World War II, Japan became an economic powerhouse and dominated this region. However, by the 1990s, Japan's economy began to suffer, and Taiwan, Hong Kong, Singapore, and South Korea surged ahead. These "Asian tigers" have achieved economic success, due in part to low wages, long hours, and other worker sacrifices.

Review Questions

1. When did the global economy begin to develop?

____

____

2. What economic challenges did Russia face after the breakup of the Soviet Union?

____

____

Name____________________________ Class______________________ Date________

CHAPTER 22 SECTION 2

Note Taking Study Guide

GLOBALIZATION

Focus Question: How is globalization affecting economies and societies around the world?

As you read this section in your textbook, use the Venn diagram to compare the effects of globalization on developed and developing nations.

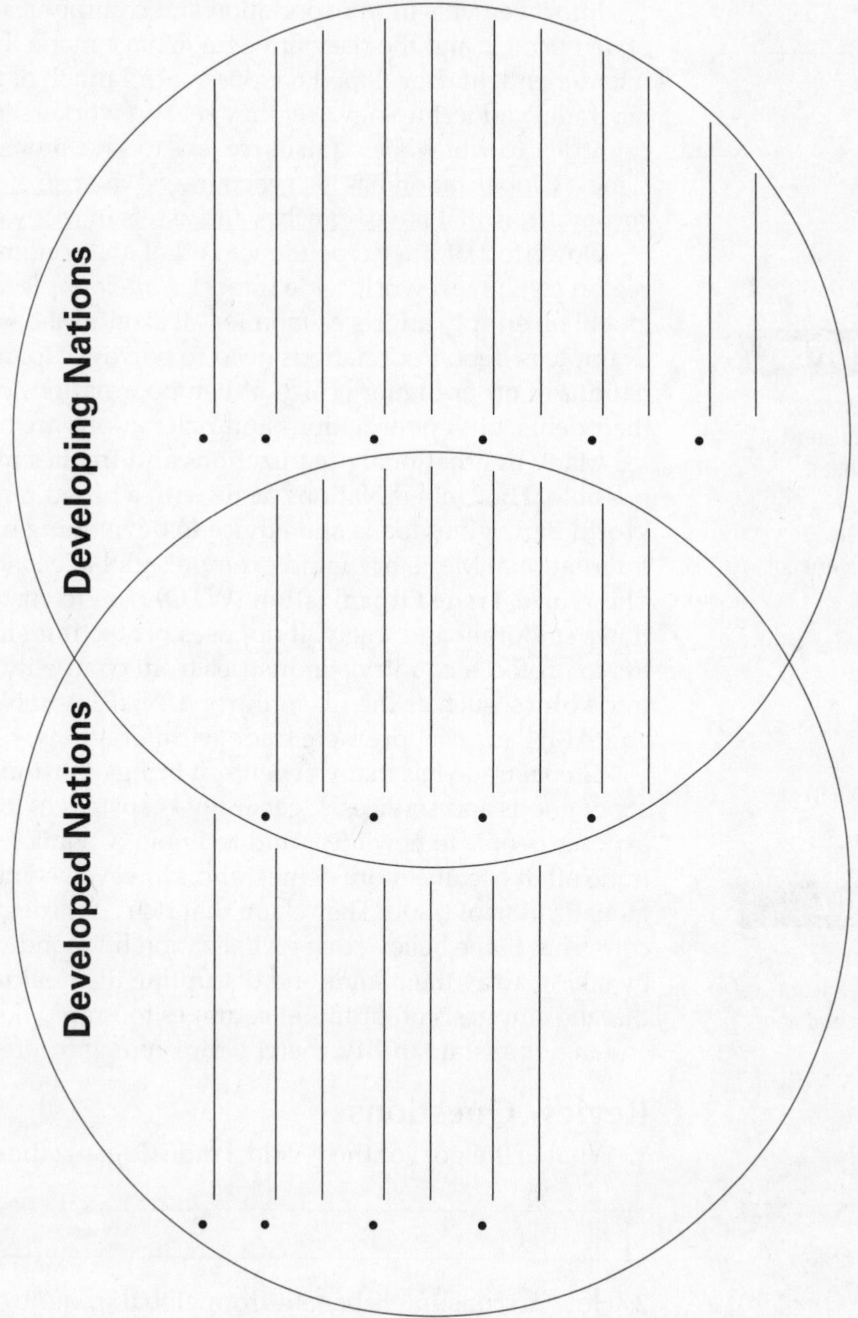

Name________________________ Class___________ Date______

CHAPTER 22 SECTION 2

Section Summary

GLOBALIZATION

READING CHECK

What is globalization?

____

____

____

VOCABULARY STRATEGY

What does the word *assets* mean in the underlined sentence? Think about what it means if someone says that you are an *asset* to the team. Use this clue to help you figure out the meaning of *assets.*

READING SKILL

Compare and Contrast Compare and contrast the effect of borrowing capital on rich and poor nations.

____

____

____

Globalization defines the post-Cold War world. It is the process by which national economies, politics, and cultures become integrated with those of other nations. One effect of globalization is economic **interdependence.** This means that countries depend on one another for goods, resources, knowledge, and labor.

Improvements in transportation and communication, the spread of democracy, and the rise of free trade have made the world more interdependent. Developed nations control much of the world's capital, trade, and technology. Yet they rely on workers in developing countries, to which they **outsource** jobs to save money or increase efficiency. Globalization has also encouraged the rise of **multinational corporations** that have branches and assets in many countries.

One effect of interdependence is that an economic crisis in one region can have a worldwide impact. For example, any change to the global oil supply affects economies all around the world. Another example is debt. Poor nations need to borrow capital from rich nations in order to modernize. When poor nations cannot repay their debts, both poor nations and rich nations are hurt.

Many international organizations and treaties make global trade possible. The United Nations deals with a broad range of issues. The World Bank gives loans and advice to developing nations. The International Monetary Fund promotes global economic growth. The **World Trade Organization (WTO)** tries to ensure that trade flows smoothly and freely. It opposes **protectionism**—the use of tariffs to protect a country's industries from competition. Regional trade **blocs,** such as the EU in Europe, NAFTA in North America, and APEC in Asia, promote trade within regions.

Global trade has many benefits. It brings consumers a greater variety of goods and services. It generally keeps prices lower. It also exposes people to new ideas and technology. Nations involved in free trade often become more democratic. However, some people oppose globalization of trade. They claim that rich countries exploit poor countries. Some believe that globalization hurts indigenous peoples by taking away their lands and disrupting their cultures. Others say that the emphasis on profits encourages too-rapid development. This endangers **sustainability,** thereby threatening future generations.

Review Questions

1. What is the goal of the World Trade Organization?

____

____

2. How do consumers benefit from global trade?

____

____

Name_________________ Class_________________ Date_________

CHAPTER 22 SECTION 3

Note Taking Study Guide

SOCIAL AND ENVIRONMENTAL CHALLENGES

Focus Question: How do poverty, disease, and environmental challenges affect people around the world today?

As you read this section in your textbook, complete the chart below to compare aspects of globalization.

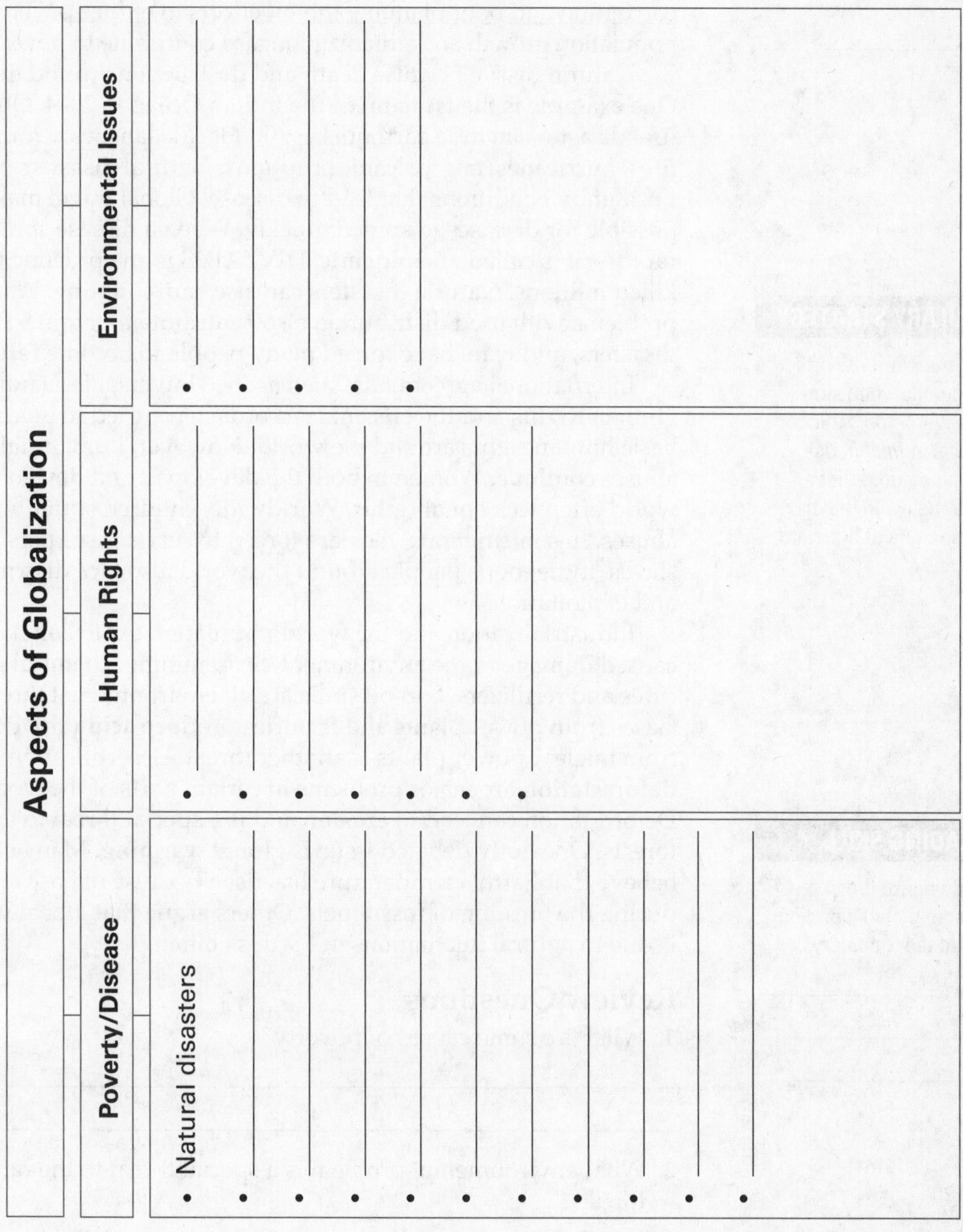

Name________________________ Class____________ Date______

CHAPTER 22 SECTION 3

Section Summary

SOCIAL AND ENVIRONMENTAL CHALLENGES

READING CHECK

What is an epidemic?

____

____

____

VOCABULARY STRATEGY

What does the word *inhibit* mean in the underlined sentence? The words *help* and *aid* are antonyms of *inhibit*. Use what you know about these antonyms to help you understand the meaning of the word *inhibit*.

READING SKILL

Compare Compare the two theories about global warming mentioned in the Summary.

____

____

____

Poverty, disasters, and disease are still challenges today. The gap between rich and poor nations is growing. Half the world's population earns less than $2 a day. Poverty is a complex issue with many causes. Many poor nations owe billions in debt and have little money to spend to improve living conditions. Political upheavals, civil war, corruption and poor planning inhibit efforts to reduce poverty. Rapid population growth and urbanization also contribute to poverty.

Natural disasters cause death and destruction around the world. One example is the **tsunami** in the Indian Ocean in 2004. Other natural disasters include earthquakes, floods, avalanches, droughts, fires, hurricanes, and volcanic eruptions. Natural disasters can cause unsanitary conditions that lead to disease. Global travel makes it possible for diseases to spread quickly. When a disease spreads rapidly, it is called an **epidemic.** HIV/AIDS is an epidemic that has killed millions. Natural disasters can also cause **famine.** Wars and problems with food distribution also contribute to famine. Poverty, disasters, and wars have forced many people to become **refugees.**

International agreements, such as the Universal Declaration of Human Rights and the Helsinki Accords, have tried to guarantee basic human rights around the world. However, human rights abuses continue. Women in both the developed and developing world often lack equal rights. Worldwide, children suffer terrible abuses. In some nations, they are forced to serve as soldiers or slaves. Indigenous people around the world also face discrimination and exploitation.

Industrialization and the world population explosion have caused damage to the environment. Strip mining, chemical pesticides and fertilizers, and oil spills are all environmental threats. Gases from power plants and factories produce **acid rain.** Pollution from nuclear power plants is another threat. Desertification and **deforestation** are major problems in certain parts of the world. Deforestation can lead to **erosion** and is a special threat to the rain forests. One hotly debated issue is **global warming.** Many scientists believe that Earth's temperature has risen because of gases released during the burning of fossil fuels. Others argue that global warming is due to natural fluctuations in Earth's climate.

Review Questions

1. What are some causes of poverty?

____

____

2. What environmental problem is a special threat to the rain forests?

____

____

Name______________________ Class______________________ Date__________

CHAPTER 22 SECTION 4

Note Taking Study Guide

SECURITY IN A DANGEROUS WORLD

Focus Question: What kinds of threats to national and global security do nations face today?

As you read this section in your textbook, complete the chart below to compare threats to global security.

Threats to Security		
Nuclear Weapons	Nuclear weapons are unsecured in Soviet Union.	

Name________________________ Class____________ Date______

CHAPTER 22 SECTION 4

Section Summary

SECURITY IN A DANGEROUS WORLD

READING CHECK

What is terrorism?

____

____

____

VOCABULARY STRATEGY

What does the word *priority* mean in the underlined sentence? Notice the sentence that follows it. What did the United States do because security was a *priority?* Use this context clue to help you understand the meaning of the word *priority.*

READING SKILL

Compare and Contrast Compare and contrast information about nuclear weapons before and after the Nuclear Nonproliferation Treaty.

____

____

____

Weapons of mass destruction (WMDs) include nuclear, biological, and chemical weapons. During the Cold War, the United States and Russia built up arsenals of nuclear weapons. To ensure that nuclear weapons did not **proliferate,** or spread rapidly, many nations signed the Nuclear Nonproliferation Treaty (NPT) in 1968. However, the treaty does not guarantee that nuclear weapons will not be used. Four nations have not signed the treaty, and other nations, such as Iran and North Korea, are suspected of buying and selling nuclear weapons even though they are treaty members. Stockpiles of nuclear weapons in the former Soviet Union are a special concern. This is because the Russian government has not had money to secure the weapons properly.

In the 2000s, terrorist groups and "rogue states" began to use WMDs for their own purposes. **Terrorism** is the use of violence, especially against civilians, to achieve political goals. Terrorist groups use headline-grabbing tactics to draw attention to their demands. Regional terrorist groups, such as the Irish Republican Army (IRA), operated for decades. They commit bombings, shootings, and kidnappings to force their governments to change policies. Increasingly, the Middle East has become a training ground and source for terrorism. Islamic fundamentalism motivates many of these groups. One powerful Islamic fundamentalist group is **al Qaeda,** whose leader is Osama bin Laden. Al Qaeda terrorists were responsible for the attacks on the United States on September 11, 2001.

Al Qaeda's attacks triggered a global reaction. Fighting terrorism became a central goal of both national and international policies. In 2001, Osama bin Laden and other al Qaeda leaders were living in **Afghanistan.** When Afghanistan's Islamic fundamentalist leaders, the **Taliban,** refused to surrender the terrorists, the United States attacked Afghanistan and overthrew them. Because President Bush believed that Saddam Hussein of Iraq was secretly producing WMDs, the United States also declared war on Iraq. <u>In addition, increased security at home became a priority.</u> As a result, the United States created a new Department of Homeland Security and instituted more rigorous security measures at airports and public buildings.

Review Questions

1. Why are nuclear weapons in the former Soviet Union a special concern?

____

____

2. Why did the United States declare war on Iraq?

____

____

Name________________________ Class____________________ Date__________

CHAPTER 22 SECTION 5

Note Taking Study Guide

ADVANCES IN SCIENCE AND TECHNOLOGY

Focus Question: How have advances in science and technology shaped the modern world?

As you read this section in your textbook, complete the chart below to compare the impacts of modern science and technology.

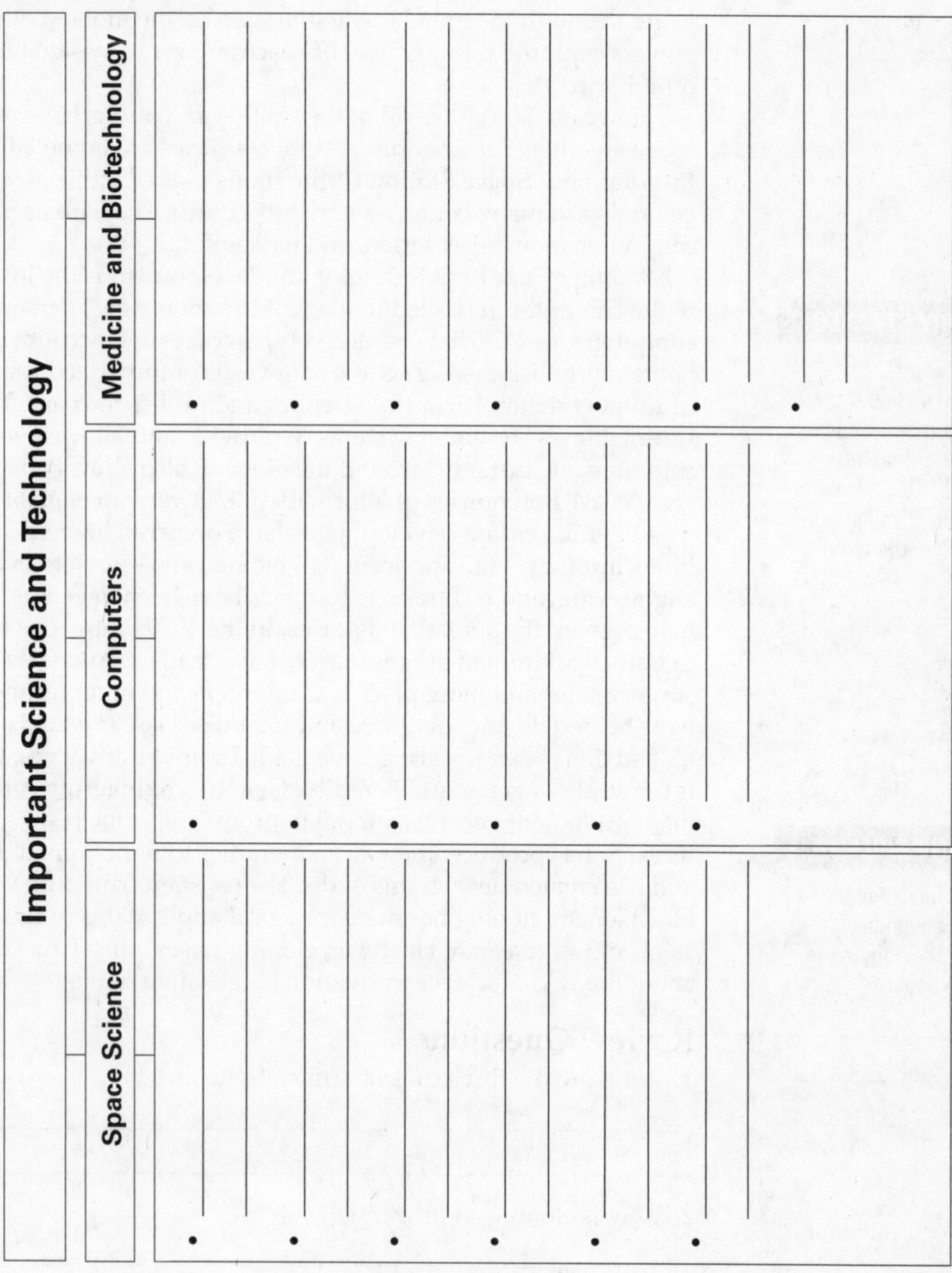

Name______________________ Class__________ Date______

CHAPTER 22 SECTION 5

Section Summary

ADVANCES IN SCIENCE AND TECHNOLOGY

Since 1945, scientific research and technological developments have transformed human existence. One example is the exploration of space. During the Cold War, the United States and the Soviet Union competed in a "space race." This began in 1957 when the Soviet Union launched *Sputnik,* the first **artificial satellite.** By 1969, the United States had landed the first human on the moon. Both superpowers explored military uses of space and sent spy satellites to orbit Earth.

However, since the end of the Cold War, nations have worked in space together. For example, several countries are involved in the **International Space Station (ISS).** Thousands of artificial satellites belonging to many countries now orbit Earth. They are used for communication, observation, and navigation.

Another important technological development is the invention of the computer. It has led to the "Information Age." **Personal computers**, or **PCs**, have replaced typewriters and account books in homes and businesses. Factories now use computerized robots, and computers remotely control satellites and probes in space. The **Internet** links computer systems worldwide and allows people to communicate instantly around the globe. It also allows people to access vast storehouses of information that were unavailable before.

Other important developments have occurred in medicine and **biotechnology**—the application of biological research to industry, engineering, and technology. Vaccines have been developed that help prevent the spread of diseases. In the 1970s, surgeons learned to transplant human organs. **Lasers** have made many types of surgery safer and more precise. Computers and other technologies have helped doctors diagnose and treat diseases. The fields of genetics and genetic engineering have made dramatic advances. **Genetics** is the study of genes and heredity. **Genetic engineering** is the manipulation of genetic material to produce specific results. Genetic research has produced new drug therapies to fight human diseases and has created new strains of disease-resistant fruits and vegetables. Genetic cloning has many practical applications in raising livestock and in research. However, cloning raises ethical questions about the role of science in creating and changing life.

READING CHECK

What is biotechnology?

____

____

____

VOCABULARY STRATEGY

What does the word *manipulation* mean in the underlined sentence? It comes from the Latin word *manus,* meaning "hand." Use this word-origins clue to help you figure out the meaning of the word *manipulation.*

READING SKILL

Compare How have people benefited from advances in science and technology since the space race began?

____

____

____

Review Questions

1. What are the three uses of artificial satellites?

____

____

2. Why is cloning controversial?

____

____

Name________________________ Class__________________ Date________

Concept Connector Study Guide

Belief Systems

Essential Question: What major belief systems have emerged over time?

A. Define *belief system.* ______________________________________

____

____

B. *Record information about the topics listed in the Cumulative Review or your answers to the questions in the Cumulative Review below. Use the Concept Connector Handbooks at the end of your textbook, as well as chapter information, to complete this worksheet.*

1. **Animism**
The belief that the world is full of spirits and forces that reside in animals, objects, or dreams is known as animism. Animism has existed since prehistoric time. Cave paintings may be evidence that early peoples held animist beliefs. The paintings lie deep in caves, far from the everyday activities of early people. They feature vivid images of deer, horses, and buffaloes. Some cave paintings show people, too. Scholars believe the paintings may have been created as part of animist religious rituals. Today animism is considered a primal-indigenous belief.

2. **Judaism**
Scholars date the origins of Judaism to around 2000 B.C. The Jews of ancient history were known as Hebrews or Israelites. The beliefs of the Israelites differed in a significant way from other ancient people. The Israelites were monotheistic, believing in one God. The Israelites believed that God had made a covenant, or promise and binding agreement, with them. If the Jewish people obeyed God's commands, God would make Israel a great nation. Today, Judaism is considered a major world religion. Judaism influenced both Christianity and Islam.

3. **The Influence of Religion on Ancient Egyptian and Ancient Israelite Society**
People in many early civilizations established belief systems that became an important force in shaping their societies. For example, religious beliefs about gods, values, and life after death affected the daily lives of ancient Egyptians. The rulers of Egypt, or pharaohs, were viewed as gods. Tremendous resources were used to prepare people for the afterlife. Israelites believed in an all-knowing, all-powerful God who was present everywhere. They believed that each event in their history reflected God's plan for them. As a result, they recorded events and laws in the Torah, their sacred text. Unlike ancient Egyptians, Jews saw their leaders as fully human and bound to obey God's law.

Name____________________________ Class____________________ Date________

Concept Connector Study Guide

4. Compare the Views of Ancient Egyptians and Ancient Indians

Different societies often have different beliefs about the results of a person's actions during his or her lifetime. The ancient Egyptians believed that after death a soul had to pass a test to win eternal life. Egyptians learned spells and formulas to use in the afterlife to prove their worthiness to the gods. Unlike ancient Egyptian beliefs, ancient Indians believed that their actions during life influenced what happened to them after they died. The beliefs of ancient Indians developed into concepts of dharma, karma, and reincarnation.

Dharma includes the religious and moral duties of an individual. *Karma* refers to all the actions of a person's life that affect his or her fate in the next life. *Reincarnation* is the rebirth of the soul in another bodily form.

5. Christianity

Christianity arose in the first century A.D. in Judea, which was part of the Roman empire at the time. It is based on the teachings of Jesus, a Jewish rabbi, or teacher. Jesus emphasized God's love and taught the need for justice, morality, and service to others. Christianity teaches that there is one God who sent Jesus to save humans. Jesus' disciples spread his message throughout the Roman empire after his death. Paul, an important early leader, traveled around the Mediterranean to set up churches. His letters form a large portion of the New Testament. The New Testament is part of the Bible, the sacred text of Christians, which also contains the Hebrew Bible. Although Christians were initially persecuted by Rome, Christianity eventually became the official religion of the Roman empire. Today Christianity is a major world religion with over 2 billion followers.

6. The Great Schism

Over time, Christianity developed differently in the eastern and western Roman empires. Christians in the east spoke Greek; Christians in the west spoke Latin. Theological differences caused controversies. During the Middle Ages, the two branches of Christianity drew further apart. In the 700s, a dispute over the use of icons, or holy images, contributed to the problems. Finally, in 1054, the popes of the eastern and western churches excommunicated each other. The event is called the Great Schism. The eastern branch became known as the Eastern, or Orthodox, Church, while the western branch became known as the Roman Catholic Church. For centuries, the two churches treated each other as rivals rather than as branches of the same faith.

7. Muhammad and the Idea of Brotherhood

Islam has been an important force in history. The sayings of Muhammad, the founder of Islam, contributed to Islam's growth. For instance, Muhammad said, "Know ye that every Muslim is a brother to every other Muslim and that ye are now one brotherhood." Islam, which developed in the 600s, became a unifying force in the Arab world. Once Arabs united, they were able to conquer huge territories from the Persian empire to Spain. Islam emphasized the equality of all believers, and many conquered people were attracted to the message of Islam.

Name______________________ Class__________________ Date________

Concept Connector Study Guide

BELIEF SYSTEMS *(continued)*

8. Shinto

Shinto developed in Japan by the A.D. 500s. Shinto is the worship of the forces of nature. Early Japanese clans honored kami, or superior powers that were natural or divine. Shinto, meaning "the way of kami," became an important religion in Japan. Hundreds of Shinto shrines dot the Japanese countryside. These shrines are located in beautiful and natural surroundings, and may be dedicated to objects such as mountains, waterfalls, gnarled trees, or oddly shaped rocks.

9. Impact of Missionaries (Chapter 12, page 417)

Name______________________ Class__________________ Date________

Concept Connector Study Guide

BELIEF SYSTEMS *(continued)*

C. Sample Topics for Thematic Essays

Below are examples of thematic essay topics that might appear on a test. Prepare for the test by outlining an essay for each topic on a separate sheet of paper. Use the Concept Connector Handbooks at the end of your textbook, as well as chapter information, to outline your essays.

1. Describe the impact of Martin Luther's ideas on the development of Protestantism, as well as on the Roman Catholic Church.

2. Discuss how the Scientific Revolution challenged or changed European belief systems.

3. Explain how belief systems can bring cultural unity to many peoples and nations.

4. Describe the roots of Judaism and its influence on both Christianity and Islam.

5. Explain how missionaries, representing different belief systems, have influenced peoples and cultures.

6. Discuss how belief systems may support or work against political and social systems. In your essay, include examples, such as the human-rights efforts of Spanish Catholic clergy in the Americas or Gandhi's embrace of Hindu traditions as he worked for India's independence.

7. Describe the beliefs of Methodism, founded by John Wesley in the mid-1700s, and its effects on industrial workers at the time.

8. Describe the influence of religion on the partition of India and Pakistan, and its role in the continuing conflicts between the two countries.

Name______________________ Class__________________ Date________

Concept Connector Study Guide

Conflict

Essential Question: What issues cause groups of people or countries to come into conflict?

A. Define *conflict.* ____

____

____

B. *Record information about the topics listed in the Cumulative Review or your answers to the questions in the Cumulative Review below. Use the Concept Connector Handbooks at the end of your textbook, as well as chapter information, to complete this worksheet.*

1. **The Persian Wars**
   Greek city-states developed different forms of government but shared a common culture and values. Greeks briefly put aside their differences to defend their freedom when the Persians threatened them. Ionian Greek city-states in Asia Minor became subjects of the Persian empire. In 499 B.C., Ionian Greeks rebelled against Persian rule, and the great city-state of Athens sent ships to help the Ionians. Then, in 490 B.C., Darius I of Persia sent his army to Greece to punish Athens. The large army landed near Marathon and was defeated by a much smaller Greek force. Ten years later, Xerxes, another Persian ruler, sent another force to conquer Greece. Finally, in 479 B.C., the Persian invasions ended when the Greeks defeated the Persians on land in Asia Minor.

2. **Compare the Persian Wars and the Punic Wars**
   Roman settlements spread throughout the Mediterranean, just as Greek city-states did around the Aegean. Both groups came into conflict with people across the sea. The Greeks fought the Persian Wars in part to preserve Greek culture when threatened by the Persians. As Rome grew in power, it came into conflict with Carthage, a great city-state in North Africa that ruled an empire stretching across the western Mediterranean. Between 264 B.C. and 146 B.C., Rome fought three wars against Carthage. These wars are called the Punic Wars. In the Second Punic War, the Carthaginian general Hannibal led his army, including dozens of war elephants, on an epic march from Spain over the Alps, to make a surprise attack on Rome. However, the Carthaginians were ultimately defeated and Rome was free to build an empire around the Mediterranean.

Name________________________ Class________________ Date________

Concept Connector Study Guide

CONFLICT *(continued)*

3. **Compare War Between Christians and Muslims in the 700s with the Crusades** The Crusades, which began in 1096, were not the first wars between Christians and Muslims. As the Muslim empire expanded west, it advanced into Europe. In the 700s, that advance was halted by Christian warriors at the Battle of Tours, in present-day France. After this, Muslim forces never again significantly threatened to take over Western Europe. Over 300 years later, invasions by Muslim Turks threatened the Byzantine empire and prevented Christian pilgrims from traveling to the Holy Land. Muslims and Christians fought for control of lands in the Middle East. These wars, called the Crusades, continued off and on, for over 200 years. Religion, desire for wealth and land, and a yearning for adventure were just some of the factors that motivated European crusaders. While the Crusades left a legacy of religious hatred, they also increased trade, the power of the pope, and the power of the European monarchs.

4. **Examples of French-British Conflict** (Chapter 2, page 105)

____

____

____

____

____

5. **Compare the American Revolution with the Thirty Years' War** (Chapter 5, page 205)

____

____

____

____

____

6. **European Revolutionaries in 1830 and 1848** (Chapter 8, page 291)

____

____

____

____

____

____

Name________________________ Class_________________ Date________

Concept Connector Study Guide

CONFLICT *(continued)*

7. **Congress of Vienna and the Paris Peace Conference** (Chapter 14, page 485)

8. **The Chinese Communists and the Guomindang** (Chapter 15, page 517)

9. **World War II** (Chapter 17, page 597)

10. **The Recent Conflict in Northern Ireland and Earlier Religious Conflicts** (Chapter 20, page 699)

Name________________________ Class________________ Date________

Concept Connector Study Guide

CONFLICT *(continued)*

C. Sample Topics for Thematic Essays

Below are examples of thematic essay topics that might appear on a test. Prepare for the test by outlining an essay for each topic on a separate sheet of paper. Use the Concept Connector Handbooks at the end of your textbook, as well as chapter information, to outline your essays.

1. Describes the results of conflicts between governments and citizens. You may wish to discuss the rise of labor unions during the Industrial Revolution, the Chartist movement in England, the Communards in France, or the Civil Rights movement in the United States.

2. Explain why nationalists in Europe fought against rulers during the revolutions of 1830 and 1848, and discuss the results of their struggles.

3. Describe the basic issues that led to the conflicts in the Balkans during the nineteenth and twentieth centuries and how the rest of the world has reacted to them.

4. Describe the issues that led to the partition of Africa by European powers in the late 1800s, and discuss how they served as the basis for conflicts between Africans and colonial powers between 1900 and 1975.

5. Compare and contrast the issues that sparked the Latin American wars of independence in the 1800s with those that created the movement for independence in Africa after World War II.

6. Describe some of the key features of the struggle between the Chinese Communists and the Guomindang (Nationalists) from the 1920s through the 1940s.

7. Analyze the issues that led to the breakup of the Soviet Union and the fall of communism in Eastern Europe in the 1980s and 1990s.

8. Describe and discuss the issues today that divide some Arabs and Arabs and Israelis in the Middle East.

Name____________________ Class__________________ Date________

Concept Connector Study Guide

Cooperation

Essential Question: In what ways have groups of people or countries cooperated over time?

A. Define *cooperation.* ______________________________

____

____

B. *Record information about the topics listed in the Cumulative Review or your answers to the questions in the Cumulative Review below. Use the Concept Connector Handbooks at the end of your textbook, as well as chapter information, to complete this worksheet.*

1. **Iroquois League**
   In Northeast America, several Native American groups spoke the same language and shared similar traditions. There are collectively known as the Iroquois. Typically, the Iroquois cleared land and built villages in the forests. While Iroquois women farmed, men hunted and fought wars against rival groups. In order to stop the constant wars, the Iroquois formed the Iroquois League in the late 1500s. The Iroquois League was an alliance of the Mohawk, Oneida, Onondaga, Cayuga, and Seneca. Nations that were members of the Iroquois League governed their own villages but met jointly in a council to address larger issues.

2. **Roads and Trade Routes**
   In different civilizations, road systems and trade routes have played important roles in connecting people. Some have connected people within a civilization, while others have connected people in different civilizations and across geographic regions. Roads and trade draw cultures together. Roads and trade also allow culture, language, and ideas to spread. For example, around 700 B.C., Phoenicians from the eastern Mediterranean set up colonies from North Africa to Sicily to Spain. Historians have called the Phoenicians "carriers of civilization" because they spread Middle Eastern civilization around the Mediterranean. Their alphabet was adapted by the Greeks—from this Greek alphabet came the alphabet we use today. Another example of the importance of roads and trade routes is the Silk Road, which began as a series of trade routes under the Han dynasty (202 B.C.–A.D. 220) in China and eventually linked China to the Fertile Crescent in the Middle East.

Name_______________ Class_______________ Date_______

Concept Connector Study Guide

COOPERATION *(continued)*

3. **Development of Medieval Trade Routes; Glorious Revolution; American Revolution** (Chapter 5, page 205)

4. **Coalitions Against Napoleon** (Chapter 6, page 241)

5. **Tactics of Abolitionist Groups** (Chapter 11, page 383)

Name________________________ Class______________ Date________

Concept Connector Study Guide

COOPERATION *(continued)*

6. League of Nations (Chapter 14, page 485)

7. United Nations (Chapter 17, page 597)

8. European Community (Chapter 18, page 647)

9. NGOs (Nongovernmental Organizations) (Chapter 22, page 765)

Name________________________ Class__________________ Date________

Concept Connector Study Guide

COOPERATION *(continued)*

C. Sample Topics for Thematic Essays

Below are examples of thematic essay topics that might appear on a test. Prepare for the test by outlining an essay for each topic on a separate sheet of paper. Use the Concept Connector Handbooks at the end of your textbook, as well as chapter information, to outline your essays.

1. Discuss cooperation as a factor in the change from nomadic to settled farming life and the beginnings of civilization.
2. Explain how cooperation is or is not a factor between developed and developing countries today.
3. Compare and contrast the Glorious Revolution with the American Revolution. For each revolution, discuss which groups cooperated, which groups were in conflict, and the forms of, or changes to, government that resulted.
4. Discuss how Enlightenment thinkers in France, England, and other European countries cooperated to refine their ideas and to spread them across Europe and beyond.
5. Describe the new level of cooperation pledged by the members of the League of Nations after World War I, and explain why the organization could not prevent World War II.
6. Describe the uneasy cooperation among Allied leaders Roosevelt, Churchill, and Stalin during World War II.
7. Describe the cooperative goals of the European Community (Common Market) and the European Union, and how it has improved the economies of its members.
8. Select two challenges the world faces in the twenty-first century, and discuss what kinds of cooperation will be needed to meet them. Consider economic, social, environmental, or security issues.

Name________________________ Class__________________ Date______

Concept Connector Study Guide

Cultural Diffusion

Essential Question: In what ways have migration and trade affected cultures?

A. Define *cultural diffusion.* ____

____

____

B. *Record information about the topics listed in the Cumulative Review or your answers to the questions in the Cumulative Review below. Use the Concept Connector Handbooks at the end of your textbook, as well as chapter information, to complete this worksheet.*

1. **Cultural Diffusion in Early Human History**
   Cultural diffusion has long been a key source of change in society. Some of the changes that took place during the Old Stone Age, the New Stone Age, and the time of early civilizations were likely the result of cultural diffusion. Developments in these periods include the use of fire, the creation of stone tools, the painting of caves, the domestication of plants and animals, and the development of early civilizations. These technologies were not invented everywhere at the same time. Knowledge traveled slowly, perhaps taking thousands of years to spread across continents.

2. **Arabic Numerals**
   The system of writing numbers that we use today was devised by Gupta mathematicians in India. The Guptas ruled from A.D. 320 to about 540. The system is commonly called Arabic; however, Hindu-Arabic is the more accurate term. Arab merchants and traders introduced the numerals as they traveled around the Mediterranean. The numerals may have been introduced in Europe via the Muslim empire in Spain. A European manuscript containing the numerals was written in Spain in 976. The superiority of the Hindu-Arabic numeral system is evident by its use nearly everywhere.

3. **Decimal System**
   Indian mathematicians also originated the concept of zero and developed the decimal system of numbers based on ten digits that we still use today. Mathematicians in the Islamic world adapted it to include decimal fractions. It was introduced to the West when a text written by the Muslim mathematician al-Khwarizmi in the 800s was translated into Latin in the 1200s.

Name________________________ Class__________________ Date________

Concept Connector Study Guide

4. Hinduism

Unlike most major religions, Hinduism has no single founder. Instead, it grew out of the overlapping beliefs of diverse groups who settled in India. Aryans began arriving in India by 1500 B.C. They added the gods of the Indus civilization to their own. Later people brought other gods, beliefs, and practices. As a result, Hinduism became one of the world's most complex religions, with many gods and goddesses, and many forms of worship. It has been said that Hinduism accepts all forms of belief and worship, and does not eliminate any.

5. Buddhism

Buddhism developed in India around 600 B.C. Its founder, Siddhartha Gautama, became known as the Buddha. Buddhism and Hinduism have some similarities, including ideas about nonviolence and reincarnation. Unlike Hinduism with its focus on priests and rituals, Buddhism urges each person to seek enlightenment through meditation. Missionaries and merchants spread Buddhism to many parts of Asia. By A.D. 500, Buddhism had spread from India into China, Tibet, Korea, and Japan. Buddhism slowly declined in India. However, Hinduism absorbed some Buddhist ideas and added Buddha as another Hindu god.

6. Evolution of the Alphabet

Even today, we can see examples of the important effects of cultural diffusion all around us. Indeed, the words on this page are the result of cultural diffusion. The alphabet we use today was developed by the Phoenicians. The Phoenician system used 22 symbols that stood for consonant sounds. The Phoenician alphabet was borrowed and modified by the Greeks. The Greeks added symbols for vowel sounds. That alphabet was then borrowed and adapted by the Romans. The alphabet was spread through trade and conquest, and because it was easier to use than other ancient writing systems, such as cuneiform or hieroglyphics.

7. The Spread of Roman Culture

Roman conquests and the empire (A.D. 27–A.D. 476) helped to spread Roman culture. That culture included language, literature, values, engineering, and laws. The Romans built roads to allow them easy access to all parts of the empire, and these roads allowed Roman culture to spread throughout Europe, North Africa, and the Middle East. The Romans developed laws to govern their large empire. Even after the empire fell, the Roman concept of law remained. Language, too, became a vehicle for spreading Roman culture. Romans wrote histories and epic poems that are read today. Latin remained the language of educated people and the Roman Catholic Church for hundreds of years.

8. The Spread of Christianity and the Spread of Buddhism

The spread of religions depends on a variety of factors, including the appeal of the religion's message and political support. Both Buddhism and Christianity spread far and wide from their original locations. Buddhism developed in South Asia in the late sixth to fourth century B.C. Today there are 373 million followers all over the world. Christianity developed in the early first century A.D. in the Middle East. There are over 2 billion Christians today. Both religions used missionaries to spread their beliefs.

Name______________________ Class__________________ Date_______

Concept Connector Study Guide

CULTURAL DIFFUSION *(continued)*

9. **The Roman and Byzantine Empires**
Byzantine rulers thought of their empire as the successor to the Roman empire. Like the Romans before them, the Byzantines spread their culture across a wide expanse of Europe. Both empires diffused language and learning, religion, art and architecture, and political ideas. The Byzantine Church, known as the Eastern, or Orthodox, Church, spread throughout Eastern Europe, the Balkans, and Russia. Byzantine scholars preserved the classic works of ancient Greece. As the Byzantine empire weakened in the 1400s, scholars left the Byzantine capital to teach in universities in the West. The work of these scholars contributed to the cultural flowering in Europe known as the Renaissance.

10. **The Spread of Islam**
Islam began in the Middle East in the A.D. 600s. Islam's founder, Muhammad, created rules that governed and united Muslims, and brought peace. As his reputation grew, thousands of Arabs adopted Islam. Islam is both a religion and a way of life. After the death of Muhammad, Islam continued to spread as the Muslim empire grew. Conquered people were treated fairly; Islam's message emphasized equality; Arab trade networks developed; and Muslim empires developed in Spain, Persia, and India. All of these factors contributed to the spread of Islam. Today, there are over one billion followers of Islam all over the world.

11. **The Spread of Ideas and Culture as a Result of Buddhist and Christian Missionaries**
Missionaries share more than their religious beliefs. They also help to spread language, values, technology, and ideas about laws and government. In the 500s, Buddhist missionaries introduced Chinese writing and customs to Japan. A Buddhist form of architecture, known as the stupa, developed into the Japanese pagoda. In the 800s, Christians from the Eastern, or Orthodox, Church adapted the Greek alphabet so they could translate the Bible into the Slavic languages. This alphabet is still used today in Russia, Ukraine, Serbia, and Bulgaria. Russians adopted other aspects of the missionaries' culture, including art, music, and architecture.

12. **The Renaissance and Islam** (Chapter 1, page 79)

____

____

____

____

____

____

____

Name________________________ Class________________ Date________

Concept Connector Study Guide

CULTURAL DIFFUSION *(continued)*

13. The Renaissance and the Tang and Song Dynasties (Chapter 1, page 79)

14. Indian Influence on Southeast Asia (Chapter 2, page 105)

15. Influence of Ancient Civilizations on Enlightenment Thinkers (Chapter 5, page 205)

Name________________________________ Class____________________ Date________

Concept Connector Study Guide

C. Sample Topics for Thematic Essays

Below are examples of thematic essay topics that might appear on a test. Prepare for the test by outlining an essay for each topic on a separate sheet of paper. Use the Concept Connector Handbooks at the end of your textbook, as well as chapter information, to outline your essays.

1. Explain how advances in science and technology are spread from culture to culture. Give examples to support your ideas.

2. Describe how the classical cultures of Greece and Rome influenced the Renaissance, and how Renaissance ideas then spread beyond Italy.

3. Discuss the importance of warfare and trade as agents of cultural diffusion.

4. Analyze the role of cultural diffusion in the modernization of Japan beginning in the 1850s.

5. Describe how the migration to Ireland in the 1600s changed the political and economic structure of the country and the impact of the Great Hunger of the 1840s.

6. Describe the ways in which Chinese culture spread to Korea during the Koryo and Choson dynasties. Give at least two examples of how the Koreans adopted certain aspects of Chinese culture, and how they adapted these cultural influences.

7. Discuss how increased trade and the demands of a global economy have changed people's lives in today's developing countries.

8. Describe at least two examples of cultural diffusion in the world today.

Name____________________ Class____________________ Date________

Concept Connector Study Guide

Democracy

Essential Question: How has the practice of democracy developed over time?

A. Define *democracy.* ____________________

____

____

B. *Record information about the topics listed in the Cumulative Review or your answers to the questions in the Cumulative Review below. Use the Concept Connector Handbooks at the end of your textbook, as well as chapter information, to complete this worksheet.*

1. **Roman Citizenship**
   Citizenship in Rome was important. In the Roman republic there was an official list of citizens. Citizenship conferred rights and responsibilities. For example, the Roman army was made up of citizen-soldiers. Roman citizens often made good soldiers because they were brought up to value loyalty, courage, and respect for authority. Rome developed one system of law that applied to citizens and another law system for non-citizens. Among the people Rome conquered, Rome gave the highly prized right of full citizenship to a few privileged groups, while other conquered people became partial citizens.
2. **Government by the People**
   In the Greek city-state of Athens, the idea of democracy first took root. Although many were excluded from the democratic process, citizens could gather and directly make important government decisions. In the Roman republic, as in the United States today, citizens were represented by a legislature. In 1215, English nobles forced King John to sign the Magna Carta. This document was another important step in the development of democracy. It asserted that nobles had certain rights. Over time, these rights were extended to all English citizens. In 1295, King Edward I summoned Parliament. For the first time, representatives of the common people were part of Parliament. This Parliament later became known as the Model Parliament. It set up the framework for England's legislature.
3. **The Magna Carta and the English Bill of Rights** (Chapter 4, page 175)

____

____

____

____

____

____

Name______________________ Class__________________ Date______

Concept Connector Study Guide

DEMOCRACY ***(continued)***

4. The American Declaration of Independence (Chapter 5, page 205)

5. The Declaration of the Rights of Man and the Citizen and the American Declaration of Independence (Chapter 6, page 241)

6. The American Revolution and Revolutions in Latin America (Chapter 8, page 291)

7. John Locke and the Expansion of Suffrage (Chapter 11, page 383)

8. The Curtailment of Citizen's Rights (Chapter 17, page 597)

Name________________________ Class__________________ Date________

Concept Connector Study Guide

C. Sample Topics for Thematic Essays

Below are examples of thematic essay topics that might appear on a test. Prepare for the test by outlining an essay for each topic on a separate sheet of paper. Use the Concept Connector Handbooks at the end of your textbook, as well as chapter information, to outline your essays.

1. What do you think were the three most important steps in the development of democracy? Explain your choices.

2. How were the American and French Revolutions related?

3. Compare the beliefs of at least three cultures throughout history regarding power, authority, governance, and law.

4. How would you define citizenship, and how have different societies viewed the rights and responsibilities of citizenship?

5. How are contemporary democratic governments rooted in Enlightenment ideals?

6. What impacts did Greece and Rome have on the development of later political systems?

7. What forces led to the nineteenth-century failure of democracy in Latin America and Russia?

8. What role does democracy play in Latin America today?

Name______________________ Class__________________ Date______

Concept Connector Study Guide

Dictatorship

Essential Question: How have dictators assumed and maintained power?

A. Define *dictatorship.* ____

____

____

B. *Record information about the topics listed in the Cumulative Review or your answers to the questions in the Cumulative Review below. Use the Concept Connector Handbooks at the end of your textbook, as well as chapter information, to complete this worksheet.*

1. **Mussolini and Hitler** (Chapter 16, page 557)

____

____

____

____

____

____

2. **Stalin and Other Russian Leaders** (Chapter 16, page 557)

____

____

____

____

____

____

3. **Communist Dictators and Other Dictators** (Chapter 18, page 647)

____

____

____

____

____

____

Name________________________ Class____________________ Date________

Concept Connector Study Guide

DICTATORSHIP *(continued)*

4. **Mobutu Sese Seko** (Chapter 19, page 677)

5. **Saddam Hussein** (Chapter 20, page 699)

6. **The Rise of Latin American Dictators** (Chapter 21, page 729)

Name______________________ Class__________________ Date______

Concept Connector Study Guide

DICTATORSHIP *(continued)*

C. Sample Topics for Thematic Essays

Below are examples of thematic essay topics that might appear on a test. Prepare for the test by outlining an essay for each topic on a separate sheet of paper. Use the Concept Connector Handbooks at the end of your textbook, as well as chapter information, to outline your essays.

1. Compare and contrast the ways in which absolute monarchs, such as Philip II, gained and used power, with the ways in which power was gained and used by modern dictators, such as Joseph Stalin.

2. Discuss why many French people supported Napoleon, even though he was essentially a dictator.

3. Describe the conditions in Mexico that led to the revolution in 1910 against the dictator General Porfirio Díaz.

4. Describe the conditions in Italy that led to Mussolini's rise to power after World War I, and the ideas and methods that kept him in power until Italy's defeat in World War II.

5. Describe Hitler's belief in a "master race," and how he used it to gain power and promote war.

6. Compare and contrast the ideas of fascism and communism and the ways in which adherents gained and maintained power in Europe and Russia before World War II.

7. Compare Fulgencio Batista and Fidel Castro. What are the similarities and differences in how they came to power and how they ruled?

8. Describe the dictatorship in China since Mao Zedong died in 1976. What has been the country's approach to economic and political freedom in this period?

Name______________________ Class__________________ Date________

Concept Connector Study Guide

Economic Systems

Essential Question: What types of economic systems have societies used to produce and distribute goods and services?

A. Define *economic system.* ____

____

____

B. *Record information about the topics listed in the Cumulative Review or your answers to the questions in the Cumulative Review below. Use the Concept Connector Handbooks at the end of your textbook, as well as chapter information, to complete this worksheet.*

1. **The Expansion of Towns in Medieval Europe**
   Before the expansion of towns, the medieval economy was based on the manor. Manors were self-sufficient estates owned by lords that produced nearly everything that was needed. Peasants were required to work for the lord in return for his protection. During the Middle Ages, towns expanded. Trade revived, stimulating new ways of doing business. Groups of merchants formed partnerships. A new middle class, made up of merchants, traders, and artisans, came into being. Towns were very different from manors. Townspeople had no lord, could move about freely, and had different economic opportunities. Nobles resented the fact that they had no control over towns. The Church was concerned that the emphasis on trade and money was immoral. Eventually the growth of towns reshaped medieval society. Peasants preferred to sell their produce to townspeople and pay rent to the lord in cash rather than in labor. By 1300, most peasants in Western Europe rented their land or were hired laborers.

2. **Mercantilism and Manorialism** (Chapter 3, page 137)

____

____

____

____

____

____

____

____

Name______________________ Class__________________ Date________

Concept Connector Study Guide

ECONOMIC SYSTEMS *(continued)*

3. **Market Economy** (Chapter 7, page 267)

4. **Centrally Planned Economy** (Chapter 7, page 267)

5. **Mixed Economy** (Chapter 7, page 267)

6. **Compare Socialism with Mercantilism** (Chapter 7, page 267)

Name________________________ Class__________________ Date______

Concept Connector Study Guide

ECONOMIC SYSTEMS *(continued)*

7. **The Commercial Revolution During the Middle Ages and the Industrial Revolution** (Chapter 9, page 325)

8. **Command Economies in Developing Countries and in Russia** (Chapter 21, page 729)

9. **Economic Systems in the Twentieth Century** (Chapter 22, page 765)

Name________________________ Class____________________ Date_______

Concept Connector Study Guide

ECONOMIC SYSTEMS *(continued)*

C. Sample Topics for Thematic Essays

Below are examples of thematic essay topics that might appear on a test. Prepare for the test by outlining an essay for each topic on a separate sheet of paper. Use the Concept Connector Handbooks at the end of your textbook, as well as chapter information, to outline your essays.

1. Discuss the importance of the merchant class in Italian city-states during the Renaissance.
2. Explain the effect of labor unions on governments and employers during the Industrial Revolution.
3. Describe how the economic systems of North Korea and China differ from the economies of the "Asian tigers."
4. List the regions involved in the triangular trade and how the Atlantic slave trade contributed to the economy of each one.
5. Contrast socialism with capitalism, and discuss the benefits early socialist reformers predicted would occur in the event that socialism replaced capitalism.
6. Discuss the role British mercantilism played in sparking the American Revolution.
7. Describe the economic changes in Eastern Europe after the fall of the Soviet Union and the challenges facing countries as they adapted from one economic system to another.
8. Contrast the Great Leap Forward of Mao Zedong in 1958 with the Four Modernizations of Deng Xiaoping in the 1980s, and discuss their results.

Name____________________ Class__________________ Date________

Concept Connector Study Guide

Empires

Essential Question: What factors allow empires to rise and what factors cause them to fall?

A. Define *empire.* ____

____

____

B. *Record information about the topics listed in the Cumulative Review or your answers to the questions in the Cumulative Review below. Use the Concept Connector Handbooks at the end of your textbook, as well as chapter information, to complete this worksheet.*

1. **Characteristics of Successful Rulers**
   To maintain control over a vast empire, it was vital that a ruler be well respected. Many characteristics or abilities make a successful ruler. These characteristics include spiritual leadership, law-giving, just punishments for crime, military power, and treatment of subjects. For example, about 1790 B.C., Hammurabi, king of Babylon, brought much of Mesopotamia under the control of his empire. Hammurabi is famous for publishing a set of laws known as Hammurabi's Code. The law code established civil law and defined crime and punishments. Hammurabi also improved the irrigation system, organized a well-trained army, and ordered repairs to temples. To encourage religious unity, he encouraged the worship of a particular Babylonian god.

2. **Empire-Building in India, China, Egypt, and the Middle East**
   Eventually empires weaken, and power changes hands. In some cases, the civilization continues. The history of ancient Egypt illustrates this. Scholars have divided Egypt's history into three main periods: the Old Kingdom (2575 B.C.–2130 B.C.), the Middle Kingdom (1938 B.C.–1630 B.C.), and the New Kingdom (1539 B.C.–1075 B.C.). Although power passed from one dynasty to another, Egypt remained united and the civilization continued. In China, various dynasties ruled from 1766 B.C. to A.D. 1911. Even as dynasties changed hands, China generally remained unified. In ancient India, however, the Maurya dynasty ruled, beginning in 321 B.C. Then in 185 B.C., battles for power destroyed the unity of the empire. It wasn't until 500 years later that a new empire, the Gupta, re-unified India. In the ancient Middle East, power passed from the Babylonians to the Assyrians, back to the Babylonians again, and then to the Persians. The culture changed under each ruling group.

Name____________________ Class__________________ Date________

Concept Connector Study Guide

EMPIRES *(continued)*

3. **Methods of Control in the Roman Empire and Han Dynasty**
The Roman empire (A.D. 27–A.D. 476) and the Han dynasty (202 B.C.–A.D. 220) in China each exerted control over a wide area and a variety of people. Roman legions maintained and protected roads, and Roman fleets chased pirates from the seas. Trade flowed freely to and from distant lands. Egyptian farmers supplied grain. Roman soldiers swiftly put down revolts. Roman officials provided spectacular entertainment for the public. Similarly, Han rulers improved roads and canals. They set up places to store grain so they could buy grain at low prices and sell it when grain was scarce. Han soldiers drove nomadic peoples out of the empire. Under the Han, trade routes to the West were opened. Both governments relied on a well-established bureaucracy to handle the details of governing a large empire.

4. **Aztec and Inca**
The Aztec (A.D. 1325–A.D. 1521) and the Inca (A.D. 1438–A.D. 1535) were two impressive civilizations of the Americas. Both civilizations could be described as empires. Through a combination of fierce conquests and shrewd alliances, the Aztec spread their rule across most of Mexico. The Aztec empire had a single ruler. A council of nobles, priests, and military leaders elected the emperor, whose primary function was to lead in war. Nobles served as officials, judges, and governors of conquered provinces. The Inca similarly used conquest and alliances to subdue neighboring groups. They used military and diplomatic skills to create their empire and established a chain of command that reached down to the family level. The Inca also imposed their language on conquered peoples. They created a network of roads across the empire, all connected to the capital. The roads aided communication. They also made it possible for the Inca to send armies to every corner of their empire.

5. **Was Charlemagne Really King of the Romans?**
The Roman empire ceased to exist in the West in A.D. 476. Germanic tribes, including the Goths, Vandals, Saxons and Franks, had conquered, or went on to conquer, parts of it. Between 400 and 700, they carved Western Europe into small kingdoms. In 768, Charlemagne became king of the Franks. He briefly united Western Europe when he built an empire reaching across what is now France, Germany, and part of Italy. In 800, Pope Leo III crowned Charlemagne emperor of the Romans. By doing so, he proclaimed that Charlemagne was the successor to the Roman emperors.

6. **The Roman Empire and the Holy Roman Empire**
The name of the Holy Roman Empire was supposed to make people think of the greatness and power of the ancient Roman empire. There were, however, significant differences between the two empires. The Roman empire lasted about 450 years. Charlemagne's empire ended with his death. However, just as Charlemagne looked to the Roman empire as an example of greatness and power, later medieval leaders considered Charlemagne's rule to be their model.

Name______________________ Class__________________ Date________

Concept Connector Study Guide

EMPIRES *(continued)*

7. **The Byzantine Empire**
The Byzantine empire (330–1453) was a powerful and influential empire. As the cities of the western Roman empire crumbled, the Byzantine empire, with its capital at Constantinople, remained secure and prospered. The Byzantine empire was the source of several important developments, such as Justinian's Code, and the spread of Christianity in Eastern Europe and Russia. For centuries, the Byzantine empire withstood attacks by Persians, Slavs, Vikings, Mongols, and Turks. The empire served as a buffer for Western Europe, preventing the spread of Muslim conquest. The Fourth Crusade in 1204 severely weakened the empire. In 1453, Constantinople fell to the Turks.

8. **The Abbasid Empire**
The Abbasid dynasty began in 750 when a Muslim leader named Abu al-Abbas captured Damascus and defeated the Umayyads. The Abbasid dynasty tried to create an empire based on the equality of all Muslims. The new rulers halted large military conquests, ending the dominance of the Arab military class. Discrimination against non-Arab Muslims largely ended. Under the early Abbasids, Muslim civilization flourished. The Abbasids moved the capital to Baghdad. Poets, scholars, and philosophers came there from all over the Muslim world. Baghdad exceeded Constantinople in size and wealth. However, around 850 the empire began to fragment.

9. **The Mughal Empire**
The Mughal dynasty (1526–1857) was the second Muslim dynasty to rule the Indian subcontinent. The Mughal dynasty was set up by Babur, who claimed descent from the Mongol ruler Genghis Khan. The chief builder of the Mughal empire was Babur's grandson Akbar. During his long reign, from 1556 to 1605, he created a strong central government, earning the title Akbar the Great. He modernized the army, encouraged international trade, standardized weights and measures, and introduced land reforms. Although a Muslim, he won the support of his Hindu subjects through his policy of toleration. He opened government jobs to Hindus of all castes.

10. **Suleiman the Magnificent**
The Ottomans were a Turkish-speaking people whose Muslim empire ruled the Middle East and parts of Eastern Europe. In 1453, the Ottomans captured Constantinople, renamed it Istanbul, and ruled from there for the next 200 years. The Ottoman empire enjoyed a golden age under Suleiman, who ruled from 1520 to 1566. Europeans called him Suleiman the Magnificent. A brilliant general, Suleiman modernized the army and conquered many new lands. He extended Ottoman rule eastward into the Middle East, and also into Central Asia. In 1529, his armies besieged the Austrian city of Vienna, causing great fear in Western Europe. The Ottomans ruled the largest, most powerful empire in both Europe and the Middle East for centuries.

Name________________________ Class____________________ Date_______

Concept Connector Study Guide

EMPIRES *(continued)*

11. The Mongol Empire

The Mongols were a nomadic people who grazed their horses and sheep on the steppes of Central Asia. In about 1200, a Mongol chieftain united rival Mongol clans. The chieftain took the name Genghis Khan, meaning "Universal Ruler." Under Genghis Khan, and his grandson Kublai Khan, the Mongols conquered an empire that spread from Europe in the west to China in the east. Under the protection of the Mongols, who controlled the great Silk Road, trade flourished across Eurasia. Cultural exchanges increased as foods, tools, inventions, and ideas spread along the protected trade routes.

12. The Ming Empire

With the death of Kublai Khan in 1294, Mongol rule in China weakened. In 1368, a new dynasty, called the Ming, took over. Early Ming rulers sought to reassert Chinese greatness after years of Mongol rule. The Ming restored the civil service system. The economy grew as new agricultural methods produced more crops. Ming China saw a revival of the arts and literature. Ming artists developed their own styles of landscape painting and created brilliant blue-and-white porcelain. People enjoyed new forms of literature, such as novels and detective stories. The Ming sent Chinese fleets to explore distant lands and to show off the glory of the Ming empire. The Ming dynasty ended in 1644.

13. The Roman Empire and the Tang Dynasty

The Roman empire and the Tang dynasty (A.D. 618–A.D. 907) in China each established a system of government to rule over their lands. Both empires had law codes and a well-developed bureaucracy or civil service. Both empires benefited from competent emperors. Rulers in both empires took steps to strengthen the central government and increase revenues through taxes. In both empires, social and economic problems, as well as invasions, weakened the governments. Both empires collapsed after a period of decline.

14. The Qing and the Yuan Dynasties (Chapter 2, page 105)

____

____

____

____

____

____

____

Name____________________ Class____________________ Date________

Concept Connector Study Guide

EMPIRES *(continued)*

15. The Roman Empire and the Spanish Empire in the Americas (Chapter 3, page 137)

16. North American Colonies and Latin American Colonies (Chapter 8, page 291)

17. The Second Reich and the Holy Roman Empire (Chapter 10, page 355)

18. The Spanish Empire of the 1500s and the British Empire of the late 1800s (Chapter 12, page 417)

Name____________________ Class__________________ Date________

Concept Connector Study Guide

EMPIRES *(continued)*

19. **Arguments Against Imperialism** (Chapter 12, page 417)

20. **The Soviet Union and Other Empires** (Chapter 18, page 647)

21. **Chechnya and Earlier Efforts to Break Away from an Empire** (Chapter 20, page 699)

Name____________________________ Class______________________ Date________

Concept Connector Study Guide

EMPIRES *(continued)*

C. Sample Topics for Thematic Essays

Below are examples of thematic essay topics that might appear on a test. Prepare for the test by outlining an essay for each topic on a separate sheet of paper. Use the Concept Connector Handbooks at the end of your textbook, as well as chapter information, to outline your essays.

1. Describe Britain's attitudes toward its colonies during the 1700s and the reasons why the Americans were able to break away from the British empire.

2. Describe the Hapsburg empire in the early 1800s and the conflicts that made the Balkans a "powder keg" before World War I.

3. Describe the reasons why the Ottoman empire was in decline by the 1700s, and explain why the Europeans were able to take control of much of the Ottoman empire in the 1800s.

4. Discuss why Great Britain was able to expand its areas of control in India after 1765 and the policies that set the stage for later independence movements.

5. Discuss reasons why Napoleon was able to build an empire in the early 1800s, and the reasons for its fall.

6. Describe the results of the Congress of Vienna in 1815 and the forces that challenged the old empires during the next 30 years.

7. Describe reasons why Western powers were able to gain control over much of the world between 1870 and the beginning of World War I.

8. Discuss reasons for the fall of communism and the breakup of the Soviet Union in the 1980s.

Name________________________ Class____________________ Date_______

Concept Connector Study Guide

Genocide

Essential Question: What factors have led groups of people or governments to commit genocide?

A. Define ***genocide.*** ____

____

____

B. *Record information about the topics listed in the Cumulative Review or your answers to the questions in the Cumulative Review below. Use the Concept Connector Handbooks at the end of your textbook, as well as chapter information, to complete this worksheet.*

1. **Native Americans** (Chapter 3, page 137)

____

____

____

____

____

____

____

____

____

2. **Indigenous People in North America, Australia, and New Zealand** (Chapter 13, page 447)

____

____

____

____

____

____

____

____

____

Name____________________ Class________________ Date________

Concept Connector Study Guide

GENOCIDE *(continued)*

3. **The Holocaust and the Armenian Genocide** (Chapter 17, page 597)

4. **Genocide in Cambodia Compared with Earlier Genocides** (Chapter 18, page 647)

5. **Genocide in Rwanda Compared with Earlier Genocides** (Chapter 20, page 699)

Name________________________ Class____________________ Date________

Concept Connector Study Guide

C. Sample Topics for Thematic Essays

Below are examples of thematic essay topics that might appear on a test. Prepare for the test by outlining an essay for each topic on a separate sheet of paper. Use the Concept Connector Handbooks at the end of your textbook, as well as chapter information, to outline your essays.

1. Describe the factors that led to the dramatic decrease of Native American populations in Latin America in the 1500s.

2. Describe the early contacts between Europeans and Native Americans in North America and how westward expansion by colonists affected the Native Americans.

3. Describe the differences between Armenians and the Ottoman Turks in the late 1800s, and discuss the factors that led to the genocide of the early 1900s.

4. Discuss Nazi attitudes towards Jews and other ethnic groups and how these views were used to justify the events of the Holocaust.

5. Describe the genocide in Cambodia under the Khmer Rouge. How does the genocide in Cambodia differ from other genocides, such as the Holocaust?

6. Describe ethnic and religious differences among groups in the former Yugoslavia and how they led to attempted genocide in Kosovo in the 1990s.

7. Discuss the reasons why genocide occurred in Rwanda in the 1990s and the international response.

8. Discuss the ethnic conflict in Sudan's western region of Darfur. Why has this conflict raised fears of a new genocide?

Name________________________ Class____________________ Date________

Concept Connector Study Guide

Geography's Impact

Essential Question: How have geographic factors affected the course of history?

A. Define *geography.* ____

____

____

B. *Record information about the topics listed in the Cumulative Review or your answers to the questions in the Cumulative Review below. Use the Concept Connector Handbooks at the end of your textbook, as well as chapter information, to complete this worksheet.*

1. **Rivers and the Rise of Civilization**
The earliest civilizations to develop were situated on major rivers. Rivers provided important resources such as a regular water supply and a means of transportation. The animals that flocked to rivers were a source of food. Most important, conditions in river valleys favored farming. Floodwaters spread silt across the valleys, renewing the soil and keeping it fertile. Examples of civilizations that developed near a major river are: Sumer, between the Tigris and Euphrates; the Indus River valley civilization, and Egypt on the Nile.

2. **The Tigris and Euphrates Rivers**
The Tigris and Euphrates rivers played an important role in the development of the world's first civilization around 3300 B.C. in a region called Sumer. Sumer was located between these two rivers. The rivers lie within the Fertile Crescent, a region in the Middle East. The rivers often flooded, destroying farmland, so early villagers learned to work together to control flooding. In the dry season, people worked together to channel water to the fields. Temple priests or officials provided leadership for these large projects. Within a few hundred years, 12 city-states were located in the region.

3. **The Aegean and Mediterranean Seas**
The civilizations of the Minoans, Mycenaeans, and ancient Greeks were greatly influenced by the Aegean and Mediterranean seas. The Minoans (1600 B.C.–1400 B.C.) and Mycenaeans (1400 B.C.–1200 B.C.) were sea traders. Through trade, both groups came into contact with Egypt and Mesopotamia. From these contacts, they acquired ideas about writing and architecture that they adapted to their own cultures. Mountains divided Greek city-states from one another. For the Greeks, the seas provided a vital link to the world outside. The Greeks became skilled sailors and carried cargoes throughout the eastern Mediterranean and, through trade, also acquired new ideas. By 750 B.C., population growth forced many Greeks to expand overseas. Greek colonies developed around the Mediterranean. Wherever they traveled, Greek settlers carried their ideas and culture.

Name________________________ Class____________________ Date________

Concept Connector Study Guide

GEOGRAPHY'S IMPACT *(continued)*

4. **Geographic Environments of Developing Civilizations**
   Rivers, seas, mountains, valleys, and rainforests have been very important to civilizations. Geographic features can encourage or discourage trade, lead to cultural diffusion and cooperation, and provide protection from attack. In Mesoamerica, the Aztec built their capital on a swampy island in Lake Texcoco. To increase farmland, the Aztec built floating gardens of earth and reeds. They created canals for transportation and linked the city to the mainland with wide stone causeways. In South Asia, the Himalayas and Hindu Kush protected the developing civilizations of Harappa and Mohenjo-Daro from invaders. Melting snow from the mountains flowed into the Indus and Brahmaputra rivers, making agriculture possible.

5. **The Ocean's Influence on the Vikings**
   The Vikings made their home in Scandinavia, in the region that now includes Norway, Sweden, and Denmark. They were expert sailors. In the 700s, they sailed down the coasts and rivers of Europe, looting and burning communities. They were also traders and explorers, setting up trade routes as far as the Mediterranean. Vikings settled across the ocean in England, Ireland, France, and parts of Russia.

6. **The Importance of Rivers to Early Cultures**
   The rivers of Russia and Eastern Europe provided highways for migration, trade, and ideas. Russia's network of rivers, running north to south, linked early Russians to the advanced Byzantine world in the south. Vikings used the rivers to trade with Constantinople, the Byzantine capital. It was from a Viking tribe called the Rus that Russia got its name. The rivers of Eastern Europe also flow north and south. Consequently, the cultures of Eastern Europe felt the influence of Russia and the Byzantine empire. When Constantinople fell to the Ottoman Turks in 1453, Eastern European cultures were influenced by the Muslims.

7. **Geography and Cultural Development in Eastern Europe and Africa**
   In Eastern Europe, geographic features such as rivers allowed easy movement of people, goods, and ideas. In Africa, geographic features were often barriers to movement. The Sahara, a vast desert, hindered trade until the introduction of the camel from Asia as a form of transportation. The interior of Africa is a high plateau. Rivers with waterfalls were barriers to trade and movement. On the other hand, the Great Rift Valley served as an interior passageway, and the Mediterranean and Red seas provided trade routes to regions in Southeast Asia and present-day Europe. Between 800 and 1600, valuable resources such as gold, salt, iron, and copper brought great wealth to African kingdoms and trading states.

Name________________________ Class__________________ Date________

Concept Connector Study Guide

8. **The Impact of Geography in Japan and Mesopotamia**
Mesopotamian civilization developed in the Fertile Crescent between the Tigris and Euphrates rivers. There were very few natural barriers. Nomadic peoples or ambitious warriors descended on the rich cities of the Fertile Crescent. The region was also a crossroads for the mingling of beliefs and ideas. On the other hand, geography set Japan apart. Japan is made up of a series of islands. Most of the land was too mountainous to farm. The seas protected and isolated Japan. They also offered plentiful food resources, and the Japanese developed a thriving fishing industry. Japan's isolation helped it develop and maintain a distinct culture.

9. **Location and the Relationship Between Latin America and the United States, 1800–1914** (Chapter 13, page 447)

____

____

____

____

____

____

____

____

10. **The Effect of Oil on the History of Saudi Arabia and the United States** (Chapter 19, page 677)

____

____

____

____

____

____

____

____

Concept Connector Study Guide

C. Sample Topics for Thematic Essays

Below are examples of thematic essay topics that might appear on a test. Prepare for the test by outlining an essay for each topic on a separate sheet of paper. Use the Concept Connector Handbooks at the end of your textbook, as well as chapter information, to outline your essays.

1. In what ways does the Middle East's location and geography make it an area of conflict today?

2. Select two cities or countries whose locations have helped in their military defense. Discuss each location and describe how geography made foreign invasions more difficult. You may consider the islands of Great Britain or Japan, or other locations.

3. How did Britain's location and climate help it rise to global prominence from 1700 to 1800?

4. Explain how the availability of natural resources helped Great Britain and the United States become leaders in the Industrial Revolution.

5. Explain how the geography of Indonesia (which was favorable for growing spices) affected the exploration of the world by Europeans in the 1400s and 1500s.

6. Describe how the location of the United States and Latin America led to the development of the Monroe Doctrine and the Roosevelt Corollary and how these policies shaped the relationship between the United States and Latin America.

7. Explain why the location of the Ottoman empire made it a desirable ally during World War I. How did its decision to join the Central Powers affect the war?

8. Describe how desertification affected early migrations in Africa and how it may affect Africa's future.

Name__________________________ Class____________________ Date________

Concept Connector Study Guide

Migration

Essential Question: What factors cause large groups of people to move from one place to another?

A. Define *migration.* ____

____

____

B. *Record information about the topics listed in the Cumulative Review or your answers to the questions in the Cumulative Review below. Use the Concept Connector Handbooks at the end of your textbook, as well as chapter information, to complete this worksheet.*

1. **Migrations of Early People**
Hominids, a group that includes humans and their closest relatives, all walk upright on two feet. Humans are the only hominids that live today. Two hominid groups, *Homo erectus* and *Homo sapiens,* migrated from Africa to Europe and Asia. Early humans were nomads, or people who move from place to place to find food. It is likely that during the periods of prehistory and very early history, the same factors influenced migration. For example, people migrated in search of plants and animals for food. Climate change and other environmental events, such as drought, landslides, earthquakes, or volcanic eruptions might also have caused people to migrate. Changes in population or competition among groups of people for resources are often factors in migration, too.

2. **Indo-European Migrations**
The Aryans were one of many groups of speakers of Indo-European languages who migrated across Europe and Asia. The migration of the Aryans into India affected the culture of India in many ways. For example, the beliefs of the Aryans influenced the development of Hinduism and the caste system in India. The language of the Aryans developed into Sanskrit, the Indian language used for sacred writings. Other Indo-European groups include the Celts, Germans, and Italics. You can see by the names of these other Indo-European groups that they influenced the development of culture in Europe.

3. **Migration and Language**
Scholars are able to trace migrations by studying language patterns. Many people of European descent speak one of the varieties of languages that can be traced to a common Indo-European language. Scholars have learned that West African farmers and herders migrated to the south and east between 1000 B.C. and A.D. 1000. They spoke a variety of languages derived from a single common language. The root language is Bantu, which gives this movement its name, the Bantu migrations. As they migrated in southern Africa, the Bantu-speakers spread their skills in farming, ironworking, and domesticating animals. The influence of the Bantu-speakers is still found in the languages of the region today.

Name________________ Class________________ Date________

Concept Connector Study Guide

MIGRATION *(continued)*

4. **Westward Movement in the United States** (Chapter 11, page 383)

5. **Factors in European Migration to the Americas** (Chapter 11, page 383)

Name________________________ Class________________ Date________

Concept Connector Study Guide

C. Sample Topics for Thematic Essays

Below are examples of thematic essay topics that might appear on a test. Prepare for the test by outlining an essay for each topic on a separate sheet of paper. Use the Concept Connector Handbooks at the end of your textbook, as well as chapter information, to outline your essays.

1. Select at least two instances between 1600 and 1950 where groups were "pushed" to migrate from one area to another. Describe the reasons why they migrated, and discuss how the groups adapted to the migration and how their move affected the area to which they moved.

2. Compare and contrast the "pull" factors that brought Europeans to the Americas between 1600 and 1800 with the "pull" factors that encouraged movement to the western United States between 1800 and 1900.

3. Identify and discuss at least three factors that "pushed" or "pulled" people into growing cities in Europe and the Americas between 1800 and 1900.

4. Identify and discuss at least three factors that cause people to migrate today. Give an example of each and describe the conditions that have encouraged migration.

5. Explain the role of religion in the partition of India in 1948 and in the migration of people that resulted.

6. Identify the "push" factor that brought the first large group of Europeans to Australia and the "pull" factors that drew others there during the late 1800s.

7. Evaluate how the potato famine in Ireland (which began in 1845) and the resulting migration of a million Irish people affected Ireland's relationships with the United States and Great Britain.

8. Compare and contrast the forced migration that occurred in southern Sudan with the movement of people in the occupied territories of Israel.

Name____________________ Class________________ Date_______

Concept Connector Study Guide

Nationalism

Essential Question: How have people used nationalism as a basis for their actions?

A. Define ***nationalism.*** ________________________________

B. *Record information about the topics listed in the Cumulative Review or your answers to the questions in the Cumulative Review below. Use the Concept Connector Handbooks at the end of your textbook, as well as chapter information, to complete this worksheet.*

1. Nationalism in the American Revolution (Chapter 6, page 241)

2. Latin American Nationalism and French Nationalism (Chapter 8, page 291)

Name____________________ Class________________ Date______

Concept Connector Study Guide

NATIONALISM *(continued)*

3. Unification and Nationalism in Greece and Italy (Chapter 10, page 355)

4. Revolts in the Balkans (Chapter 10, page 355)

5. English Nationalism (Chapter 12, page 417)

6. Nationalism in the United States (Chapter 12, page 417)

Name______________________ Class__________________ Date_______

Concept Connector Study Guide

NATIONALISM *(continued)*

7. **Pan-Arab and Pan-Slav Nationalism** (Chapter 15, page 517)

8. **Expansion in Japan, the United States, and Britain** (Chapter 15, page 517)

9. **Hindu Nationalism of the BJP in India** (Chapter 19, page 677)

Name________________________ Class__________________ Date________

Concept Connector Study Guide

NATIONALISM *(continued)*

C. Sample Topics for Thematic Essays

Below are examples of thematic essay topics that might appear on a test. Prepare for the test by outlining an essay for each topic on a separate sheet of paper. Use the Concept Connector Handbooks at the end of your textbook, as well as chapter information, to outline your essays.

1. Compare and contrast the ways in which nationalism helped Napoleon create an empire and how it also encouraged resistance against that empire.

2. Discuss the role of nationalism in the revolts by slaves, creoles, and others in South and Central America in the late 1700s and early 1800s.

3. Describe how Bismarck used nationalism to attack both the Catholic Church and socialists in the late 1800s and the results of those attacks.

4. Explain the effects of nationalist movements on the Hapsburg empire before and after 1848 and how the success of the Hungarians after 1866 continued to weaken the empire.

5. Describe the British response to nationalists in India before and after World War I and how Mohandas Gandhi helped inspire Indians to work for an independent nation.

6. Discuss how Mussolini used nationalism to gain and keep power in Italy.

7. Describe how Adolf Hitler used nationalism to help him gain control of the country and establish the Third Reich.

8. Describe the role of nationalism in the conflict that broke out in the former Yugoslavia in the 1990s.

Name______________________ Class__________________ Date________

Concept Connector Study Guide

People and the Environment

Essential Question: What impact have people had on the environment?

A. Define *environment.* ____

____

____

B. *Record information about the topics listed in the Cumulative Review or your answers to the questions in the Cumulative Review below. Use the Concept Connector Handbooks at the end of your textbook, as well as chapter information, to complete this worksheet.*

1. **Stone Age Hominids and Neolithic Farmers**
Stone Age people were nomads who moved from place to place to find food. In general, men hunted or fished while the women and children gathered berries, fruits, nuts, grains, and roots. Although Stone Age people depended on their environment for survival, they also adapted their surroundings to their needs. They made tools from stone, bone, or wood—materials they found at hand. They made clothing from the skins of animals. They may have used boats or canoes to travel across water. Neolithic farmers adapted the environment to a greater extent than did earlier Stone Age peoples. They settled in one place, selecting particular plants to cultivate for food. They used animals such as oxen or water buffalo to plow the fields. They used clay to create pottery and wove cloth from animal hair or plant fibers.

2. **Farming Methods**
Civilizations in the Americas developed different farming techniques based on their environment. The Maya of Mesoamerica developed two farming methods that helped them grow crops in their tropical environment. In the first method, farmers burned down forests, then cleared the land to plant it. In the second method, farmers built raised fields along the banks of rivers. This lifted the crops above the annual floods. The Aztec settled on an island in a lake. They developed a farming method that allowed them to grow crops on human-made islands. On these artificial islands, the Aztec grew maize, squash, and beans. The Inca lived in the mountains of South America. To farm, they carved terraces, or flat strips of land, on steep hillsides. Stone walls held the terraces in place. The terraces provided flat land for crops and kept rains from washing the soil away. The Hohokam lived in the deserts of southwest North America. To grow crops they created a complex irrigation system. Canals carried river water to fields as far as ten miles away.

Name________________________ Class____________________ Date________

Concept Connector Study Guide

3. **The Building of Tenochtitlán**
The capital city of the Aztec, Tenochtitlán, was built on an island in a lake. The Aztec built temples, palaces, zoos, and floating gardens, turning the island into a magnificent city. As they filled the lake with floating gardens called chinampas, they created canals for transportation. To connect the city with the mainland, they built wide stone causeways. From this city, the Aztec governed a complex, well-ordered empire.

4. **Geoglyphs**
The way that people affect the environment does not always appear to have a practical application. For example, between 500 B.C. and A.D. 500, the Nazca people lived along the southern coast of Peru. They etched geoglyphs in the desert. A geoglyph is a figure or line made on Earth's surface by clearing away rocks and soil. Some Nazca geoglyphs extend for miles. The designs include giant birds, whales, and spiders. Most researchers think the geoglyphs had spiritual significance.

5. **Cliff Dwellings and Earthworks**
In North America between A.D. 1150 and A.D. 1300, the Anasazi constructed huge housing complexes on cliffs along the sides of sheer canyon walls. These cliff dwellings offered protection from enemies. The Anasazi cut blocks from stone to build the dwellings. They used ladders to reach their fields on the flatlands above or the canyon floor below. One of the largest dwellings had more than 200 rooms. Other Native American groups, the Adena and the Hopewell, affected the environment in a different way. They built giant earthworks by heaping earth in piles and shaping them. Some of the earthworks were burial mounds; others were used as the platforms for temples, or formed defensive walls. Some were in the shape of an animal. The Adena's Great Serpent Mound twists in the shape of a snake for almost a quarter of a mile.

Name________________________ Class________________ Date______

Concept Connector Study Guide

C. Sample Topics for Thematic Essays

Below are examples of thematic essay topics that might appear on a test. Prepare for the test by outlining an essay for each topic on a separate sheet of paper. Use the Concept Connector Handbooks at the end of your textbook, as well as chapter information, to outline your essays.

1. Explain how the development of farming during the Neolithic Period led to changes in the environment and how people lived. How would you compare these changes to the changes brought by the Industrial Revolution thousands of years later?

2. Discuss the relationship between the natural environment and industrialization in the period between 1750 and 1914.

3. Explain how British rule in India affected the natural environment.

4. Evaluate the positive and negative effects of automobiles on people's lives and on the environment.

5. Compare and contrast the conditions in North American and European cities during the Industrial Revolution with those in South American and Asian cities today.

6. Discuss how increased industrialization has threatened air and water quality and how governments have responded.

7. Discuss how nuclear power could help the environment as well as ways it could harm it.

8. Describe how global warming might harm the environment as well as how limiting emissions of greenhouse gases could hamper economic growth.

Name________________________ Class____________________ Date_______

Concept Connector Study Guide

Political Systems

Essential Question: How have societies chosen to govern themselves?

A. Define *political system.* ____

____

____

B. *Record information about the topics listed in the Cumulative Review or your answers to the questions in the Cumulative Review below. Use the Concept Connector Handbooks at the end of your textbook, as well as chapter information, to complete this worksheet.*

1. **Oligarchy**
   In ancient Greece, between 750 B.C. and 500 B.C., different forms of government evolved. The first cities were ruled by kings. A government in which a hereditary ruler has central power is called a monarchy. Wealthy landowners could afford bronze weapons and chariots. They were the military defenders of the city. Gradually they won power for themselves; this resulted in an aristocracy, or government by a hereditary landholding elite. As trade grew, a new middle class of wealthy merchants, farmers, and artisans developed in some cities. They challenged the aristocracy for power. The result in some city-states was a form of government called an oligarchy. In an oligarchy, power is in the hands of a small, wealthy elite.

2. **The Roman Republic and the Oligarchies of Ancient Greece**
   In the oligarchies of ancient Greece, power was in the hands of a small, wealthy elite. Ancient Romans set up a different form of government. In 509 B.C., wealthy Roman landowners overthrew the king. In place of a monarchy, the Romans established a republic. Men who were citizens could elect their officials. Three groups of citizens helped govern the republic—the senate, the magistrates, and several assemblies. Early Rome was made up of two social orders: the wealthy landowning patricians and the plebeians. Although both plebeians and patricians voted, only patricians could be elected to office. Even in the republic, power remained in the hands of a wealthy ruling class.

3. **Religion and Rulers in Egypt, China, and the Inca Empire**
   In early civilizations, religious beliefs and political systems were often linked. In ancient Egypt, the chief god was the sun god, Amon-Re. The pharaohs, whom Egyptians viewed as gods as well as kings, were believed to receive their right to rule from Amon-Re. In China, rulers were not considered gods. Instead, the Chinese developed the idea of the Mandate of Heaven. This was the divine right to rule. As long as a dynasty provided good government, it was believed the gods wanted that dynasty to continue. If rulers became corrupt or weak, the Chinese believed that heaven would withdraw its support. In the chaos that followed, a new leader would seize power. If the new leader was successful, it showed the people that the new dynasty had won the Mandate of Heaven. In South America, the Inca believed their emperor was divine, descended from the sun itself. Incan emperors had absolute power, and they also served as the religious leaders of the empire.

Name________________________ Class____________________ Date________

Concept Connector Study Guide

POLITICAL SYSTEMS *(continued)*

4. **Feudalism and Building a Strong Empire**
Feudalism was a political system in which powerful lords divided their landholdings among lesser lords in exchange for loyalty and service. Around 220 B.C., the emperor Shi Huangdi abolished feudalism in China in order to create a strong central government. He felt that allegiances to local lords weakened the central government. Feudalism was the political system of medieval Europe for hundreds of years. Knights owed military service to their feudal lords. Warfare was constant as rival lords battled for power. Gradually feudalism declined. Monarchs became more powerful. Knights were replaced by professional armies. Towns and cities provided revenue for kings. Kings gained the right to tax their subjects, and strong centralized governments began to form. In both China and Europe, monarchies replaced the political system of feudalism.

5. **Absolute Monarchy Under Louis XIV and Imperial Rule in Ancient Rome** (Chapter 4, page 175)

____

____

____

____

____

____

6. **The Federal Government** (Chapter 5, page 205)

____

____

____

____

____

____

7. **Enlightenment Ideas About Democracy and Totalitarianism** (Chapter 16, page 557)

____

____

____

____

____

____

Name______________________ Class__________________ Date________

Concept Connector Study Guide

C. Sample Topics for Thematic Essays

Below are examples of thematic essay topics that might appear on a test. Prepare for the test by outlining an essay for each topic on a separate sheet of paper. Use the Concept Connector Handbooks at the end of your textbook, as well as chapter information, to outline your essays.

1. Describe the effects of the Reformation on European political systems of the era in England, the Holy Roman Empire, Switzerland, and Spain.

2. Compare and contrast how Spain governed its American colonies with how Britain governed its American colonies. Which ruling nation offered greater opportunities for self-government to its colonists, and in what ways?

3. Compare oligarchy to autocracy. How are these two political systems similar? How are they different? Include an example of each from history in your essay.

4. Describe the relationship between the Industrial Revolution and the ideas of Karl Marx, and discuss the reasons why communism appealed to many workers of this time.

5. Describe the changes to Argentina's political system that occurred between the early 1900s and the late 1900s.

6. Analyze the conditions in Eastern Europe and the Soviet Union late in the Cold War that led to the collapse of communism and the breakup of the Soviet Union.

7. Describe the democratic political system in South Africa after the end of apartheid and the approval of a new constitution in 1997.

8. Describe the changes that occurred in the Iraqi political system after the defeat of Saddam Hussein in 2003. With what challenges were new political leaders in Iraq having to deal?

Name________________________ Class________________ Date______

Concept Connector Study Guide

Revolution

Essential Question: Why have political revolutions occurred?

A. Define ***revolution.*** ____

____

____

B. *Record information about the topics listed in the Cumulative Review or your answers to the questions in the Cumulative Review below. Use the Concept Connector Handbooks at the end of your textbook, as well as chapter information, to complete this worksheet.*

1. **The Transfer of Power in England, 1377–1688** (Chapter 4, page 175)

____

____

____

____

____

____

2. **The German Peasants' Revolt of 1524 and the French Revolution** (Chapter 6, page 241)

____

____

____

____

____

____

3. **Latin American Revolutions** (Chapter 8, page 291)

____

____

____

____

____

____

Name________________________ Class____________________ Date________

Concept Connector Study Guide

REVOLUTION *(continued)*

4. **The Russian Revolution and the French Revolution** (Chapter 14, page 485)

5. **European Colonial Independence Between 1946 and 1970 and the American Revolution** (Chapter 19, page 677)

6. **Recent Rebellions in Latin America and Earlier Revolutions** (Chapter 21, page 729)

Name________________________ Class____________________ Date________

Concept Connector Study Guide

C. Sample Topics for Thematic Essays

Below are examples of thematic essay topics that might appear on a test. Prepare for the test by outlining an essay for each topic on a separate sheet of paper. Use the Concept Connector Handbooks at the end of your textbook, as well as chapter information, to outline your essays.

1. Discuss the basic dispute between monarchs and Parliament in England in the 1600s and how it resulted in the English Civil War and the Glorious Revolution.
2. Discuss the economic problems of the Third Estate before the French Revolution and how these problems inspired people to revolt.
3. Compare the revolutions of 1848 in Europe with the revolution led by Simón Bolívar and José de San Martín in South America. Be sure to include a discussion of causes and effects.
4. Describe the causes of the Meiji Restoration, which swept the shogun from power in 1868 in Japan.
5. Discuss the causes and effects of the revolution and civil war that put Vladimir Lenin in power in Russia by 1921.
6. Contrast the tactics used by Mohandas Gandhi during the struggle for independence in India with tactics used by other revolutionary leaders before World War II.
7. Describe the social and economic conditions in South Africa during most of the twentieth century and how other countries around the world helped bring about change there.
8. Describe the causes and effects of the revolution in Iran that drove Shah Mohammad Reza Pahlavi into exile in 1979.

Name____________________ Class________________ Date______

Concept Connector Study Guide

Science

Essential Question: How has science changed people's lives throughout history?

A. Define *science.* ____

____

____

B. *Record information about the topics listed in the Cumulative Review or your answers to the questions in the Cumulative Review below. Use the Concept Connector Handbooks at the end of your textbook, as well as chapter information, to complete this worksheet.*

1. **Advances in Mathematics**
   Advances in mathematics and science developed by early civilizations benefit us today. The Greeks contributed geometry, astronomical observations, and practical inventions based on physics. Indian civilizations contributed the system of writing numbers, including zero, that we use today. In China during the Han dynasty, scientists wrote texts on chemistry, zoology, botany, and other subjects. The Chinese also pioneered advanced methods of shipbuilding and invented the rudder to steer. Other practical inventions from China include fishing reels, suspension bridges, and a method for making paper. Why were such advances possible in these ancient societies? They all had stable governments, periods of peace and prosperity, and opportunities for education.

2. **Incan Surgery**
   Civilizations of the Americas made many important advances. The Inca, for example, practiced medical procedures that are similar to those currently used in modern medicine. Surgical techniques practiced by the Inca included surgery on the human skull. They cleaned the area to be operated on and gave the patient a drug to make him or her unconscious. These procedures are similar to the modern use of antiseptics and anesthesia.

3. **The Ideas of Copernicus and Newton** (Chapter 1, page 79)

____

____

____

____

____

____

____

Name__________ Class__________ Date__________

Concept Connector Study Guide

SCIENCE *(continued)*

4. **The Scientific Revolution and the Scientific Ideas of the Late 1800s** (Chapter 9, page 325)

5. **Newton's Theories and Einstein's Theories** (Chapter 16, page 557)

6. **Louis Pasteur's Medical Advances and Those of World War II** (Chapter 17, page 597)

Name____________________ Class________________ Date________

Concept Connector Study Guide

SCIENCE ***(continued)***

C. Sample Topics for Thematic Essays

Below are examples of thematic essay topics that might appear on a test. Prepare for the test by outlining an essay for each topic on a separate sheet of paper. Use the Concept Connector Handbooks at the end of your textbook, as well as chapter information, to outline your essays.

1. Discuss how the Scientific Revolution that began in the mid-1500s marked a profound shift in the thinking of Europeans and how that shift is still reflected in the work of scientists.
2. Explain how science and technology aided European exploration and imperialism.
3. Describe how "germ theory" helped improve health in the 1800s, and discuss how new medical and health practices contributed to the growth in population.
4. Discuss the scientific knowledge that changed medical care in hospitals during the 1800s and how it improved health care, especially for poor people.
5. Describe the scientific discoveries made during the 1900s by Marie Curie, Albert Einstein, and Enrico Fermi. What were the effects of these discoveries?
6. What did the work of genetic researchers in the 1950s reveal about DNA? What were the implications of these discoveries?
7. Explain how science has been used to explore and make use of space.
8. Discuss the effect of computers on society and modern life and the reasons why this period is sometimes called "The Information Age."

Name_________________________ Class____________________ Date________

Concept Connector Study Guide

Technology

Essential Question: How has technology changed the way people live and work?

A. Define *technology.* ____

____

____

B. *Record information about the topics listed in the Cumulative Review or your answers to the questions in the Cumulative Review below. Use the Concept Connector Handbooks at the end of your textbook, as well as chapter information, to complete this worksheet.*

1. **Paleolithic Stone Tools**
People of the Old Stone Age, or Paleolithic Period, made tools out of materials at hand, such as stone, wood, or bone. Tools were often made from flint because the stone is relatively easy to shape by chipping flakes from it. Once chipped, these stones have sharp edges. Creating a tool required patience, skill, strength, and a number of other tools. The toolmaker would use a hard stone to strike flakes off another stone, and then use other tools, such as a small chisel, to refine the tool's shape. Even stone tools from locations far apart were made with similar techniques. The use of tools indicates early hominids were developing complex technologies to survive and probably used spoken language to communicate techniques.

2. **Advances During Prehistory and Technological Advances in Egypt and Mesopotamia**
During prehistory, technological advances such as the development of stone tools, domestication of animals, and farming allowed early humans to radically expand the possibilities for their lives. The peoples of ancient Mesopotamia and Egypt also made important advances. In Mesopotamia, people turned iron into powerful weapons and developed a writing system called cuneiform. Egyptians made a type of paper from plants and developed a cursive writing system. Medications made from plants helped to heal and ease symptoms. Did the advances of prehistory or the advances of Mesopotamia and Egypt have a greater impact? You could make the argument that all later advances are just improvements or refinements of technologies developed during prehistory.

3. **Military Technology and the Ottoman and Safavid Empires**
The Ottoman and Safavid empires benefited from advances in military technology. The Ottoman fleet helped to conquer Constantinople. Both empires used cannons to blast defensive walls, while muskets increased the effectiveness of their foot soldiers. The new military technology helped the Ottomans expand in the lands surrounding the Mediterranean, while the Safavids built a strong empire in Persia. As a result, the period from about 1450 to 1650 is sometimes called "the age of gunpowder empires."

Name________________________ Class____________________ Date________

Concept Connector Study Guide

TECHNOLOGY *(continued)*

4. **The Printing Press**
   The invention of the printing press in Europe changed the course of history. Because of this technology, books became cheaper and more readily available. Literacy increased. As presses were established in Europe, printed books exposed literate Europeans to new concepts and encouraged the exchange of ideas. Many of the first printing technologies, however, were not developed in Europe but in China. For example, in the 700s the Chinese developed block printing. In block printing, a full page of characters was carved onto a wooden block. Later in the 1040s, they invented movable type. With movable type, precut characters were combined to form a page.

5. **Gunpowder**
   Gunpowder was developed by the Chinese about 850. The earliest form of gunpowder was made from a mixture of saltpeter, sulfur, and charcoal, all found in abundance in China. The gunpowder was first used in fireworks. Later, gunpowder was used in cannons. The use of cannons during the Hundred Years' War in Europe helped to end feudal society. Castles could not stand up to the more destructive firepower. Monarchs needed large armies, not feudal vassals to fight their wars.

6. **The Compass** (Chapter 2, page 105)

7. **The Printing Press and the Steam Engine** (Chapter 7, page 267)

8. **The Agricultural Revolution and the Industrial Revolution** (Chapter 9, page 325)

Name______________________ Class__________________ Date________

Concept Connector Study Guide

TECHNOLOGY *(continued)*

9. **First and Second Phases of the Industrial Revolution** (Chapter 9, page 325)

10. **Nuclear Power** (Chapter 17, page 597)

11. **Coal Mines, Factories, and Railroads in Europe and North America in the 1800s and Hydroelectric Power in Africa Today** (Chapter 21, page 729)

12. **The Telephone and Computer Technology** (Chapter 22, page 765)

Name________________________ Class____________________ Date______

Concept Connector Study Guide

TECHNOLOGY *(continued)*

C. Sample Topics for Thematic Essays

Below are examples of thematic essay topics that might appear on a test. Prepare for the test by outlining an essay for each topic on a separate sheet of paper. Use the Concept Connector Handbooks at the end of your textbook, as well as chapter information, to outline your essays.

1. Discuss how improved technology helped Europeans explore the world beginning in the 1400s and to establish distant colonies.

2. Describe the "putting-out system" used to produce textiles in Britain in the 1600s and how it was changed by new technology in the 1700s.

3. Discuss how the use of steam power changed land and sea transportation during the 1800s and how it expanded business opportunities and personal travel.

4. Compare the benefits of industrialization with the problems it created.

5. Describe the role of artificial satellites in the modern world, and discuss at least two ways they affect everyday life.

6. Discuss how improvements in transportation technology have contributed to the success of Japan and "the Asian tigers" since the end of World War II.

7. Discuss the reasons why the United States used the atomic bomb in World War II and how its development by the Soviet Union within a few years affected world politics.

8. Describe some benefits of biotechnology and genetic engineering, as well as some issues that create debate about these topics.

Name________________________ Class____________________ Date______

Concept Connector Study Guide

Trade

Essential Question: What have been the major trade networks in world history?

A. Define *trade.* ____

____

____

B. *Record information about the topics listed in the Cumulative Review or your answers to the questions in the Cumulative Review below. Use the Concept Connector Handbooks at the end of your textbook, as well as chapter information, to complete this worksheet.*

1. **Phoenician Sea Traders**
While powerful rulers controlled large empires in the ancient Middle East, the smaller state of Phoenicia made its own contribution to civilization. The Phoenicians gained fame as both sailors and traders. They produced glass from coastal sand, and a luxurious dye called "Tyrian purple" from a tiny sea snail. The Phoenicians traded all around the Mediterranean Sea, and as far as Britain. To promote trade, they established colonies in North Africa, Sicily, and Spain. The Phoenicians spread Middle Eastern civilization all around the Mediterranean. One of their most significant cultural contributions is the Phoenician alphabet. It is the basis of the alphabet we use today.

2. **Phoenician Trade Network and the Silk Road**
The Phoenicians were Middle Eastern sea traders who sailed around the Mediterranean and as far as Spain. The Silk Road was a land-based network of trade routes that connected China to the Mediterranean. Both trade routes connected multiple cultures. The Phoenician trade network depended on Phoenician ships, traders, and the trade posts and colonies they set up. The Silk Road, on the other hand, was not controlled by any one group. In addition, trade goods on the Silk Road exchanged hands often because they passed from trader to trader on the extensive route. Small, expensive, luxury items were traded, including silk and spices from the east, and Roman glass from the west. They took up less space, were easier to carry, and had high value.

Name________________________ Class____________________ Date_______

Concept Connector Study Guide

TRADE *(continued)*

3. **Trade in Ancient Greece and Phoenicia**
The culture and economy of ancient Greece was greatly influenced by trade. With hundreds of bays offering safe harbor for ships, and thousands of miles of coastline, it was only natural that Greeks became expert sailors. Greek ships carried cargoes of olive oil, wine, and marble throughout the eastern Mediterranean. They returned not only with grains and metals but also with ideas, which they adapted to their own needs. By focusing on the eastern Mediterranean, Greek sailors never traveled as far as the Phoenicians. Phoenicians, who made their home on the eastern shore of the Mediterranean, sailed across the length of the Mediterranean into the Atlantic Ocean to reach the west coast of North Africa and as far north as Britain.

4. **Traders and Merchants in Feudalism and the Manorial System**
Medieval Europe was dominated by feudalism and the manorial system. Feudalism was a political system; the manor, or lord's estate, was an economic system. Both systems were based on mutual obligations. The manor was intended to be self-sufficient, producing everything needed by the lord's family, and the peasants and serfs who lived there. How did trade develop during this period? Around the 1100s, people began to travel more; crusaders brought luxury goods back to Europe. Nobles wanted goods that could not be produced on manors, and peasants needed iron for farm tools. Traders formed merchant companies that traveled together and set up trade fairs near major crossroads. Slowly, small trade settlements in Europe developed into towns and cities. Meanwhile, Europe's population was growing. Manors became overcrowded. Lords often allowed peasants to buy their freedom and move to towns.

5. **Trade in the Byzantine Empire, Russia, and Phoenicia**
Trade was at the heart of the prosperity and power of Constantinople and the Byzantine empire. In Russia, trade contributed to the rise of Kiev and Moscow. Earlier, trade had been just as important to the ancient Phoenicians. Location helped each of these cities or regions develop trade. Phoenicia was located on the eastern coast of the Mediterranean. In addition, Phoenicia had a resource that people wanted: a valuable purple dye. The Byzantine empire had a strategic location between Europe and Asia, in an area linking the Mediterranean and Black seas. From this location, the empire commanded key trade routes. Merchants bought and sold wheat from Egypt, silks from China, spices from Southeast Asia, and furs from Vikings in Scandinavia. Rivers connected Vikings with Kiev and Russia. Russia's network of rivers connected it to the advanced Byzantine world Eventually, Russia adopted many aspects of Byzantine culture.

Name________________________ Class__________________ Date________

Concept Connector Study Guide

TRADE *(continued)*

6. **Coastal Peoples and Trade**
   Naturally, many coastal peoples became skilled sailors and developed major trading cultures. Greek, Viking, and East African traders all sailed great distances using their nautical skills, and exchanged goods and ideas with new cultures. The Mediterranean and the Aegean seas were central to the development of Greece, and the seas provided a vital link to the world outside. The Greeks traded primarily in the eastern Mediterranean. Farmland was limited in Greece. When the population grew, the Greeks set up colonies throughout the Mediterranean, including in Spain and Egypt. These colonies expanded trade opportunities for the Greeks. The Vikings of Scandinavia were warriors, skilled shipbuilders, and sailors. They constructed shallow-draft ships that could sail up European rivers, which allowed them to attack far inland. Eventually, Viking groups settled outside of Scandinavia and influenced the development of cultures in Russia and Normandy, among other places. East African trading cities flourished in the 600s. From ancient times, Phoenician, Greek, Roman, and Indian traders traded in the region. Later, African rulers allowed Arab and Persian merchants to set up communities. East African trading cities benefited from the monsoon winds that carried ships between Africa and India. Goods from the interior of Africa, Persia, Arabia, India, China, and Southwest Asia flowed on and off the shores of East Africa.

7. **Chinese Trade in Southern China and Up Coast**
   During his reign, the famous Han emperor Wudi (141 B.C.–87 B.C.) opened up a vast trade network, later called the Silk Road, that linked China to the West. Under both the Tang and Song dynasties, foreign trade flourished, with Chinese merchants carrying goods to Southeast Asia in exchange for spices, rare woods, and a faster-growing type of rice. Between 1405 and 1433, a Chinese admiral named Zheng He commanded a series of sea expeditions to promote trade. He sailed to the Red Sea and the Persian Gulf and visited ports in East Africa. As a result of trade, Chinese merchants settled permanently in Southeast Asia and India, bringing their culture with them.

8. **The Dutch Trading Empire** (Chapter 2, page 105)

____

____

____

____

____

____

____

____

Name________________________ Class________________ Date______

Concept Connector Study Guide

TRADE *(continued)*

9. Indian Trade in Southeast Asia (Chapter 2, page 105)

10. European Approaches to Trade in the 1500s and 1600s (Chapter 2, page 105)

11. Earlier Slave Trades and the Atlantic Slave Trade (Chapter 3, page 137)

12. Railroad Travel and Travel on the Silk Road (Chapter 7, page 267)

Name____________________ Class__________________ Date________

Concept Connector Study Guide

TRADE *(continued)*

13. The British and Dutch Trading Empires (Chapter 13, page 447)

14. United States Trade in the Twentieth Century (Chapter 22, page 765)

15. Fears About Foreign Trade Dominance (Chapter 22, page 765)

16. Modern Free Trade and Mercantilism in the 1600s and 1700s (Chapter 22, page 765)

Name________________________ Class____________________ Date_______

Concept Connector Study Guide

TRADE *(continued)*

C. Sample Topics for Thematic Essays

Below are examples of thematic essay topics that might appear on a test. Prepare for the test by outlining an essay for each topic on a separate sheet of paper. Use the Concept Connector Handbooks at the end of your textbook, as well as chapter information, to outline your essays.

1. Describe the spice trade in the 1400s and how it helped spur European exploration.
2. Discuss the importance of trade in the Spanish and Portuguese conquests of Latin America and its effects on the lives of Native Americans and Africans.
3. Describe the triangular trade that began in the 1500s and its effects on each of the three regions it linked.
4. Describe the British trade in cotton before the Industrial Revolution and how it was changed by the factory system.
5. Describe the importance of trade in Latin American nations before and after independence. How did trade have both positive and negative effects?
6. How was a favorable balance of trade an important part of Japan's growth after World War II?
7. Describe the development of the Common Market and European Union, and evaluate their impact on trade among member nations.
8. What are the benefits of global trade? Why do some people oppose globalization?